Mike Thornton has d… life of Gaston Barnab… It adds new and previously unknown facts concerning Cashwell's life and ministry. I recommend this to everyone interested in early Pentecostalism in the United States.

—Vinson Synan
Dean Emeritus
Regent University School of Divinity

Having grown up in the 20th Century Pentecostal revival, I have heard stories about Crumpler, Cashwell and others all my life. Until now, I never had a way to sort out fact from fiction. When a book so well researched from primary source documents comes along, you have to take it all in. Even with the struggles of the movement, I am honored to stand on the shoulders of the Pentecostal leaders who have come before me. I am equally thrilled to know there are leaders in the current generation like Mike Thornton who still value those men's efforts. I highly recommend *Fire in the Carolinas* to you!

—Dr. Jim Wall
The Acts 2 Network

FIRE *in the* CAROLINAS

THE REVIVAL LEGACY OF G.B. CASHWELL *and* A.B. CRUMPLER

MICHAEL THORNTON

CREATION HOUSE

Fire in the Carolinas by Michael Thornton
Published by Creation House
A Charisma Media Company
600 Rinehart Road
Lake Mary, Florida 32746
www.charismamedia.com

Scripture quotations marked KJV are from the King James Version of the Bible Design

Director: Bill Johnson
Cover design by Terry Clifton

Library of Congress CataloginginPublication Data: 2013952182
International Standard Book Number: 978-1-62136-704-8
E-book International Standard Book Number: 978-1-62136-705-5

While the author has made every effort to provide accurate telephone numbers and Internet addresses at the time of publication, neither the publisher nor the author assumes any responsibility for errors or for changes that occur after publication.

First edition

14 15 16 17 18 — 9 8 7 6 5 4 3 2 1
Printed in Canada

CONTENTS

INTRODUCTION AND ACKNOWLEDGMENTS

In August 2005, the Lord called me to attend Heritage Bible College in Dunn, North Carolina. This college was spawned out of Rev. G.B. Cashwell's historic revival meeting held in Dunn, North Carolina, during January 1907. I first heard the name *G.B. Cashwell* from theology professor Dr. Herbert Carter, who is a founder of the college. Fascinated with Cashwell's story, I sought to know more about the famed revivalist. I even searched for the historic site where G.B. Cashwell's famous meeting took place.

At the time, there was still some debate as to where this well of revival was located. Compelled by the Spirit, I got in my car and drove frantically around the small town looking for the Azusa Street of the east coast! Suddenly, I heard a voice say, "Turn right here and stop." The invisible message led me to a small Pentecostal Church and a vacant lot right beside it. As soon as I got out of my car, my entire body, mind, and soul were accosted with something that can only be described as lightning. Immediately, I broke out into tears and wept from the inside out. I recalled asking myself, "Could this really be the place where it happened?" Hearing nothing, I got back in my car, drove off, and soon forgot about the whole experience.

For the next five years, I continued to further my education and ministry assignments. In August 2010, I received a startling news article from *The Dunn Daily Record*. The article featured a cover story, which revealed the exact location where G.B. Cashwell held his historic Dunn meeting in January 1907. The news story also disclosed new information regarding a negative response from the local government during that revival. While reading the article, I was once again revisited with the lightning experience that I had felt five years earlier. The name *Cashwell* seemed to burn in my mind! At the time, I was a graduate student at Regent University and lived on campus in Virginia Beach, Virginia. Unable to shake the Cashwell name from my thoughts, my father and I set up a meeting in Dunn with the outstanding researchers who re-dug the Cashwell story. After the meeting, they took us to the newly discovered site where G.B. Cashwell initiated "Azusa East." To my surprise, it was exactly where the voice of God's Spirit had led me six years earlier.

Returning home, I was consumed with the name G.B. Cashwell. I fell to my knees and began to ask the Lord what I was supposed to do with all of this. His response: "Write a book about Cashwell and all things that I will reveal to you." Having never written a book before, I immediately felt unqualified and ignorant to write such a story. After assuring the Lord He had made a huge mistake, He quickly reminded me that He doesn't make mistakes. Suddenly, His presence began to fill my apartment in the most powerful way. "Take your pen and write," He said. This is what followed:

> I want you to write a book about all the things I have revealed to you about Cashwell—a book to expose the thrones of iniquity working over Eastern North Carolina. Michael, I have chosen you for this task. I have anointed you for this purpose, and I will show you tremendous favor if you write according to My voice and My ways! For I am calling you to finish what G.B. Cashwell started in 1907! And that is to reveal and destroy the opposition to revival in the land. This book will not only serve to reveal the inner-working of the enemy over North Carolina, but it will also serve as a blue-print for other states and regions where the same thrones of iniquity have established their rule! I will supernaturally awaken many people to a desire to read this work who will be starving for its every word and use it as a heavenly strategy to take back the land. Trust in Me, my son, and do not fear. Do not worry about consulting with men, but listen to My voice, and I will direct you in the ways in which you should go. Michael, I have kept certain documents hidden for this reason, but the time has come for the "truth" to be revealed in the right way. That is, with My anointing and My presence.

Following this word, I began the long and grueling process of researching everything I could about Rev. G.B. Cashwell. Surprisingly, within one year's time, the Lord had put into my possession photographs, land deeds, letters, and other "hidden" documents that church historians and scholars have been searching for over one hundred years! Adding to the excitement, I also discovered that I am a distant blood relative of G.B. Cashwell through my great-great-great-great-grandfather Thomas Cashwell, G.B. Cashwell's uncle. Needless to say, I was burning with enthusiasm! I soon realized that there was more to this than writing a book about Cashwell, it was my personal appointment with destiny!

Why A.B. Crumpler? Some may wonder why I chose to include A.B. Crumpler's life story with G.B. Cashwell's. Traditionally, it has been written that G.B. Cashwell and A.B. Crumpler disliked each other over the issue of the Pentecostal baptism experience. I also took this approach after reading volumes of information about these two spiritual giants. However, as I began to dig for myself, I noticed that I could not separate the two no matter how hard I tried. They always seemed to be together. Whether appearing in each other's family photo albums, or being saved in the same revival, A.B. Crumpler and G.B. Cashwell seemed inseparable in every nook-n-cranny I searched. I just followed the evidence.

Interestingly, it opened my eyes to see that Crumpler and Cashwell were not enemies but friends. Moreover, I learned that there ministries in the Southern United States were based on something that was intended to be forgotten: racial and denominational healing among a segregated nation. To this end, Crumpler and Cashwell were pioneers. Gripped with a spiritual power unknown to our generation, these men turned a region upside down and nearly defeated the ideology of "separate but equal" through their powerful meetings. Therefore, the purpose of this work is to honor the revival legacy of G.B. Cashwell and A.B. Crumpler—two spiritual giants who transformed a nation and shifted Christianity on a global scale.

There have been many people who have inspired me to complete this book. I wish to first thank God, the Holy Spirit, and Jesus His son, who chose me for this assignment. Without God's love, I would have given up a long time ago. I sincerely thank Amber, Jordan, Abigail, Briella and Bethany Thornton, my beautiful wife and four daughters, who sacrificed so much for me to complete this book—without them this means nothing. I love you all! Richard and Esther Thornton, who funded my countless trips between Virginia and North Carolina, drove me anywhere I needed to go, and assisted me in researching cemeteries, old records, and numerous libraries. A special thanks to my dad for all of those late night conversations in trying to figure out the Stanly woods mystery. I will never forget it. Thank you, Pastor Tom Hauser and my Global River Church family. Thanks to historians such as Elizabeth Crudrup and Thomas Ellis II, whose hard work and diligent research sparked a fire in my heart. Thank you for lighting the flame. I also give a thank you to a special friend of our family, Karen Lucas who continued to challenge my research and offered much of her free time to assist me in this endeavor. My thanks also to Gary Barefoot whose endless emails and thoughtful contributions added greatly to this work. Thanks to Robert Lindsey and Moses King for helping me break one of the G.B. Cashwell mysteries. Thanks to Terri Holler for her excellent insights. Special thanks to Dr. Vinson Synan and Dr. Doug Beacham, whose hard work on Cashwell inspired me to write this book.

Thank you to a very special lady, Jane McGregor. I will never forget the day that my father and I spent with you at the Clinton J.C. Holiday Library. Thank you for your memories and the chance to pray over one very significant Bible. I would also like to thank all of A.B. Crumpler's descendants, both past and present.

Above all, I would like to thank Mr. Stanley Carr. Whether showing up at his door step unannounced or speaking on the phone for hours, Stanley Carr's insights had a tremendous impact on my quest to know the truth about G.B. Cashwell. Without him, this story would have never been written. Many times I wanted to throw in the towel and quit. Stanley, however, refused to give up on me. From the very beginning, Stanley knew that God had called me to write this story. His confidence in me is overwhelming and humbling. Thank you, Stanley, for believing in me and not giving up. I will always treasure our conversations and friendship!

May the Holy Spirit's fire leap off of the page and into the heart of anyone who reads this story. Lord, I ask for the impartation of G.B. Cashwell and A.B. Crumpler's mantle of ministry for any reader who is called to lead their generation into global revival. Let the fire of your love, and the significance of this story, consume them just like it has consumed me!

PREFACE

IT IS ESTIMATED that there are over 600 million Pentecostal Christians living on the earth today. With the exception of the Roman Catholic Church, global Pentecostalism has exploded to become the largest Christian church in the world. It is a world-wide movement that is still evolving and impacting every race, nation, and culture. Approximately 70 million of those believers can trace their Pentecostal roots back to one extraordinary meeting, held by Rev. G.B. Cashwell on December 31, 1906, in Dunn, North Carolina. Dubbed "Azusa East" by authors, G.B. Cashwell's historic Carolina meeting is known as the Azusa Street of the East Coast. Under Cashwell's leading, this revival phenomenon ripped through the entire southern regions of the United States during the turn of the twentieth century. In less than three years, G.B. Cashwell personally spread the Holiness-Pentecostal Movement to over a dozen states and brought some twelve denominations into the Pentecostal Movement, including: The Assemblies of God, Church of God (Cleveland, Tennessee), Church of God of Prophecy, International Pentecostal Church of Christ, International Pentecostal Holiness Church, Pentecostal Free Will-Baptist, and several others.

Cashwell's predecessor and close friend, Rev. Abner Blackmon Crumpler of Clinton, North Carolina, was also a powerful revivalist who roved the Carolina countryside with Cashwell. Ten years before the outbreak at Azusa Street in Los Angeles (1896), A.B. Crumpler was trailblazing North Carolina, with the fires of Holiness during the late 1890s. Tens of thousands were converted and national interest was stirred as a result of his legendary tent meetings. In their own ways, both G.B. Cashwell and A.B. Crumpler sought to establish the Holiness-Pentecostal Movement everywhere they traveled. With this message burning in their bones, these two Tar Heel revivalists even set their sights on tearing down one of the South's biggest strongholds, racism.

Regrettably, just as fast as Cashwell's and Crumpler's historic ministries began, they would mysteriously end. For over one hundred years, researchers have been baffled and unable to come up with a solid answer as to what happened to these revival pioneers. Their thundering voices were silenced, and their impact on Christianity has largely been forgotten. In recent years, however, there has been a growing hunger to know the truth about Cashwell, Crumpler, and why their ministries ended so abruptly. Thus, this book will attempt to unravel an ancient old mystery while bringing honor to the revival legacy of G.B. Cashwell and A.B. Crumpler; two of the South's greatest revivalists.

PART I:

SECRETS IN THE GRAVEYARD

Chapter 1

CASHWELL AND CRUMPLER: FAMILY ORIGINS

GASTON BARNABAS CASHWELL is one of the most significant, dynamic, and powerful revivalist that has ever thundered upon American pulpits. To the general public, however, he still remains as the most misunderstood, unknown, and forgotten figure in American church history. Like Samson of the Bible, G.B. Cashwell was a very large man who possessed an incredible ability to captivate all who would listen to his message. Standing well over six feet and weighing over 250 pounds, this powerhouse shifted the entire atmosphere of the room when he entered through the door.[1]

Stepping into the pulpit, Cashwell often began services by raising his hands high in the sky proclaiming, "Praise the Lord!" The power flowing from his voice was enough to baptize an entire generation into the Holy Spirit. Even so, family members remembered that when Gaston Cashwell spoke, a "spellbinding" type of anointing followed. Enough to convict the hardest of hearts, yet sweet enough to fill the room with kindness, Cashwell's messages penetrated the human soul with unthinkable power. Under his preaching, people all over the Southern United States were swept into the blazing message of Pentecostal love.[2]

Dubbed the "Apostle of Pentecost to the South," his soul was set on fire at the Azusa Street Mission during the November of 1906. Upon returning from Los Angles, California, where he had been baptized into a deeper love for Christ, he held a multi-racial and inter-denominational revival in Dunn, North Carolina that shook the world. So powerful was this meeting that entire churches and denominations were consumed by its flames. Even today, the impact of what he did is still being felt in the South and around the world. Millions of people have been brought into the Kingdom because of his willingness to take a 3,000 mile train ride of faith one hundred and fourteen years ago. Yet, not everyone would be so receptive to his arrival back in Dunn, North Carolina.[3]

What many do not know is that this world-wide-reaching awakening that took place in the heart of Carolina would end just as quickly as it started due to outside influences. Little did Mr. Cashwell know that this revival would not only spark life in local churches, but would also provoke an ancient evil that had been gaining strength in the South, white supremacy. Perhaps, this is why no one really knows who G.B. Cashwell is. Maybe this is why he remains one of the most forgotten revivalists in church history. Could it be possible that there were those who wanted him to remain forgotten? If so, then who and why? Why would there be a need to extinguish the flames of this fiery preacher?[4]

Before diving into the amazing life of G.B. Cashwell, it seems appropriate to examine the lives of G.B. Cashwell's parents—the Cashwells and the Stanleys. Their stories will help shape our understanding of who Gaston B. Cashwell really was, and why God chose him to ignite one of the most powerful revivals ever recorded within church history.

THE CASHWELL TRIO: THOMAS JR., WILLIAM, AND HERRING CASHWELL

According to Cashwell family history, the son of Pentecost, G.B. Cashwell, descended from a long line of Cashwells in southeastern North Carolina. Cashwell's father's name was Herring Cashwell. Herring, along with two brothers William, and Thomas Jr., were the children of Thomas Sr. and Catharine Cashwell of Bladen County. During the 1850s, the three Cashwell brothers left Bladen County, North Carolina, and settled in neighboring Sampson County. Reasons explaining their departure are generally rooted in the belief that their father, Thomas Sr. Cashwell, and mother, Catherine Cashwell, separated.[5]

Apparently, this Cashwell family separation drove all three bothers over the Bladen County line to make better lives for themselves in a new country, Sampson County. The first brother to cross over was the oldest of the three, Thomas Jr. Cashwell. Thomas Jr. was born in Bladen County in 1820 and died in Sampson County sometime between 1880 and 1900. According to the 1860 Federal Census, Thomas Jr. married Christian Cashwell and had several children. They reared their family on a small farm in McDaniel's Township which is situated in southern Sampson County. At the present time, there are no written accounts revealing dialogue between Herring Cashwell and his oldest brother, Thomas. However, to say that Thomas lived a boring life would apparently be a big mistake.[6]

According to The Heritage of Sampson County, North Carolina, Thomas Jr. Cashwell served in the Civil War. He enlisted as a private on November 12, 1861, in the city of Clinton. Thomas Cashwell Jr. was discharged soon after on February 15, 1862, due to his age and disability. It seems Thomas was wounded while serving in an artillery regiment. This appears to have cut his military career short and limited his service to the Confederate cause to just three months.[7]

Unlike Thomas Jr. Cashwell, there are a few more records which paint a clearer picture of Herring's other brother, William Cashwell. William Cashwell, the youngest of the Cashwell trio, was born around 1825 in Bladen County and died July 17, 1863. Sometime between the years 1851 and 1853 both William and Herring Cashwell settled upon the Brewer lands in Sampson County. The Brewer farm provided an opportunity for the brothers to live and work as farmers. Subsequently, William met a young woman named Susan Bass. It wasn't long before these two tied the knot. By 1860, William and Susan Bass were married with two small children.[8]

Sometime after their marriage, Herring Cashwell assisted his brother, William, and his new family. In a land deed dated August 15, 1855, Herring Cashwell sold his nine acre plot of land on the Brewer farm to his brother, William. After meeting a wife of his own, Herring Cashwell quickly relocated and moved about one mile north. The deed also shows that the William Cashwell family settled and farmed on the Brewer estate. It wouldn't be long, however, before this young family would go through a life changing process.[9]

On May the 16, 1862, William Cashwell also enlisted as a farmer in the Confederate Army. He joined the service as a private and served in the Fifth Calvary. From this point, nothing else is known about William except that he died on July 17, 1863, in the Goldsboro Hospital. He was just thirty-eight-years-old. There are no other records revealing how he died or if he was wounded in a battle. Certainly, there are numerous possibilities that could be suggested at this point. What should be remembered about William Cashwell is that he gave the ultimate sacrifice for his country. On account of William's death, his wife, Susan Bass Cashwell, became a widow and his two small children orphans. Nevertheless, as a testimony to the strength of southern families who survived the Civil War, Susan and the small Cashwell children would not be alone nor forgotten. They would soon find refuge and a home on another farm under the care of William's brother's family, Herring and Susan Stanley Cashwell.[10]

Herring Cashwell, the father of Gaston Barnabas Cashwell, was born in Bladen County, North Carolina on May 9, 1824, and died in Halls

Township on October 14, 1878. Sometime shortly after the family separation, Herring left the Cashwell farm and was hired to work the Willie Hall farm in Bladen County. In approximately 1853, Herring made his way into Sampson County onto the Abraham Brewer estate and lived with his mother's side of the family. Up until this point, nothing else is known about Herring except that he lived on a nine-acre plot of land. While living on the Brewer farm, however, Herring Cashwell would cross paths with another remarkable woman in the community, Susan Stanley.[11]

Traditionally, some have believed that Herring Cashwell served in the Civil War and was present in Appomattox when General Lee relinquished command of his troops. However, a search in the Appomattox courthouse records reveals no such name on any of its rosters that day. The North Carolina Troops Index Rosters also never record any soldier from North Carolina by the name Herring Cashwell. According to these records, the only two Cashwell names from Sampson County were William and Thomas Jr. Cashwell, Herring's brothers. Furthermore, Herring and Susan's third child, Ann Pender Cashwell, was also born just about the same time General Lee surrendered at Appomattox. Family tradition states that Herring Cashwell was home when she was born. Most likely, family members got Herring confused with his brother, William Cashwell. Over the years, this has probably led some to believe that Herring marched with the Confederates. Current family members believe it was Herring's disability that prevented him from joining. According to them, Herring suffered from a leg injury which physically prevented him from enlisting in the armed forces at that time.[12]

There are several things that we can learn from the lives of the Cashwell brothers. Early census records reveal that their father, Thomas Sr. Cashwell, was a very wealthy land owner. This does not mean that he assisted them, however. Through researching all of the Cashwell family deeds during that time, it is very likely that the Cashwell trio received nothing from their father.

Without an inheritance, the Cashwells most likely worked extremely hard for next to nothing. In addition, they also probably had to work side by side with freed slaves. Under this atmosphere, Caucasian, African American, and local Native Americans would forge close partnerships. This was not uncommon, given the South's devastated economy during the reconstruction period. Today, many Americans have grown up not knowing or understanding the difficulty of living during the reconstruction period. Most of us have a hard time trying to comprehend what life would be like without owning our own land, houses, cars, etc. However, for those who grew up during this period in the South, times were extremely difficult and living conditions were brutal.[13]

This appears to have been the everyday life of the Cashwell trio, especially the father of G.B. Cashwell. Although little has been recorded about Herring and G.B. Cashwell's relationship, it should be noted that Herring Cashwell was a humble man who entered into Sampson County under humble circumstances. Overcoming his difficulties, Herring married a highly respected woman in the community. Incredibly, from these small beginnings, one of America's greatest preachers would burst onto the scene sweeping thousands into his fiery message of brotherly love.

The Stanley Girls: Harriet and Susan Stanley

Although G.B. Cashwell's father's side has provided us with some thoughtful insights, it seems Cashwell's mother's side of the family is what shaped his identity. His mother, Susan Stanley Cashwell, was the youngest of three girls. She, along with her three older sisters, Harriet, Rebecca, and Patience Stanley, were all reared on the Stephan Stanley farm during the mid-1800s. Situated just south of Kenner crossroads, the Stanley farm was located in Halls Township of Sampson County. Today, it is commonly referred to as the "Stanley Woods."[14] There is not much known of Susan's middle sisters, Rebecca and Patience Stanley. They both went on to marry farmers in the Halls Township area and lived peaceful lives with their respective families. On the other hand, there is a lot more to be said of Harriet and Susan Stanley.

Their outstanding reputation in the community rivaled even that of Mother Teresa's. Both Harriet and Susan were extraordinary women who possessed incredible talents and surpassing medicine knowledge. However, what really set this dynamic duo apart from everyone else in the community was there deep-rooted love for all people. Chosen to lead a global inter-racial movement, G.B. Cashwell, no doubt, inherited the mantle of love from both his mother and aunt who helped raise him and the other four Cashwell children.[15]

Harriet Stanley, the eldest sibling of the Stanley girls and aunt of Gaston B. Cashwell, was born on July 2, 1823, in the Stanley Woods. Harriet, more commonly known as "Aunt Harriet," never married and remained single all her life. She left the Stanley Woods at the same time Susan and Herring Cashwell did. Having very little of material value, Aunt Harriet moved into a small cabin and dedicated her life to assist her sister's family, the Cashwells. The 1860 census reveals that her new home was situated on the Cashwell farm adjacent to the old Herring and Susan homestead. Over the next fifty years, both Harriet's and Susan's homes would serve as a base command for all the ministry operations in which they would take part in.[16]

Without question, Aunt Harriet was remembered and cherished for her many contributions of selfless service. Perhaps one of her greatest offerings of love was witnessed in her unyielding dedication to seeing new life spring up into the community. Dr. Joseph T. McCullen Jr., Harriet's great nephew, remembers that his aunt Harriet was most famously known as "Halls Township Midwife." According to Dr. McCullen, she delivered countless babies into the region for over fifty years. She was so well known for this wonderful attribute, that whenever Aunt Harriet donned her black robe and headed out with her satchel, folks used to say: "Soon there'll be another amongst us."[17]

Besides bringing new babies into the world, Aunt Harriet was also well-known for comforting people who were dying. Like pre-modern chaplains, both Harriet and Susan Stanley Cashwell attended the deathbed of many family members and neighbors. Using their gifts of encouragement, they reassured many weary souls that the Lord would "see them through to a land even better then Persimmon College, Heaven itself." Her relationship with her nephew, Gaston Cashwell, is something to be noted as well.[18]

According to Dr. McCullen, Harriet and Gaston Cashwell lived to play pranks on one another. Annie Lee Gore, also known as Poca, seemed to enjoy these stories more than anyone else in the family. Poca, Cashwell's niece, knew Gaston B. Cashwell first hand and recounted a time when Gaston and his friends sawed a foot log across a stream between the homes of Susan and Harriet in two and then hid in the brush. Rounding the corner and singing "Amazing Grace," Aunt Harriet strolled by, stepped onto the log, and fell into the water. Soaking in the middle of the stream, she yelled, "Come out of those bushes, Gaston and you other scoundrels!" Aunt Harriet Stanley lived to be eighty-years old and passed away on November 12, 1903. Though she has been long gone, her legacy still lives on in the community she so loved and served for over half a century.[19]

Although Aunt Harriet played a major role in helping raise Gaston Cashwell, it would be his mother, Susan Stanley Cashwell, that most impacted Gaston's life. Susan can be adequately compared to Mother Teresa, who once said, "Being unwanted, unloved, uncared for, forgotten by everybody, I think that is a much greater hunger, a much greater poverty, than the person who has not anything to eat." This statement embodied the life of Susan Stanley Cashwell. Susan, better known as Granny Susan and the Medicine Women of Persimmon College, appears to have been a remarkable woman. Having a unique love for all, Granny Susan's heart was perhaps larger than the Tar Heel state itself.[20]

Susan Stanley Cashwell was born on November 20, 1830, and died June 19, 1913. She also grew up in the Stanley Woods under the care of Stephan and Edney Stanley. There is not much known of her early childhood years except that she possessed an uncanny wealth of knowledge about early tobacco and medicine. Family tradition states, "She knew how to locate and soften first-rate black gum brushes for dipping."[21] Knowledge of this kind was extremely rare during this time in Sampson County. So rare that tobacco wouldn't be introduced in this part of North Carolina as a cash crop for at least another thirty years. In terms of early medicine, many of the early settlers were ignorant on how to cultivate local herbs and gardens for the purpose of producing strong penicillin, but not Granny Susan.[22]

According to her grandson, Dr. McCullen, Granny Susan was going around the local community and taking care of the sick at the age of fourteen. She also was accustomed to growing local herbs and spices for medical purposes. By applying her remedies to the sick, Susan quickly gained the reputation of being Halls Township's doctor. Keep in mind, this is before modern hospitals and local urgent cares arrived. People born into this generation did what they had to do in order to survive. This does, however, surface some interesting questions. Where did Granny Susan learn this knowledge? How did she acquire this unique understanding of medicine and tobacco, especially at an early age? Strangely, no one knows. It is at this point that Cashwell family history grows uncomfortably silent.[23]

Susan's knowledge, coupled with a genuine love for others, eventually led her into an act of kindness that would forever alter her life. In a will dated January 1853, by W. Everett Bass of Sampson County, Granny Susan was generously rewarded for medical services rendered to him throughout his life. Won over by her devotion, this wealthy planter decided to give her 205 acres of land and $1,000 dollars in cash. This is a gift that is still sufficient even by today's standards. However, in 1853, these gifts were no less than a small fortune. Granny Susan was just twenty-three years of age when this occurred.[24]

Shortly following, Granny Susan and the young Herring Cashwell met and were quickly married. Unfortunately, there is no record of how they met or the date of their marriage. Nonetheless, with a handsome bank account, the mother and father of G.B. Cashwell sought to begin a new life together. According to a land deed in 1855, the Cashwell couple purchased just a little over one hundred acres of farm land from Joshua Bass (the son of the same Mr. Bass who left an inheritance to Susan) and moved into a small cabin. During the next seventeen years, the old Cashwell homestead witnessed the birth of eight Cashwell children, including the future Apostle of Pentecost to the South, G.B. Cashwell.[25]

In retrospect, Susan Stanley Cashwell's life was nothing short of astonishing. Born in a time that was ruthless, Granny Susan and her sister, Harriet Stanley, overcame much adversity, such as the Civil War, reconstruction, famines, and many infant deaths. Susan and Aunt Harriet did not wish to abide in big houses or dress in fancy clothing. They were ordinary women who lived extraordinary lives. Living a simplistic lifestyle, G.B. Cashwell's mother and aunt gave themselves to everyone in need without prejudice. This was the spiritual heritage that G.B. Cashwell and the other Cashwell children would be brought up in.

Rooted in Justice: The A.B. Crumpler Family Tree

If Gaston B. Cashwell is now being recognized as the Apostle of Pentecost to the South, then it is only to fair to say that his counterpart, Abner Blackmon Crumpler, should also be recognized as the Apostle of Holiness to North Carolina. Together, these two companions, friends, and Sampsonians altered the entire spiritual landscape of the Southern United States. A.B. Crumpler, the forerunner of G.B. Cashwell, is most famously recognized for bringing the great National Holiness Movement to eastern North Carolina in 1896. The waves of his ministry produced powerful revivals which swept entire denominations in its violent wake.[26]

Despite the fact that A.B. Crumpler won thousands to the holiness cause, established over thirty different churches, empowered local preachers by the dozens, and started a denomination, most people living in his home town have never heard of his name. In fact, besides the years 1896-1908, there is virtually nothing known of his life. Both his early and later years have remained in a desert of obscurity just as G.B Cashwell's have. Yet, in seeking to honor the late Rev. A.B. Crumpler, new facts have emerged that will add depth and understanding to the legacy he left behind. As in G.B. Cashwell's case, it seems appropriate to explore A.B. Crumpler's family history. No doubt, this will shed light on how A.B. Crumpler became such a powerful force for the Holiness Movement.[27]

Abner Blackmon Crumpler descends from a long line of Crumpler's who first arrived in Sampson County, North Carolina, around 1750. John Sr. Crumpler, A.B. Crumpler's great-great grandfather, was the first known Crumpler to settle in this region. Considered the Patriarch of the North Carolina Crumpler family tree, John was born about 1724 in Isle of Wight County, Virginia, and died in Duplin County, North Carolina, in 1782. In 1749, he married Nancy Holmes, also of Isle of Wight County, and together they traveled down into southeastern North Carolina. In a deed dated May of 1757, John Crumpler and his bride purchased one hundred acres of land worth about twenty pounds of gold from Henry Easterling and settled in Duplin County, North Carolina. This land would later be known as Honeycutt Township of Sampson County in 1784. During this same time, the Crumpler's also expanded their wealth by acquiring more land. According to the first Sampson County tax list in 1784, the Crumpler plantation was noted as containing "700 acres of farm land."[28]

Afterwards, the newly-arrived Crumplers most likely built a house and began to focus their efforts on raising their family. John, who apparently had a taste for local government, was appointed first as Sheriff of Duplin County in 1765, and then as an "overseer of roads" by the local justices. Serving as the County Sherriff for the next seventeen years, John Sr. Crumpler established himself as a strong law man within the community he served, and went on to set a historic precedent of justice that would flow through the veins of succeeding Crumplers in the Sampson County area, including his great-great grandson, A.B. Crumpler.[29]

Nearing the end of his life, John drew up his will and dispersed a very fair and even amount of his wealth to his children. John Jr. Crumpler (A.B. Crumpler's great-grandfather) was the oldest single male left of the children and was given the responsibility of managing the Crumpler homestead as well as caring for his younger sisters. In order to accomplish this, John Sr. left John Jr. the plantation house, 230 acres of land, as well as all of his father's slaves. John Jr. Crumpler apparently answered the challenge and grew up to be a successful farmer. The death of John Sr. Crumpler marked the beginning of a new generation of Crumplers to emerge within the newly formed Sampson County. Although it cannot be established with certainty whether or not he went to church, what is known is that his offspring would begin to cover the landscape and engage in religious affairs, civil matters, and government.[30]

John Jr. Crumpler was born about 1753 in Duplin County, North Carolina, and died May 12, 1803, in Sampson County. It appears that John Jr. did not follow in his father's footsteps as being Sheriff, but rather was appointed to an even higher office, County Magistrate. Being appointed in December of 1785, John Jr. Crumpler served as the Sampson County Magistrate for the next six years. Besides serving in government, John Jr. also maintained his identity as a wealthy southern planter by overseeing the Crumpler plantation. After receiving his father's estate, he married a local woman, Elizabeth Blackmon, in 1783, approximately. Together, they raised several children, including Blackmon Crumpler, A.B. Crumpler's grandfather.[31]

Blackmon Crumpler, who was born in Sampson County in 1784, grew up on his father's plantation and also became a wealthy farmer. He, like his father and grandfather, was also appointed to a governmental position. On August 20, 1819, Blackmon was appointed as Sampson's post master. Although it is not certain how he long served as Sampson's postmaster, it is certain that the Crumplers were definitely beginning to make their mark in the local government of Sampson County. Also, during this time, Blackmon married Janet Holmes and sought to leave the original John Sr. Crumpler plantation. Apparently, the young couple decided to take some of their wealth and purchase land several miles south.[32]

In a deed dated December 2, 1812, Blackmon Crumpler purchased 282 acres of land at five hundred dollars from Thomas Sutton and his wife, Bathsheba Crumpler Sutton, sister of Blackmon. This track of land would traditionally become known as the Crumpler farm where A.B. Crumpler would grow up. Located on highway 24, between Clinton and Roseboro, North Carolina, this land resides right next to a little town today known as Bonnetsville, North Carolina. Here Blackmon and his wife, Elizabeth, established themselves as respectable farmers and helpers of the community.[33]

One of the ways that Blackmon contributed to the community besides being postmaster was by giving land to build a local Methodist Church. During February of 1842, Blackmon gave a piece of his property to several men who identified themselves as "trustees of the Methodist Episcopal Church." According to the deed, Blackmon gave the land for the "purpose of building a house of worship" which was to be situated somewhere on Highway 24 between Clinton and Fayetteville.[34]

Whether or not the church ever materialized is not known. However, it is known that A.B. Crumpler's grandfather had a warm heart to the Lord and prophetically sowed a seed for his grandson. Years later that seed would mature into a strong righteous oak that would win many souls to Jesus. Blackmon Crumpler passed away on August 5, 1868, and was buried in the Blackmon Crumpler cemetery located next to the Crumpler homestead. To him and Janet were born six children, including George Washington Crumpler, A.B. Crumpler's father.

A.B. Crumpler's Father and Mother

George Washington Crumpler, the father of Abner Blackmon Crumpler, was born on March 30, 1823, at the Blackmon Crumpler plantation and died there on April 21, 1895. There is not much known of his childhood years except that he worked on his father's farm; however, farming was not to be his only occupation. George W. Crumpler also had a passion for government and justice as his great-grandfather did, John Sr. Crumpler. By the age of twenty-three, the young aspiring George Crumpler was already working as a county officer. After holding that position faithfully for at least five years, George W. was promoted to Sheriff of Sampson County in 1855. This office enabled him to secure a great deal of governmental authority within the region. He served the community as Sheriff for the next six years until a tragic turn of events took him from policing the county to fighting in the nation's deadliest conflict, the Civil War.[35]

Just prior to the war, around 1855, George fell in love and married a woman who lived nearby. Her name was Margret Lafayette Crumpler. Born on October 23, 1824, Margret L. Crumpler was a distant cousin of George W. Crumpler and grew up nearby. Margret also descends from John Sr. Crumpler, the North Carolina Crumpler patriarch, but through a different Crumpler line. Records and family stories concerning Margret have been scarce. What is known, however, is that her father, John II Crumpler, also took up the role of government in Sampson County during the early 1800s.[36]

John II Crumpler, A.B. Crumpler's grandfather and great uncle on his mother's side, was born about 1787 in Sampson County, North Carolina, and died February 23, 1830. According to the *Heritage of Sampson County, North Carolina* and *The Sampson County Historical Society*, John II Crumpler was also appointed as Sheriff of Sampson County in 1810. One short story that has been preserved and recorded about his term as Sheriff includes him, "protesting the people as being inefficient, and ordered James Holmes to build a house on the courthouse grounds for his personal use to sell spirits (liquor) and other things of value John went on to serve the community as Sherriff for the next eleven years until he stepped down and took the next step in furthering his political career as a North Carolina State Representative during 1824-1825.[37]

It is quite clear that the Crumpler's of Sampson County were rooted in justice. Beginning with John Sr., the patriarch, different Crumpler's throughout the generations have made great contributions to their communities. Many have benefited from their mark on history. Over the years, Crumplers of Sampson County have become involved with law enforcement and seats of congress, while others have become educators within schools and churches. Indeed the Crumpler family tree, which was planted during Colonial times, is one of the most respected families within that region.

In reviewing the G.B. Cashwell and A.B. Crumpler family origins, it seems much has been learned. Whether discussing the lives of their parents, social upbringing, or roles in the community, it is clear that both Cashwell and Crumpler revived their unique identities from their ancestors. No doubt, these genealogical insights will help deepen our understanding of G.B. Cashwell and A.B. Crumpler's powerful revival ministries.

Chapter 2

THE OBSCURE YEARS

Understanding the Times and Seasons

Gaston Barnabas Cashwell was born on April 28, 1862. He was the second of eight children born to Herring and Susan Cashwell. His other siblings included: William Herring (Billie) Jr., Ann Pender (Sis Penny), Susan, and Lettie (Docia) Cashwell. Unfortunately, Gaston's three other siblings died as infants. The surviving five Cashwell children grew up together and lived on the Cashwell farm. As a result, the Cashwell children formed a very close relationship with one another. It seems this family bond is what would see them through some of their most difficult years. Thus, it is important to remember the intense atmosphere that G.B. Cashwell was born into, the reconstruction period.[1]

In the wake of America's bloodiest war, which claimed the lives of over 600,000 men and brought about the assignation of President Lincoln, the nation, both north and south, laid devastated. Many wives were made widows and their children, orphans. An awful sense of hopelessness and despair seemed to descend upon the land with great heaviness. Christianity and the local church also suffered immensely. Without hope, many began to abandon their Christian faith. Almost overnight, the Civil War had ripped apart America's largest denominations, such as the Methodists and Baptists, over racial matters. Though many textbooks and historians have tried to pin the war on economic issues, what should be remembered is that the war was always about one issue that divided America: slavery.[2]

From the fountains of slavery flowed the moral, economic, and political ills that forced America into this horrific battle of brother against brother. The aftermath of such violence and bloodshed brought about a dark era within American history. Hailed by some as the second Civil War, reconstruction, in all its glory, attempted to do the impossible—reconcile 300 years of hatred between one race and another. Its failure would create another platform for private and secluded organizations to arise and take matters into their own hands.[3]

With a broken economy, political upheaval, and millions of freed slaves living in a white dominated country, the South's atmosphere following the war was like a page right out of the Bible:

> How deserted lies the cities, once so full of people! How like a widow is she, who once was great among the nations! She who was queen among the provinces has now become a slave. Bitterly, she weeps at night, tears are upon her cheeks. Among all her lovers there is none to comfort her. All her friends have betrayed her; they have become their enemies. After affliction and harsh labor, Judah [Southern Tribe] has gone into exile. She dwells among the nations; she finds no resting place. All who pursue her have overtaken her in the midst of her distress.[4]
>
> —Lamentations 1:1–3

For many, this was a perfect picture of the South's condition after the Civil War. Southerners all over were longing for something that would bring closure to the pain that both sides were experiencing.

The government's approach was not working. How can one treat a three hundred- year-old wound with forty acres and a mule? The great American democracy machine was failing her people. What could possibly ease the suffering? These are some of the issues and questions that a young Gaston B. Cashwell encountered as he grew up on the Cashwell farm. It would be through these trying times that G.B. Cashwell would shine on the national stage and move the entire South towards a spiritual revival of racial reconciliation.[5]

G.B. Cashwell's Early Years

While the war was coming to a close and reconstruction was entering into its early stages (1870's), G.B. Cashwell was growing up as a small boy on the Cashwell farm in Halls Township, North Carolina. One of the earliest accounts about Gaston B. Cashwell is found on the 1870 and 1880 Federal Census of Halls Township. According to the 1870 census, G.B. Cashwell is recorded as being eight-years-old. The census also reveals that he, along with his older brother William Herring Cashwell Jr., were both workers on the family farm. Growing up in rural North Carolina during this time, there weren't many other options. Times were extremely difficult, and most families ate, slept, and lived off the land they farmed. Without having the luxury of modern day grocery stores, farmers heavily depended on their crops for survival. Therefore, it was very common to see younger children assisting older family members with the usual tasks of farm life.[6]

In terms of education, Cashwell attended a local school in the area. This is also verified on his death certificate, which discloses that he had a "common education." Although it is uncertain when he started his schooling, it is important to remember that Cashwell received an education in the rural South. For many in Sampson County during reconstruction, this was a rare opportunity. This would prove to be very helpful in Cashwell's later years, as he became a prolific writer and defender of the Pentecostal Movement.[7]

Besides farming their lands and going to school, the Cashwells also demonstrated an entrepreneur spirit by establishing a local general store for neighbors and travelers. Situated on the Old Raleigh road (highway 701), the Cashwell store generated all kind of business. After residing in their original home for seventeen years, Herring and Susan Cashwell decided to build a new home on a newly acquired piece of land directly north of the store. Instead of trying to sell their old home, they decided to turn it into a store which was commonly referred to as the "old country store." It was, according to Dr. McCullen, a place where "farmers could blow the noon heat" and exchange tales about one another.[8]

Among other things, the store's purpose was to provide local farmers with a place to sell and purchase goods without having to make a trip to town. Their establishment offered simple items that would be found in any other typical general store. Store items most likely included drinks, meat, animal feed, and farming tools. On the other hand, there was another item found in the Cashwell store that would not be found anywhere else: tobacco.[9]

Due to Granny Susan and Aunt Harriet's extensive knowledge of tobacco, the Cashwell family knew how to "locate and make early tobacco snuff." This was an entirely new product that the Cashwells had been introducing into Sampson County at the community level. This kind of early success is what enabled the country store to run for nearly forty years. During the 1870s, when this store began, it was most likely operated first by the Cashwell children, especially the two oldest Cashwell brothers: William Herring Jr. and Gaston B. Cashwell. After they both left the Keener area, their sister, Docia Cashwell Gore, and her husband, Jerry F. Gore, took over the store. Dr. McCullen notes that his "Ma and Pa Gore" operated it until the store closed sometime after the turn of the twentieth century.[10]

While there are not many other documented reports of Cashwell's childhood years, what we do know about young Gaston Cashwell has been revealed to us through the family historian, Dr. Joseph Thomas McCullen

Jr. "J.T.," as the family would call him, was G.B. Cashwell's great-nephew and had wonderful insight into Cashwell's early and later years. He was a prolific writer who authored several unpublished books, specifically for family members. Some even provide answers to the mysteries surrounding G.B. Cashwell and the revival movement he led. We are indebted to his scholarship because without it, the story of the Cashwell family would have slipped into oblivion.

Concerning Cashwell's younger years, Dr. McCullen wrote three published articles in the *Heritage of Sampson County, North Carolina*. These wonderful accounts reveal the early years of Cashwell's life. All three articles identify the young G.B. Cashwell as being quite the prankster. Buddie, as the family referred to him, seemed to always play pranks and jokes on family members as well as neighbors in the Keener community. For instance, McCullen writes:

> As a young man, Uncle Gaston and his cohorts enjoyed pranks played on people assembled for prayer meeting. Once near the door of a room filled with singing crowd, there was a well. The pranksters first moved the curb, and then started a commotion among the horses and mules tied a few yards away. Rushing out to determine what wild beast was among their livestock, some of the worshipers tumbled into the well.[11]

Another story includes Cashwell and his Aunt Harriet Stanley playing jokes on one another. Dr. McCullen recounts the dialogue shared between Auntie Harriet and Gaston Cashwell:

> "This is the worst year for gardens I've seen since the war. My animals are puny, too-chickens not laying, shoats all runts, cow dried up! What's next? Sometimes, I wish I was dead." A knock at the door distracted the attention of Aunt Harriet from worry as she called, "Who is it?" A voice that rasped "DEATH!" revived her old self. "Sakes alive!" she exclaimed. "Things are worse than I thought. Nowadays, a body can't even crack a joke round here anymore." It wasn't death that had responded, but her nephew Gaston, "Buddie" as the family referred to him. He was full of pranks, some of which he played on Aunt Harriet. Sis Penny said he was probably evening scores after Aunt Harriet sounded a false alarm one night.[12]

Aunt Harriet's home was situated just south of the old Cashwell house. She lived alone and her cabin, which was located off the main road that connected Raleigh to Wilmington (Old Raleigh Road).

Once more, McCullen writes, "Gaston was returning from Clinton with two other drunks, and the trio dismantled two or three hundred yards of rail fence that kept livestock then roaming freely out of fields owned by Mr. Abe Hobbs." Dr. McCullen adds, "Sis Penny said the next day, a Sunday, her sister Docia Cashwell Gore, and their mother Susan Stanley Cashwell had to rebuild that fence." These family stories are both colorful and insightful in gaining a better perspective into G.B. Cashwell's early years. It is apparent that he was a jokester who enjoyed getting innocent kicks at some of the family member's expense. What is noteworthy to mention though, is that Gaston Cashwell was quite the character who made impressions everywhere he went.[13]

Although there is not an exact dates given to reveal what age Cashwell was when these events transpired, what can be established with certainty is that they all transpired before he was twenty-three-years-old. Doug Beacham, G.B. Cashwell's biographer, believes that these wilder years were the result of growing up without a father. Herring Cashwell passed away in 1878. G.B. Cashwell was only fifteen-years-old when he died. Most likely, Cashwell surrounded himself with those less likely to succeed causing him to display this type of behavior. Yet, what teenager wouldn't follow this path given the early loss of their father?[14]

A.B. Crumpler's Younger Years

Abner Blackmon Crumpler, better known by locals as "Blackmon Crumpler," was born on June 9, 1864, in Honeycutt Township, North Carolina. Recognized later as the Apostle of Holiness amongst his peers, Rev. A.B. Crumpler was also destined for spiritual greatness just as his counterpart G.B. Cashwell was. With the message of holiness burning in his bones, A.B. Crumpler took North Carolina by storm during the late 1890s. Known for having iron lungs, Crumpler's voice could be heard over a mile radius during the height of his ministry. Underneath his preaching, the Carolina's would be consumed in holy fire, and countless souls would be won over to its ranks. Like John the Baptist, A.B. Crumpler's holiness ministry prepared an entire generation to receive the message of Pentecost that would be brought to them through G.B. Cashwell several years later. Ironically, these two spiritual giants emerged onto the national stage from rural Sampson County, North Carolina.[15]

Being nearly the same age as G.B. Cashwell, A.B. Crumpler also grew up under the difficult times of reconstruction. According to the 1880 Federal Census, young Blackmon Crumpler is found working on the Crumpler family farm in the heart of Sampson County, North Carolina. Located in Honeycutt Township, the Crumpler farm rested at the basin of the Coharie swamp. This area had been largely settled and populated by the county's Native American population. Interestingly, the Crumpler farm was also positioned only seven miles away from the G.B. Cashwell farm. Being the same age and practically neighbors in the same farming community, it is very likely that A.B. Crumpler and G.B. Cashwell were friends while growing up.[16]

Unfortunately, besides early census records, there is very little known about A.B. Crumpler's younger years. Thankfully, one more insightful detail has surfaced about Mr. A.B. Crumpler. According to his personal study Bible, Crumpler followed in his family's legacy by going to law school. His Bible records indicate that he graduated from the prestigious Law School of Duke University in 1888, at the age of twenty-four. Known at that time as Trinity College, Duke University was founded by the famous Duke family of Durham, North Carolina.[17]

Interestingly, Crumpler must have made quite the impression on one of its founders. For a graduation present, B.N. Duke, brother of J.B. Duke, presented the young aspiring law student from Sampson County with this massive study Bible, which he personally signed. Another insightful detail we can gleam from Crumpler's tenure at Duke Law School was that the school was a part of the Methodist Church.

It has widely been known that A.B. Crumpler came through the ranks of Methodism when he ignited the Holiness Movement in eastern North Carolina during 1896. Yet, no one has ever discovered how he first came to the Methodist Church. Surprisingly, it came through the hands of a burning preacher that staged perhaps one of the most significant revivals in North Carolina's history. Crumpler, however, would not be alone in his remarkable salvation experience. Another extraordinary young man from Keener would also be present for the "revival that would change everything" in the summer of 1885.[18]

Chapter 3

THE REVIVAL THAT CHANGED EVERYTHING

A PASTOR ONCE STATED, "It would indeed be a remarkable privilege to meet the world renowned evangelist Billy Graham, but for me, it would be an even greater privilege to meet the man who led him to the Lord!" This well-spoken statement also applies in describing the man who initiated perhaps the greatest unknown revival in Sampson County, North Carolina, since its inception. As a newly appointed Methodist circuit riding preacher, Rev. James T. Kendall arrived at the heart of Keener, North Carolina, during the summer of 1885. While there, he ignited a powerful revival that would reap two of the South's greatest revivalists.[1]

Through Kendall's Cotton Gin Revival, the young G.B. Cashwell and A.B. Crumpler would be brought to the fountains of salvation. Traditionally, it has been assumed by revival scholars that G.B. Cashwell was saved while on a farming trip in Georgia during 1893. Although it is true that Gaston Cashwell did have a "theological changing" experience while in Georgia in 1893, his salvation experience did not occur there, as some believe. Surprisingly, G.B. Cashwell was saved in his own backyard: Keener, North Carolina. Likewise, no documents have ever emerged revealing where A.B. Crumpler was first saved either. Incredibly, both men were brought to salvation under Kendall's ministry in Keener, during August 1885. Before discussing the Keener revival in further detail, it seems appropriate to meet the preacher responsible for their conversion.[2]

REV. JAMES T. KENDALL

With the exception of Gaston B. Cashwell, possibly no other minister during this time frame is surrounded by such mystery as the Rev. James T. Kendall. Records revealing who he was and what his ministry was like are scarce and rare. The 1900 Federal Census shows that Kendall was married and had two small children. Additionally, the census lists Kendall's occupation as a "Preacher," and says that he born somewhere in North Carolina around the year 1859. At some point in his youth, he gave his heart to the Lord and felt a call to the ministry. Although it cannot be proven with certainty when this occurred, what is known is that Kendall became an ordained and licensed minister with the Methodist Episcopal Church South. This occurred at Winton, North Carolina, in the year 1880, when Kendall was just twenty-one years of age.[3]

As a young minister of the Methodist church during this time, Kendall was appointed to preach at various church circuits consolidated in a specific area. His first circuit in 1880 was located in the Brunswick section of North Carolina. The following year he was assigned to the Onslow circuit, placing him further up the northeast part of Cape Fear in what is now known as Richland's, North Carolina. In 1882, however, young Kendall was admitted in the Raleigh Conference where he was appointed to the newly formed Cape Fear circuit which was centered out of Fayetteville, North Carolina. By 1885, Kendall was re-assigned to another region that would ultimately shift the direction of his ministry and alter Carolina's spiritual landscape forever: Sampson County's Clinton circuit.[4]

Kendall's first objective, arriving on the Clinton Circuit, was to hold a series of revival meetings in a little town known as Persimmon College (Keener). Why he selected Keener to hold the revival is not known. However, what is known is that Keener was a wise choice because of its strategic location. With miles of rural woodlands all around, this junction possessed a well of water for weary travelers to stop and rest. It also had a cotton gin and saw mill that provided goods and services for local farmers.[5]

The Keener stop was also the half-way point between Wilmington and Raleigh, the two biggest cities at that time in North Carolina. In terms of timing, 1885 was a tough year due to reconstruction. People, both white and black, were spiritually hungry for something greater that would perhaps unify their efforts in rebuilding the South. With the White Supremacy movement emerging through the rich and aristocrat Democratic Party, racism was beginning to boil over into the poor white and black communities as well. The separation of races was well under way. Nevertheless, the twenty-six year old burning preacher arrived and preached the Gospel without prejudice. By doing so, Kendall started a fire that is still blazing in the hearts of some 125 years later.[6]

G.B. Cashwell's Salvation Experience

The revival that changed everything is not something to be taken lightly. With hundreds in attendance, this personal visitation of God's Spirit upon Halls Township literally swept multitudes into the sweet presence of the Almighty God, including G.B. Cashwell and A.B. Crumpler. Fortunately, recent records have surfaced which a paint a clearer picture of what happened during this historic meeting.

According to the Keener United Methodist Church records, a great and mighty revival swept through the area in August of 1885 under the ministry of Rev. James T. Kendall. It reads as follows:

> In August of 1885, the Revered J.T. Kendall, Pastor of the Clinton Circuit conducted a revival meeting in the Keener Community. At the conclusion of the revival a Methodist Church was organized with 108 charter members and was called Keener Chapel, named in honor of the presiding Bishop of our Methodist Conference, Reverend John C. Keener. However, all available quarterly conference records give the name as Keener Methodist Church. The revival and other church meetings were held in a cotton gin owned by Mr. B.C. Weeks, but were later moved to the Persimmon College School across the road from the cotton gin until the church could be built.[7]

Cashwell family historian, Dr. McCullen also agrees with these records by writing a brief article in one of his unpublished books entitled, "Keener and Its Schools." He states:

> Keener community, the center of which is located at the junction of the Old Raleigh Road (now 701) and State Road 1746 (Keener Rd.) lies midway between Clinton and Newton Grove. Its name (Keener) derives from the Reverend John C. Keener, Methodist Bishop presiding when, during the summer of 1885, a revival was staged at the junction of these roads and Keener Methodist Church was founded.[8]

Both accounts testify that a great and mighty outpouring of God's Spirit was occurring in Keener, and many souls were being brought into the Kingdom. There are several facts that can be noted from these revival meetings.

First, the Keener Methodist Church history records 108 charter members who were all impacted by Kendall's revival. The list of 108 only seems to include the heads of local families represented. It doesn't take into account the children of these family members, some of which had ten or more. From this, we can speculate that there could have been several hundred or more people in attendance throughout its duration.[9]

Second, the churches history discloses that the meetings were moved from the "cotton gin to the Persimmon College School across the street."

This school building was used to educate children of the community. At the time, this was probably the biggest structure that could house the most people. Nonetheless, the meetings continued in the school house for five months until a house of worship was constructed by local families in 1886.[10]

Third, Rev. J.T. Kendall was the church's original pastor during its first year of existence. This is documented in the church's history and on the original land deed. Given by Mr. B.C. Weeks and his wife to the "trustees" of the new Keener Methodist Church, the land was situated right off Keener Road. The Keener church was built in 1886, and was initially pastored by Rev. J.T. Kendall. Although a mighty revival was breaking out in Keener during this time, how do we know for sure that G.B. Cashwell was a part of it? The answer is also found in the Keener church history.[11]

To ensure the continuation of revival fire burning on Keener's alter, it had to be sustained by local leaders. Church records reveal five men were listed as its first trustees. Among the five trustees mentioned, three of them were connected with the Cashwell family: G.B. Cashwell, A.H. Brewer (Gaston's Uncle), and Jerry F. Gore (Gaston's brother-in-law). Gaston Cashwell, therefore, was not only converted at this meeting, but elevated to the position of trustee. Cashwell family history also agrees that J.T. Kendall's revival in 1885 is what brought G.B. Cashwell to the waters of salvation.[12]

To gain a better understanding of the role Cashwell played in the church as trustee, a further search into Methodist Church history is appropriate. The *1881 North Carolina Methodist Handbook of Church Discipline* gives some insights of what trustees of the local Methodist church were expected to do:

Trustees were appointed by the presiding preacher.
Trustees had to be at least twenty-one years of age.
Trustees were shareholders in church property and assets.
Trustees generally looked over the churches finances.[13]

Even though there are more functions that the trustees perform, the four mentioned here allows us to understand where Gaston's life was spiritually immediately following this six month revival. Notice that in order to be a trustee, Gaston Cashwell and the other four gentlemen had to be hand selected by Rev. J.T. Kendall himself and placed in that position. They had to be at least twenty-one-years-old, which speaks of having some degree of maturity, and they had to be trusted with overseeing the financial needs of the church. Of course, the biggest requirement was that one had to be saved and make a public profession of faith. Certainly, for this to transpire, Gaston Cashwell must have made quite the impression but, now, in a positive way. His wild youth years were being put behind him, and now at the age of twenty-three, his life was being awakened to the destiny that awaited him.[14]

G.B. Cashwell: Methodist, Southern Baptist, or Neither?

Given these early records that reveal G.B. Cashwell was saved and presided as a trustee of Keener Methodist Church, it is very easy to assume that Gaston B. Cashwell joined, and emerged out of, the Methodist camp. However, this is an assumption and mistake that many researchers and scholars have made over the years (including myself). This is not to discredit the Methodist church. Without the wonderful efforts and sacrifices of circuit riding preachers like J.T. Kendall, the Holiness-Pentecostal message would have never come into existence. Yet, in searching to discover the truth about G.B. Cashwell's unknown years, an ancient question must be answered: was G.B. Cashwell really a Methodist?

Exhaustive searches in the North Carolina Methodist archives reveals that Gaston B. Cashwell was never a member, affiliated, or received ordination through the Methodist Church. Yet, Keener Methodists church history reveals Cashwell was a trustee of the church. How could this be? Amazingly, this mystery can be cleared up rather easily.[15]

Even though Gaston Cashwell and three of his family members were listed on the initial roll call of the church's history as trustees, this does not necessarily constitute that they were active members of the church. *The North Carolina Methodist Discipline of 1881* also specified that "trustees did not have to be members of the church." They could come from an outside church body. If this is true, then what church body did G.B. Cashwell and his other family members come from? The answer is quite revealing.[16]

Prior to Kendall's arrival in 1885, Granny Susan Cashwell and other concerned parents in the area "pulled their resources together" and built a school/church meetinghouse in the same vicinity that Kendall held his revival. The mother of G.B. Cashwell did this so that folks in her community could attend church and school. Dubbed "Persimmon College," the meetinghouse had served the community as meeting place for two local Missionary Baptist congregations. Dr. McCullen alludes that weekly prayer meetings were held there for many years before Rev. J.T. Kendall arrived. It is very likely that G.B. Cashwell attended these meetings when he was a child. However, given his wilder years, he probably sat in only as a spectator. Family history remembers that it was not until J.T. Kendall's arrival in 1885, that G.B. Cashwell really made a decision to give his heart to God.[17]

Observing his heart change, J.T. Kendall nominated G.B. Cashwell to assist in the establishment of Keener Methodist Church. Once established,

STATE OF SOUTH CAROLINA **JUROR SUMMONS FOR CIRCUIT COURT**

COUNTY OF: **Greenville County**	FOR TERM BEGINNING WEEK OF: **March 14, 2016**	JUROR NUMBER: **29**

You are hereby summoned to appear at **Greenville County Courthouse, 305 East North Street Greenville, SC, 29601-** on **Monday, March 14, 2016 at 9:00 am** to answer this summons to serve as a petit juror for the Court of Common Pleas and General Sessions. Failure to appear at the address above at the specified time may subject you to penalties as prescribed by law.

Panel: MAR_14_2016

Clerk of Court, **Paul B. Wickensimer**

Phone: (864)467-8553

NAME AND ADDRESS OF JUROR	IMPORTANT INFORMATION AND INSTRUCTIONS
COVINGTON, INGRID M 312 STILLWATER CT SIMPSONVILLE, SC 29681	Fill in the requested information in the "Juror Information Section" and the appropriate contact information below. After reading all the conditions listed in the "Juror Response Section," mark any condition that applies to you Separate the top and bottom portions of this page at the line indicated below and WITHIN THREE DAYS OF RECEIPT return the bottom portion of the form using the self-addressed envelope provided

Separate this top portion from bottom portion at the dotted line. Retain this top portion for your reference.

however, G.B Cashwell, Jerry Gore, and A.H. Brewer ceased in being Keener Methodist's trustees. Cashwell quickly returned to the Missionary Baptist congregation of Persimmon College and began to embrace his calling to preach the gospel to all people. Cashwell's religious affiliation as being a member of the Missionary Baptist church is further evidenced on his funeral record. Although Cashwell was saved under J.T. Kendall's ministry, he would not rise out of the ranks of Methodism. His climb to the top would emerge from the loosely-affiliated Missionary Baptist church that his mother built, Persimmon College.[18]

A.B. Crumpler: Conversion and Church Affiliation

As the sounds of Heaven continued to explode throughout Keener, it was becoming quite apparent that this was shaping up to be a revival of the ages. Quite possibly, not sense the county's formation in 1784 had anyone seen such a display of God's wondrous power as those who attended these meetings. Under the dynamic preaching of Kendall, and the testimonies of people like Gaston Cashwell, hearts were being stirred for Christ. Even before the revival had come to a close, fruit was already appearing. Hundreds had been converted, a church was being planted, and the future "Apostle of Pentecost to the South," had now been won to Christianity. Strange as it may sound, God was not finished. There was yet another young man from a neighboring township also being drawn to the great Keener revival during the summer of 1885, A.B. Crumpler.

For over a century no one has discovered where or how A.B. Crumpler first came to the Lord. Authors and historians descending from his own church recorded that his "sanctification experience" occurred while he was residing in Bismarck, Missouri, during the year 1890. Though it is true that A.B. Crumpler was theologically transformed in 1890, the date of his salvation experience has always remained a mystery. Due to the emergence of new sources, there is an excellent reason to conclude that A.B. Crumpler was saved in the exact same meeting that G.B. Cashwell was, the Keener Revival! Several key observations support this claim:

The first key source is taken from Abner B. Crumpler's Holiness revival in Dunn, North Carolina, during the year 1896. At this revival, Crumpler preached a sermon on Holiness that was recorded in the Dunn local newspaper. Entitled "Sparks Caught at the Tent Meeting: Crumpler's Hot Shots," this insightful article reveals A.B. Crumpler's year of salvation. Crumpler states, "I came to the Lord eleven years ago and have not bothered Him anymore." According to this article, Crumpler distinguishes very clearly between the year of his sanctification (1890), and the year of his salvation

(1885). Amazingly, Crumpler announces that 1885 was the year when he first "came to the Lord."[19]

The second key source derives from the historical records of the First United Methodist Church of Clinton, North Carolina. Rev. J.T. Kendall, who initiated the great Keener revival of 1885, could not be present every day to maintain the six month-long revival. He had other preaching obligations to fulfill. One of those appointments was being pastor of the Clinton Methodist Church. According to Mrs. Grace Crumpler Vann (A.B. Crumpler's daughter), Rev. Kendall led the church from the years 1885–1887. Mrs. Vann also states that A.B. Crumpler "joined the North Carolina Methodist conference in 1888" as an ordained minister of the M.E. Church South. After being converted in the revival held at Keener, A.B. Crumpler sought to further his faith by joining this church. Seeing the unique call of God on his life, it appears that Kendall took him under his wing and helped disciple him. Given the insight of these records, it is probably safe to say that A.B. Crumpler was not only saved, but also ordained through Rev. J.T. Kendall's ministry.[20]

Another solid key source to substantiate A.B. Crumpler's salvation connections with J.T. Kendall is found in Crumpler's study Bible. Crumpler used this Bible throughout his sixty years of ministry. In the family records section, Crumpler's marriage to his first wife, Lillie J. Underwood Crumpler, is recorded as taking place on September 26, 1886. This was only a few months after the Keener revival had come to a close. The minister who married them was none other than, Rev. J.T. Kendall. The records kept in this Bible were written by A.B. Crumpler himself and also reveal some very insightful information concerning his younger years following his conversion at Keener during the summer of 1885.[21]

The last and perhaps most concrete record of A.B. Crumpler's salvation experience comes from Rev. J.T. Kendall's own pen. In a lost issue of J.M. Pike's *Way of Faith*, J.T. Kendall wrote an article revealing his relationship with some of the major catalysts for the National Holiness Movement, including A.B. Crumpler. He states: "My address will be Goldsboro, N.C., and I refer to Rev. W.S. Rowe, Goldsboro, N.C., my last presiding elder; or to Rev. B Carradine, D.D; or Rev. A.B. Crumpler, Clinton, N.C., who was converted under my ministry."[22]

According to these records, it is certain that A.B. Crumpler was saved under J.T. Kendall's powerful revival held in Keener during August 1885. In addition, A.B. Crumpler, G.B. Cashwell, and J.T. Kendall all seem to have known each other during this time. After the North Carolina Holiness Movement erupted in the 1890s, all three of these men staged revivals, organized churches, and preached the gospel to bi-racial congregations. Surprisingly, it now seems that they may have done it together.[23]

Certainly, this was the revival that changed everything! Through the amazing efforts of an unknown Methodist preacher, James T. Kendall, many in Sampson County had been converted. In a time when North Carolinians were suffering through the pain of reconstruction, and Christianity was disappearing from the landscape, a great and mighty revival broke out in Sampson County during August of 1885. Kendall's ministry emerged like a rushing and violent tornado, swept through the entire county, and disappeared just as quickly as it began. The aftermath of this perfect storm during a three year period (1885–1887) accomplished many feats.

It re-awakened a desire for Christianity; brought hundreds, possibly even thousands, to Christ; established multiple churches in the area; and converted two of the South's greatest preachers. Enough could never be said of the sacrifice of Kendall's efforts in reforming an entire community. He is definitely an unsung hero in this story. Although information concerning his life is scarce, it should be remembered that God used him to usher in one of the greatest and forgotten revivals in eastern North Carolina's history.

Another noteworthy observation worth mentioning is the conversion and church affiliation of both G.B. Cashwell and A.B. Crumpler. Through this revival, it can be noted that both Crumpler and Cashwell, young men in their early twenties, accepted Christ and began to pursue God with all their hearts. Following Crumpler, we learned that he entered into the Clinton Methodist Church after being saved and immediately pursued a law degree at the outstanding Law School of Trinity College (Duke University). After graduating in 1888, he also became a licensed and ordained preacher through the Clinton M.E. Church, South. Cashwell, on the other hand, took a different route after coming to the Lord.

Instead of joining the Methodist ranks as Crumpler, he returned to Persimmon College, the small Missionary Baptist meetinghouse founded by his mother, Granny Susan Cashwell. Here, it seems that he took up a leadership role. Following no creed but Christ and believing in no doctrine but the Bible, G.B. Cashwell began to pastor this congregation with incredible passion after his conversion. His days spent at Persimmon College would go on to shape his understanding of the Gospel, and prove to be essential in the Pentecostal Movement that he was chosen to lead. Cashwell remained in the Kenner area until an unlikely trip took him to Georgia in 1893.

This is the home that G.B. Cashwell and his seven other siblings were born and raised in. The Cashwells lived in the home for approximately seventeen years until it was later used as a country store. Courtesy of Stanley Carr.

Granny Susan Cashwell, mother of Rev. G.B. Cashwell. Known in and around Keener as the "Medicine Woman of Persimmon College," Granny Susan is most recognized for establishing the school/church that G.B. Cashwell emerged from, The Persimmon College Meetinghouse. Courtesy of Stanley Carr.

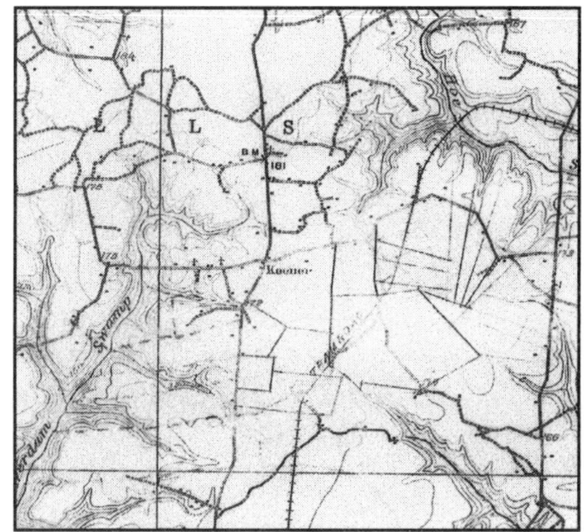

This is a 1909 map of Keener, N.C.(Persimmon College). The main intersection (right above the "K" in Keener)is the site where Rev. J.T. Kendall staged the historic revival in 1885 that saved A.B. Crumpler and G.B. Cashwell The first cross on the left marks Keener United Methodist Church. It started out of J.T. Kendall's revival and was organized by several Cashwell family members including G.B. Cashwell The second cross to the left is believed to be the site of Persimmon College Meetinghouse. This was the church/school in which Granny Susan Cashwell helped build, and where G.B. Cashwell emerged from. The Crumpler family farm was located just seven miles southwest of Keener. Courtesy of John Aman.

This photo is believed to be a young A.B. Crumpler. Courtesy of John Aman.

Rev. J.T. Kendall is the man responsible for bringing both G.B. Cashwell and A.B. Crumpler to Salvation in 1885. He was a Methodist circuit riding preacher who organized churches all up and down the Cape Fear region. Courtesy of Clinton United Methodist Church.

Rev. G.B. Cashwell is standing holding the Bible. The man sitting down is G.B. Cashwell's brother, William "Billy" Cashwell. This is one of the only known photographs ever taken of Rev. G.B. Cashwell. It was taken in the late 1880's after his salvation experience at Keener in 1885.
Courtesy of Stanley Carr.

Rev. Abner Blackmon Crumpler, founder of the Holiness Church of North Carolina. Photo was taken in Goldsboro 1900. Courtesy of Mt. Olive College Archives.

PART II:

A.B. CRUMPLER, G.B. CASHWELL, AND THE HOLINESS MOVEMENT

Chapter 4

ANCIENT WELLS OF REVIVAL

BETWEEN THE YEARS 1896–1906, perhaps no other state in America would experience as much revival fire as North Carolina. During this supernatural decade, the Tar Heel state would burn hot with the flames of the Holiness Movement. From Carolina's crystal coast to the mountains of Cherokee, tens of thousands would be swept into the new message of sanctification. These meetings, which often were recorded in local newspapers, were almost identical to the Great Awakenings led by John Wesley and George Whitfield in the 1700s. Even so, A.B. Crumpler and G.B. Cashwell would awaken an entire generation from their spiritual slumber. Motivated by their sanctified experiences, Crumpler and Cashwell worked tirelessly to establish the Holiness Movement in the Carolinas. Uniting divided denominations as well as divided races, both of these Sampson County natives would be pioneers in sparking the fires of holiness in their own ways.[1]

In order to place their holiness ministries in the proper context, one must revisit the place where the National Holiness Movement first began. Most scholars pinpoint the movement's origins to the extraordinary camp meeting held at Landis Park in Vineland, New Jersey, during 1867. Here, tens of thousands gathered to seek the Lord for a national spiritual awakening. As a result, the National Camp Meeting for the Promotion of Holiness was conceived. Accordingly, this organization became responsible for spreading the Holiness Movement all around the globe during the late 1800s. By the 1890s, it had swept in thousands of ministers all over the country, including A.B. Crumpler and G.B. Cashwell.[2]

Following the impressive camp meeting revival held in Vineland, during 1867, organizers decided to dig two more wells of holiness—one in Manheim, Pennsylvania, during August, 1868, and the other in Round Lake, New York, the following summer. By the close of the Round Lake meeting, national interest for holiness would be stirred. Therefore, a brief study of these revivals is appropriate for several reasons. First, they provide insight into the holiness messages Crumpler and Cashwell were preaching. Second, they identify methods of ministry used by the Tar Heel revivalist. Finally, and perhaps most importantly, they reveal the audience in which they targeted.

Vineland, New Jersey: 1867

Two years after the Civil War, during July 1867, approximately 10–15,000 people of multiple denominations gathered at Landis Park in Vineland, New Jersey, for a massive solemn assembly. Broken and devastated due to the aftermath of the war, people were hungry for a spiritual awakening. Their appetite for the supernatural, however, would be satisfied through the remarkable camp meeting in Vineland. The encampment, which was designed from a prophetic revelation of Ezekiel's wheel within a wheel, was strategically laid out to accommodate the seas of people destined to arrive there. Coming in horse and buggies, campers began to pitch several thousand tents with excitement in the Ezekiel-wheel formation all around the main stage.[3]

Once this occurred, Dr. Kenneth O. Brown states, "The National Camp Meeting at Vineland, New Jersey, officially opened on July 17, 1867, at 3:30 p.m. in the spacious Kensington Tent. Persons from several states and at least six denominations attended the opening services." Even before the services started, however, an incredible sense of God's presence was beginning to manifest around the grove that afternoon. Sensing an invasion of Heaven upon the encampment, John S. Inskip, one of the founders of the movement, took the stage and declared with power the following statement:

> It is evident to me, and it must be to all, that God is present in this place, and the fact of His special presence is to us a clear indication of His approval of this meeting. As for me, I desire no clearer proof of the Divine favor than the evidence of special Divine presence. I am just as sure that this movement is of God, as it should be had it been written as a specific command in God's Word, that the purpose for which they have come; and I confidently believe that the object of our assembling will be accomplished.[4]

Inskip then encouraged everyone to set aside their differences and come together in the spirit of love. He continues:

> We have not come here for that purpose, but for a nobler one of holding up a banner that has written upon it, "Holiness to the Lord." Let us point the people to that. Let every sermon aim at it, every

> exhortation urge it, all prayer embrace it, and the life of every man and women present exemplify it.[5]

Immediately following his message and prayer, it seemed as if the veil between heaven and earth was ripped in half, and God's powerful presence filled the trees that surrounded them. Thousands laid prostrate on the ground for hours, others were found weeping with indescribable joy, while some remained paralyzed with awe as to what they were witnessing. Incredibly, seas of people were encountering the Almighty God all at once.

Having acute prophetic insight, leaders brilliantly organized teams of preachers and local churches to assist in the meetings. Under Vineland's atmosphere, Methodists, Presbyterians, and Baptists were one. Leading national figures, such as Phoebe Palmer, Bishop Matthew Simpson, and William McDonald, were also present and assisted with different encampment services, although the meetings were not dependent on them.[6]

Progressing simultaneously, eight different ministry tents were positioned around the park, forming a giant eight-spoke-wheel with the main stage at the hub. They provided salvation opportunities for children, young adults, married couples, as well as divine healing. There was also a very special place in the encampment which was dedicated as the place of intercession. Known as the "Bower of Prayer," campers assembled at this sacred spot morning, noon, and night in order to sustain the fire of God's presence. If Inskip sparked the initial flame at Vineland that morning, surely the "Bower of Prayer" sustained it for the next few weeks. These sets of intercession were led by prayer warriors like Phoebe and Walter Palmer.[7]

During the morning hours, massive love feasts were held all around the camp. The love feast was first instituted by the Moravian revival in Germany during 1727. It was a time of fellowship where campers broke bread and shared fresh testimonies about their own revival experiences. Impacted directly by the Moravians, John Wesley adopted many of their ministry methods, including the love feast. Being mostly Methodists, Vineland leaders also organized these love feasts during the encampment. This became one of the major catalysts for allowing God's Spirit to fan the flames of revival even brighter. Besides the love feasts, thousands were also experiencing a divine resurgence of what John Wesley had called the "second blessing."[8]

What is the second blessing? According to Wesley, the second blessing, or "second work of grace," occurred when the inbreed sin is purged away from the life of a believer. Wesley identified that this experience took place following salvation. He believed that when this action occurred within the heart, a person was sanctified, or set apart, for Christian service. Building upon this foundation, Wesley would use terms like, "heart purity," "perfect love," and "Christian perfection" to describe the work of sanctification and the life of Holiness in the believer. For many at Vineland, this experience was described like an invisible fire burning within their hearts. Sensing the Spirit of God moving in this direction, leaders began to expound upon the beautiful experience of sanctification that was sweeping through the grove.[9]

Prior to this 1867 meeting, there had been smaller outbreaks of holiness revivals in the country. Charles Finney, Phoebe Palmer, and others were carrying the holiness mantle before the Vineland meeting was conceived; however, something very different was occurring at Vineland, New Jersey. Working together in unity, believers from six different denominations came together in light of the horrific war that had just ripped the nation a part. Assembled as one in mind, body, and spirit, campers lifted up their cry and with one voice asked God for the "descent of the Spirit upon ourselves, the church, the nation, and the world." Pleased with their prayer, the Lord answered by sending wave after wave of His glory upon the whole city of Vineland.[10]

As the Vineland meeting came to a close, organizers met together on their knees in prayer during the final day. Hearing the voice of the Lord, they arose from prayer and formed a leadership committee. Made up of leaders such as John S. Inskip, Alfred Cookman, William Osborn, and others, the committee identified themselves as the "National Camp Meeting Association" and the movement they founded, the "National Camp Meeting Association for the Promotion of Holiness." The committee's first objective was to hold another massive camp meeting the following year. After discussions, they chose the beautiful rolling hills of Mennonite country in Manheim, Pennsylvania. Thus, the National Holiness Movement was born and very soon, would set the nation on fire with the message of holiness.[11]

Manheim, Pennsylvania: 1868

One year after the monumental revival at Vineland, New Jersey, tens of thousands gathered together in Lancaster, Pennsylvania, just outside of a little town known as Manheim. Situated in the heart of the Amish, Mennonite, and Quaker country, Manheim's beautiful rolling hills were chosen to host the second annual National Holiness Camp Meeting. Coming off a glorious revival at Vineland, word was beginning to spread throughout the entire country about this encampment. The leadership committee began to prepare the grounds by securing a twenty-five acre tract of land and placing the Rev. Barlow Gorham in charge of the camping lay out. Just a few miles north of Manheim, this spiritual well of revival was nestled between corn fields and a small Mennonite Church.[12]

Gorham, laying out the grounds similar to the Vineland meeting—an Ezekiel's wheel within a wheel, did so because of one reason: to honor the ancient Jewish festival known as the feast of tabernacles. According to his camp meeting manual, this was the most Biblical way to construct a massive holy convocation that would honor God as the Israelites did. Assembling in small booths (tents), ancient Hebrews would sanctify themselves from the everyday luxuries for a brief period of time and worship the Almighty God. This was also Rev. Gorham's aim for the first three national Holiness Camp Meetings (Vineland, Manheim, and Round Lake).[13]

Dr. Brown writes that by opening day of the meeting, over six hundred tents had been erected on the grounds and thousands of people were flooding onto the property. A centralized worship area larger than a modern NFL football field had been prepared. Backless pews filled this seating area which would host a crowd of at least 5,000. Dedicating every aspect of ministry to the Lord, the committee also had a very large piece of canvass stretched across the camps entrance which read, "Worship the Lord in the Beauty of Holiness." Just like Vineland, the people came in droves.[14]

With 25,000 in attendance, over four hundred different preachers showed up. With a range including Methodist, Baptist, African Methodist Zion, and even the Amish, all sects of Christianity were welcomed and had a part to play in Manheim's camp meeting. Every sector under the nation was represented by leading voices of revival power. Among them were Bishop Matthew Simpson, personal friend of President Lincoln; Bishop Henry Boehm, the ninety-three-year-old Holiness Mennonite Bishop; and Bishop Alexander Waymen of the African Methodist Episcopal Church. Bishop Waymen of Philadelphia was noted for his preaching and playing a leading role in the Manheim Camp Meeting. Being a powerful leader with the African Methodist Church, his presence furthered the cause of racial harmony between the races at this encampment.[15]

Manheim was a success from the beginning. The Spirit of unity and power that prevailed there was astounding. Author William Kostlevy captured the revivals significance by writing an article revealing Manheim's impact upon the local Dutch community. He states:

> The *Lancaster Daily Express* noted, "The scene was beyond all description. It was one of the most wonderful manifestations of divine power we have ever be held. Several thousand people seemed to be prostrate under the mighty influence of supernatural power." On Wednesday one observer remembered that "the slain of the Lord covered the land." For many, it was, as one noted, "a little Pentecost," as Methodist,

> Baptists, Presbyterians, Dutch Reformed, Congregationalists, Quakers, United Brethren, Evangelicals, and Episcopalians became indistinguishable as they sought and received the Baptism of the Holy Spirit.[16]

Like Vineland's atmosphere, Kostlevy writes that all were one during the Manheim camp meetings. Kostlevy also notes that Manheim's influence even altered the fate of one local denomination, the Mennonites.[17]

Accordingly, C. H. Balsbaugh, an influential leader of the Anabaptists, would be converted to Holiness by the early 1870s due to this camp meeting. Balsbaugh, who always remained true to his Amish and Mennonite roots, preached the message of holiness for years amongst his brethren. He is credited for transforming the once secluded Mennonite church into the evangelistic army they are today.[18]

The Manheim holiness revival is without a doubt, one of the greatest mass religious convocations of the nineteenth century. Indeed, it became a living well of fire for the growing National Holiness Movement. Unfortunately, only a handful of people know what took place in those hills one hundred and forty years ago. With momentum building, however, and a movement born, leaders of the National Holiness Association sought to further the revival by establishing the next historic gathering at Round Lake, New York, the following summer. Between the Vineland and Manheim Camp Meetings, an estimated 50,000 people were in attendance. Strange as it may sound, the Round Lake Camp Meeting was destined to host twice as many people than the previous two camp meetings, and without failure, keep the fire burning.

Round Lake, New York: 1869

Within two years of the Vineland Camp Meeting, the Holiness Movement was exploding all over the United States. People all around the nation were discussing the Vineland and Manheim meetings. Newspapers, religious periodicals, and journals of all kinds were reporting the impacts of this movement. The National Holiness Association, although made up of powerful revivalist, pastors, and evangelists, really did not know what to do next. The young Holiness Movement breaking out under their leading was new territory. However, they all seemed to be in one accord and trusted the Holy Spirit for prophetic direction.

After waiting upon the Lord, the Association was called upon by Joseph Hillman. Hillman, who was the founder of the Round Lake Camp, requested the committee to host their next annual Holiness Camp Meeting at Round Lake during the summer of 1869. Found in the beautiful Adirondack Mountains of upstate New York, this forty acre camp ground proved to be the ideal location for the third Holiness Camp Meeting. Local newspapers were reminding its readers of the "Manheim Pentecost" and urged campers to come with great expectations.[19]

According to Dr. Brown, the *Methodist Home Journal* published an article stating, "We have no new measures, no doctrinal novelties to prose. Our aim is to press Christian believers onward to a better spiritual life and to urge them to endeavor to be sanctified wholly as well as justified freely." By opening day of the encampment, 800 to 1,000 tents had already been erected. Over 100,000 thousand people were carried in on the local rail road alone. Although an exact number was never recorded, Dr. Brown writes that an estimated 250,000 people attended the meeting in Round Lake in the summer of 1869. During the "roll call" of the encampment, twenty-eight states were represented, as well as those from Canada and London.[20]

As in both the Vineland and Manheim revivals, the Round Lake camp grounds were laid out in the "wheel within the wheel" formation in order to honor the ancient Jewish feasts of tabernacles. Dubbed "A Modern Pentecost," Round Lake also brought together over seven different denominations. Even some leaders at the beginning of the meeting were concerned because they felt the revival was only about the Holiness message. John Chaplin, one of the Round Lake leaders, confessed this prejudice before a great mighty throng of people once the meetings began. Dr. Brown remembers that after he attended the meetings and "paused to see the hand writing on the wall," Chaplin found the Round Lake Revival to be identical with Acts chapter two when the Spirit of God was poured out through Pentecost.[21]

First, he observed how Jews from many countries attended the feats of Pentecost. Chaplin then claimed how people from twenty-eight different states and foreign countries came to the Round Lake meeting. He stated that this attendance included over seven different denominations. Second, the Jews in Jerusalem at Pentecost heard the Apostles speak in their own tongue, and at Round Lake, Chaplin wrote, "God gave them one language." Third, a special time of waiting, prayer, and unity preceded the Biblical Pentecost, and all three of these sources were found to be extremely powerful during the Round Lake encampment. Although there is no record of speaking in tongues during the encampment, Chaplin and other leaders seemed to be more impressed with the unity aspect of Pentecost, rather than the manifestation of glossolalia.[22]

At the closing service, John S. Inskip and Bishop Matthew Simpson walked arm in arm leading twenty-five thousand campers around the entire forty acre property. Like Joshua and the Israelites at Jericho, Inskip and

Simpson marched the people around the camp seven times. On the final lap, the mighty crowd assembled together and with one voice, shouted the shout of victory! The Joshua marching tradition had started in Vineland, and continued through the first three National Holiness Camp Meetings. Prophetically speaking, the famous Jericho march seemed to be an act of spiritual war. By declaring victory through holiness, leaders began to sense the walls of racism and denominationalism were crumbling around them.[23]

The Fire Spreads

Due to the success of the first three National Holiness Camp Meetings, invitations began to pour in from all over the nation. It seemed that every state wanted the Holiness Movement to invade their city. Realizing the importance of this work, the National Holiness Association (NHA) committee began to abandon their pastoral positions and accepted the charge of becoming global revivalists for the cause of Holiness.[24]

In response to requests they were receiving, John S. Inskip, William McDonald, and a few other leaders secured a large Holiness Tabernacle (canvas tent) that would seat three thousand people. After consecrating this massive tent for the purpose of holiness evangelism, the committee sealed the tent's assignment through Isaiah 35:8 which states, "And a highway will be there; it will be called the way of holiness." Immediately, leaders began to extend the movement westward. Preaching the message of holiness without prejudice, these burning revivalists used their massive tent to cross over both racial and denominational barriers throughout the Midwest.[25]

Gripped by a spiritual power unknown to our generation, these holy pioneers even took their tent to Mormon headquarters. By invitation from the Church of Latter Day Saints, the same crew that was burning with Holiness from the North positioned the three thousand man holiness tabernacle right in the middle of Salt Lake City, Utah, during June of 1871.[26]

For ten days, a powerful holiness revival broke out within the Mormon Camp causing thousands of Mormons to abandon the teachings of Joseph Smith and the Book of Mormon, and follow Christ wholly. Dr. T. DeWitt Talmage, a minister who visited Salt Lake City some weeks after the revival, stated:

> We found the track of the Methodist tent all the way across the Continent. Mormonism never received such a shot as when, with Brigham Young and his elders present in the tent, the party of wide-awake Methodist ministers preached righteousness, temperance, and judgment to come in great Salt Lake City...A few poles and a big

> piece of canvas, and four or five Christians on fire with zeal, have proved themselves to shake Brigham's Tabernacle.[27]

Brigham Young attended the revival meetings and listened to fiery messages being preached by Inskip, McDonald, and others. Obviously, Young did not abandon Mormonism; however, many who were in the Mormon priesthood had been largely affected. This caused a great controversy over the truth of Mormonism among the leadership. Though it seemed as if war was going to erupt during services, Godly order prevailed and the Holiness firebrands carried out their heavenly assignment. When the dust settled, many Mormon leaders had been converted, seeds had been planted, and an invitation of fellowship was extended to the Mormon Church. Perhaps this is an invitation still waiting to be revisited.[28]

In retrospect, the Vineland, Manheim, and Round Lake gatherings were indeed the beginning steps towards a series of supernatural events that reshaped Christianity. When the nation was spiritually bankrupt following the Civil War, over fifteen thousand people assembled at Vineland, New Jersey, and, with one voice cried, out for a national healing revival. Moved by their cries, God answered by sending the fires of holiness upon the vast multitude. This overflow of divine love and His presence resulted in what is now called the Nineteenth Century Holiness Movement. Thus, something occurred through these meetings that man could never have done; healing was brought to a nation and a church that had been divided by the Civil War.

Thankfully, no one got credit for these historic meetings but God Himself. The National Holiness Association committee never sought to organize this fresh outpouring of revival. Instead, they promoted the healing power of Christ through the message of holiness and sanctification to all races, creeds, and denominations. Evidence of their fruit is seen through successfully reaching Methodists, Presbyterians, Baptists, African Methodists, Amish, Mennonites, and even the Mormon Church with their message. As the movement spread, it would only be a matter of time before the holiness fires beckoned the attention of two young preachers from Sampson County, North Carolina.

A.B. Crumpler's Sanctified Experience

When the National Holiness Movement broke out in Vineland, New Jersey, and traveled to the Midwest states, it was drawing attention from all regions of the globe during the 1870s and 1880s. During this period, a young Abner Blackmon Crumpler was becoming restless and yearned for something greater than what he was observing in the organized church.

Having just been admitted into the North Carolina Methodist Conference in 1888 as a local elder, Rev. Crumpler began to hear accounts of the great Midwest Holiness meetings. Grace Crumpler Vann, A.B. Crumpler's only daughter, notes that her father in this same year "transferred his credentials to the St. Louis Conference." Subsequently, Crumpler along with his new bride, Lilly Underwood Crumpler, decided to follow the Spirit's leading and relocated to Missouri between the years 1888 to 1894. During their tenure in the "show me state," the Crumplers witnessed the birth of their first child, Lawrence Crumpler, and would soon become spiritually impregnated with the fires of holiness.[29]

Rev. Blackmon Crumpler's restless pursuit of something more occurred two years later in a revival meeting held by Rev. Carradine in 1890. Carradine, who was ministering directly with some of the very leaders of the Vineland Holiness revival, preached a sermon that would forever alter the destiny of A.B. Crumpler's life as well as the state of North Carolina. Rev. Crumpler recorded this experience in a paper he later published entitled, *The Holiness Advocate*. He states:

> I was sanctified in 1890 at Bismarck, MO at the District conference, under a sermon preached by Beverly Carradine, D.D. I came to North Carolina, my native state, to preach the blessed doctrine of full salvation to my own people, and in 1896, the great Holiness Movement broke out in North Carolina chiefly under my own ministry, in which hundreds and thousands came into the experience of salvation.[30]

Indeed, A.B. Crumpler underwent a transformational process during this time in his life and began to embrace the mantle of holiness in which he was destined to carry. Additionally, his words disclose that in 1896, the North Carolina Holiness Movement broke out "chiefly under my ministry." However, Crumpler fails to mention when he returned to the Tar Heel state, and how he began his quest to sanctify his native land under the banner of holiness. This has remained a mystery until now.[31]

According to *The Democrat,* Rev. A.B. Crumpler returned to Clinton, North Carolina, from the state of Missouri in the summer of 1894. By September of the same year, he was preaching in his home church, Clinton Methodist. During this time, Rev. Crumpler was still an ordained minister for the Clinton M.E. Church South, and in good standing, although he was preaching the new message of "entire sanctification." However, something was strangely different about Rev. Crumpler after returning home. He began to notice that great power and conviction was accompanying his preaching. The people to whom he was preaching also began to express a deep hunger for this new message that was sweeping the land. Word of mouth was spreading all over Clinton about A.B. Crumpler's sermons, and soon things began to shift in the town. Just as massive crowds were drawn to the revival wells at Vineland, Manheim, and Round Lake, equally large crowds were beginning to assemble around Rev. Crumpler's early holiness meetings.[32]

From a ministry perspective, this appeared to be a critical point in Rev. Crumpler's life. A choice was developing before his very eyes. He could return to practice law and quietly serve the local church as an elder, or he could forsake everything and follow the voice of the Spirit that was compelling him. Thankfully, he chose the latter. Being highly intelligent, Crumpler realized that God was calling him to something radically different. In trying to piece this together, Crumpler fulfilled the fire in his heart by following in the footsteps of his predecessors, the National Holiness Association.

Consumed with a passionate vision to see North Carolina burn with holiness, four walls and a pulpit could not contain him. He was on fire and needed to expand his new ministry. Crumpler soon began to hold outdoor meetings where his powerful voice thundered freely throughout the Carolina countryside. The lawyer turned evangelist immediately invested in a tent that would hold up to one thousand people and began to stage interracial and inter-denominational holiness revivals within Sampson, Duplin, and Bladen Counties during the year 1895.[33]

Fortunately, Mr. Crumpler wrote of his new revival adventures in a holiness magazine entitled, *Way of Faith* that was published by John M. Pike. Some of these early issues are still missing; however, in locating the earliest writings from A.B. Crumpler's pen, an article can be found on December 4, 1895. Holding a holiness meeting in Parkersburg, Sampson County, an excited A.B. Crumpler reveals some insightful information regarding his early meetings. Crumpler writes:

> Dear Bro. Pike, The last time I wrote to the dear Way of Faith, I mentioned the fact that I was going to aid Rev. J.T. Kendall in a meeting near Warsaw, N.C., an account of which I was to give in my next letter. We held the meeting in the school house, which was by far too small to accommodate the hungry crowds that came to hear the gospel of full salvation. We had a most glorious time. There were eight sanctified and about thirty converted. The people in this community never had heard any one shout until this meeting. Bro. Kendall is the popular pastor of the Kenansville circuit. He is a whole soul man, a good worker and is in full sympathy with the Holiness Movement. I want all the readers of the Way of Faith to pray that he may be wholly sanctified...Well you want to know about the meeting at Parkersburg. The fire fell on the first service and continued for ten days, until the close of the meeting. There was a good deal of opposition at first, but very soon that was all gone and the Power of the Holy Ghost was sweeping

> the country. Methodists, Baptists, and Presbyterians swept alike into the glorious experience of perfect love... People are getting converted and sanctified all over the country. Hallelujah! The meeting closed on Sunday, the 16th, with a congregation estimated at 1,800 people. I commence another meeting at Elizabethtown, count seat of Bladen, N.C., on Thursday night before the first Sunday in December.[34]

Several things can be drawn from this article that will shed some light on the North Carolina Holiness Movement's infancy years.

First, we learn that Rev. Crumpler was working with Rev. J. T. Kendall, who was responsible for bringing both G.B Cashwell and A.B. Crumpler to the Lord in 1885. Although Crumpler does not mention Gaston, it does reveal the he had a good relationship with his former mentor and mutual friend of Cashwell, Rev. James T. Kendall.

Second, the article reveals that Kendall had not yet experienced sanctification as Crumpler preached it, though he did not oppose it. It was quite common for preachers who did not yet receive the "second blessing" to be sympathetic towards the Holiness Movement and support it. Perhaps it would be this open-minded view towards holiness that would eventually claim Rev. Kendall in its ranks in just a few short months.

Finally, the greatest conclusion that can be drawn from this early letter is the fruit of the meeting. The excitement of Crumpler's words reveals what would become the core or centralized purpose of the holiness revival: denominational and racial reconciliation through the powerful message of sanctification. This was the theme that seemed to dominate the initial three Holiness Camp meeting revivals that took place in Vineland, Manheim, and Round Lake. In the days to follow, it would also become the dominating theme of both A.B. Crumpler's and G.B. Cashwell's holiness ministries in the South.

G.B. Cashwell's Holiness Encounter

For nearly ten years of his life (1897–1906), Gaston gave himself to the love burning message of entire sanctification by preaching to an audience whom most believed should have no rights, no liberties, and no place among the southern elite. However, it has never been established with certainty how or when he first came into contact with the inter-racial and inter-denominational Holiness Movement that was sweeping the country. Thankfully, Dr. McCullen left behind some clues that may be able to shed some light on this unanswered mystery.[35]

According to Dr. McMullen, G.B. Cashwell encountered the Holiness Movement while working as a tobacco demonstrator in Georgia in 1893.

Eight years prior, in 1885, John Inskip and other national holiness pioneers had organized the Georgia State Holiness Association in Augusta. By the time Cashwell made his business trip the Peach State in 1893, Georgia was burning from the inside out with holy fire. Dr. McCullen also noted that while there, G.B. Cashwell's holiness conversion came under the preaching of an unknown dynamic Georgia evangelist. Who was this great Georgia evangelist that made a lasting impression on G.B. Cashwell and connected him with the National Holiness Movement? Although no exact documentation exists to give a solid answer, there is convincing evidence that suggests an unlikely candidate, Rev. Pleasant Hilliard Crumpler.[36]

Better known as Rev. P.H. Crumpler, this Georgia native was a fiery holiness evangelist. Ironically, he is a cousin of A.B. Crumpler and also descended from the Crumpler family tree in Sampson County, North Carolina. In tracing his roots, early census records reveal that sometime during the 1840s, Pleasant's father, James H. Crumpler of Sampson County, moved his family to Dooly County, Georgia.[37]

According to South Georgia's Methodist conference records, P.H. Crumpler was born in Dooley County, Georgia in 1851, and died on February 28, 1920. In 1873, he joined the South Georgia Conference as an ordained Methodist minister. By 1876, he was married to Miss Linnie Cox and had five children. At some point, Rev. P.H. Crumpler embraced the holiness message that was coming down from the north. Quite rapidly, he became a leading voice for holiness throughout the peach state. Conference records also show that P.H. Crumpler embraced the new doctrine of entire sanctification and was well known for holding massive holiness crusades all over Georgia.[38]

Pleasant Crumpler would not just be confined to Georgia's boarders. Early North Carolina newspapers, as well as J.M. Pike's *Way of Faith,* also reveal that when A.B. Crumpler ignited his famed 1896 North Carolina Holiness Campaigns, his cousin, Rev. P. H. Crumpler, assisted him for over two years. Preaching in places such as Clinton, Dunn, Fayetteville, and Smithfield, these two Crumplers lit the Carolinas on fire with holiness during the late 1890s.[39]

On Thursday, July 23, 1896, *The Fayetteville Observer* reported that a great holiness revival broke out in Clinton, North Carolina, under the leadership of A.B. Crumpler. It states, "Ministers of several denominations are assisting [A.B. Crumpler] in the meeting, among them being Methodist, two Missionary Baptist, and a holiness minster from Georgia."[40]

Several months later, in the same newspaper, another article was written that recorded another historic holiness revival that took place in Fayetteville, North Carolina. Dated February 11, 1897, *The Fayetteville*

Observer declared, "Rev. A.B. Crumpler, the sanctification evangelist, has last arrived and in his own language 'is going to stay until he has driven the Devil out of Fayetteville'…Mr. Crumpler is accompanied by Rev. Pleasant H. Crumpler, Georgia's great sanctificationist."[41]

In December of the same year, *The Raleigh News and Observer* records a powerful revival in Smithfield, North Carolina. The paper states, "Crumpler is here, and he says he is here to stay until a tidal wave of pure old time, old fashioned religion, spreads over the old historic town of Smithfield. The original Sampson County Crumpler and his cousin began a series of meetings here at the courthouse…"[42]

Without a doubt, Rev. P.H Crumpler was identified as Georgia's great holiness evangelist. He is also is credited as being one of A.B. Crumpler's cousins. However, how do we know that he is the person responsible for bringing the flames of holiness to G.B. Cashwell? The answer to this question may be also found in the 1920 South Georgia's conference records.

Being a circuit riding preacher for the Methodist church, P.H. Crumpler was often placed on numerous circuits that served the South Georgia area. Accordingly, the great Georgia Holiness evangelist was placed on the Tifton, Georgia, circuit in 1892 and 1893. While serving this district, he conducted numerous holiness revivals all over the area.[43]

Interestingly, Tifton, Georgia, is in the exact vicinity of where G.B. Cashwell was living during the year of 1893. Working as a tobacco demonstrator from North Carolina, Gaston Cashwell had been sent to Georgia to teach farmers how to crop the newly developed "golden weed." Unfortunately, there are no records to reveal where Gaston stayed during his tenure in Georgia. We do know, however, that he stayed in the Tifton area for at least six months during 1893. Having already been an acquaintance of the A.B. Crumpler family, it is very likely that G.B. Cashwell attended holiness meetings staged by Rev. P.H. Crumpler. Later, after marrying Lovie Lee Harrison in 1899, Gaston Cashwell would return to south Georgia and preach holiness revivals.[44]

Is it possible that A.B. Crumpler's cousin, Rev. P.H. Crumpler, is the preacher responsible for bringing Cashwell in contact with the Holiness Movement? Given these accounts, along with other interesting facts concerning the Cashwell and Crumpler connection, there are good reasons to believe so.[45]

Another interesting note is the fact that A.B. Crumpler's mother and father used tobacco. "I propose to make an improvement over my father and mother. They used snuff and tobacco," said A.B. Crumpler in his famous Dunn holiness revival in May 1896. Knowing this, it would not have been uncommon for Crumpler's family to own a tobacco patch of their own. If Gaston Cashwell was hoping to make some extra cash farming this crop as a traveling tobacco demonstrator, then it is very likely that A.B. Crumpler's family in Sampson County is who connected him with the Crumpler's in Georgia.[46]

Intense searches throughout the Cashwell family tree reveal that he had zero connections to the state of Georgia prior to 1893. Therefore, it is very intriguing to learn that out of all the places in the southeastern United States Cashwell could have traveled to, he chose Berrien County, Georgia, where an extension of the Sampson County Crumpler's lived. Nevertheless, while there, it is clear that Cashwell had a theological change, and converted to the holiness ranks through the great Georgia evangelist.

The Student Converts the Teacher

When A.B. Crumpler was beginning to ignite holiness throughout eastern North Carolina, it is quite evident that he was never alone. Even in his earliest meetings he was always accompanied by a tight knit holiness team. Following the ministry methods of the NHA, Crumpler organized envoys of preachers, worshipers, and intercessors to storm eastern North Carolina's gates. One of the first candidates on his list was his former pastor, Rev. J.T. Kendall.

Noted previously, Kendall was in full sympathy with Crumpler's revival meetings, although, he had not received the second blessing experience. This would all change at the Warsaw Schoolhouse revival conducted by A.B. Crumpler, P.H. Crumpler, and others in August of 1896. According to A.B. Crumpler, after the meeting had come to a close, "300 precious souls converted and sanctified. Among these were Rev. J.T. Kendall and wife and Rev. John Rouse." Crumpler went on to say, "These men will make themselves felt for holiness in the future." How is that for irony? In 1885 Rev. J.T. Kendall staged a revival at Kenner, North Carolina, and ushered in G.B. Cashwell and A.B. Crumpler to salvation. Now, eleven years later, the student (A.B. Crumpler) was leading the teacher (J.T. Kendall) to the cleansing stream of holiness.[47]

After this point, Kendall entered into the evangelistic field with Crumpler and began to hold holiness crusades up and down the Cape Fear River. Taking up his new role, Kendall announced his new calling to the public by writing a brief article in J.M. Pike's *Way of Faith.* Entitled "A New Evangelist on a New Line," Kendall informs readers of his new field. He states:

> I have been thirteen years an itinerant Methodist preacher, and have been station preacher, circuit preacher, and presiding elder. Have some tact as a financier and will cheerfully help my brethren financially as well as win souls to the Master. My address will be Goldsboro, N.C.,

> and I refer to Rev. W.S. Rowe, Goldsboro, N.C., my last presiding elder; or to Rev. B. Carradine, D.D; or Rev. A.B. Crumpler, Clinton, N.C., who was converted under my ministry. In the thirteen years of my itinerancy? I have added over 3,000 to the church. I expect to preach a full salvation—one that saves from sin.[48]

According to his letter, Kendall was a well-seasoned firebrand for Christ and answered the holiness charge. Having left the Methodist church to fulfill this call, Kendall still had a covering or accountability group of ministers he subjected himself too. This impressive list includes Rev. Carradine, the same minister who introduced the message of sanctification to A.B. Crumpler in Missouri. Yet it seems that Kendall was closest to A.B. Crumpler, whom he led to the Lord.

Perhaps the most interesting thing about this letter stems from Rev. Kendall's move to Goldsboro, North Carolina, in 1897. Goldsboro had become a point of interest for Crumpler during this time. Over the next two years, both A.B. Crumpler and G.B. Cashwell would also live in or around Goldsboro. Interestingly, all three men would be in the same location when the first Pentecostal Holiness Church would be organized in 1898. Thus, Kendall's move to Goldsboro in 1897 to begin work on "A New Line" would be strategically significant.[49]

Chapter 5

CAROLINA FIRE

As the fires of holiness began to spread throughout America, the spiritual landscape of the nation was beginning to experience a paradigm shift. Through this movement, unity between churches was becoming a reality. Color barriers were being dismantled, and denominational walls were being destroyed as revival power from the North was flooding the country. Holiness was becoming the cry of a generation who was hungry for more of the Lord. It would only be a matter of time until this powerful movement erupted in the great Tar Heel state. Although A.B. Crumpler, G.B. Cashwell, and others spread the Holiness Movement within eastern North Carolina during the late 1890s, another group would be chosen to birth it, the African-American United Holy Church.

North Carolina's African-Americans Birth Holiness

A decade before A.B. Crumpler would initiate the famed 1896 holiness crusades in the eastern part of the state, a small holiness meeting broke out in Method, North Carolina. Accordingly, on the first Sunday in May of 1886, among African-Americans, holiness broke into North Carolina's boarders. In his book, *The Untied Holy Church of America: A study in Black Holiness-Pentecostalism,* Dr. William Turner Jr. informs readers of North Carolina's first holiness outbreak and the ministers who were involved.

Men such as L.M. Mason, G.A. Mials, Isaac Cheshire, and H.C. Snipes all of which hail from Raleigh, North Carolina, were chosen to host this significant and strategic holiness meeting. The fruit of this revival meeting would later produce the United Holy Church of America. Dr. Turner writes, "This account establishes the very early date for the meetings out of which the Untied Holy Church (Black Holiness Church) sprang. Indeed, the date (May 1886) is among the earliest given by a modern Holiness-Pentecostal denomination." Interestingly enough, this meeting was not just a freak accident or a heightened emotional prayer gathering, but rather the holiness revival in Method was the real thing.[1]

Following this powerful move of God's Spirit among the African American saints of North Carolina, holiness began to permeate throughout the entire Raleigh/Durham area. Dr. Turner states:

> The first meeting in Method was followed immediately by the organization of churches, conventions, associations, and revivalist campaigns. One of the first churches to be organized was in the home of Elder and Mrs. C.C. Craig of Durham, North Carolina. Inspired by the Method meeting, they proceeded to build a church edifice, which was completed in 1889 on a lot adjacent to their home. This church, which came to be known as Durham Tabernacle, was a center for holiness and became a focal point for the convergence of several groups throughout the state. In addition, it became a seedbed for numerous churches in the Durham area. Indeed, it was in the city of Durham that pioneers from Method, and others who joined them, held the first convocation of Holy People in North Carolina in 1894. This convocation had among its leaders L.M. Mason, who was to become the first president, along with G.A. Mials and H.C. Snipes, who were also present at the early meeting in Method. Other leaders, such as D.S. Freeman and G.W. Roberts, were joined by the many delegates who attended. Out of the first convocation of the Holy Church of North Carolina came the impetus that would bring other "Holy People" throughout the state into a untied fellowship.[2]

This account establishes several important aspects worth mentioning:

First, it reveals that God chose unknown African American forerunners of the Raleigh/Durham area to birth North Carolina's first Holiness Movement. Equally intriguing, is that through this revival, Durham was transformed and became a powerful stronghold for the cause of holiness within the young church.

Second, it reveals that the African-American "Holiness Convocation" was far more advanced by the time Crumpler ignited his revival campaign ten years later. This is something that Crumpler's co-editor, T.M. Lee, would also acknowledge in the columns of the *Holiness Advocate* during 1901.[3]

Lastly, these African American pioneers would eventually form a close interracial and inter-denominational relationship with A.B. Crumpler's Holiness Church. In addition, the United Holy Church would also work closely with other independent white holiness ministers stationed in the Carolinas. Together, these different streams of holiness would, in Vineland fashion, carry the banner of "perfect love" to white, black, Indian, and the mixed multitudes. Under their leading, fires of holiness would rage throughout the Carolinas.[4]

Pre-Fire Baptizers

Besides the "Colored Holiness Convocation" and Rev. A.B. Crumpler's holiness team that would burst onto the scene in 1896, another group of holiness ministers began to emerge in the early 1890s. This holy remnant was found hanging around the boarder of North and South Carolina. Equally burning with compassion to see the lost saved and sanctified, these ministers were known for roaming around counties such as Bladen, Columbus, Roberson, Brunswick, Hoke, and New Hanover. In South Carolina, they held revivals in Powellville, Cool Springs, and Marion.[5]

Among them were S.D. Page, W.W. Avant, T.J. Browning, S.C. Perry, J. A. Williams, Rev. Brooks, Miss Mattie Perry, Edward Kelly, and H.F. Schulken. All of them, with the exception of W.W. Avant, came out of the Methodist Church. Avant, who was a sanctified Baptist, was put out of the Baptist church for failing to renounce the doctrine of sanctification. Four years after he had claimed the holiness experience, Avant turned to holding outdoor meetings. He states, "Since June, 1895, I have been in the tent work with S.D. Page, and have been trying to do the little things for Jesus."[6]

Although there are very little documented accounts of their early revivals, what is known can be found within the early editions of J.M. Pike's *Way of Faith.* Most of them knew each other quite well and were often seen in the columns of the paper working together for the cause of holiness. In the same article, both W.W. Avant and S.D. Page wrote:

> We closed on the 12th inst with victory to the Lord. As at all places we had some opposition, but we praise the Lord for the victory He gave us. As Far as I know all the opposers bid us good bye with "God bless you on your way." At least fifty people testified that they had been converted or sanctified. May God build a wall around Bladenboro, N.C., that they may stand the test of temptation, and win a crown at last. We organized a lady's prayer meeting every Friday afternoon; also a cottage prayer meeting to meet every Sunday night, composed of the different denominations. May love and union abound. Everybody pray for the good people of Abbottsburg and Bladenboro. Pray for us that God may use us to His glory.[7]

Avant, Page, along with many other holiness evangelists, traveled from town to town and pitched their tents to proclaim holiness. This was before holiness churches were organized. Therefore, many of them who joined the Holiness Movement had to leave the comfort of paid pastoral positions and subject themselves to a difficult lifestyle of faith. Some even dared to cross racial lines in the South to bring forth the Wesleyan message of burning love to people of color. In fact, between the years 1890–1895, most of these independent firebrands staged inter-racial and inter-denominational revivals working with their "colored" holiness brothers and sisters.[8]

Early letters also reveal that these Carolina independent holiness ministers also had formed an underground network with each other. In a day when there were no e-mails, cell phones, Facebook, twitter, etc., most of them would utilized the *Way of Faith* to announce future meetings and establish centralized locations for regional gatherings. Such a place was chosen in Bladen County at a little town known as Vineland, North Carolina.

Located one mile form Whiteville, North Carolina, Vineland was named because of the large amount of grapes that were exported and in later years would become one of the nation's leading wine-producers. Prophetically speaking, Vineland was also the name of the New Jersey town that produced the National Holiness Movement in 1867. Although the town itself was never incorporated, it contained a very significant transportation system, the Wilmington and Manchester railroad. Encompassing one hundred and sixty-three miles, this railroad strategically stretched from the port of Wilmington almost to the port of Charleston, South Carolina. Since some of these preachers were from South Carolina, this rail road carried them back and forth between North and South Carolina, enabling them to hold massive holiness meetings. Therefore, Vineland served as a rendezvous point for many of them to meet and became an agreed center where holiness gatherings could be established.[9]

A.B. Crumpler Embraces the Mantle of Holiness

Although he would not be alone in initiating the North Carolina Holiness Movement, Crumpler quickly became one of its most popular and controversial figures. Dubbed as the "Father of Holiness," A.B. Crumpler's ministry took center stage and accelerated in 1896. Newspapers all over North Carolina described him as being, "The Preacher of Sanctification who has Hypnotic Power." He was also noted for being the minister who "possesses a strange power." Like John Wesley, George Whitefield, or Jonathon Edwards, Rev. Crumpler carried a certain presence or charisma that literally changed the atmospheres of cities when he arrived to preach the gospel.[10]

Authors in recent years have been drawn to the supernatural manifestations that were occurring during Crumpler's meetings. Indeed, it was quite common for masses of people to fall into trances for hours and experience heavenly visions. Others dropped like dead men at the alter under the powerful preaching of this young revivalist. Divine healing was also taught and practiced by Crumpler and his mighty men. However, there was another aspect of Crumpler's early ministry that has not been explored, his disposition towards African Americans.[11]

Before the Holiness Movement reached eastern North Carolina through Crumpler's campaigns in 1896, "separate but equal" was already taking its toll among small rural churches. Racial segregation had just triumphed within the halls of Justice through the Supreme Court Case *Plessey vs. Ferguson,* and it was only a matter of time before strict Jim Crow Laws would be enforced with violence and bloodshed within North Carolina towns. This did not seem to hinder the Sampson County preacher one bit. Burning with the same flames that were lit on Vineland's alter in 1867, A.B. Crumpler was numb towards racial hatred.[12]

Like G.B. Cashwell, Crumpler believed the new message of heart purity should be shared with all people regardless of color and social status. Bold and fearless, this preacher penetrated the racially charged South by holding massive inter-racial tent meetings. Charging whites for not living the religion of their forefathers while inspiring and encouraging "colored" audiences during his famous meetings, Crumpler's ministry demanded the attention of the mixed multitudes.

His first meeting of 1896 took place in January at Ingold, North Carolina, which resides in Sampson County. According to Crumpler, this is where "Jesus Triumphs." One month prior to this meeting, Crumpler wrote that he had attended the Methodist conference in Elizabeth City. On his way home, he stopped at New Bern where he "accidently preached to the colored people in the morning" and for the white people in the evening at "Hancock Street." According to him, the meetings at both places extracted the same results. He writes, "There was much prejudice and strong opposition to overcome, but hallelujah the Lord honored the preaching of his word." Crumpler also added, "This meeting (Ingold) was among the best I ever held and the victory the most complete; 105 were converted and 110 wholly sanctified. Among those converted, were Methodists, Baptists, and Presbyterians. Surly God is no respecter of persons."[13]

As fame of his reputation began to spread through Carolina newspapers, Crumpler soon found himself with a loaded itinerary. In May of 1896, this schedule took Crumpler to the newly formed city of Dunn, North Carolina, where a revival of epic proportions would erupt. Over a month before he was to arrive, The Dunn local newspaper *The County Union,* was already advertising the meeting. It announced, "We understand that Rev. Mr. Crumpler, the great sanctification preacher of Sampson County, will start a meeting in Dunn about May 15. He has a tent that will cover about 2,500 people." Judging by the tone of the article, Dunn was full of excitement in anticipating his arrival. Both fans and critics were curious to experience a Crumpler meeting. Being the bold and tenacious preacher that he was, Rev. Crumpler did not disappoint.[14]

Over the next three weeks, he took the stage and proclaimed a message that shook the foundations of the city. Many of the headliner statements that caught the attention of the public were printed off in the newspaper under a section entitled, "Sparks caught at the Tent Meeting." Rev. Crumpler's statements included colorful phrases such as, "I expect to pull the hide off of some of these fellows around Dunn. Expect it will split for it is no doubt rotten." He added, "You little bow backed possum eared Methodists haven't any religion." Keep in mind, at this time he was still a Methodist minister in good standing. Crumpler also revealed his purpose for coming to Dunn. Unashamedly, he proclaimed, "I am a preacher to the poor people that it is why I came to Dunn." Though these statements would begin to shape his audience's understanding of him and the movement itself, nothing prepared them for what Crumpler would declare to the "colored saints" attending the Dunn meeting.[15]

In preaching his "Sermon to the Colored," whites began to crowd in with blacks under the tent and eagerly awaited Crumpler's response. Surprisingly, Rev. Crumpler opened his message by declaring with power, "I have the reputation of being the best Negro preacher in eastern North Carolina. I hope to sustain my reputation this evening." He went on to say, "I am afraid for some of these white people to go up to heaven. They would be cutting up the streets. If the white people had been left in your condition after the war they would have stolen the world." These statements may not mean much in the 21st century; however, in 1896 in Dunn, North Carolina, this was a declaration of war![16]

Speaking in the face of underground secret societies such as the Freemasons, Red Shirts, and the Ku Klux Klan, A.B. Crumpler was sending a clear statement. He was challenging the mindset of the entire South. Most southern whites at this time viewed both blacks and Native Americans as being sub-human or inhuman. Yet, because of his sanctification experience, A.B. Crumpler did not see them as an illiterate, ignorant, or sub-human sect of people, but rather as his own brothers and sisters.[17]

During these early years of Crumpler's ministry, most people followed his example, until a revival of racism would erupt in 1898 on the streets of Wilmington. Nevertheless, by identifying himself as Carolina's best "Negro Preacher," Crumpler inspired both poor blacks and whites. After his departure, Dunn's black population continued to sustain holiness fires by holding all night sanctified prayer meetings within the town. Other reports of this historic meeting also began to pour into the local paper. Within a week, numerous articles began to appear which praised Crumpler and his team for coming to Dunn.[18]

Amazingly, most of the whole town was impacted by the revival, and responded with their full approval of Crumpler's ministry. Merchants and store owners were closing their places of business down, and multiple small group prayer meetings began to appear throughout the city. Thousands who attended the meetings were testifying that they had never seen or experienced anything quite like it. Most importantly, what happened in Vineland, New Jersey in 1867 was now occurring in Dunn, North Carolina in 1896. In light of this, *The County Union* made the following statement regarding this historic revival:

> Since Dunn first had an existence, there never has been witnessed so much interest in religious circles as there has been during the past few weeks. Her people are awakened and aroused, enthused and are at work. The Christian people are turning their back upon the *prejudice* and *strife* that has long been the ruling power among our church members. The people are coming together and seem to be determined in their efforts to put down the common enemy of our country. Prayer meetings continue at some house nearly every night in the week and at nearly every meeting some soul is benefited.[19]

Another story that was printed following this statement stated:

> As evidence of the Christian spirit and brotherly love that abounds among our people, the Baptist and Methodists and other churches worshiped together Sunday. It is pleasant to know that this spirit prevails among our churches. It shows the true Christian Spirit. Christ did not recognize any denominational lines, but simply went about doing good and attending to His Father's business. Let our people lay aside prejudice and dwell together in unity and love and try as best we can to follow in the footsteps of the meek and lowly Savior and all will be well in the end.[20]

Other articles included a child's prayer meeting in which four eleven-year-old little girls banded themselves for intercessory prayer, African-American holiness services, and a brief write up that declared, "When you come in to Dunn now you can hear the people singing and praising God."[21]

Indeed, a well of revival had been dug and now streams of living waters were flowing through virtually the entire city. Dunn, which was now burning hot with the fires of Holiness, was not the first or last city Crumpler and his team set ablaze. It was only to become the pattern by which dozens and dozens of Eastern North Carolina cities would be consumed.

Following the Dunn meeting, Crumpler continued to stage inter-racial and inter-denominational holiness revivals all throughout eastern North Carolina.

Some of these cities and townships include: Clinton, Keener, Goshen, Dunn, Mt. Olive, Goldsboro, Elizabethtown, Smithfield, Fayetteville, Lumberton, Vineland, Whiteville, Burgaw, Richland's, Magnolia, Rose Hill, New Bern, Greenville, Chocowinity, Elizabeth City, Wilmington, Statesville, High Point, Raleigh, and many others.[22]

Where is Gaston Cashwell? Presently, there is no exact written record that places Cashwell at the Dunn meetings in May 1896. Most Pentecostal scholars believe that he was not present during Crumpler's 1896 holiness crusades which were held in eastern North Carolina; however, at best this is only based on speculation. There is no documented and proven evidence that shows Cashwell to be absent from these great and historic revivals either. Instead, new evidence is surfacing to prove that Cashwell was attending these meetings and may have even taken up a role in assisting Crumpler's ministry team during the years of 1896–1898. This shall be discussed further in chapter eight.

A.B. Crumpler's Influence

Certainly, the coming of A.B. Crumpler to Dunn, North Carolina, was like the ark of the convent coming to the city of Jericho. Just as the walls around Jericho shook and crumbled before God's presence, so it was that walls of racial hatred and denominationalism began to crack and break in Dunn under the ministry of A.B. Crumpler and his sanctified warriors. Thousands in and around the surrounding area had been awakened to the reality of heaven's glory invading eastern North Carolina. In light of this, Crumpler sought to unite all Christians through this wonderful new message of holiness. Early records reveal that Crumpler's ministry was winning people from both the Methodist and Presbyterian camps; however, it was from another denominational stream that Crumpler would have his greatest victory, the Free Will Baptist's of the Cape Fear Conference.[23]

The Free Will Baptists of North Carolina trace their history to Paul Palmer, who, during the 1720s, began to establish Free Will Baptist churches in the north eastern section of North Carolina. As the movement spread south, Free Will congregations started appearing all along the eastern part of the state, especially along the banks of Cape Fear. By 1855, the Free Will Baptist Conference was organized at Stoney Run Church, which is now located in Sampson County. The original conference included Stoney Run, Long Branch, Free Union, Fayetteville, Shady Grove, Bethsaida, Prospect, and Elbethel. The conference flourished for many years and won many converts to the Lord. Their wonderful efforts in preaching the gospel are too many to count. Yet the conference underwent a transformational process when A.B. Crumpler came to town in 1896.[24]

Primarily through the Dunn meeting, nearly every Free Will minister in the conference was swept into the Holiness Movement during 1896. Florence Goff identified some of these ministers: R.C. Jackson, J.A. Blalock, William Byrd, H.W. Jernigan, E.L. Parker, C.J. Carr, J.F. Owen, H.H. Goff, and many others. Following this revival, these love burning Baptists returned to their churches and shared what they had experienced under Crumpler's big tent. Through their evangelistic zeal, the holiness message ripped through local congregations like lightening. Soon, almost every congregation within the conference became holiness believing Free Will Baptists. Like Crumpler, these ministers also began to canvass eastern North Carolina's counties holding tent revivals wherever they went. Although most of them stayed within the conference, many joined Crumpler's ministry team through the inter-denominational holiness convention.[25]

Over the next several years, many of them traveled alongside A.B. Crumpler. Together, sanctified Methodists, Presbyterians, Free Will-Baptists, and Missionary Baptists brought forth one of the greatest revivals that North Carolina had ever witnessed. It was a great win for Crumpler, and an even greater victory for the holiness cause.

Chapter 6

MERGING HOLINESS STREAMS

FOLLOWING REV. A.B. Crumpler's whirlwind tour of North Carolina in 1896, many converts had been won over to the holiness ranks. Between his meetings, the African-American holiness revivals, and the Independent Southeastern Tar-Heel ministers, North Carolina was burning from the coast to the mountains with the message of holiness. It's very critical to understand that during the first two years of this movement, 1896–1897 there was great harmony among many churches. Denominations that had been bitter enemies were reconciling and working to form closer relationships. Under the banner of revivalism, Methodists, Baptists, and Presbyterians in the Carolinas were becoming one.

A.B. Crumpler most likely had no idea that this revival was going to materialize as quickly as it did. Taking advantage of this unique opportunity, he, along with some of his peers, decided to form loosely structured holiness associations. These associations, which heavily resembled camp meetings, would provide centralized locations for the holiness people while building stronger inter-denominational and inter-racial relationships between churches impacted by this revival. Therefore, in initiating this venture, Rev. Crumpler and others would pattern local holiness associations by using the Vineland, New Jersey, meeting of 1867 as their model.

THE VINELAND MODEL

No one ever anticipated that when the holiness revival exploded at Landis Park in Vineland, New Jersey, during the summer of 1867, a major precedent would be established for future holiness organizations. The camp meeting itself had been around for decades. Many scholars trace its beginning to the great Cane Ridge Revival in Kentucky during the year 1800. Dr. Synan notes, "America's first camp meeting (1800–1801) was in Cane Ridge, Kentucky, where thousands experienced manifestations of the Holy Spirit."

Following this massive revival which witnessed some 25,000 in attendance, camp meetings began to appear all over the country. Yet, the camp meeting, and all its glory, would come to a grinding halt with the advent of the Civil War. After the war, the camp meeting began to slip into oblivion along with Christian fervor and revivalism; however, it would be the divine explosion at Vineland, New Jersey, in 1867 that camp meetings would be "born again."[1]

Along with that explosion came strategic revelation in how to accommodate seas of people who would attend. Barlow Gorham, who revolutionized the camp meeting, utilized several key elements at Vineland, New Jersey, that would constitute a successful encampment and association. This included: location, relationship-building, Jewish formation of the meeting, love feasts, unity, and many others. A detailed outlook on some of Gorham's strategies is listed as follows:

Location: First, a strategic location had to be found that would be convenient for travelers. Vineland, New Jersey, therefore, was chosen because it was ideally situated between Philadelphia and New York and still close to the Baltimore/Washington D.C. area.

Relationship Building: Second, relationships were often built up prior to the meetings between leaders of the holiness association and local pastors, bishops, and church elders of other denominations and races. Their aim was to unite all local church leaders through their message. This resulted in local preachers and pastors playing a major role in the camp meeting itself.

Jewish Formation: Third, the formation of the grounds had to be created. As noted previously in chapter five, Rev. Gorham strategically laid out the first three National Holiness camp meetings in a gigantic wheel formation taken from Ezekiel's vision. The hub of this wheel would be where the 3,000 men tent would be positioned and the main stage erected. Making a perfect circle around the main tent, thousands of small family tents would also be erected. In its completion, this flaming wheel of holiness would encompass fifty or more acres of land accommodating crowds numbering in the hundreds of thousands. Gorham, who brilliantly constructed this, did so for one reason—to honor the ancient Jewish festival known as the Feast of Tabernacles.

Love Feats: Fourth, the resurgence of the Moravian love feasts, which fueled the fires of the meetings. Typically, when initiated, these meetings consisted of a church style service three times a day with prayer, worship, and preaching. Between services, people would erect large tables and garnish places to eat in which the large crowds would enjoy a meal together. During the feasts, testimonies, prophetic words, words of knowledge, etc., would be delivered by those attending the meetings. It has been noted that some of the greatest outpourings of heavenly rain would occur during these massive love feasts.

Unity: Fifth, above all else, these meetings were intended by the National Holiness Association to be unifying to the entire body of Christ. Unity among believers, pastors, and denominations was even placed above Christian perfection or the doctrine of holiness itself. This was the primary reason leaders chose to meet in Vineland, New Jersey, in the first place. Aware of the difficult times they had been born into, these men and women stressed the significance of perfect oneness, or unity, with the saints of every race, color, and creed.

Thus, the pattern of ministry revealed through this historic camp meeting in Vineland, shaped and influenced state holiness associations all around the country. At that time, this was the fresh prophetic insight used to sustain God's extraordinary presence throughout regions. As a result, the Iowa Holiness Association, Texas Holiness Association, Georgia Holiness Association, and the North Carolina Holiness Association emerged. Incredibly, all of these holiness organizations mirrored the same characteristics and methods used in the great revival of Vineland, New Jersey, in 1867.[2]

From Vineland to Vineland: The First North Carolina Holiness Association

Traditionally, authors have suggested that A.B. Crumpler was the first to establish the North Carolina Holiness Association in May 1897, at Magnolia, North Carolina. G.F. Taylor, one of the original founders of the Pentecostal-Holiness Church and convert of Crumpler, believed this to be true. However, Mr. Taylor, who wrote the entire early history of the Holiness-Pentecostal church from memory, did so over twenty years after it occurred. Possibly, he might have forgotten some details that would shed additional light on the Holiness Movement's early years in North Carolina.[3]

This seems to be the case because according to J.M. Pike's *Way of Faith*, the first North Carolina Holiness Association did not begin in May of 1897, but sometime in the spring of 1896 in Vineland, North Carolina. While Rev. A.B. Crumpler did organize an association in May of 1897, it would be his peers down in Columbus and Bladen Counties that conceived the first known white Holiness Association in North Carolina.

Moving in fashion with the National Holiness Association, independent Carolina ministers S.D. Page, W.W. Avant, T. J. Browning, S.C. Perry, Miss Perry, and others chose a strategic center for the North Carolina Holiness Movement. Ironically, that center was Vineland, North Carolina, where organizers first established the Browning Tabernacle Holiness Association.

The Browning Tabernacle Association consisted of a small local body of holiness believers (local church), who sought to solidify a more permanent stronghold of holiness in North Carolina during the early 1890s. It cannot be proven with certainty when the Browning Tabernacle Holiness Association was founded. Yet, we do know that there were meetings taken place as early as 1895.[4]

The first known president of this local association before Rev. T.J. Browning was W.W. Avant, the sanctified Baptist minister. He, along with secretary S.D. Page, petitioned readers to join them in their cause. Appearing in the November 27, 1895, issue of the *Way of Faith*, these fiery preachers wrote;

> Please say to your readers that the Browning Tabernacle Holiness Association will convene the last Sunday in April, 1896, and run ten days. Everybody invited, especially the itinerant and local preachers of all denominations in reach. The renowned Dr. W.B. Godby will have charge of the forces and give a series of Bible readings. The Tabernacle is located one mile from Whiteville depot, between the Wilmington, N.C., and Florence, S.C., forty-six miles from former. The Lord gives us a grand Pentecost. Yours for holiness, S.D. Page, sec'y W.W. Avant, Pres.[5]

Having closed their meeting in the fall of 1895, these ministers were already beginning to advertise the spring session of their association. Typically, these early holiness associations, as well as A.B. Crumpler's associations, would meet twice a year—once in the spring and again in the fall.

Early articles in the *Way of Faith* also reveal that "conventions" were taking place while holiness association meetings were occurring. The best way to distinguish between holiness associations and conventions is to understand that the conventions, although open to the public, were primarily geared for the local ministers impacted by holiness revivals. Early convention meetings were also "inter-denominational" in nature and extended open invitations to preachers. Through joining the convention, preachers from other denominations were given opportunities to proclaim the holiness message without leaving their church.[6]

The holiness associations, on the other hand, were generally for the people. Seeking to expand the doctrine of sanctification and the flames of the holiness revival, the associations provided converts of local communities a place to worship, grow, and fellowship with others. They (associations) were patterned after the great Vineland, New Jersey, holiness camp meeting that occurred in the summer of 1867. Generally, when these associations took place twice a year, the conventions (leader's meeting) would also meet during encampment services and plan to organize the next association meeting. Such was the case in Columbus County, North Carolina, with S.D. Page and W.W. Avant.[7]

Apparently, Page and Avant's efforts in planning the 1896 spring holiness meeting at Vineland, North Carolina, did not disappoint either. Dr. W.B. Godbey, who was requested to lead the revival meetings, reported that the meeting was full of success. So impressed with the ministry work of Avant and Page, Dr. Godbey likened them to David and Jonathan of the Bible and described them as being, "red-hot, faithful, and true, able preachers, good singers and exceedingly efficient alter workers." Certainly, this revival was producing much fruit through the conversions of countless souls; however, Dr. Godbey also noted that the most significant aspect of the meeting occurred when leaders met together and established the very first North Carolina State Holiness Association. Dr. Godbey writes:

> The presence of the Lord in all the meetings made our visit to dear old North Carolina memorable and precious. Probably the most hopeful work we saw was the organization of the North Carolina Holiness Association. Rev. T.J. Browning (President) of Wilmington, N.C., Rev. D.H. Tuttle (Vive-President), Rev. Etheredge, Rev. Edward Kelly of Cerrogordo, and Rev. Shulken (Treasurer) of Vineland are the officers elected to conduct the enterprise. All the holiness people pray constantly for the Association. O, the work in North Carolina. Evangelists in Kentucky, Georgia, and other states who feel led of the Lord in this direction, address Rev. Edward Kelly, of Cerrogordo, N.C., secretary, or Rev. T.J. Browning, of Wilmington, N.C., in reference to field labor.[8]

Following this meeting, these organizers came together in one accord and sought to make Vineland, North Carolina, the center rallying point of holiness for the entire state. With Rev. T.J. Browning leading the charge as the new president, plans were already being made for the fall session to be held again at Vineland, in August 1896. Interestingly, during that meeting there would be a significant changing of the guard.[9]

With the exception of the African-American Holiness Convocations in the Raleigh/Durham area, Vineland, North Carolina, was the original birthplace of the Holiness Association within the Tar Heel state. Progressing from random tent revivals to having a more permanent location where holiness believing people could gather and worship freely, this association was the first of its kind that provided inter-denominational relationships between local churches.

Seeking to strengthen this new venture, ministers such as Browning, Kelly, Page, Avant, and others incorporated the Vineland, New Jersey, model and Gorham's camp meetings strategies into these first encampment services. It wouldn't be long, however, before this stream of holiness would merge with another holiness stream that was gaining strength in Sampson County, North Carolina. Very soon, under the dynamic ministry of A.B. Crumpler, these two streams, along with the African-American United Holy Church, would unite to forge a mighty river of holiness that would literally wash over every "tribe and tongue" within the Old North State.

Two Streams Become One

Just a few months after the Vineland, North Carolina, encampment ended and the first North Carolina State Holiness Association was formed, A.B. Crumpler held a massive holiness revival in his hometown of Clinton, North Carolina. Crumpler, whose fame was spreading faster than the movement itself, also caught the attention of North Carolina Holiness Association leaders down in Vineland, especially Rev. Edward Kelly. Kelly had heard of the young Methodist evangelist burning with holiness and decided to seek him out during the Clinton meeting. To his amazement, he found Crumpler brilliantly organizing a "three in one" meeting within the town limits. Seeking to reach every class of people, the A.B. Crumpler ministry team attacked different points of the city simultaneously. *The Fayetteville Observer* notes:

> It was our pleasure to attend, with quite a number of the people of Dunn, the Crumpler meeting at Clinton Saturday and Sunday. The meeting is largely attended every day and on Sunday the crowd was unusually large and much interest was taken. Every service brings renewed interest from all classes of people. On Saturday afternoon three services were being held in the town; one at the tent to the colored people one at the Methodist Church and one in the jail. Some of the prisoners had requested special prayer. The people of Clinton are kind and hospitable and are doing all they can for the accommodation of the visitors. This is better than some towns do when this strange doctrine of sanctification is first preached. Some of the best people of Clinton were brought under its influence and power Sunday night and we learn that many more have since become interested. Ministers of several denominations are assisting in the meeting, among them being a Methodist, two Missionary Baptist, and a holiness minister from Georgia.[10]

Some interesting observations can be made through this amazing revival.

First, A.B. Crumpler and his team possessed a high-level of prophetic insight in how to take the city with the new message of sanctification. Given his family's legacy, Crumpler also had great local government connections which enabled him to manifest his prophetic mantle of ministry and government.

Second, this account also identifies the core theme of the Holiness Movement: racial and denominational reconciliation through the message of sanctification. Having organized services for "all classes of people," Crumpler continued to exemplify his willingness to bridge the gap between blacks and whites, Baptist and Methodists, and so forth.

Third, Crumpler was not a one man show. He always encouraged unity and often empowered other pastors to lead. This is evident through the Free-Will Baptists, Missionary Baptists, and Methodists ministers working side by side during the Clinton revival.

Amazingly, one of these Methodists was Rev. Edward Kelly, who couldn't believe his eyes when he witnessed the bond of unity that was present among these workers. Relaying what he witnessed back to his brethren in Vineland, North Carolina, Kelly wrote,

> On the 6th inst. (July 6, 1896) I left Chadbourn for Clinton, N.C., to attend the Crumpler meeting and I am so thankful that God let me go. My! My! How the fire fell on the people during those services! Glory to God! Some of the brightest faces the writer ever looked in, and some of the brightest testimonies he ever heard, were in Clinton. When we left Saturday morning there had been seventy or seventy-five conversions and sanctifications, about equally divided, and the meeting going on with increasing power. The first Baptist preacher I ever heard was Bro. Ed. Parker, on Friday night. How he did preach! And how his face beamed! Glory…A.B. Crumpler is truly a holy man of God. God is blessing him and his labors much. Holiness is in North Carolina to stay. Glory![11]

A.B. Crumpler also weighed in on this meeting by writing to the *Way of Faith* about the results of this strategic revival. In identifying those helping him, Crumpler adds:

> We had several ministers from a distance who gave us a helping hand. I am indebted to Bro. Edward Parker, of the Baptist Church, and Bros. Edward Kelly and D.H. Futrell, of the Methodist, for a good sermon each. I want to say right here that I was ably assisted all through the meeting by Rev. P.H. Crumpler of Ashburn, Ga., and of the South Georgia conference. He preached at least a third of the time with his consecrated and accomplished wife at the organ, to the delight of everybody who heard him. He is a strong preacher, a fine singer and a pure Christian. He is a revivalist…Since the Clinton meeting closed I have held another glorious meeting with Rev. J.T. Kendall, in which we had about 40 converted and 65 sanctified. Hallelujah! Salvation

> sill rolls on over ignorance, prejudice and opposition. We commence at Warsaw the first Sunday in August. Pray for us.[12]

What's very intriguing about the partnership of this revival is that Crumpler unveils the identity of those helping him, such as Kelly and Futrell (Methodists), P.H. Crumpler (Crumpler's cousin and Georgia evangelist), J.T. Kendall (Crumpler and Cashwell's friend), and Ed Parker (Free-Will-Baptist). However, there were two Missionary Baptist workers assisting in the meetings that Crumpler failed to unmask. Who are they? Why didn't Crumpler identify them?

Most likely this was G.B. Cashwell and his brother-in-law Jerry Gore. Both Cashwell and Gore were members of Persimmon College, the loosely affiliated Missionary Baptist Church. G.B. Cashwell was also the only known Missionary Baptist preacher to ever become a part of Crumpler's movement. Moreover, family tradition suggests that G.B. Cashwell was home during this time. His farm was located only four miles away from the site of the revival, but why the secrecy? Maybe it was Cashwell who was leading the "tent for the colored." Certainly, this would have been up his ally. If so, why didn't Crumpler include him in this article, or any other early article within the *Way of Faith*? Perhaps it was Cashwell's request to remain hidden from the spotlight given his church affiliation. An interesting suggestion no doubt, yet this is a suggestion that will have to tarry for now.[13]

Nevertheless, from all vantage points, the Clinton meeting appears to be the one that connected the North Carolina Holiness Association in Vineland, North Carolina, with Rev. A.B. Crumpler's movement in eastern North Carolina. Following this meeting, Crumpler, along with Rev. Kelly, began to build strong networking relationships with each other. Soon, pages of holiness publications would be littered with joint services between these two rushing streams of holiness. Separate and distinct though they were, these streams would begin to finally merge into one body. Therefore, A.B. Crumpler, having made an unforgettable impression on Rev. Edward Kelly, was extended an invitation to the newly formed North Carolina Holiness Association in Vineland, North Carolina, during the fall of 1896.

Fortunately, Rev. Kelly recorded this meeting. In describing its results, an excited Kelly writes, "The Lord was present, and saved and sanctified thirty or more souls." Among attendance were T.J. Browning, S.D. Page, S.C. Perry, W.W. Avant, Miss Mattie Perry, Edward Kelly, J.M. Pike, and A.B. Crumpler. Besides having an extraordinary revival meeting under the canopies of the large tent positioned one mile from Whiteville, this band of warriors also went on the offense.[14]

Probably following the gigantic love feast, a group of holiness believers decided to pay a visit to the "County Home" or poor house. Surrounded by suffering, but overflowing with holy love and compassion, these faithful few brought Jesus into the hearts of everyone present. While in the home, some even noted that "brother Jesus is with us today!" making this evangelistic endeavor a major highlight of the association meeting. Though this outing was indeed a significant moment for the holiness warriors, it was not the only one. At the conventional meeting of this same gathering, a changing of the guard took place. Rev. Ed Kelly writes:

> The following officers were elected for the ensuring term: Rev. A.B. Crumpler, President; Rev. T.J. Browning, Vice President; Edward Kelly, Secretary; and H.F. Schulken, Treasure. Plans are being made to make the ground a permanent camp ground, for the purpose of preaching holiness. If anyone desires to put up a tent for the "camp," they can write H.F. Schulken, Treasure, Vineland, NC, and he can arrange for them to do so. The land will not cost them anything. We hope to go in camp there the first in September, 1897 (D.V.), with Rev. A.B. Crumpler to lead us.[15]

According to Kelly's assessment, we can conclude that there was great harmony between the North Carolina Holiness Association of Vineland and Rev. Abner Blackmon Crumpler of Sampson County. Being elected president, leaders obviously placed a great deal of confidence in A.B. Crumpler. Accordingly, they thought he was the best minister to "lead the way" for the 1897 year. Perhaps even more significant than this, however, was the location of first State Holiness Association. Even before the cities of Goldsboro and Falcon would become holiness centers, Vineland, North Carolina, was chosen as the original "wheel within the wheel" for the Tar Heel Holiness Movement.

With this strategic meeting behind them and a new partnership formed through the Vineland Holiness Association Meetings, these Tar Heel holiness preachers began to ransack every North Carolina county with the message of perfect love. Throughout the entire year of 1897, holiness teams would travel the Carolinas as Paul and Barnabas did in the book of Acts. Roving the countryside, these ministers often worked together interchangeably with the purpose of forming as many local Holiness Associations as they could. Many of them would sleep in each other's house, share tents and meals together, and of course, endure verbal and physical persecution from the white aristocrat community. Despite initial opposition, they stayed the course and continued to establish strongholds of holiness everywhere they traveled.

This would be true of Rev. A.B. Crumpler and his dynamic team of twenty plus preachers who arrived at Magnolia, North Carolina, on May 15, 1897. After preaching in the local Methodist Church, Crumpler invited the large crowd to a massive testimony and love feast service the next day. The service, which was to be held under Crumpler's 2,500 men gospel tent, drew in thousands from around the countryside. As the great throng of people rushed the tent, a great and mighty outpouring of God's Spirit ripped through this small rural town. The meeting resulted in another North Carolina Holiness Association being founded.[16]

G.F. Taylor, a local resident of Magnolia, was one of the many spectators that day who experienced the holiness flames. Taylor, who was destined to become an original founder of the IPHC, and one of Crumpler's preachers, was also known for being an educator at the local school. This is a position that would land him at Falcon, North Carolina, exactly ten years later under the leadership of J.A. Culbreth. Through the Magnolia Association, however, Rev. G.F. Taylor entered into the Holiness Movement and began his journey. Eventually, he too would be destined for the national spotlight.[17]

Three Streams Become One

There is not much evidence in linking the third holiness stream, The African American United Holy Church, with these other holiness groups, probably because at the time, opposition was mounting against the idea of mixing white and black conventions through revivalism. However, this does not mean that it didn't happen. Noted previously, the African-American Untied Holy Church was chosen to birth the Holiness Movement in the great Tar Heel State. Having been established as the original fathers of this movement, these forerunners often sought to have fellowship with their white brethren. Though they had been experiencing substantial growth and development, many of them did not know how to fully articulate the doctrine of sanctification amongst their more conservative peers. In seeking to do so, G.A. Mials, one of the leading ministers of this group, wrote to J.M. Pike's, *Way of Faith* requesting help.

Mials, who was the church secretary for the young African-American holiness congregation, wrote a compelling letter humbly requesting ministers, "regardless of color," to aid them in constructing the second blessing doctrine. Amazingly, two white southern holiness evangelists responded to Mials's request. They were Rev. J.A. Williams and Rev. Brooks of South Carolina, who, according to Mials, "came to Raleigh with a tent and stayed for four weeks."[18]

The first two weeks were spent preaching to the white people; however, both Williams and Brooks always made a point to mix the audiences together during the meetings. During the last two weeks, Williams and Brooks focused on preaching and teaching holiness primarily to the "colored people" of the Raleigh/Durham area, although the meeting quickly became inter-racial. By the time it was over, Mials reported that a "great and wonderful revival had occurred amongst all those who attended."[19]

Other articles in *The Way of Faith* also reveal that P. H. Crumpler, A.B. Crumpler, and both J.A. Williams and Rev. Brooks went on to stage many more inter-racial revivals in the southeastern section of North Carolina during the late 1890s. Rev. Williams and Rev. Brooks were both affiliated with the North Carolina Association that meet in Vineland, North Carolina, until a theological cyclone rolled through in 1898 and split the Carolina Holiness Movement in half.[20]

Another strong connection between the white and black holiness people of North Carolina can be found within the columns of A.B. Crumpler's, *Holiness Advocate.* Rev. T.M. Lee, who was a dear friend of Crumpler's and fellow holiness minister, frequently attended the United Holy Church's early convocations. In 1901, when the "Colored Convocation" met in Winston-Salem, North Carolina, Rev. Lee wrote about his intergraded experiences with his peers. In a very compelling letter, Rev. T.M. Lee states:

> The Colored Holiness Convocation of North Carolina meets here from the 1st to the 8th in St. Paul's M.E. church, of which Bro. J.D. Diggs is pastor. It has rarely been my privilege to attend a meeting where the presence and power of the Holy Ghost were more manifest. There were a number of visiting workers. Two of the central figures were Bro. Robinson, of Pittsburg, Pa., and Bro. Collet, of Charlotte. It was gracious to see the power of God... [rest of sentence unclear.] It was my privilege to speak to them one morning. If the work here, and at this convention, is a fair sample of the general work in the hearts of the colored people in the holiness ranks in North Carolina, than so far as I can judge, their white brethren will have to spur up or they'll find themselves behind in this blessed race. May God pour out his Spirit on both the white and colored people in our State.[21]

Despite mounting racial tensions, Rev. T.M. Lee established a strong relationship with the African American Holiness pioneers. Obviously, Lee was impressed with the depth and character that the Convocation carried. What's interesting to note, however, is Lee's active role within the meetings. Although he most likely a played a small part during the convocation, it is significant that Lee participated by speaking to these precious saints. Judging from his words, one gets the sense that Mr. Lee was well aware of God's hand upon the infant church. In closing the letter, Rev. Lee prophetically prays for an outpouring upon both races. Little did he know that God would answer this prayer through the Azusa Street Mission Revival just five years later.

Chapter 7

GOLDSBORO: THE GATEWAY CITY

WHILE THE FIRST original Holiness Association was birthed in Vineland, North Carolina, other holiness associations began to spring up all over eastern North Carolina. As defined earlier, these associations were loosely affiliated pre-holiness churches, where converts could assemble, pray, worship, and fellowship. There establishment would sustain the holiness flames that had been lit by roving evangelists. One of these associations, however, was destined to outgrow the Vineland, North Carolina, organization and form a new strategic center for holiness activity in the Tar Heel state. Under A.B. Crumpler's leadership, that center would be situated in Wayne County, North Carolina, in a city known as Goldsboro.

Known to many Carolinians in Crumpler's day as the "Gateway city of Eastern North Carolina," Goldsboro was incorporated on January 18, 1847. Its "advantageous location" and natural well-drained plateau made the landscape perfect for building up homes and businesses. Agriculturally, the town was surrounded by unusual, fertile soil and would be known in later years for producing crops such as tobacco, apples, cherries, cabbage, beets, hay, cowpeas, beans celery, strawberries, huckleberries, melons, peaches, plums, and many others. But perhaps what made this town strategically significant to Crumpler's ambitions and worthy of being dubbed the gateway city was its relationship with the early railroad system.[1]

Goldsboro, at this time, was the only North Carolina city seated between the intersections of several major railroads. Running throughout both the state and the nation, this transportation system enabled passengers to reach cities such as New York, Philadelphia, Baltimore, Washington, and Atlanta within a "daylights journey." Here, one within a thirty hour ride could reach the cities of Boston, Quebec, Toronto, Buffalo, and Chicago, not to mention nearly every city throughout the state. The railroad systems, thus, made Goldsboro an excellent choice to plant and grow the fires of holiness.[2]

Spinning violently like Ezekiel's wheel within the wheel between the years 1896 to 1906, the city of holiness hosted mighty revivals and dynamic ministers during the late nineteenth century. They included L.L. Picket, G.D. Watson, Seth C. Reese and Sam Jones, all of which were acquaintances of Rev. Crumpler. During these years, thousands of seekers were often seen standing in the streets hoping to experience the spiritual phenomenon breaking out. However, very little is known of Crumpler's involvement with the town prior to 1898.[3]

The Unknown Goldsboro Revival of 1896

Today most Tar Heels, especially those living within the city's limits of Goldsboro, are unaware that a gripping inter-racial revival meeting exploded within their midst during 1896. Bringing an entire city to its knees, this gathering was the initial step that A.B. Crumpler took in building a holiness empire. Indeed, during the month of June 1896, A.B. Crumpler and his entourage conducted an earth shaking revival in a Goldsboro tobacco warehouse. So great was this heavenly visitation, the *Goldsboro Weekly Argus* continued to run ads of it nearly two years after it closed. Through this meeting, the spirit of revival was loosed in the atmosphere. It was so compelling, that it caused business owners to close their shops. Churches of all denominations abandoned their services. Regardless of race, social status or gender, all came to experience the powerful presence of God that Crumpler and his team carried into their city.[4]

Beginning on June 3, 1896, and running for several weeks, Rev. Crumpler and his team of prophetic warriors bum rushed the gateway city of eastern North Carolina with incredible spiritual power. They pulled down strongholds of dead religion and racism. Crumpler's words cut through the heart of sinner and saint, vagabond and statesman, black and white, with unprecedented authority. Crying out like a "voice in the desert," Crumpler's message ushered many people into the powerful presence of God. Mr. H.J. Faison, being one of those touched, was a prominent business owner who traveled from nearby Duplin County to hear the burning evangelist. Mr. Faison, who was described as a "man of intelligence," experienced the heart purity that Crumpler and others were preaching about. Soon after, Mr. Faison was burning just as Crumpler was and began testifying to the great throng of listeners who were crowding in the warehouse.[5]

It wasn't that A.B. Crumpler was preaching a deep and dynamic sermon that only spiritually mature people could understand, but rather Crumpler's words were powerfully truthful. In becoming transparent with his audience, Crumpler learned to articulate his own weaknesses through the message of holiness. The *Way of Faith*, in recounting this revival, captures the essence of this by stating, "His sermon was a mirror into which each one of his hearers could look and see portrayed their individual charter." Perhaps this is why Rev. Crumpler could relate so well to both the wealthy merchant and the poor tenant farmer. He, like the prophets of old, didn't just preach a message on holiness; he was the message of holiness![6]

With the gospel being preached, signs and wonders following, Crumpler began to focus his attention on breaking down the alters of racial indifference. In an evening service lead by local African-American converts, Rev. A.B. Crumpler, the "best negro preacher in eastern North Carolina," stirred the broken hearts of his black brothers and sisters. The *Goldsboro Weekly Argus* reports:

> At 3:30 o'clock the service for the colored people took place. The vast tabernacle building was filled with both races, the colored representatives having the right of way. Mr. Crumpler claims to be a follower of the "old time religion," and it was expected at this service that the old gray-descendants of Africa, whose forms are now bent with years of toil, would fill the air with shouts of joy and songs of praise. All that had been anticipated of shouting saints and happy hearts transpired. The heart of every idle spectator to this scene was made to swell with emotion when that vast concourse of musical voices was lifted in song and the old familiar tune of "When the Gin'l Roll is Called" was wafted to the afternoon breeze and that vast building seemed to sway in accord with the melodious notes that tried to burst its confines. Mr. Crumpler preached to them for an hour, and they shouted and sang sweet songs. It is estimated that 3,000 people were present last night. His sermon was one of his sanctification series and was interspersed with Scriptural citations bearing on the subject. At every service now there are a large number of seekers after sanctification. This doctrine, so new to the Goldsboro people in the light that Mr. Crumpler puts it, has been endorsed by a great numbers of our citizens of all classes and has been exemplified in their lives. Is it possible that this gracious experience has been withheld from Christian people all these years and it was left for this man to reveal it to this community? Recent observations seem to evidence this fact.[7]

This meeting, like the Dunn meeting a few weeks prior, accomplished many wonderful things. First, it brought many unbelievers in contact with the almighty God for the first time. Second, it refreshed the old Methodist doctrine of sanctification within the hearts of many hearers such as Mr. Faison. Thirdly, in the face of racial hatred, it sought to bring unity between two brothers that had been divided since the American establishment of slavery. Lastly, this meeting, which left behind holiness converts, laid the foundation of what would become the first Pentecostal-Holiness church and the center for eastern North Carolina's Holiness Movement.

To say that this would be the last visit Mr. Crumpler and his entourage made to Goldsboro would be a farce. Truthfully, it appears that this revival immediately spawned a North Carolina Holiness Association like the ones in Vineland and Magnolia, North Carolina. Unfortunately, no articles have been found to elaborate upon this early Goldsboro association; however, we do know that it existed.

Rev. Ed. Kelly, personal friend of A.B. Crumpler and co-leader of the Vineland, North Carolina State Holiness Association, placed on his itinerary that he would be attending the North Carolina Holiness Association in Goldsboro, during November of 1897. Rev. H.W. Jernigan, a holiness Free-Will Baptist preacher, was found in *The County Union* as having attended the "holiness convention" in Goldsboro during the first week of April 1897. The Rev. J. T. Kendall, in transitioning from pastor to holiness evangelists, also moved to Goldsboro in January of 1897, where he began a holiness work on "A New Line." Therefore, it is very likely that following the great tobacco warehouse revival in June 1896, another North Carolina Holiness Association was formed at Goldsboro between 1896 and 1897.[8]

The First Church Organized

Following the massive outbreak of the holiness revival under Crumpler's ministry during 1896, Carolina leaders began to sense that a more permanent organization was needed. Unfortunately, not everyone was welcoming to this movement, especially the Southern Methodist Church. Having declared war on the Holiness Movement in 1894 over its doctrines, stances on tobacco, inter-racial gatherings, and its evangelistic campaigns, the M.E. Church South began to expel its members for professing holiness. This same attitude also began to appear within other established churches such as the Baptists and Presbyterians.[9]

Remarkably, the movement would be accepted more within the African-American and Native-American churches of North Carolina then white established churches. G.F. Taylor noted that because "colored folk" were allowed to participate in the meetings, many opposers did not believe this revival to be a healing movement between different races or denominations. Instead, they believed it was not of God. Having acquired a large following of "poor folks and Negros," Crumpler began to lose popularity. Perhaps this is why he was crowned as "Eastern North Carolina's Best Negro Preacher," because he was willing to do something that most Southern whites could not, "loving your brother."[10]

With holiness converts being turned out of their churches and the lost having no place to go, Crumpler and other leaders began to organize small holiness congregations. Located mainly in the country of eastern Carolina, Crumpler's churches accommodated "poor folk and Negros," as well as anyone else looking for a church home. Crumpler did this so that many "who belonged to no church, and had been turned out of their churches for professing holiness might have a congenial home."[11]

One of these early inter-racial and inter-denominational congregations came off the heels of the massive Goldsboro tobacco warehouse revival of 1896. Two years later, another historic revival hit Goldsboro's streets. It was referred to as the Court House Square Revival of 1898. Traditionally, nothing has ever been written about these early Goldsboro meetings through A.B. Crumpler's ministry. Having already observed the tobacco warehouse meeting of 1896, let us now turn to the great Court House Square revival of 1898, which produced, in Dr. Synan's words, "the first church to ever bear the name, Pentecostal-holiness."[12]

After canvassing North Carolina in 1896 and 1897, A.B. Crumpler found himself once again in Goldsboro during the spring of 1898. Occupying the pulpit of St. John's Church in January 1898, Crumpler and his sanctified team began to prepare the people's hearts for another historic Goldsboro revival. This meeting was set to take place two months later, on March 27, 1898. At the same time, writers of the *Goldsboro Weekly Argus* also announced that Rev. Stephan Merritt, and Dr. Peck, and Dr. Wilson of New York, "will hold a union service in this city on Thursday and Friday the 24th and 25th of this month in the Court House." These northern ministers, who were national officers of the Christian Alliance, descended upon Goldsboro to preach holiness and prepare the city's residents for another monumental Crumpler revival.[13]

As March 27 approached, pre-revival services began in the courthouse. While services were running, "Uncle Jim Crumpler" was erecting his cousin's 2,500 men tent directly outside on the courthouse square. Before the days of stadiums, convention centers, and mega churches, the courthouse square is where one went to be heard. Like the Old Testament temple in Jerusalem, the courthouse was generally situated in the middle of the town and was often surrounded by crowds of people who were visiting the city for whatever reasons. The *Argus* further records that there was an excitement in the air, while many of the holiness adherents anticipated the coming of the "chief exponent of that doctrine (sanctification as second work of grace) in this section in the state."[14]

Besides Rev. Merritt, Dr. Peck, and A.B. Crumpler, the Rev. Collett was also in town preaching a holiness revival to the African-American believers at the same time. "The noted colored divine" was one of the first African-American holiness evangelists in N.C. Rev. Collett was widely recognized for his role within the organization of the Untied Holy Church that began in Method, North Carolina, in 1886. Although the newspapers do not elaborate, it seems that both Rev. Crumpler and Rev. Collett were working together, along with the Yankee ministers. Their objective: to establish a solid and lasting foothold of holiness within the "gateway city."[15]

Certainly, this revival was going to be one for the ages; however, the *Goldsboro Weekly Argus* for whatever reasons, failed to carry any detailed accounts of this meeting. It quietly stated that, "After three weeks of preaching day and night, Rev. A.B. Crumpler has folded his tent and gone to fill engagements elsewhere." Unfortunately, the silent treatment from local newspapers would become a reoccurring theme towards Crumpler and the North Carolina Holiness Church. Progressing towards the new century, this inter-racial movement would not only feel opposition from established churches, but also from local government authorities. In just eight months following this revival, an overwhelming outpouring of racial hatred and bloodshed would fill the streets of Wilmington, North Carolina.[16]

The so called explosion of Wilmington's "race riots," however, was not just a sudden flash of emotion. The riots, as we shall see, reflected years of hatred, bitterness, and vengeance that had been building within the hearts of some since the close of the Civil War. What does that have to with a Goldsboro newspaper running A.B. Crumpler's courthouse revival? Interestingly, it has everything to do with it. The political war that would consume dozens of innocent African-Americans at the hands of angry white citizens on November 1898 evolved around one issue, the local newspaper.[17]

During the nineteenth century, the local newspaper was the only form of mass communication. With the rise of "white supremacy" through the Democratic Party in 1898, there would be a war for control over what was placed in it is columns. Regardless if the Goldsboro paper reported the results or not, the courthouse revival at Goldsboro in March of 1898 did manifest some long-lasting fruit, namely the organization of the first Pentecostal Holiness Church, a church that was both white and black.[18]

There has been much debate as to when this organization took place. The two prevailing opinions both agree that it was in Goldsboro, in 1898. Rev. W. Eddie Morris, in his book, *The Vine and the Braches John 15:5: Holiness and Pentecostal Movements,* addresses this unsettled debate by contrasting conflicting accounts given by IPHC charter members, Rev. A.H. Butler and Rev. G.F. Taylor.

Both Butler and Taylor joined Crumpler's church in 1903, and would later recount from memory the history of the North Carolina Holiness Movement. According to Morris, Butler says, "The Pentecostal Holiness Church was organized in the year of our Lord, November 4, 1898, in a gospel tent on the Court House grounds in the city of Goldsboro, N.C.," According to Dr. Synan, Butler was supposedly present for the historic meeting and, from memory fourteen years later, recorded the charter members involved on a small piece of fly leaf paper. The problem with this account is that the courthouse revival did not occur in November, but eight months before in March 1898.[19]

The Goldsboro newspaper also stated, "After three weeks, Crumpler folded his tent and went to fill engagements elsewhere." Furthermore, searches through the city's newspapers for the fall of 1898 announce nothing in relation to a revival, meetings, or Crumpler himself visiting the town. Although newspapers would cease to run the results of Crumpler's meetings in 1898 and 1899, they would always briefly mention any time he would visit or hold a revival.[20]

Rev. G.F. Taylor, on the other hand, believed that the first church organized was "in Goldsboro, on Sunday morning, April 3, 1898." Rev. Morris, as well as other IPHC scholars and historians, has always generally agreed that Butler's account was more accurate because he recorded it before Taylor did. However, as the *Goldsboro Weekly Argus* shows, the historic courthouse Goldsboro revival took place starting on March 27, and lasted approximately to the third week of April 1898. Using this primary source as a plumb line, it stands to reason that the church was organized in April of 1898.[21]

After organizing a holiness church in Goldsboro, holiness ministers involved chose the name "Pentecostal Holiness" to give the new congregation an identity. Rev. Crumpler, who was still listed in good standing as an itinerant preacher with the Clinton Methodist Church, appears to have been the churches first leader at this point. Yet it wasn't long before Crumpler was back roving the Carolina countryside preaching revivals.[22]

Even without Crumpler at the helm, this racially mixed congregation, made up of mostly tenet famers, seems to have maintained their identity as the Pentecostal Holiness Church of Goldsboro between the years 1898–1900. Perhaps its leadership during this time was shared by multiple holiness ministers who would take turns preaching and leading the people while Crumpler was evangelizing. Nonetheless, this is the earliest documented account of a local church organization under A.B. Crumpler's ministry.

Crumpler Launches the Pentecostal Holiness Church

After A.B. Crumpler and others organized the first church in Goldsboro, the Southern Methodist Church began to take the war against holiness to the next level. Receiving both verbal and physical threats, Crumpler's ministry began to experience persecution. One of these threats surfaced when it was reported that on Christmas night, Crumpler's large gospel tent had been severely slashed and destroyed. Sadly, most of this early persecution seems to have come through the hands of Methodist bishops and elders. Many of them were becoming strongly dissatisfied with Mr. Crumpler and his efforts to help the poor, homeless, and despised.[23]

Unhappy with his fiery messages being aimed at their "dead churches" and "dead circuits," Methodist leaders devised a way to hinder the roving evangelist and "check the Holiness Movement." This plan of attack culminated in the creation of Rule 301, a rule which ultimately drove Crumpler out of organized religion. According to Dr. Synan, the M.E. Church South, in 1898, passed rule 301 which stipulated that:

> Any traveling local preacher or laymen who shall hold public religious services within the bounds of any mission, circuit or station when requested by the pastor not to hold such services, shall be deemed guilty of imprudent conduct, and shall be dealt with as the law provides in such cases.[24]

This rule, which was a premeditated church law, was intended to silence the thundering voice of Abner B. Crumpler. Having already scheduled a holiness meeting in Elizabeth City during the summer of 1898, the son of holiness now found himself in a heart-wrenching dilemma. Being an ordained Methodist preacher, Crumpler was forced to either break the law and continue on with his appointment, or withdraw from the beloved church in which he had been a member since 1886.

Sensing that his call to carry the mantle of holiness was more important than obeying the rules of men, A.B. Crumpler decided to temporally withdraw from the Methodist Church by surrendering his preaching credentials. For over one hundred years, no one has really known how this exactly transpired, or how Crumpler himself felt about the situation when it occurred, until now.

In a lost issue of the *Way of Faith*, a frustrated Crumpler pours out his heart and true feelings about rule 301 and the decision he made to go "on with the revival!" He writes:

> It seems that Southern Methodist Church is bent on crushing out the Holiness Movement by ridicule, abuse, legislation or any way they can.

> On the 9th of June, the day I started to my appointment in Elizabeth City, I went to my pastor and withdrew from my church. I had it to do or be turned out for doing what I believed with all my heart God was leading me to do.[25]

Despite the opposition, Rev. A.B. Crumpler, in this letter, made a critical decision. Rather than to surrender his call to preach, he chose to surrender the benefits and comfort that came along with being an ordained minister within an established church. Yet not all Methodist pastors would be against the flaming evangelists and his mission to preach the "glorious doctrines of Methodism."

Recognizing his unique call and gifting, Crumpler's own pastor, D.C. Geddie was saddened to see him withdraw. Interestingly, he wrote Crumpler a powerful letter of dismissal on the same day Crumpler withdrew from the church. Using this letter to any pastor who would evoke rule 301 against him, Crumpler carried it in his pocket wherever he went. The letter, written by D.C. Geddie, stated:

> We take pleasure in stating that Rev. A.B. Crumpler has been a local elder in the M.E. Church, South, for some time, and that he has been quite abundant in labors and has accomplished great good. He is a great and good man. We are sorry to note that for reasons on to himself he withdraws in good standing from our Church. We most heartily recommend him to any people whom he may be led of the Spirit to serve in the future. Respectfully, D.C. Geddie, Preacher in charge of Clinton Circuit, June 9th, 1898.[26]

This so called "letter of dismissal" reveals that Crumpler not only had enemies, but friends within his beloved church during these turbulent times. Perhaps it was relationships like these that enabled Crumpler to rejoin the church throughout his fifty plus years of ministry.

Over the next year, between June 1898 and June of 1899, Crumpler stayed out of the Methodist church to avoid future conflicts with rule 301. Although being free to evangelize wherever he pleased, and whenever he pleased, Rev. Crumpler never severed his ties with the Methodist Church. Rejoining the church in June of 1899 and thinking that rule 301 had "about died of its own weight," Crumpler continued to hold holiness meetings.[27]

In July of 1899, A.B. Crumpler planned to pitch his tent at Cedar Creek near Steadman, North Carolina. To his surprise, the local Methodist pastor enforced rule 301 upon Mr. Crumpler and his team. Rather than temporally withdrawing from the church as he did previously, Mr. Crumpler decided this time to remain steadfast and to "go on with the revival!" Responding back to the local pastor, Crumpler writes, "The call to preach God's Word comes, or should come, from God and not from the church...I cannot allow you to come between me and what I conceive to be my duty towards God and man."[28]

Several months later, on November 11, 1899, Rev. Crumpler found himself before a jury of five men at the Clinton Methodist Church. Having been charged with violating rule 301 at Cedar Creek, Crumpler found himself facing trial. He believed it to be a monstrosity. The jury found Crumpler guilty of holding the Cedar Creek revival, but acquitted him of any charges violating church law. Thus, he was subjected to no penalties. Although Crumpler remained as an ordained preacher in good standing with the Church, he soon withdrew again from the ranks of Methodism to avoid any more conflicts. Subsequently, the Carolina revivalists began to fully devote his efforts in carrying the mantle of holiness throughout North Carolina.[29]

Having been forced out of the Methodist Church, Crumpler sought to organize the movement that was ripping throughout North Carolina. Meeting in Fayetteville, North Carolina, in the early part of 1900, Rev. A.B. Crumpler and several ministers who had been converted under his ministry began to strategize how to "provide new bottles for new wine" that was being poured out.[30]

During this meeting, ministers also drew up a church *Discipline* which consisted of both doctrines and rules. As a result, the holiness bunch formed a loose style of church government. According to A.B. Crumpler, this government would run "on the order of the Missionary Baptist's." Being the leading denomination in Eastern North Carolina during this time, the Missionary Baptist's were a congressional church that allowed each church to operate autonomously. Fearing against a tyrannical form of church government, A.B. Crumpler established the Holiness Church as a self-governing congregation to minimize any one leader from taking control.[31]

Ambitious though they were, these burning pioneers never intended to church the Holiness Movement into a denomination. Instead, they organized independent holiness congregations. Operationally, these congregations were independent, inter-denominational, and inter-racial. Regardless of social status, gender, race, or creed Crumpler and others were bent on providing for these despised and destitute saints a "congenial home" where they could be free to worship, free to dance, free to shout, and free to proclaim the message of holiness without fear. Their mission was simple:

> Not only does the holiness church furnish a home for the homeless; but she has a peculiar and very sacred mission in this earth while we tarry for the Bridegroom. That mission is to "spread scriptural holiness over these lands" and to carry the gospel of full salvation to the

> despised, the poor, the downcast, the outcast and neglected ones for whom our precious Savior shed his life's blood![32]

The Fayetteville meeting was a great success. Upon its close, leaders developed this core objective, and began the process of embracing the "despised, poor, downcast, and outcast" people of North Carolina.

Moving with Heaven's army behind them, Crumpler and his band of warriors began to organize these small holiness churches throughout eastern North Carolina. Some of these churches included: Goshen, Antioch, Magnolia, and Goldsboro, which would become a city of holiness.[33]

Crumpler's Headquarters: The Goldsboro Tabernacle

Sensing he could lead the movement more efficiently from the gateway city, A.B. Crumpler became the first pastor of the congregation in Goldsboro during the early part of 1900. Initially, the Goldsboro church started meeting regularly in a small building. After Rev. Crumpler's arrival, the little meeting house became inadequate to host the large crowds attending. This problem was alleviated when a leading business man offered to lend a large sum of money towards the construction of a large new tabernacle. At sixty by ninety feet, this plain wooden structure was surrounded by windows and was able to accommodate an audience of over one thousand. For the next several years, this tabernacle would become known as the Pentecostal Holiness Church of Goldsboro, and hosted some of the strongest and influential holiness revivals the South has ever witnessed.[34]

Although a membership of one hundred and fifty would be recorded on paper, nearly one thousand seekers attended the Sunday night services on a regular basis. Traditionally, in both A.B. Crumpler and G.B. Cashwell's holiness meetings, Sunday night services were always reserved for the "colored saints." The Goldsboro church was no different. It was mostly made up of both black and white poor tenet farmers who, according to Mr. Crumpler, "did not even own a home." Though attendance would be high, income for the church would always remain low and humble. This lack of finances would prove to be an enormous problem for the holiness church in the days ahead.[35]

Shortly after taking on the head pastoral position in Goldsboro, Rev. A.B. Crumpler contracted the deadly typhoid fever and nearly died. The *Goldsboro Weekly Argus,* in following Mr. Crumpler's status, recorded his bout with the deadly virus. One article published on August 9, 1900, stated, "The serious illness of Rev. A.B. Crumpler, the pastor of the Pentecostal Holiness church in this city, is reported here from his home in Clinton." Being "confined to his home," Mr. Crumpler's condition gave much alarm to his wife, Lilly Jane, and their two small children, Lawrence and Grace Crumpler.[36]

Nearly two weeks later on August 16, 1900, J.J. Street was reported to have received a letter from Mrs. Lilly Jane Crumpler. Written by Mrs. Crumpler, she stated that her husband "is not improving but on the contrary is growing weaker." The letter ended in requesting the church and the entire city to pray for his recovery.[37]

With his assignment yet to be fulfilled and waves of intercession going up before the Lord, Rev. Crumpler's fever broke and he soon returned to "filling his appointments." On September 6, 1900, Rev. Crumpler wrote from Clinton that he was now "convalescent and will fill his pulpit in the holiness church here next Sunday and his appointment in Pikeville." Though the dangerous typhoid fever claimed thousands of lives during this time, it did not claim Abner Blackmon Crumpler. His time would not come for another fifty years.[38]

Although Crumpler was absent for a few months, it did not stop the folks of the Goldsboro Pentecostal Holiness Church from accomplishing their mission. While Mr. Crumpler was confined to his bed with the fever, the *Argus* carried a brief write-up of the evangelistic work that was being done by Crumpler's congregation. Published on August 9, 1900, it reads:

> The Sunday school of the Pentecostal Holiness church held their picnic last week at Kelly's Springs, about two miles from Mt. Olive. A large crowd of children and grown people were in attendance and all report a most pleasant trip. They were treated to a free watermelon feast by the country people in the vicinity, which was highly enjoyed by the children.[39]

Despite the fact that their pastor was sick, the young congregation remained active in the community. A noteworthy observation from this account reveals the Goldsboro church, like the Missionary Baptists, were self-sufficient. Being a self-governed ministry, the Goldsboro congregation helped the community without the presence of their pastor for some time. Although sources never reveal if anyone co-pastored during this time, it is very likely that one of the elders in the church continued the preaching, Sunday schools activities, and ministry operations while Rev. Crumpler was recovering.

In January of 1901, a renewed and refreshed Rev. Crumpler decided to relocate his family from Clinton to Goldsboro. He made this move in order focus on shepherding the Holiness Movement. It was also during this time, that Rev. Crumpler began a newspaper called *The Holiness Advocate* which was printed by the "Holiness Publishing Company" of Lumberton, North Carolina. Running bi-monthly, this publication informed readers of the North Carolina Holiness Movement between the years 1900–1908. It existed to "promote the cause of the Pentecostal Holiness Church" and was a representation of J.M. Pikes, *Way of Faith.* Like most holiness papers of that era, it contained editorials, sermons, holiness teachings, itineraries of preachers, supporters, and local testimonies. However, perhaps the most controversial items were found in discussions concerning church issues of the day, such as tobacco, divorce, and secret societies. The *Holiness Advocate*, which was created and edited by A.B. Crumpler and T.M. Lee, was freely circulated to the Methodist, Free-Will Baptists, and other church groups. This also made the paper inter-denominational that ran on non-sectarian principles. Without it, most of Crumpler's work would have been entirely lost. Even so, nearly half of the *Advocate* is still missing.[40]

Having acquired the largest holiness church, Carolina's best "negro preacher," and a major holiness publication, Goldsboro quickly became a major well for the holiness revival. Indeed, it was chosen to prophetically steer the movement of "scriptural holiness" that was sweeping the land

Chapter 8

G.B. CASHWELL'S MISSING HOLINESS YEARS

ONE OF THE most divisive issues that ripped through the North Carolina Holiness Movement during Crumpler and Cashwell's time was tobacco. However, between the years 1895 to 1901, tobacco was not a major issue for A.B. Crumpler and the Holiness Church. Although some of his early sermons would condemn its personal use, for the most part the burning evangelist remained silent about the "filthy weed" until he was forced to act. Having witnessed both his parents use tobacco, Rev. Crumpler was very likely sensitive to poor farmers who made their living on the cash crop. He understood that if farmers gave up growing tobacco, many would be brought to starvation.[1]

G.B. Cashwell also seems to have taken up Crumpler's position on the divisive issue. Yet, before he abandoned the tobacco industry, his life was dominated by two major themes: tobacco farming and preaching. Given the influence tobacco would have on the Holiness Church and Cashwell's involvement with the southern "cash crop," a brief overview of G.B. Cashwell's farming career is necessary. No doubt, it will give additional insight into this extraordinary life of G.B. Cashwell.

CASHWELL FARMING

Tobacco, to the Cashwell's, was more than just plugging your mouth with a "chaw" or two to pass the time away. As for most southern families during that time, tobacco was a way of life. When Granny Susan Stanley Cashwell received her fortune in 1854 for medically assisting the wealthy William Bass, she did so with the help of tobacco. Being the "Medicine Women of Persimmon College," Granny Susan exercised her medical expertise through her extensive knowledge of this most interesting plant. Using tobacco as the "cure-all" for diseases that would plague family and friends during the nineteenth century, Granny Susan and Aunt Harriet cultivated this natural herb and applied its healing power to cure dropsy, rheumatism, constipation, gout, asthma, and convulsive coughing. Like Native-Americans of old, these exceptional women learned the ways of an ancient people whose medical contributions to early white settlers have long been forgotten. During the 1860s and 1870s, all of the Cashwell children, including Gaston, were raised to view tobacco from this perspective.[2]

In the 1880s, tobacco as a cash crop was virtually non-existent in Sampson County. Sensing the time was right, however, Granny Susan started encouraging family members to explore ways on how to grow tobacco in greater quantities. At that time, Gaston's sister, Pender "Penny" Cashwell, married another young local famer by the name of John R. Bass. As we will later see, this marriage proved to have both positive and negative affects upon the Cashwell family.

In 1888, Gaston Cashwell's new brother-in-law (John R. Bass) traveled to Edgecombe County, North Carolina, where tobacco was being raised in mass quantities. Upon returning home, Mr. Bass brought a tobacco demonstrator back to the Keener area with him. This demonstrator introduced the concept of tobacco farming to the Sampsonians, and instructed the Cashwell family on how to raise it as a cash crop. Forecasting the financial success this would bring to their family, Gaston Cashwell and John R. Bass became business partners. This partnership made the Cashwell-Bass families among the first to grow, sale, and manufacture tobacco in the county.[3]

As the tobacco business began to expand for the Bass-Cashwell families of Keener, a thirty-one-year-old G.B. Cashwell traveled to south Georgia as a private tobacco demonstrator. He arrived in Berrien County sometime in the early spring of 1893. In Georgia, Cashwell sought to demonstrate to local farmers the concept of raising tobacco in large quantities. While he was there, Mr. Cashwell made headline news in *The Atlanta Constitution,* a local Georgia newspaper. Author Doug Beacham records the article in his book, *Azusa East: The Life and Times of G.B. Cashwell.* Beacham reveals that Gaston harvested 20,000 lbs. of tobacco during his demonstration. However, he also writes that "all was not pleasant for the tobacco 'demonstrators' and the Berrien County locals."[4]

According to Beacham, another article surfaced nearly two months prior to Cashwell's story. Appearing in the *Tifton Gazette*, this account recited problems occurring between local merchants and one "North Carolina tobacco demonstrator." The writer states that a conflict arose between the different business parties over an issue that centered on blackmailing. The article insinuates that the North Carolinian was "demanding payment on goods and services" from a local merchant who never placed an order. Gaston Cashwell was never implicated or charged with criminal behavior or activity in these matters; however, this may not necessarily mean he was completely innocent either.[5]

Family historian Dr. J.T. McCullen wrote an article entitled "Prayer Meeting at Persimmon College" which suggests that Gaston may very well have been a part of these accusations. McCullen makes a reference that Persimmon College's most famous leader was caught up in a swindle that has the makings of the Georgia conflict. He also writes that this swindle brought about a great spiritual change in the heart of this particular leader. "Brother Clute," as McCullen calls him, returned to Persimmon College and gave "the prayer meetings such zest as they have never known before." Could this be G.B. Cashwell? McCullen does not specifically name G.B. Cashwell or any other family member in the prayer meetings, but does give unmistakable clues to the identity of each Cashwell family member. These clues give an excellent reason to believe that "ole brother Clute" was indeed Uncle Gaston Cashwell. Perhaps it was the swindle that brought about a conviction in Cashwell's heart and led him to his first encounter with the Holiness Movement while in Georgia.[6]

Though details of this swindle appear to have fallen between the cracks of time, what has not is Cashwell's heart-changing, sanctified experience in Georgia. As noted previously, Gaston Cashwell was converted to holiness while staying in Georgia in 1893. By all accounts, his conversion seems to have come through the dynamic ministry of Rev. P.H. Crumpler, cousin of A.B. Crumpler. Nevertheless, Cashwell returned to Keener, North Carolina, at the close of 1893, and picked up where he left off as the spiritual leader of Persimmon College. Testifying to mostly family and close friends, G.B. Cashwell shared his sanctification experience with exceptional power.[7]

Indeed, G.B. Cashwell had encountered the flames of holiness while in Georgia, but he did not yet abandon the trade by which he and his family made a living on. Cashwell, after returning from his trip in Georgia, traveled across the Tar Heel state with another family member. Together, they learned how to raise tobacco barns for the purpose of applying the newly discovered "flue-curing" technique upon their harvest. Dr. McCullen also writes: "My grandfather, Jerry Gore, and his brother-in-law, Gaston Cashwell, observed farmers utilizing flue-curing barns up in Caswell County and, returning home, erected the first 'modern' tobacco barn in Sampson County."[8]

Using the inheritance of land given to him by his father, Herring Cashwell,

Gaston raised this barn on Cashwell land right off the Old Raleigh Road (Now 701) close to where Halls Fire Department is today.[9]

Once the days of using tobacco barns had arrived in Sampson County, someone was needed to stay up during the night and cure the crop, making tobacco farming a full time job. Gaston Cashwell, as it appears, continued to do this job for the next several years (1894-1897) while leading prayer meetings at Persimmon College. Yet with the flames of holiness growing ever so stronger, Cashwell began to sense God was calling him to a greater work.

When did G.B. Cashwell Join Forces with A.B. Crumpler?

Before diving into this intriguing question, let's discuss another big mystery that has always surrounded Cashwell's preaching career, his ordination. Having learned that the "Apostle of Pentecost to the South" emerged from the Missionary Baptist Church, it seems very likely that this too is where he was ordained. Unfortunately, back then most country churches did not keep written records.

The Persimmon College Meetinghouse, after G.B. Cashwell's death in 1916, appears to have died out due to lack of leadership. No trace of a written church history has ever been found. In fact, without the amazing work of Cashwell's great nephew, Dr. McCullen, any existence of the Persimmon College Meetinghouse would have slipped into oblivion. In view of this, an intriguing question begins to surface. Is it possible that G.B. Cashwell, the dynamic preacher who swept the entire Southern United States into his powerful message, was never officially ordained and licensed? The likely answer might be surprising.[10]

Emerging out of this loosely affiliated meetinghouse, Gaston Cashwell seems to have never received a formal ordination as most ministers did during that era (This explains why exhaustive searches into church records have always proved fruitless). Recognizing the unique call upon his life, it seems that church members of the meetinghouse informally ordained G.B. Cashwell as a holiness evangelist. Most likely, this oral ordination service took place in the mid-1890s. This account also agrees with Cashwell's own pen. Cashwell later noted that he "had been preaching holiness for nine years" before traveling across the country to the Azusa Street Mission in 1906. This puts the origins of Cashwell's charge to preach holiness around the year 1897.[11]

Although Rev. A.B. Crumpler had been dubbed as Eastern North Carolina's "best negro preacher" in the eyes of the public, Rev. G.B. Cashwell began to earn the exact same reputation, only without the spotlight. Preaching to all people groups, G.B. Cashwell started his holiness ministry by ministering to ex-slaves, Native-Americans, and poor white sharecroppers. Based on his audience, he really did not need a formal license to preach. Even so, his church services were held in one room shacks, poorly built slave quarters, and old run-down meetinghouses.[12]

Ordination or not, G.B. Cashwell was burning hot with holiness and believed that "all people should have an opportunity to hear the gospel." Regardless of skin color or denominational background, Cashwell urged everyone within the local community to live a holy life. Heading in this direction, it was only a matter of time before A.B. Crumpler and G.B. Cashwell joined forces. With Crumpler being a sanctified Methodist and Cashwell a sanctified "M. Baptist," the two independent holiness ministers assisted each other numerous times during the infancy years of the Holiness Movement.[13]

Traditionally, it has been taught by scholars that Rev. G.B. Cashwell joined A.B. Crumpler's Holiness Church in Dunn during the 1903 convention. Written by G.F. Taylor, a personal acquaintance of Gaston Cashwell, this article has gone unchallenged since Taylor wrote it from his memory in 1921. However, it seems to be highly inconsistent with recent records that have surfaced concerning Cashwell's involvement with Crumpler's Holiness Movement.[14]

G.B. Cashwell's church affiliation always seems to have been placed in the Missionary Baptist church. Though his theological views towards Christianity would change over time, his Baptist roots never did. It seems Cashwell never left the church in which his mother helped established, Persimmon College. This is proven on his funeral record which states at the time of his death in 1916, Cashwell's religious affiliation was with the "M. Baptist Church."[15]

On the other hand, Rev. G.B. Cashwell did join A.B. Crumpler's inter-denominational holiness convention in February 1900. As far as we know, the only established holiness church at this time, under A.B Crumpler's banner, was in Goldsboro. Even so, the holiness church in Goldsboro was initially congregational, inter-denominational, and interracial. It was a meeting-house type of church where other denominations could come and celebrate the holiness message while retaining membership in their existing churches. Besides the Goldsboro congregation, there were independent holiness congregations like it all over eastern North Carolina. Holiness ministers were in great demand. It didn't matter if you were a Baptist, Methodist, Presbyterian, Quaker, and so on. Just as long as you accepted, practiced, and exemplified holiness of life, then you were given access through the Holiness Convention to minister within "Holiness Tabernacles."[16]

Under A.B. Crumpler, it seems the creation of the Holiness Convention also gave ministers the opportunity to transfer their credentials without coming out of their original churches. In doing so, holiness preachers from different denominations were able to exercise their evangelistic gifts among congregations that had been organized by Crumpler and Cashwell's efforts. A great example of this is seen through ministers such as H.H. Goff and R.C. Jackson. Both Goff and Jackson were apart of A.B. Crumpler's holiness churches while retaining their church membership in the Free Will Baptist Church. This also seems to be the case for G.B. Cashwell.[17]

According to the 1907 Holiness Church minutes, G.B. Cashwell was admitted into the Holiness Convention in Goldsboro during February 1900. Interestingly, the minutes also reveal that A.B. Crumpler admitted himself into this same convention meeting. Crumpler's arrival to the convention was announced in the *Goldsboro Weekly Argus.* It states, "Rev. A.B. Crumpler, the Sanctification apostle, and father of the Holiness Movement in this section, is in the city, attending the Holiness Convention." Amazingly, these records reveal that both G.B. Cashwell and A.B. Crumpler joined the Holiness Convention at the same time and same place—Goldsboro, North Carolina.[18]

Prior to the 1900 convention, however, G.B. Cashwell was believed to be heavily involved with A.B. Crumpler's holiness campaigns during 1896–1900. There are several claims to support this:

First, when the Holiness Movement began to break out under Crumpler's preaching in 1896, it did so in Sampson County, North Carolina. Yet before the apostle of holiness would canvass the Old North State, his first major revivals occurred in Ingold, Parkersburg, Goshen, and Clinton. All of these initial meetings, which hosted thousands, transpired within a fifteen mile radius of the Cashwell farm. By 1896, Cashwell was a holiness lay preacher leading the Persimmon College congregation. It is hard to believe that Cashwell was not present for these meetings that attracted so many of his neighbors in the early part of 1896.[19]

Second, in March 1896, A.B. Crumpler pitched his massive gospel tent at Goshen and held a powerful revival. Incredibly, Crumpler's tent only stood a few miles from the home of G.B. Cashwell. Surprisingly, four years later in March 1900, both G.B. Cashwell and A.B. Crumpler organized the Goshen folks into a holiness church. In its early years, the Goshen Holiness church most likely retained both black and whites. Cashwell served the church as its first pastor in 1900.[20]

Third, Rev. Crumpler erected his tent in the middle of Clinton for another incredible revival in June 1896. The famous "three in one" meeting also took place just five miles from the Cashwell farm. The *County Union* records several ministers assisting Mr. Crumpler that day. Two of them were from the Missionary Baptist church. This is believed to be Gaston Cashwell and Jerry

Gore. At this time, G.B. Cashwell was the only known M. Baptist minister to ever join or assist in Crumpler's holiness convention throughout its early years.[21]

Fourth, two years following the Goshen and Clinton revivals, the city of Goldsboro was preparing to host the great courthouse revival on March 27, 1898. This revival, which spawned the first organized Pentecostal-Holiness Church, also contains another fascinating secret, the involvement of G.B. Cashwell. Accordingly, Cashwell family history remembers Gaston giving A.B. Crumpler, "a helping hand in organizing the first Pentecostal Holiness Church."[22]

Fifth, when A.B. Crumpler established the holiness church's early form of government, he did so based upon the "order of the Missionary Baptist."[23] Some believe this was done in fear of the tyrannical structure of Methodism that Crumpler was battling. However, it seems possible that Crumpler was also influenced by Cashwell's Missionary Baptist background.[24]

Sixth, sometime between the years 1897–1899, Gaston Cashwell became recognized as an official ordained and licensed preacher outside of the Persimmon College community. This is confirmed through several sources such as his marriage certificate and his wedding announcement in the Dunn *County Union*. Even though Cashwell was never one for church titles, his identity as full-time minister at this point, was becoming increasingly clear. Yet it did so only after he started preaching the "doctrines of holiness" around 1897.[25]

Although these claims shed light on Cashwell's obscure years, they also conjure up more questions. Namely, one in particular: If G.B. Cashwell was never officially ordained, how did he transfer into the Holiness Convention in 1900? That answer seems to be buried underneath something that was never intended to surface; the close relationship shared between G.B. Cashwell and A.B. Crumpler.

Having both been converted by J.T. Kendall in the same revival in 1885, Crumpler knew G.B. Cashwell longer than he did any other minister within the holiness convention. Most likely, he also knew Cashwell's family, friends, and most importantly, his mysterious background. Conducting inter-racial and inter-denominational meetings during a time when white preachers could be "strung up," A.B. Crumpler had more in common with G.B. Cashwell than anyone may have ever believed. Besides being a preacher, Rev. Crumpler was also an intelligent lawyer who knew the law, judges, and leading county officials very well.[26]

Therefore, knowing G.B. Cashwell's background, it seems evident that Mr. Crumpler allowed G.B. Cashwell to transfer his oral ordination from

Persimmon College without making much fuss about it. From this, we can conclude that G.B. Cashwell, while assisting Crumpler in organizing holiness churches, was given an informal holiness certificate to preach the holiness message. This certificate would have given Cashwell access to holiness congregations all over eastern Carolina, although he still remained an independent holiness evangelist with Missionary Baptist roots.[27]

G.B. Cashwell and Lovie Lee

It's no surprise that G.B. Cashwell found a beautiful bride during his early preaching years. What most do not know is that Cashwell's wife, Lovie Harrison Lee, would be driven into the arms of this powerful preacher though the Holiness Movement. At the age of thirty-seven, the Rev. G.B. Cashwell both met and married this amazing woman who also hailed from Sampson County. Lovie's story, which has never been explored, answers a lot of missing questions that have lingered over the Cashwell mystery. It is both insightful and interesting to see how her life was interwoven into the fabric of the Pentecostal-Holiness Movement. Thus, it is imperative that we view her history, and how she came to meet the future "Apostle of Pentecost to the South."

Lovie was born on January 19, 1874, to Erasmus and Lucinda Allen Lee of Sampson and Harnett counties, North Carolina. According to her obituary, Lovie was "born into one of Dunn's leading families." Her father, Erasmus Lee, her uncle L.H. Lee, and other Lee family members were all part of the Freemason brotherhood. The Lee's were also noted for being wealthy land owners in eastern North Carolina.[28]

After moving from Sampson County (Mingo Township) sometime in the 1860s, Erasmus Lee settled the large Lee family in the Black River Township of Cumberland County. Situated approximately ten miles from the new booming town of Dunn, North Carolina, this land was located very close to what is now Falcon, North Carolina. Another prominent and wealthy family also moved to the Black River Township around this same time. They were William and Nancy Culbreth of Sampson County. The Culbreth's, who were the founders of Falcon, North Carolina, also had several children,n including Julius A. Culbreth. Both the Culbreth and Lee children were practically neighbors and apparently shared a close relationship while growing up together.[29]

Lovie Lee, who grew up in this general area, was very active in church affairs from her youth. She was well-known for playing the organ in the local Presbyterian Church, though she was not a member. Lovie, like her father, was a member of the Free-Will Baptist Church. This is what most likely led her to her first marriage with another well-known and beloved Free-Will Baptist minister, T.F. Harrison.[30]

Rev. Harrison and his brother were famously known in eastern Carolina as being the "twin preachers." Besides being evangelists, they were instrumental in leading the entire Cape Fear Conference. T.F. Harrison, who began preaching at the age of eighteen, held a high position in the church and was a published author. He, along with J.M. Barfield, wrote the early history of the Free-Will Baptist Church conference history. Incredibly, Rev. Harrison accomplished these things before his twenty-fifth birthday.[31]

On April 24, 1895, the twin preachers came to Dunn, North Carolina, and held a series of revival meetings. The local newspaper, *The County Union,* advertised the meetings by announcing, "T.F. and T.H. Harrison the twin brothers and evangelists of the Eastern Free Will Baptist Conference began a series of meetings at the Free Will Church Sunday night and they continue to have large and attentive congregations."[32]

Apparently, T.F. Harrison must have made quite the impression on Dunn's residents, especially Lovie Lee. Fifteen days later, the two would be married. Their wedding announcement was also recorded in the same paper on May 15, 1895. It reads as follows:

> Last Sunday was the day the marriage right was to be performed which brought together two lives that are now one. At 9:30 a.m. Elder T.F. Harrison led to the hymeneal alter Miss Lovie Lee the lovely and accomplished daughter of Mr. Erasmus Lee, a wealthy and highly esteemed farmer of Cumberland County. Elder Harrison came to Dunn 15 days previous to this marriage and he and his brother, known as the twin preachers held a protracted meeting at which time he met Miss Lee and her winning ways and pleasant manners seemed to captivate him. It seems to be love at first sight. The match was made short order. Elder R.C. Jackson, pastor of the Free Will Church at this place performed the marriage ceremony. May their life be surrounded with comfort, and their days know no sorrow.[33]

Following the marriage the two moved back to T.F. Harrison's house which was located in Ayden, North Carolina. Ayden, which would also be a town where G.B. Cashwell and Lovie would move to in the future, was home to the Free Will Baptist Seminary School. This school, which is now Mt. Olive College, proved to be a centralized location for the Eastern Free Will Baptist Conference. It seems Elder Harrison was preaching to three churches in the area and owned a home not far from this institution of higher learning.

Though their relationship and marriage seemed like a page out of fairy tale story, it was destined to end just as quickly as it started. Rev. Harrison succumbed to the dangerous typhoid fever and died on Sunday afternoon October 24, 1897. He was just twenty-four-years-old leaving Lovie Lee Harrison a widow at the age of twenty-three and with no children. Just before he died, however, a remarkable spiritual encounter occurred within both Mr. and Mrs. Harrison's life.[34]

After the historic holiness revival that took place in Dunn during May of 1896, Rev. A.B. Crumpler continued to make several trips back to the young city. Returning in June of the same year, Crumpler held another powerful holiness revival. Against her husband's wishes, Lovie attended the services. T.F. Harrison was in Ohio at the time, and could not stand the thought of his wife attending one of those "Crumpler meetings." As noted previously, not everyone was welcoming to the new Holiness Movement being led by A.B. Crumpler and G.B. Cashwell. Rev. Harrison despised the doctrine of sanctification and its stand against using tobacco.

Harrison, a smoker himself, would begin to see things a little differently when he returned from his trip. To his amazement, his new bride Lovie Lee claimed the holiness experience. Torn between believing his wife's testimony and his own prejudices towards the rapidly growing movement, Harrison began to seek for himself the experience of burning love. He got it soon thereafter! His testimony was printed in J.M. Pike's *Way of Faith* in which he declares:

> On February 8, 1897, I was on my way home from one of my appointments riding along in my buggy. I began to pray for entire sanctification with a cigar in my mouth. The angel of Conscience whispered and said, "You will never get it as long as you use tobacco." I instantly threw the cigar down promising God never to use it again. At that instant I was baptized with the Holy Ghost and fire. I have been perfectly happy ever since. Hallelujah to the Lamb! I will close for it is impossible for me to tell you what good things the Lord hath done for me. Yours saved, sanctified, and cleansed in the blood of Christ, Rev. T.F. Harrison Ayden, N.C., March 27, 1897.[35]

Amazingly, Rev. Harrison, who was so adamant against this movement, was now won over to holiness through his wife, Lovie Lee Harrison. From this point on, Harrison subscribed to the *Way of Faith* newspaper and began to follow A.B. Crumpler and the Holiness Movement very closely.

Unfortunately, for the young preacher, Lovie Lee Harrison, and the entire Cape Fear Conference, Elder Harrison passed away just eight months later. Being a major leader and respected preacher in the Free Will Baptist Church, there is just no telling how his leadership might have inspired the entire North Carolina Free Will-Baptist Church towards the holiness revival. Rev. Crumpler had already had a significant impact in the Cape

Fear Conference by winning many of them to holiness. Free Will ministers such as H.H. Goff, R.C. Jackson, Ed Parker, J.A. Blalock, and a host of others had already succumbed to the movement sweeping the land.

Their conversions, however, eventually lead to a great divide within the Free Will Baptist conference during 1912. The split would center over the doctrines of "sanctification" and the baptism of the Holy Spirit with the initial evidence of speaking in tongues." If Harrison hadn't died so young, it is very possible that the division may not have occurred. Nonetheless, at best this is speculation, and such assumptions can only be left up to the providence of God. Besides, if things would have worked out this way, Lovie would have never met another stunning and powerful man of God destined to sweep her off her feet, Rev. Gaston B. Cashwell.[36]

After Harrison's death, Lovie appears to have stayed in the house at Ayden, North Carolina. Two of her sisters, Emma and Kizzie Lee, were also known to have Ayden ties. In April 1896, Kizzie Lee married Mr. Willie Taylor, "a prominent young merchant" from Ayden. Emma Lee, Lovie's other sister, took a teaching job at the Free Will Seminary School. The Lee family members, therefore, were not strangers to the little town residing in Pitt County. Unfortunately, there are no formal documents informing us how Gaston Cashwell and Lovie met. Still, there is a solid family story which may shed some additional light.[37]

According to the Lee family tradition, while Lovie was visiting her family in the Dunn area, she heard a voice that caught her attention. The voice belonged to Rev. G.B. Cashwell who was also preaching in the area. Given the untimely death of her first husband, local newspapers reported that Lovie came home after the funeral. Apparently, Lovie stayed with her mother in Dunn for an extended period of time. Interestingly, at the same time Lovie was staying in Dunn, A.B. Crumpler and his ministry associates held meetings between Benson and Dunn. Could this have been the meeting in which Lovie "heard a voice that caught her attention?"[38]

Although the answer may never be known, it is certain that Gaston Cashwell and Lovie Lee Harrison met during this time frame. Ironically, it seems Lovie fell in love with the gentle giant from Keener, just as she did with Rev. T.F. Harrison. Like her marriage with Harrison, Lovie's engagement with G.B. Cashwell did not last long. Accordingly, Gaston and Lovie "tied the knot" on March 8, 1899, through a mutual friend of holiness, Rev. H.H. Goff.[39]

H.H. Goff was a Free Will Baptist Church minister, who had been swept into Crumpler's Holiness Movement. From all points of view, H.H. Goff and his wife Florence Goff, appear to have been good friends with the Cashwells until changing times would sever their relationship. Prior to this, it seems that the Cashwells and Goffs had a lot in common. G.B. Cashwell and H.H. Goff were both Baptists and known for being ministers. Both were affiliated with A.B. Crumpler's holiness convention, although they belonged to other churches. After the Pentecostal revival would occur in Dunn during 1907, the Goffs and Cashwells spent time in each other's homes praying down the Spirit of heaven.[40]

It has always been assumed that Gaston and Lovies's wedding announcement was never carried in the local Dunn newspaper. Searches for its existence have always seemed to come up short. The answer to this mystery, however, lies with the editors of *The County Union*. Apparently, someone dropped the ball, and the Cashwell's wedding announcement was "forgotten" and not placed in the paper on the designated day. Nearly three weeks later, the newspaper finally publicized the newlywed's private marriage, which took place in the city of Dunn at the Lee's residence on March 22, 1899. It reads:

> We failed to announce the marriage of Mrs. Lovie Harrison to Rev. G.B. Cashwell, on the evening of the 8th at the residence of Mrs. Erasmus Lee, mother of the bride, in this city, Rev. Mr. Goff officiating. Mr. and Mrs. Cashwell took the train here next day for the home of the groom's mother near Clinton. They have our best wishes.[41]

Being short and sweet, the announcement does contain two insightful components. First, the marriage was private and held in the evening. Second, following the wedding, Gaston took Lovie to meet his family in Keener, most likely for the first time. According to the Cashwell history, none of Gaston's relatives attended the ceremony. Both the article listed here, and the Cashwells' wedding certificate, confirms this by revealing that only friends of the bride were present. Nonetheless, the newlyweds did pay a visit to Granny Susan and Gaston's side of the family.[42]

Sometime after this, the Cashwells left for Georgia. It seems preaching engagements is what lead Cashwell back to the peach state. Doug Beacham also notes this Georgia preaching trip in his book. In searching another branch of Cashwell family history, Beacham adds, "Family history (Cashwell) speculates he (Gaston) was in Georgia preaching" during the latter part of 1899. Apparently, when Cashwell was converted to holiness in 1893, he made some connections in Georgia with certain holiness ministers. Ironically, these connections seem to always lead back to one man, Rev. P.H. Crumpler.[43]

During this time, Rev. P.H. Crumpler also left Clinton, North Carolina, and headed back home to south Georgia. Upon his arrival, Georgia newspapers reveal that P.H. Crumpler held massive revivals that attracted thousands. Yet, between the years 1896–1898, Rev. P.H. Crumpler assisted A.B. Crumpler and most likely G.B. Cashwell while staying in the Carolinas. This seems to be the only reasonable connection between Cashwell and Georgia in 1899. Most likely, G.B. Cashwell went back with Rev. P.H. Crumpler and assisted him in preaching tent revivals throughout south Georgia. Nevertheless, while in Georgia, the Cashwell's had their first child, Ruth Cashwell, in the fall of 1899.[44]

Cashwell Spreads Holiness

After returning from Georgia with their firstborn child, the new family settled back in Ayden, North Carolina, sometime around 1900. Their move to Ayden was confirmed through *The Democratic Banner*, which was Dunn's new leading paper between 1900 and 1902. According to the "local dots" section, Lovie was in town visiting her family. It reads, "Mrs. Lovie Cashwell, of Ayden, is visiting her mother, Mrs. Erasmus Lee." While Lovie was in town probably showing off the new baby to the Lee side of the family, Gaston Cashwell was on the move burning hot with the flames of holiness.[45]

The earliest documented account of Cashwell's holiness career shows him organizing the Goshen Pentecostal Holiness Church along with his counterpart, A.B. Crumpler. Up until this point, there has never been a documented account of G.B. Cashwell's holiness ministry prior to 1903. It reads:

> Goshen Pentecostal Holiness Church was organized in the month of March 1900 by Rev. A.B. Crumpler and Rev. Gaston Cashwell with twenty members. The land was donated by G.W. Sutton. During these years the following ministers have served as pastors; Reverends Gaston Cashwell, John Rouse, A.H. Butler, C.B. Strickland, H.E. Oxendine, W. J. Noble, M.H. Alexander, Gustave Sigwalt, S.A. Fann, Jerome Hodges, J.W. Berry, N.J. Medford, V.W. Callahan, H.M. Pope, J.G. Crocker, Samuel J. Williams, W.L. Mayo, and our current pastor, Vernon Clark and his faithful wife, Mrs. Clark.[46]

Amazingly, this record shatters nearly every account of G.B. Cashwell's early relationship with A.B. Crumpler and the Holiness Movement. In years past, historians and scholars have wrote that Cashwell was largely absent from Crumpler's movement until 1903. However, the Goshen history, along with Dr. McCullen's work, discloses a different Crumpler-Cashwell relationship. They reveal that Cashwell and Crumpler worked together in establishing the Holiness Movement in eastern North Carolina during its early years (1896–1900).

After a brief tenure as founding pastor of the Goshen Holiness Church in

1900, Rev. G.B. Cashwell began to "enlarge his tent pegs" beyond Sampson County. Canvassing Wayne, Lenoir, Green, Wilson, and Edgecombe counties, G.B. Cashwell's holiness ministry began to accelerate during 1900–1902. Roving around eastern Carolina, Cashwell preached to black and white audiences everywhere he went. There is just no telling how many other holiness congregations he helped organize. At this time, Ayden served as a home base for the Cashwell's ministry. This would prove to be a strategic choice for Gaston.[47]

Being a major hub for the Free Will Baptist Conference of North Carolina, Ayden enabled Gaston to develop strong ties with his Baptist brethren while living there. Having just been admitted into A.B. Crumpler's newly formed Holiness Convention in February of 1900, Rev. Cashwell's ministry evolved heavily around the holiness believing Free Will Baptist ministers. Working closely with preachers such as H.H. Goff, J.F. Owen, C.J. Carr, M.M. Johnson, J.A. Blalock, and others, Cashwell appears to have really strengthened the bond between the Baptist and holiness groups. This Holiness-Baptist relationship was something A.B. Crumpler desperately wanted to pursue. Crumpler always sought to keep the movement both inter-denominational and inter-racial. Thus, Gaston's efforts in collaborating with other Free Will evangelists added depth to the rapidly growing movement. His work around Ayden would ensure A.B. Crumpler's ecumenical vision for the young aspiring North Carolina church.[48]

Since G.B. Cashwell's holiness meetings never appeared in North Carolina newspapers for obvious reasons, Crumpler's *Holiness Advocate* has become the only source to verify Gaston's holiness ministry. Being an interdenominational newspaper, the *Advocate* allowed all denominational ministers to publish articles. Cashwell's first reference within this paper begins in August of 1902. Here, Cashwell along with Free Will Baptist minister J.F. Owen were found holding a most powerful meeting near Zoar Free-Will Baptist Church in Salemburg, North Carolina.[49]

Shortly following, the *Advocate* boasted of Gaston and M.M. Johnson holding another meeting at Snow Hill, North Carolina. A month later, A.B. Crumpler wrote of Cashwell, "Bros. G.B. Cashwell and M.M. Johnson have just closed a meeting at Aaron, North Carolina." Though the success of these meetings was never recorded, it seems that Cashwell's preaching was making an impact within eastern North Carolina.[50]

By October of 1902, G.B. Cashwell was erecting the "tent" at Hood Swamp in Wayne County, and held a powerful tent revival. Returning to Hood Swamp a year later, Cashwell continued to proclaim holiness amongst the mixed multitudes. In preaching to the "colored saints at 4 o'clock," Rev.

Cashwell reported a glorious meeting, where the "Spirit of the Lord was present" among both races.[51]

Traditionally, what little has been written concerning Cashwell's holiness years, has limited his role within this movement. Being labeled as an evangelist, most have thought that this was his only function. On the contrary, G.B. Cashwell was not only evangelizing during these years, but was planting churches, organizing prayer meetings, and pastoring multiple congregations. Besides the Goshen P. H. church history, evidence confirming this is found through a letter written by Rev. C.B. Strickland.

In April 1904, Rev. C.B. Strickland, another holiness minister, was sent to hold a holiness revival at the Goshen Holiness Church. This is the same congregation that Cashwell had pastored after organizing it with A.B. Crumpler. Recording his journey, Strickland wrote: "Dear Advocate family: We are here in battle for precious souls. Brother Cashwell, the pastor, began the meeting last Friday night, March 4, and stayed until we came."[52]

Based on this account, G.B. Cashwell transitioned again from evangelist to pastor for the holiness cause in 1904. Equally intriguing is that the Goshen Holiness Church and the Persimmon College Meetinghouse were only a few miles apart. Cashwell family tradition also suggests that Gaston was still mindful of his congregation back home and continued pastoring it as well.[53]

Besides Persimmon College and the Goshen Holiness Church, there was a third holiness congregation in the area, St. Matthews Holiness Church. St. Matthews, according to its history, was organized by Rev. A.H. Butler in 1903. Butler served as its first pastor until 1904. Yet the history also states that the church existed prior to 1903. Although the exact date is unknown, St. Matthews was started through a "brush arbor revival."[54]

Congregants met in an old ran down shanty known as the "Old Cindy House." Similar to Persimmon College, the Cindy House hosted sanctified prayer meetings in the Sharecake area during the 1890s. It was here that the Rev. A.H. Butler bowed down to an impoverished alter under the preaching of an unidentified sanctified boy in 1895 and gave his heart to the Lord. Just who was this boy?[55]

These records fail to mention who was responsible for initiating the "Brush Arbor Revival" that lead to the Cindy House meetings. This leaves behind a serious question. If Rev. Butler organized the church in 1903, then who started it? Fortunately, Cashwell family history has an answer.

According to Cashwell's descendants, St. Matthews Pentecostal-Holiness Church was started under the preaching of G.B. Cashwell through a brush arbor revival. Certainly, this would have been right up Cashwell's ally. The Cindy House meetings seemed to be identical to Cashwell's home church,

Persimmon College. Leading these sanctified prayer meetings was a natural fit for Gaston by this time, but could it be possible that the boy Rev. A.H. Butler referred to was Gaston?[56]

Nevertheless, Persimmon College, St. Matthews, and the Goshen churches seemed to have made up a small holiness circuit around the Keener area. Incredibly, this seven mile circuit surrounded the Cashwell farm during the 1890s and early 1900s. Considering Cashwell's involvement with these churches, it is very likely that Gaston spent a majority of his holiness career right in his own backyard.[57]

Considering these observations, we can now view G.B. Cashwell's obscure holiness years in a different light. Being sanctified in 1893 and preaching holiness by 1897, G.B. Cashwell's holiness experience predates all other holiness ministers who would go on to organize, join, or be affiliated with the North Carolina Holiness Church. This list includes, Revs. J.T. Kendall, D.A. Futrell, W.A. Jenkins, J.A. Rouse, W.F. Galloway, E.L. Parker, R.B. Jackson, J.A. Blalock, H.H. Goff, R.C. Jackson, J.A. Culbreth, G.F. Taylor, A.H. Butler, C.B. Strickland, and S.D. Page. In fact, the only other minister whose sanctified experience predates G.B. Cashwell's within the North Carolina Holiness Church is none other than A.B. Crumpler (1890).

What can we learn from this? That both A.B. Crumpler and G.B. Cashwell were among the first to pioneer the powerful Holiness Movement in eastern North Carolina. Surprisingly, they were always together. Together they were saved, joined the North Carolina Holiness Convention, staged revivals, organized churches, and served as pastors over inter-racial congregations during the movement's infancy years. More importantly, it can now be asserted that G.B. Cashwell and A.B. Crumpler both founded the church which bears the name Pentecostal Holiness.

For whatever reasons, IPHC founders G.F. Taylor, A.H. Butler, J.H. King, and J.A. Culbreth failed to mention this when they wrote the churches first history. Their silence has always left a huge gap within the Crumpler-Cashwell mysteries. Thankfully, that gap is beginning to close

This rare photograph was taken at the First National Holiness Camp Meeting in Landis Park, Vineland, New Jersey 1867.

Rev. Pleasant H. Crumpler. Cousin of A.B. Crumpler, Pleasant is believed to have introduced G.B. Cashwell to the holiness way. Courtesy of archives from Georgia's United Methodist Church.

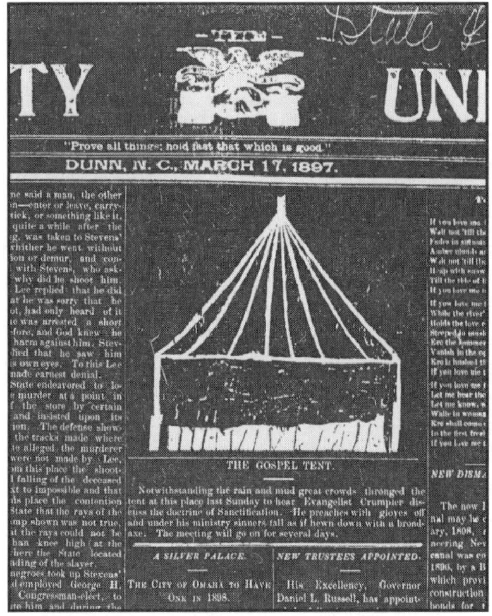
TY UNI

"Prove all things: hold fast that which is good."

DUNN, N. C., MARCH 17, 1897.

THE GOSPEL TENT.

Notwithstanding the rain and mud great crowds thronged the tent at this place last Sunday to hear Evangelist Crumpler discuss the doctrine of Sanctification. He preaches with gloves off and under his ministry sinners fall as if hewn down with a broad-axe. The meeting will go on for several days.

A SILVER PALACE.

The City of Omaha to Have One in 1898.

NEW TRUSTEES APPOINTED.

His Excellency, Governor Daniel L. Russell, has appoint-

This was taken from a front page article in The Dunn County Union newspaper during March 1897. This was A.B. Crumpler's Holiness Tent that came to Dunn, North Carolina in May 1896, and shook the entire city.

A.B. Crumpler Co-founder of the Goshen P.H. Church. This is a never before seen photo of the Apostle of Holiness. Taken during early 1900's. Courtesy of John Aman.

PART III

THE HOLINESS CHURCH VS. RACISM, RELIGION, AND SECRET SOCIETIES

Chapter 9

THE EXTERNAL WAR: WHITE SUPREMACY vs. HOLINESS CHURCH

While Crumpler, Cashwell, and others were establishing an inter-denominational and inter-racial church in the Goldsboro area in 1898, racial tensions were beginning to escalate seventy miles south in Wilmington, North Carolina. These tensions exploded on a chilly November morning when a heavily armed caravan of white men marched in military-fashion into the black neighborhoods of Wilmington. Fueled by hatred, they shot down and murdered dozens of innocent black residents in the name of white supremacy. The fierce mob then overpowered the local black newspaper office and burned it to the ground. Their bloody coup did not stop until many successful black citizens and their so called "white nigger" allies were banished from the city. This tyrannical political mob made of North Carolina's wealthiest and so called finest citizens did not stop here. Their lustful desire for control and power only ended when they achieved something that had never been done in America's history: a violent overthrow of an existing government.[1]

Indeed, the Wilmington race massacre of 1898 was a crucial turning point in the history of North Carolina. It was an event that stirred national interest and forced governments in the South to enforce brand new laws that would segregate the races. Following the Wilmington model of brutality, other southern states began to enforce white supremacy in their cities. Soon, every state in the south would begin to study and apply Wilmington's methods of mob violence and implement it within their own towns. After all the bullets had ceased and bodies were removed from hanging trees, the South once again laid devastated. Wilmington's political aggressions, which had been funded and supported by North Carolina organizations such as the Ku Klux Klan and Freemasons, finally culminated when state lawmakers ushered in one of the most horrific and darkest eras in our nation's history, the Jim Crow south.[2]

For nearly a century this story and how it relates to the Holiness Movement of North Carolina has never been explored. Yet it would be these critical events in Wilmington, North Carolina, that would inspire a war between white supremacy and the North Carolina Holiness Church. Prior to November of 1898, the Holiness Movement, being led by A.B. Crumpler, seemed to experience only minimal persecution; however, as Jim Crowism began to deepen its roots in the Carolinas, Crumpler's new organization would quickly find itself loosing key members and leading ministers.

The so called "revolution of 1898" did not begin overnight. It was a premeditated and well thought-out strategy which consisted of several key players and organizations. Rev. A.B. Crumpler and others, however, would not remain silent over these political forces that were sweeping through the land. Before searching for his response to this wave of sin, let us briefly examine the movement which fooled many good people into giving into the cause of white supremacy.

The Origins, Rise, and Explosion of the White Supremacy Campaign of 1898:

Following the Civil War, during the reconstruction period, white planters and wealthy business men dominated politics in North Carolina up until the 1890s. A shift in government occurred, however, when in the early 1890s, white farmers and African Americans formed a coalition known as the Fusion movement. This movement consisted of two major political parties (Republicans and Populist) which sought to dethrone the wealthy and elite Democrats of North Carolina. Although they did not agree on everything, this partnership made a courageous attempt to establish an interracial democracy within the Old North State. Populists, also known as the "people's party," was formed in response to widespread economic pressures during this period. Being founded by mostly farmers and poor sharecroppers, this party pressured Democrats to bring relief to the local famer.[3]

Despite their efforts, the Populist could not turn the interests of Democrats from big corporations and railroads towards the poor rural farmer. Being led by North Carolina Senator Zebulon Vance, who was a powerful Freemason, Democrats viewed the people's party as a threat to remove them from office. Sensing they could not defeat Democrats alone, the Populists created a plan to fuse with the Republicans who still enjoyed a strong backing from African American voters. The Republicans had been the party of Abraham Lincoln and strongly supported the 13th, 14th, and 15th amendments to the U.S. Constitution. These amendments abolished slavery and recognized the voting rights of African Americans. It was also during this reign 1867–1898 that North Carolina African Americans, besides having voting rights, held very prominent and high positions in Carolina cities and towns.[4]

Incredibly, fusion politics achieved great success in both the 1894 and 1896 elections. For the first time in twenty years Democrats lost control of the State Assembly. Having been backed by 87 percent of black voters, Fusionists elected into office Republican Daniel Russell as North Carolina's new governor. Populists also shared in the victory by electing Marion Butler, another Sampson County native, as Senator in 1894. Together this union passed legislation that brought relief to farmers, both white and black. By cutting taxes on farmers and increasing tax rates on big corporations and railroads, the Fusion movement struck hard at the core of the Democrats policies, but, this attack would fail in comparison to the Fusionists next move, political integration.[5]

Being an interracial political movement, this "new order" gave people of color a chance to excel in high places of government. By increasing the number of African American officials in the state, the movement seated many African Americans in government positions. While very few were elected to the State Assembly, most were given opportunities to serve public office on the local level. In fact, according to Dr. Jerry Gershenhorn, "over 1,000 black officials served in public office in North Carolina during the fusion era as magistrates, deputy sheriffs, and county commissioners." Under this government, cities like Greenville, Wilmington, and Raleigh would witness a great surge of African American businesses, churches, and community centers.[6]

Outraged by what Democrats called, "Negro domination," party leaders did not remain silent for long. Beginning in 1898, most of the wealthy and elite of North Carolina sought to destroy and crush this reproach against the white man. Being led by Furnifold Simmons, Charles B. Aycock, and Josephus Daniels, the Democrats of North Carolina organized an evil political revolution that would end in a bloody massacre upon the streets of Wilmington. Moving across the Carolina landscape like Adolf Hitler's Third Reich, the Democrats of North Carolina sought to humiliate an entire race of people through media manipulation, intimidation, and just plain murder. Basing their campaign upon "white supremacy," these leaders sought to disenfranchise fusionists by launching a well-coordinated massive assault upon African and Native Americans in North Carolina. By taking over the media, these leaders were able to sway public opinion in believing that white people everywhere were in danger to "Negro Rule." Capitalizing on this fear, Democrats often rushed Carolina cities and organized family barbecues, church dinners, and other forms of family entertainment to spread their vial message.[7]

In Wilmington, former Democratic Congressman Alfred M. Waddell rallied a mass meeting of prominent white citizens and boldly declared, "We will never surrender to a ragged raffle of Negroes, even if we have to choke the Cape Fear with carcasses." Waddell, who was destined to lead the Wilmington massacre, rose quickly to prominence in 1898 and was close friends with James Sprunt, Charles B. Aycock, Robert Glenn, and Furnifold Simmons, all of which were leading North Carolina government officials and Freemasons. Calling for statewide murder against blacks, Waddell took his message to Goldsboro where eight thousand white Democrats came to cheer the fiery Master-Mason of Wilmington. Waddell set the tone early by promising to throw enough black bodies into the Cape Fear to block its passage into the Atlantic Ocean. Ironically, about the same time Waddell's arrival in Goldsboro occurred, North Carolina's most famous white "Negro preacher" A.B. Crumpler, along with G.B Cashwell and others, were there promoting large interracial holiness meetings. The unknown war had officially begun![8]

One of the major ways that Democrats were able to expand the message of white supremacy during 1898 was through secret societies. According to the membership records of the Grand Masonic Lodge of North Carolina, Charles B. Aycock, Furnifold Simmons, Alfred M. Waddell, James Sprunt, Robert B. Glenn and many other key Democratic leaders were all active Freemasons when this bloody plan was devised. It has also been noted that during this time, Waddell was also allegedly a part of North Carolina's Invisible Empire.[9]

What many do not know however, is that groups like the Freemasons, Shriners, Odd fellows, and the Klan all shared similar values and morals during this period. The Klan, which was originally founded by several Freemasons in Tennessee, including Nathan B. Forrest, incorporated many of the same principles of Freemasonry such as, secret passwords, hand grips, taking oaths etc. Besides lynching innocent people of color, this group (Klan) boasted that they were above all a "fraternal and charitable organization," and were especially charged to look after orphans and widows of fallen confederate soldiers.[10]

The Freemasons of North Carolina also adopted this policy by building Masonic orphanages all over the state. Providing food, shelter, water, and even education during hard times was how these brotherhoods could push their political agenda. Appearing as sheep in wolves clothing, these societies seemed to have approached pastors of local churches, community leaders, and white families promising to help them if they would become advocates for white supremacy by joining the Democratic Party.[11]

The Red Shirts, like their Klan brethren, was yet another organization that struck fear in the black community. Known for their brutish tactics of lynching and murder, these so called vigilantes of justice often disrupted black churches and sought to punish white preachers who assisted them. Donning bright red shirts in honor of the confederate dead, these men of violence became the right arm of force for the North Carolina Democrats in 1898.[12]

On November 9, 1898, Dunn's leading newspaper, *The County Union,* ran an article entitled, "A Great Red Shirt Parade" in which a large following of red shirts were spotted moving across the southern parts of North Carolina. Armed and dangerous, this white militia would canvass nearly every North Carolina county throughout 1898. Taking direct orders from leading North Carolina Freemasons, this unruly group intimidated black voters by threatening to shoot them if they showed up to vote on Election Day.[13]

In Wilmington, the Red Shirts patrolled every street in the city days before the election and would often attack black citizens. Alfred M. Waddell of St. John's Masonic lodge, in a speech to his fellow Red Shirts the night before elections, stated:

> You are Anglo-Saxons. You are armed and prepared, and you will do your duty. If you find the Negro out voting, tell him to leave the polls, and if he refuses, kill him, shoot him down in his tracks. We shall win tomorrow if we have to do it with our guns.[14]

These guns were not just limited to hand pistols, but heavy artillery. Also right before the elections, the Democrats spent a jaw-dropping $1,200 on a new, rapid-fire Gatlin gun. If black voters were to show up, they would have had to face hundreds of large bullets that had the capacity of blowing them into smithereens.[15]

The following day, November 8, 1898, many African Americans in Wilmington and surrounding areas avoided the polls. The Democrats won in the Port City by six thousand votes, a massive swing from two years before when Fusionist earned a five thousand vote advantage. Surprisingly, no violence was reported and all seemed well as the white supremacists celebrated their victory. However, with hundreds of mobilized Red Shirts on standby, and thirty years of built up white anger towards blacks, violence erupted two days later on November 10, 1898. With Hugh McRae, Alfred Waddell, James Sprunt, and others leading the way, an organized and highly dangerous mob stormed the local African American newspaper office ran by Alexander Manly. Mr. Manly, who looked more white than black, was forced to leave the city and his newspaper offices were burned to the ground. After it was destroyed, Wilmington's streets were filled with both angry blacks and whites. At once, Red Shirts poured an enormous amount of gunfire at the intersection of fourth and Harnett streets, and the massacre had begun.[16]

Author Timothy Tyson's account of the Willington massacre is extremely provocative. He writes: "Using a pipe to knock down Daniel Wright, a well-known black politician, the mob shouted, 'String him up to a lamp post!' But, rather than to see him hang, the mob turned him loose and yelled, 'Run nigger, run!' Wright ran for fifteen yards or so until about forty shots ripped through his body." Riddled with bullet holes, and his blood rushing through Wilmington's streets, Daniel Wright's murder was only but a small glimpse of the evil that prevailed in Wilmington that day.[17]

Storming the black sections of town, the Red Shirts screamed, "Kill every damn nigger in sight," and used their Gatlin gun to enforce their command. "What have we done, what have we done?" one black man cried out in desperation. At the end, no one knew for sure just how many had died. Leaders of the assault estimated around twenty blacks had been killed, while others put the death toll at ninety. Yet, according to oral tradition from ancestors of the victims, the number was more like three hundred; unfortunately, because the city just wanted to forget this monstrosity, the exact number will most likely never be known.[18]

Besides the dead, fourteen thousand blacks immediately fled the city's limits. Being forced to take shelter in the woods and surrounding pine forests, African American men, women, and children huddled together in freezing temperatures. Starving and fearful of angry whites, these innocent victims had neither money nor sufficient clothing for survival. Children cried in the cold, their parent's hesitant to light fires for fear of the mobs patrolling the city. Indeed, it was a terrible day for the African American community of Wilmington. With fear reigning and dead bodies everywhere, the armed militia headed by Waddell did not stop there. Their mission was not complete until they rounded up dozens of Republican and Fusionists leaders, both white and black, and dismissed them from their jobs. Rather than being handed a pink slip, these public officials were forced at gun-point to relinquish the reigns of control over Wilmington. Alfred M. Waddell, the bloodthirsty Masonic politician, felt it necessary to make himself the new Mayor of Wilmington. Being backed and supported by the good ole' boys, also known as the "Secret Nine of Wilmington," Waddell and others soon drafted the "White Declaration of Independence," which became the foundation of racial discrimination for the next seventy years.[19]

Subsequent to the elections of 1898, North Carolina stripped the vote from black men in 1900. By 1910, every state in the South had taken the vote from its black citizens using Wilmington, North Carolina, as their model. When Georgia, in 1906, sought to remove the black vote from its colored citizens, they personally consulted men who came to power during the North Carolina white supremacy campaign of 1898. During that year, Hoke Smith, Georgia's would-be white governor, urged whites to prepare for bloody violence. If whites could not disfranchise blacks legally, Smith promised the citizens of Georgia publically that, "We can handle them as they did in Wilmington, where the woods were left black with their hanging carcasses." In the end, Wilmington, North Carolina, marked the beginning of the Jim Crow South for the nation. Although legally, racial segregation had become the supreme law in 1896 through *Plessey v. Ferguson,* it was the Wilmington Massacre of 1898 that brought it to national prominence. Like falling dominos, southern states would follow Wilmington's example in creating laws banishing blacks, Native Americans, and even those with "mixed blood" from hundreds of white establishments including schools, businesses, churches, and even cemeteries.[20]

In North Carolina, this meant that, "No child with Negro blood in its veins, however remote the strain, shall attend a school for the white race, and no such child shall be considered a white child." No marriage shall be legally binding "between whites and Negroes or Indians or persons of Negro or Indian decent up to the third generation." Cemeteries holding the bones of both white and colored had to be excavated and separated into white and black resting places. Established churches like the Baptists, Methodists, and Presbyterians not only banished blacks from attending, but prohibited them from using the same Bible. Courthouses followed this same policy and had two Bibles for the people to swear on, one white and one black. For the Native Americans of the state, it also meant that a third establishment of schools, churches, and businesses had to be created. No longer were North Carolina counties filled with peace and a mutual respect between the races, but rather streets were now flowing with blood, trees remained full of lynching victims, and two brothers were once again divided.[21]

To substantiate their claim of victory, the Freemasons of North Carolina, along with the Daughters of the Confederacy, Colonial Dames of America, and other kindred fraternal organizations, all united at the turn of the century and went on a state wide campaign erecting large Masonic obelisks. From Wilmington to Raleigh, from Ashville to Kinston, these markers were strategically placed at either the center of Carolina cities or at the courthouse. By "marking their territory," white supremacy leaders deliberately handpicked dozens of historic North Carolina sites to situate these so called statues of honor. Linking the South of old with the new South of Anglo-Saxon supremacy, leaders such as Waddell, Aycock, Simmons, Daniels and other Democrats, raised these monuments with ulterior motives.[22]

To the natural eye, they are big and beautiful monuments that bear inscriptions of honor for those Americans who sacrificed their lives, in both the War for Independence and the Civil War. But, what most have failed to realize is that these man-made alters were really erected to commemorate the political revolution of 1898, which was only successful because it exalted one race while trampling upon another. By identifying themselves with the patriots of old, and establishing these huge landmarks, these Masonic and fraternal leaders wanted to distinguished themselves as some of the finest Tar Heels that ever lived. With Wilmington's new self-appointed Mayor Alfred M. Waddell leading as the main orator for White Supremacy, he and his fraternal entourage, would help lay the Masonic corner stone for dozens of these monuments all around the state.

Sadly, Charles B. Aycock, Furnifold Simmons, and Joseph Daniels are names which are now immortalized and exalted upon North Carolina's biggest landmarks. Building upon the mass murder of "poor Negros" and their "white-nigger" allies, these so-called great "Tar Heel Patriots" would go on to climb high into government positions. Many of them would become reformers in their respective fields; however, let it always be remembered that their ascension into the Governorship (Aycock), the Senate (Simmons), and Secretary of Navy (Daniels) only came at the expense of those unknown black North Carolina citizens whose innocent blood and life-less carcasses laid in the dust of the White Supremacy Campaign of 1898.

Masonic Orders Harbor White Supremacy

With the "Color Line" now being sharply drawn throughout North Carolina and the South, due to Wilmington's racial Massacre, things began to quickly change for A.B. Crumpler, G.B. Cashwell, and the North Carolina Holiness Church. As a result, the interracial Pentecostal Holiness Church, going into 1900, began to encounter fierce opposition. White supremacy, which had now evolved into racial segregation, found a home within the secret orders of North Carolina. These societies, or Masonic organizations, would now become the main emphasis of war between white supremacy adherents and the holiness people.

Crumpler, who strongly opposed Freemasonry, Shriners, Odd fellows, the Klan, Red Shirts, and all other fraternities, would use his holiness newspaper to inform the public against the "evils of the lodge." Traditionally, it has always been written that tobacco and divorce were the issues that divided the newly established Pentecostal Holiness Church. While these topics did cause points of disagreement, it would be Freemasonry, secret societies, and the race issue that would generate a great falling away from A.B. Crumpler's ranks. Filling nearly two-thirds of the existing issues of Crumpler's paper, articles against these secret orders were published more than both tobacco and divorce combined. Since Crumpler and others were so passionate about teaching against Freemasonry, it is only befitting that we briefly observe the love affair that North Carolina has shared with these secret societies, and how that relationship affected the North Carolina Holiness Church.[23]

The relationship between secret orders and North Carolina is as old as the state itself. In 1663, nearly seventy years before North Carolina was to become recognized as a colony, it was known as the Province of Carolina. Belonging to King Charles I of England, the Carolina province covered an extensive amount of land ranging between the thirty-six and thirty-one degree north latitude from the Atlantic to the Pacific oceans. This encompassed every state in the South, from present day North Carolina to Los Angles, California. Having been beheaded due to the English Civil War, the Province of Carolina passed from King Charles I to his son, Charles II. Charles II, better known as the "merry monarch," was famously remembered for his involvement with England's most powerful secret societies. With the English Monarchy in shambles, however, Charles II desperately wanted to regain control of the throne. To do this, he needed help. Meeting in English secret lodges, Charles II devised a plan which called upon the financial and political support of a group of men known as the eight Lord Proprietors. In return for their assistance, the would-be king offered them the entire Province of Carolina with full rights to do whatever they desired; however, there was a small problem with their flawless plan, the Native-Americans of North Carolina.[24]

This problem was alleviated when the newly installed king of England, Charles II, drew up the Carolina Charter of 1663. Besides having the full right to establish governments, courts of law, and public officials, the charter also permitted the eight Lords to murder all of Carolina's Indian population for the apportion of their lands . For the next sixty-six years, under this charter, both the Tuscarora and Yamasee wars would erupt between colonist and Indians on Carolina lands. Hundreds of Indians would be slaughtered, leaving the fate of their wives and children in the hands of cruel white slave masters. Royal governors, who were hand selected from the eight Lords, were the leaders responsible for bringing these policies into reality. Stationed in Edenton, North Carolina, the royal leaders were usually a part of two organizations, the state church of England and the Masonic lodge.

Although the Carolina Charter of 1663 did pave the way for many settlers, its doctrines, like the White Supremacy Campaign of 1898, resulted in the shedding of innocent blood. Interestingly enough, both the Carolina Charter of 1663 and the white supremacy crusade of 1898, would both be conceived and executed through the secret order of fraternal fellowship.[25]

After 1729, when North Carolina became a colony, the state began to witness a surge of immigration from settlers located in England, Scotland, and Ireland. Navigating upon the currents of the Cape Fear, these Brits and Scot-Irish pioneers established small towns and cities all along the banks of the river. Besides bringing their accents and families, these countrymen also brought with them Freemasonry. Having been conceived in England, the Masonic lodge flourished in North Carolina due to its many English and Scotch-Irish settlers. Soon, these meeting halls began to emerge everywhere.[26]

By the time 1801 arrived, southern Freemasonry birthed The Supreme Council of Ancient and Accepted Scottish Rite, more commonly known as "The Mother Supreme Council of the World." This grand lodge was founded as the head Masonic Temple for lodges all around the world. Interestingly, the location for this supreme lodge was founded on the 33 degree latitude line (Scottish Rite Masonry has thirty-three degrees) at Charleston, South Carolina. Charleston or Charles-town was named of course after King Charles II. For the next one hundred years, The Mother Supreme Council of the World would stand within Carolina jurisdiction until plans were made to move it to Washington D.C. where it presently sits today.[27]

Although this massive boom of Freemasonry was beginning to gain ground throughout the state, not everyone could be a part of this elitist group. Candidates had to meet several requirements before joining. These requirements could generally range from various things, but every lodge typically agreed that you had to be wealthy, a prominent citizen, of lawful age, white, and by 1898, a supporter of the Democratic Party. Such exclusive membership allowed the society to boast many business men, powerful politicians, and wealthy land owners. It would also become the perfect vehicle for white supremacy to inhabit.[28]

Before the campaign of 1898, however, white supremacy first manifested itself through the Ku Klux Klan in the 1870s. Surprisingly, three of the four founding members of the Klan were both Freemasons and Scotts. Joining forces following the Civil War, these ex-confederates often contained members that belonged to both organizations. With their advent, lynchings and murders against blacks began to appear everywhere. Accordingly, in 1870, Congress passed the Ku Klux Klan Act, which made Klan activity unlawful. Due to this legislation, the Klan would begin to decline in North

Carolina, but not after they had a significant impact within the state legislature. Helping Democrats regain control because of their night raids, the Klan assisted the Democratic Party back to power for the next two decades. Being outlawed to burn crosses and mask themselves, most members would return back to Freemasonry, Odd Fellows, or the Knights of Pythias, which were all leading secret orders during the mid to late nineteenth century.[29]

A.B. Crumpler's Response

By the time the Holiness Movement broke out under A.B. Crumpler's preaching in 1896, nearly every North Carolina city contained more lodges than it did churches. This is evidenced in several eastern North Carolina newspapers during the early 1900s. Some of them are: *The County Union, The Democratic Banner, The Goldsboro Weekly Argus, The Evening Light, The Caucasian*, and many others. So great was the influence of the lodge in 1900 that Rev. W.A. Forbes, Dunn's Baptist pastor, was recorded as having "preached an excellent sermon and defined the origins of Masonry" to large congregations. The following night, Rev. Forbes would also go on to preach about the "Independent Order of Odd Fellows" in honor of their eighty-second anniversary. Rev. J.A. Campbell, another leading Baptist figure in the area, was also known to be a high-ranking Mason. Noted most famously for founding Campbell University, this fraternal brother would often bring in Masonic teachers from around the state to spread the message of the lodge to the public.[30]

Masonic infiltration was not just confined to the Baptist camp, however. Methodists, Presbyterians, and others were also full of Mason friendly pastors, elders, and deacons; Perhaps there is no greater illustration demonstrating the amount of influence the lodge had over eastern North Carolina, then the following Dunn news article entitled, "The Man with the Button:"

> The man that wears the button of a Fraternal Order is a good man to tie to. He belongs to the progressive class. He sees the world move, and he moves with it. He wears the button as a matter of pride in the organization in which he holds membership. He wants to advertise facts of that membership as well as his confidence in that order. He wants his friends and the whole world to know it... You will find the button everywhere in the ranks of good citizenship. It is found among the toilers of the fields, the workshops, the counting house, and the busy marts of trade, the employers, and the employed, in the hall of legislature, on the judicial bench and in the executive departments of government everywhere. No good man can afford to be without the protection and a fraternity that the button represents. Wear the Lodge button proudly...Prove your faith by wearing it.[31]

Despite the fact that lodges were everywhere and Freemasonry embodied local governments, churches, and businesses, imagine their surprise when a Sampson County native arose and, under the power of God, preached against their establishments. Condemning the teachings but never the people, A.B. Crumpler took a strong stand against the Freemasons, Odd Fellows, and every other fraternity that would "Wear the Lodge button proudly."

To expose these evils of the lodge among his followers, Crumpler published a large and in-depth series teaching against the order that was harboring white supremacy. Spanning over two years and taking up dozens of pages within the Advocates columns, these intense articles revealed many of the lodge's secrets. Fearlessly, Crumpler attacked nearly every aspect of Freemasonry doctrines including the first thee Masonic degrees of membership, specific oaths and vows, passwords, hand grips, tools, symbols, and the Masonic apron. In describing the Master Mason's initiation ceremony, Crumpler writes:

> He (candidate) is at once stripped of his clothing to his shirt, puts on the old lodge drawers which are rolled up above both knees; both breasts are bared and both arms to elbows. Generally the shirt is taken off entirely. The cable-tow is put three times around his body; the hood wink is securely fastened over his eyes; a white apron is tied on, with bib turned up, when he is Masonically considered to be "Duly and Truly Prepared" for the third or Master's degree in Free-masonry.[32]

A.B. Crumpler goes on to add:

> Is there a wife in the world who would not be ashamed and disgusted to see her husband in this sort of garb? Is there a preacher in the world who could look his congregation in the face on Sunday morning after he had been put into this kind of mess if he thought they knew it?[33]

In seeking to dethrone the Masonic order, Crumpler would go on to publish many more of these intriguing articles, but where his pen would stop, his thundering voice picked up. In that, "strange meeting at Richland's," North Carolina, Rev. Crumpler preached openly and tenaciously against Masonry. Mr. Royall, who at one time labored over lost souls in the tent with A.B. Crumpler, attended the meeting that night. After hearing Crumpler abuse the fraternal order, Mr. Royall decided he had heard enough and wanted nothing more to do with the eastern North Carolina Apostle of Holiness.[34]

Crumpler, however, was not alone in his convictions. Appearing also within the pages of the Advocate was Rev. J.M. Foster, who wrote so eloquently how the "lodge belittles men" in his article, "Christian Manliness vs. the Lodge." Then there was the letter sent by Dr. Blank, called *Holiness and Masonry*, which was the powerful testimony of a pastor who had left the Masonic lodge because he felt that his character was being compromised. After leaving and renouncing its oaths, the pastor states, "And having promised my Savior never again to enter the lodge, I soon received the Baptism of the Holy Ghost." Yet, as strong as these articles were, nothing could prepare lodge members for A.B. Crumpler's secret weapon against Masonry, Rev. T.M. Lee.[35]

Rev. T.M. Lee, who became Crumpler's co-editor, was first saved and sanctified under Crumpler's ministry around 1900. Descending from a prominent northern Lee family, this young and intelligent fireball was a prestigious lawyer before turning holiness evangelists. Naturally, Lee and Crumpler had a lot in common. Both were extremely intelligent and had practiced law, but what really set Lee apart from Crumpler and every other holiness minister was his astounding testimony. Crumpler writes:

> Bro. Lee was a young lawyer of promise and belongs to one of the best families of the state, and was a member of the Episcopal Church and the Masonic order. A year or so ago God wonderfully saved Bro. Lee and called him out of the Episcopal church and the Masonic order and away from his law practice and into the ministry of His own blessed word.[36]

However, what Crumpler failed to mention was the fact the T.M. Lee wasn't just a low-level member of the fraternal brotherhood. Rather, Lee, in 1896, was the Worshipful Master of Clinton's Masonic order known as Hiram's Lodge no. 98 AF and AM. Being a Worshipful Master, Lee possessed an extensive knowledge on the practices, rituals, and teachings of Masonry. My, what his Masonic brothers must have thought when he left the order he used to lead and began to publically preach against it.[37]

Besides Crumpler's teachings and other miscellaneous articles against Masonry, T.M. Lee was remembered as writing provocative accounts of how lodge members operated this charitable organization. The financial structure, membership requirements, their views, and many other interesting aspects of the lodge that only an ex-Worshipful Master could provide were just some of the details Lee wrote about. In hoping to discourage another promising young man from joining this secret fellowship, Lee's pen flowed with piercing truthfulness and extraordinary conviction upon the pages of the Advocate. Entitled, "Secret Societies," this extensive article written by Lee literally destroyed the theological and ethical foundations of the lodge. Lee declares:

> The initiation and succeeding degrees of almost every order are full of nonsense and tom-foolery. Think of a sensible man, much less a man of deep spirituality, being led around the room of a lodge with very little clothing on, a rope around his neck and blind fold over his eyes while ever and anon something is said or done to frighten

> him, thinking, to impress him with solumity (?) of the degree he is taking...Now, beloved if you can get down on your knees, and looking up into the face of Jesus, say, "I know dear Lord, that you would engage in just such foolishness and nonsense as this," then you will be free to join. Foolishness has always been a foe to spirituality, therefore no spiritually minded Christian can unite or remain with secret societies without there being a decided leakage in his spirituality...Can't you see that the secret orders are full of the unsaved, wicked men, and yet you are yoked together with them...We have heard them (Current Masons) say, "If a man will be a good Mason or Odd Fellow he will be saved." Such stuff as that is blasphemy for it puts the secret order in the place of Christ, and makes the initiation take the place of his blood. The whole scheme of secret societies is an inauguration of the Devil, to deceive unwary souls. May God guide his children clear of these things.[38]

If any preacher during the North Carolina Holiness Movement had a right to declare such things, it would have been T.M. Lee. Having been a Worshipful Master who was now baptized with the flames of holiness, Bro. Lee's testimony was virtually indisputable and unstoppable.

Imagine the thoughts of those Masonic candidates that Lee initiated himself, or his brother Robert E. Lee, who remained in the lodge even after Rev. T.M. Lee dropped out. What were they to think? How could one of the lodge's most powerful and influential teachers of Masonry abandon his fraternal brothers to join a group of crazed holiness believers made up of "poor folks" and Negros?" The answer can only be found in the supernatural transformation that takes place when a broken man is brought before the glorious riches of Christ's love. Such was the case of Bro. Lee who went on to hold many more holiness revivals and edit Crumpler's paper, while strengthening inter-racial relationships between the African American Untied Holy Church of Raleigh and the North Carolina Holiness Church of Goldsboro.

Due to his limited role in the spotlight of the Holiness Movement, there are no records revealing G.B. Cashwell's own words towards Masonry. However, we do know that Gaston despised the white supremacy campaign of 1898 that swept through the area. We also know that he was never a part of the lodge nor did he ever condone it. Being a part of Crumpler's convention, it seems pretty evident what Gaston's position was on the subject. Yet, the lodge seemed to always follow Gaston around no matter where he went or what he did. Before he became a holiness preacher and was farming tobacco, his business partner and brother-in-law, John R. Bass, joined the Freemasons in 1888. In addition, Gaston's father-in-law, Erasmus Lee, was a very wealthy land owner and prominent Mason of the Mingo Lodge in Sampson County. Both his father (Erasmus Lee) and brothers were also

Masons, making the Lovie Lee family one of Dunn's leading Masonic families at that time. Fortunately, there are no records indicating how the Lee's felt about Gaston Cashwell's position against Masonry. Perhaps it is just better for some things to be left unsaid.[39]

Despite the fact that these Masonic orders contained powerful white supremacy leaders within its lodges, Lee, Crumpler, Cashwell, and a few others never backed down. Boldly and unashamedly, they took their stand against this ancient fraternity and the evils of white supremacy. To them, the doctrines of Masonry were complete foolishness and deceptive, causing many to be led astray. Seeing beyond the veil, these holiness pioneers understood that behind the orphanages, shelters for widows, and so called "high standard of morals," many members were manipulative, controlling, Democratic, and racist. In a war for the "lost sheep" of eastern North Carolina, the Holiness Movement and the Lodge would go toe to toe. Initially, the Holiness Church appears to have won the battle, but as the years pushed forward and the reality of legalized racial segregation set in, the great white snake of racism would eventually squeeze all of the color out of Crumpler's holiness church.

Chapter 10

THE INTERNAL WAR: THE FIRE-BAPTIZED CHURCH vs. THE HOLINESS CHURCH

Just as A.B. Crumpler, T.M. Lee, G.B. Cashwell, and the Holiness Church of North Carolina, were beginning to engage in an underground war with the Masonic Order, another disastrous conflict quickly arose within their ranks. Moving in cyclone fashion, this internal holiness war erupted between the Rev. B.H. Irwin and Rev. A.B. Crumpler. The results of this theological crisis would prove to be tragic for many of the original founders of the North Carolina Holiness Church. Many ministers would be forced to join sides causing a massive divide within the infant Tar Heel congregation. Internally, relationships would be either severed or strongly tested. This war for truth is a war that many do not know even existed. Apparently, in writing their early church history, both Rev. G. F. Taylor and J.H. King left out many of these insightful details. Thankfully, the local newspapers recorded it giving us insight into this forgotten dispute that would turn brother against brother. Having already introduced the champion (Crumpler) of holiness within eastern North Carolina, let us observe the holiness champion of the mid-west, B.H. Irwin, and explore how the showdown of 1899 erupted in Dunn, North Carolina.

B. H. Irwin and Strange Fire

When the holiness pioneers of Vineland, New Jersey, stormed the continent in the 1870s, they ignited holiness fires everywhere. Moving their massive tent along the heartland of the nation, these burning revivalists soon found themselves near Cedar Rapids, Iowa, where a great and mighty revival broke out. Coming off the heels of this fiery meeting emerged a minister by the name of

Isaiah Reed. Rev. Reed, who was a powerful Presbyterian leader, soon organized the Iowa Holiness Association in 1879 which was destined to become one of the strongest state holiness associations in the country. Dr. Brown noted that the Iowa holiness camp meeting was one of the largest encampments in the west, and the Iowa Holiness Association had created its own school, Central Holiness University, now called Vennard College. In addition, the Iowa Holiness Association licensed its own evangelists and other holiness workers that shook the mid-west. It was under one of these holiness bands that Baptist minister, B.H. Irwin, became "sanctified wholly."[1]

Benjamin Harden Irwin was born and grew up in Mercer County, Missouri. As a young adult he moved to Lincoln, Nebraska, where he began to study law. At some point, he accepted Christ into his heart and joined the Baptist church. Rising to the position of elder or local pastor, Rev. Irwin began to shepherd a small congregation. It was here, in his own pulpit, right before he was to preach, that Irwin received a confirmation of the sanctified experience he had experienced just twelve hours prior on May 16, 1891.[2]

Several years later, Irwin wrote to Pike's *Way of Faith*, and described in vivid detail this interesting encounter. Irwin writes:

> Four years ago, the 16th of last May, about 11 o'clock at night, I was sanctified wholly by faith, and immediately I entered soul-rest. My heart was cleansed from all interior pollution by the precious blood of Jesus Christ. Twelve hours later, while sitting in my own pulpit, and they were singing the last hymn before preaching, I received the witness of the Spirit; the conscious baptism with the Holy Ghost. I was at the time expressing to preach a definite holiness sermon, and my mind was drawn to my text—"Let us go up at once and possess it, for we are well able to overcome it" (Num. 13:30),—when suddenly I was melted, as it seemed to me, into a flood of tears, which continued all through that sermon, and all that afternoon. I had a new Bible and the church has a new preacher. The Holy Ghost in his fullness had come into my soul. The flood gates of heaven were opened wide, and there came into my soul successive waves and mighty inundations of light and love and joy and faith, and power and glory and loyalty to God, and from that moment to this my soul has been kept on a constant stretch for God.[3]

Soon after he was "sanctified wholly by faith," Rev. Irwin was dismissed from the Baptist church for professing the doctrine of holiness. Ministering as an evangelist, B.H. Irwin began to hold holiness meetings all around the state of Nebraska. Yet, as powerful as his experience was, it did not quench the spiritual hunger deep within his soul. By reading Upham's *Life of Madame*

Guyon, and Dr. Watson's *Coals of Fire*, Rev. Irwin began to sense that some of his brethren were experiencing a "third blessing" beyond the sanctified experience known as the "fire." In the same article, Irwin continues:

> And that single word (fire) seemed to linger about my soul and in my dreams and deepest mediations, everything seemed to gather about that single word FIRE, and while I knew and enjoyed the experience of entire sanctification and had the baptism of the Holy Ghost upon my soul, yet I knew that some of my brethren enjoyed an experience of fire to me unknown, and I felt sure that many holiness people, whom I believe…(Sentence unclear). I believe Miller Willis had it, and C.P. Carkuff and Jesse Buthurst and Geo. M. Henson. And if these enjoyed it (fire) why not myself? I became convinced and satisfied that there was an experience of fire for me, and that it was my privilege and duty to ask for and receive it. God has sent Bro. C.P. Carkuff two hundred and fifty miles, all the way from Ness City, Kansas, to tell me his experience, and while he was relating it to me, about 12 o'clock in the night, of the 23rd of October, 1895, as we lay together and alone, I saw in the room above me a cross of pure transparent fire. It was all fire…Thee very walls of the room seemed to be on fire. But as yet there was no sense of heat connected with it; not until the night of the 25th, when on the train, en route for home from Enid, all at once I became conscious of the fact that I was literally on fire…My entire being, spirit, soul, and body seems literally conflagrant. I feel at this moment dashing over my soul, these blissful, burning, leaping, love-waves of living fire. It was not cleansing; it is not the witness of the Spirit; it is not the baptism with the Holy Ghost; it is not a dream; it is not a delusion or a deception; it is none of these. It is the baptism of fire.[4]

Emerging from this encounter burning from the inside out, Irwin quickly began constructing a "third blessing" theology which consisted of three steps: salvation (justification by faith), sanctification (second work of grace subsequent to salvation), and the baptism of fire (baptism of the Holy Ghost with fire).[5]

The Holiness Movement in general taught that the baptism of the Holy Ghost was included in the sanctification experience; therefore, when many holiness leaders began to hear of this third blessing, they were appalled. Disregarding their thoughts, Rev. Irwin believed that he had experienced a real transformation and wasted no time, preaching this doctrine everywhere he went. Surprisingly, the "baptism of fire" took root in many hearts around the Midwest.[6]

Holding revivals in tents, holiness churches, and brush arbors, Irwin, in whirlwind fashion, declared with boldness this fiery message. Bizarrely, Rev. Irwin began to extend his new theology by adding several more baptism experiences. Dr. Hunter notes, "Irwin came to teach that beyond the baptism of fire there were other 'fiery baptisms' which he designated by chemical names like dynamite, lyddite, and oxidite." Besides this, Irwin also began to preach unconventional views on topics like divine healing and the pre-millennial second coming of Christ, doctrines that had not been highlighted within the Holiness Movement prior to the 1890s.[7]

Detecting these extreme theological patterns developing within his messages, major holiness leaders of the Midwest began to denounce Irwin's teachings as heresy. In time, the Iowa Holiness Association "invited Irwin and his followers to disassociate themselves from the organization." Wasting no time, Irwin began to organize small local "Fire-Baptized Holiness Associations" to gather up those who had made professions of the fiery baptism. The first organization took place at Olmitz, Iowa, in the year 1895. By the early part of 1896, Fire-Baptized Holiness Associations were springing up in states such as Kansas, Oklahoma, Iowa, and Texas. Naming himself as General Overseer of the new church, Irwin began to empower other fire-baptized ministers to spread the doctrines of fire, dynamite, lyddite, and oxidite all throughout the states.[8]

With his "own soul bathing in an ocean of fiery of love" Irwin took his message to the South where he landed in Piedmont, South Carolina, and began meetings on December 19, 1896. Following this meeting, the South Carolina Fire-Baptized Association was organized where he left Rev. R.B. Hayes as president. By 1897 and into 1898 this large and charismatic fiery preacher was extending the movement into Georgia, Canada, and North Carolina. With so many associations now organized, Irwin thought it best to give the movement a little more structure. Meeting in Anderson, South Carolina, from July 28 to August 8, 1898, the fire-baptized crowd came together and formed a new denomination. Here, Irwin presented the church with a more thorough church constitution which contained some interesting features. Topping the list, however, was Irwin's unique position on church government. Donning himself with the absolute power to appoint all state ruling elders, pastors, and ordinations, and to dismiss anyone he disliked, Rev. Irwin made himself a Tyrant and his church government tyrannical. Irwin also created the general overseer position (his position) for life, making himself superior to anyone else in the church.[9]

In terms of rules and regulations, the Fire-Baptized had a few things in common with A.B. Crumpler's holiness of North Carolina. For instance, they both promoted inter-racial meetings; forbade joining secret societies and the wearing of excessive clothing, jewelry, and feathers. On the other hand, they had a lot of disagreements. Unlike Crumpler's church, they pushed holiness to radical extremes. Believing that the ceremonial laws of the Old Testament were still binding, many Fire-Baptized followers condemned the eating of pork or any other prescribed dietary food laws. They also damned the use, growth, and selling of tobacco in all its forms; whereas Crumpler's followers remained neutral about tobacco until 1903. Neckties and mustaches were also condemned by these fiery zealots. Capitalizing on this point, Dr. Synan notes, "A favorite expression heard from F.B.H.A. pulpits was, 'I had rather have a rattlesnake around my neck than a necktie.'" Such extremism would eventually lead to a climatic holiness battle between both A.B. Crumpler and B.H. Irwin in Dunn, North Carolina, during the spring of 1899.[10]

The Showdown: B.H. Irwin vs. A.B. Crumpler

Between the years 1896 to 1899, A.B. Crumpler and his sanctified army of warriors established a stronghold of holiness in eastern North Carolina. While not everyone was welcoming towards the movement, the general public, for the most part, both loved and revered the man with iron lungs. They not only admired his preaching, but also his willingness to be a legal advocate in the halls of justice for such cases dealing in alcoholism, homelessness, and rescue shelters. His ability to network with other denominations was also a positive factor that local residents respected. Echoes of this admiration can be found within dozens of North Carolina newspapers ranging from the *Dunn County Union*, *Goldsboro Weekly Argus*, *Clinton Dispatch*, *Robesonian, Fayetteville Observer,* and many others between 1896 and lasting into 1920s.

Based on these accounts, the North Carolina Apostle of Holiness had won over their hearts. Though he would be hated by the white empowered secret societies and Democrats, he was always regarded as a champion in the eyes of the poor, humble, and despised. So what were they to think when another "crazed" religious group appeared on the scene preaching about the "fire" while strongly condemning both A.B. Crumpler and the movement he was leading? Better yet, what was A.B. Crumpler to think when he realized that many of these fire preachers who opposed him where some of his closest companions and friends? To this end, we turn to the press where the battle between Irwin and Crumpler was destined to erupt.

Arriving in Dunn, North Carolina, on April 23, 1899, Rev. B.H. Irwin pitched his fire-baptized gospel tent and publicly bashed Rev. A.B. Crumpler and all his followers. Accusing them of being "tamed holiness devils," Irwin and his following informed Dunn's residents that Crumpler was not even saved and went as far as praying for his death. Condemning the movement that had broken out under Crumpler's preaching three years earlier, these ministers sought to humiliate the North Carolina Apostle of Holiness. Appearing on May 3, 1899, *The County Union* published an extensive article revealing the verbal abuse A.B. Crumpler and others suffered at the hands of these tyrannical wild-fire preachers. Entitled the "Fire-Baptized Crowd," it reads as follows:

> The "Fire Baptized Holiness Association" struck our town Monday of last week and pitched their tent Tuesday and commenced to preach. There came some 18 or 20 men, 8 or 10 women and one colored woman…They preach against everything that is not "fire-baptized." Every church and church member who is not "fire baptized" receives the wrathy excoriations of these "fire" preachers. They preach against the eating of hog-meat, wearing of mustaches, neckties, jewelry and fine clothing. One of their favorite prayers was for "God to kill the hog-meat eating devils, the mustache wearing devils, the whiskey drinking devils, the tobacco-chewing devils, the snuff-dipping devils, the tame-holiness devils, etc." Some of them confess of having been in jail for various causes; of being forgers, liars, drunkards, and thieves before they got converted. They tell the deeds of their misdoings as if it were something nice to tell. All of them were converted, than sanctified holy, and then baptized with the Holy Ghost and with fire. This last degree (fire) they claim is the highest gift to a Christian, and when he is thus favored he has had all the devils knocked out of him by the "dynamite of God." They take no stock with Rev. A.B. Crumpler and his believers in sanctification. They call them "tame-holiness devils," and that they cannot be saved unless they get the "baptism of fire." Their meetings, to our mind, are not healthful morally or religiously to any community. They made few converts here.[11]

Cleary, the fight was on. In taking no stock with Rev. A.B. Crumpler or his believers in sanctification, these wild preachers sent the young holiness church of North Carolina an obvious message. Unless they get the baptism of fire and preach doctrines of the dynamite, lyddite, and oxidite, the gift of salvation, in their eyes, was unacceptable for Crumpler and his followers. Oh, how this must have made Crumpler's blood boil with righteous anger; yet, as furious as this attack may have seemed, what probably hurt Crumpler more was the fact that many of these "fire" preachers were once his close friends.[12]

Two years before this scathing revival meeting, Rev. Irwin struck North Carolina with force and established a North Carolina Fire-Baptized Holiness Association in the southeastern part of the state. Joining his ranks was the entire North Carolina Holiness Association at Vineland, North Carolina. This is the very same association that A.B. Crumpler had been elected president of in the fall of 1896. Vineland, North Carolina, Holiness ministers like S.D. Page, W.W. Avant, Ed Kelly, S.M. Payne, and others that had personally assisted Rev. Crumpler in the past were now caught up in Irwin's cyclone ministry of fire. In 1898 many of them began to disassociate themselves from Crumpler and his following. By 1899 they were preaching against him and believed he had erred in his holiness views.[13]

This great falling away within the North Carolina Holiness Movement generated strong feelings between both Crumpler's church and Irwin's fire movement. Unity, which had once prevailed in Vineland, North Carolina, during 1895, 1896, and 1897 was now replaced with division, accusations, and religious conflicts in 1898 and 1899. In trading their friendships with Crumpler for positions in a church, their relationships became severely damaged. Crumpler, in refusing to remain silent, belted a loud and powerful response in the next issue of Dunn's *County Union* newspaper.

Sensing that the good people of Dunn and Fayetteville had been deceived by Irwin, he felt it necessary to respond and state his personal view of the Fire-Baptized movement that was sweeping the land. Making front page headlines on May 10, 1899, was Rev. Crumpler's personal letter to the citizens of Dunn. The North Carolina Apostle of Holiness declared:

> I want a little space in your valuable paper that I may disabuse the minds of some of the good people of Cumberland and Harnett counties who may think that I am in sympathy with the Fire Convention that recently assembled in Fayette (ville) and Dunn. I want the people among whom I have labored and to whom I have preached, to know that I disclaim any connection to the "Fire Movement" or any sympathy for it. I believe there are some good people mislead by it and mixed up with it; and against them or any experience they may have felt that has made them more Christ-like and more useful, I have not a word to say, let them call it what they will. But from what I have seen of the work and spirit of the Fire Movement as it was carried on in Fayetteville, Dunn and elsewhere in the State, I am convinced beyond a doubt that the thing is not of God. Anything that has the spirit of our blessed Savior in it is not bitter; but is long suffering and kind. It envieth not, vaunteth not itself, is not puffed up, doth not behave itself unseemly, seeketh not her own, is not provoked, thinketh no evil. But a thing or spirit that spends its time and force denouncing everything and everybody that does not feel as it does or who cannot subscribe to its narrow views in toto (?) is not of God. Some of those fire-baptized brethren made a wholesale denunciation of all preachers and people who do not claim a special experience of fire after they were sanctified and who has not seen fit to tear off their neck tie and cut off their mustache. I am frank to say that I believe that spirit is born of the rankest kind of fanaticism. Paul tells us that the kingdom

of God is not meat and drink; but righteousness and peace and joy in the Holy Ghost. Now if there are any of my friends who have received a special baptism of fire after you were sanctified (I got it like the Apostles and Isaiah in order to be sanctified) and not after I was sanctified, Acts 2:1–2, Isa. 6:6–7. I hope you got a sufficient quantity to keep you sweet while you read these lines and make you love me and pray for me always. A.B. Crumpler.[14]

After receiving the initial blow from the "rankest kind of fanaticism" there was, Rev. Crumpler took off the gloves and struck back hard at the foundations of B.H. Irwin's movement. Charging them with preaching a condemnation gospel rather than a convicting gospel, A.B. Crumpler made it perfectly clear that he was strongly against the Fire-Baptized Movement. Being convinced, "beyond a doubt that the thing is not of God" Mr. Crumpler distinguished himself, along with the most of his followers, as having nothing to do with Rev. Irwin or his tyrannical organization. Unfortunately, in just a few years, A.B. Crumpler would be ousted from the church he founded. The fire-baptized crowd that he bitterly opposes here in 1899 would be found merging with the remaining members of his own converts in 1911, forming what is today known as the International Pentecostal Holiness Church (IPHC).

On the third page of the same issue, Mr. J. P. Pittman, the proprietor of The County Union, published an additional article which adds more insight into this spiritual battle. It states:

On the first page of this issue will be found a letter from Rev. A.B. Crumpler. He takes no stock in the "fire baptized" gang that preached their strange doctrine here. If we remember aright some of these "fire" preachers claimed to have been converted under Mr. Crumpler's preaching. They tried to adopt a good many of Mr. Crumpler's pulpit manners and expressions.[15]

No doubt, these articles reveal that an internal war was brewing within the North Carolina Holiness Movement. Accordingly, these accounts, plus some additional ones not mentioned here, all share a common theme. That being, a majority of the people, and not just Crumpler, opposed the Fire-Movement in eastern North Carolina. For many, Crumpler had become their champion and voice. They trusted him because of his consistency to minister in their towns several times a year, but when the unknown fire-baptized company swept town, the North Carolina Holiness Movement became sharply divided.[16]

The people were put into a position to choose sides according to their own experiences. This seems to be why A.B. Crumpler and others called for the first state Holiness Convention in Goldsboro, on October 26, 1899. They wanted to distinguish themselves from the Fire-Movement that was sweeping through. In this meeting, leaders made it profoundly clear that they disagreed with the "third blessing" theology Rev. Irwin had developed. Furthermore, they decided they would not endorse or support a group just because they professed holiness, but only those who were united on the doctrine of salvation and sanctification.[17]

Surprisingly, not every one of Crumpler's followers would share in their leader's convictions about Irwin and the fire movement. Such was the case with Falcon leader and personal friend of A.B. Crumpler, Julies A. Culbreth. Most famously recognized for establishing the town of Falcon and the Falcon Camp Meeting Association, J.A. Culbreth was a man destined to bask in the spotlight. He was born to the wealthy William and Nancy Culbreth in 1873. Being another Sampson County native, J.A. Culbreth also grew up near the Crumpler and Cashwell farms in the northern regions of Sampson County. During the 1880s, the Culbreths moved to Black River Township where the town of Falcon is presently located.[18]

J.A. Culbreth's father, William Culbreth, was an extremely wealthy merchant and was remembered in Dunn as the man who carried the city's debt. After dying a premature death, moneys owed to William Culbreth by hundreds of people were published in the local newspaper at Dunn. As an administrator of his father's estate, J. A. Culbreth inherited these debts and decided to sell them off in a public auction. By selling the debts, Culbreth inherited a fortune and became one of the region's wealthiest and most popular figures. Additionally, J.A. Culbreth received a significant amount of land in several North Carolina counties including multiple lots situated in downtown Dunn. During this time, Culbreth also established himself as a prominent businessman of Dunn and Falcon by owning two stores and working at the Dunn First National Bank.[19]

Prior to A.B. Crumpler's arrival to Dunn in 1896, Culbreth was remembered as being arrogant and flamboyant, often lighting his cigars with dollar bills to show off his father's wealth. However, like so many others in the Dunn revival, Culbreth would have a "Damascus Road" experience in which his life would be changed. Following his conversion, Culbreth and A.B. Crumpler appeared to have shared a very close friendship. Yet, as times would change, Culbreth and Crumpler's relationship would become strained.[20]

Although converted in 1896, J.A. Culbreth continued to dive deeper into local politics and local government following his sanctification experience. Many are unaware that Mr. Culbreth served as the "Commissioner of the Superior Court" within both Cumberland and Harnett Counties between the years 1896 and 1905. Such a tenure in a government position persuaded Mr. Culbreth to be consumed with local politics. As a strong supporter of the all-white and aristocratic North Carolina Democratic Party, Culbreth and Crumpler would seemingly clash over the issue of race. Thus, Culbreth's holiness conversion would have both positive and negative affects upon Crumpler and Cashwell's ministries in the years that followed.[21]

According to Joseph E. Campbell, right before Rev. Irwin struck Dunn, North Carolina in April of 1899; Mr. J.A. Culbreth's wife became critically ill with appendicitis. Due to her weak physical condition, it was not advisable to operate. Even with two doctors by her side treating her illness, she showed no signs of improvement. Mr. J.A. Culbreth was praying day and night for her recovery, but to no avail, his wife remained completely sick. In tracking the Holiness Movement, J.A. Culbreth, like many others, followed J.M. Pikes *Way of Faith* very closely. Interestingly, they had been reading about the remarkable faith healings that were taking place under Rev. B.H. Irwin's fire-baptized preaching. Mrs. Culbreth, amazed at some of the testimonies, expressed her desire to have the Rev. B.H. Irwin come personally from the Midwest to the Culbreth's house in Falcon, North Carolina, and pray over her. Within one week's time on April 23, 1899, the Rev. B.H. Irwin was in Dunn holding the infamous revival that centered upon degrading A.B. Crumpler and his ministry. Most likely, it was by J.A. Culbreth's personal request that Irwin accepted the invitation to Dunn in 1899.[22]

Out of desperation for his wife, J.A. Culbreth attended the meeting, probably against Crumpler's wishes. Culbreth, who had been one of A.B. Crumpler's biggest financial supporters and personal friends, now found himself in a peculiar dilemma. Instead of turning away and leaving after Irwin attacked his friend, J.A. Culbreth remained throughout the entire service waiting patiently to see Mr. Irwin. Mr. Campbell records what happened next. "Mr. Culbreth attended the service, and immediately after the service, Mr. Irwin and a man by the name of Harper from Durham went with him to pray for his wife." Strangely enough, after Rev. Irwin anointed her with oil and prayed over her, she was miraculously healed. Utterly impressed by Rev. Irwin's ability to release healing though prayer, the Culbreths would forever immortalize this moment by having it etched upon their spectacular mausoleum after they died. It reads, "1899, Wife seriously sick, two Doctors said she would die, God instantly healed and added 44 years to her life."[23]

From this point, J.A. Culbreth never turned his back on the fire-baptized movement but embraced it. Soon, he would be hiring some of their most influential leaders to come and work for him. This turn of events, however, leads us to a burning question. Just what was A.B. Crumpler to think about all of this? Is it possible that Crumpler and Culbreth's friendship became one of those relationships damaged by this fiery movement? Given these new facts, as well as the mutual partnership these two bodies would take, it certainly seems so. Conceivably, one thing is for certain. With A.B. Crumpler leading the Holiness Church, affiliation between his organization and the fire-baptized crowd would be strongly discouraged. As we shall see, this is something not every member of Crumpler's church would agree with. Perhaps this is one of the mysterious reasons why A.B. Crumpler would be forced out of the church he helped start in November of 1908.

B.H. Irwin's Demise, J.H. King's Rise, and Everything in Between

Besides teaching that there was a baptism of the dynamite, lyddite, and oxidite, Rev. B.H. Irwin's ministry also taught "that an open public confession of all grades of sin was necessary to evidence genuine repentance; that restitution must be made of the most minute and insignificant things; that the wholly sanctified could not succumb to temptation; that those filled with the spirit needed no one to instruct them; that doctors should be denounced as imposters and their remedies as poisons." These things, along with wearing no facial hair, neckties, and eating zero pork quickly made him a target for spiritual pride. Clearly, it seemed that the charismatic Irwin was treading on thin ice. Ultimately, such loss of self-control would eventually lead to his demise as general overseer of the Fire-Baptized Association.[24]

In 1900, just one year after the holiness war between A.B. Crumpler and his followers, it became known that Rev. B.H. Irwin was living a double life. According to Dr. Synan, the "discovery was definite, and the proof appeared conclusive" that Rev. Irwin had become involved in what was to be labeled as "open and gross sin." Accordingly, he wrote to J.H. King and requested that he would assume the editorship of *Live Coals of Fire*, the short-lived, fire-baptized newspaper. After taking over its editorship, King was soon anointed as the new general overseer of the Fire-Baptized Association. Although details surrounding Irwin's defection have never surfaced, it is unfortunate that such a gifted preacher and holiness evangelists fell to the temptations set before him. Let his story always remind us that no matter how anointed, gifted, or talented a person might seem, they are only one step away from life-destroying sin.[25]

Joseph Hillary King, the man who replaced Rev. Irwin, was born on August 11, 1869, in Anderson County, South Carolina. Becoming saved and sanctified at the age of sixteen, the young King was destined to bask in the

Holiness-Pentecostal spotlight. After joining the M.E. Church South, Mr. King was granted a license to preach in the month of March 1891. Eventually, this highway of holiness led the young preacher to the consolidation of the Fire-Baptized Association that met in Anderson, South Carolina, from July 28 to August 8, 1898. It was here that Kings says, "I became a member of this church, and entered out into new fields of labor from that time and onward as the Lord led me." For the next two years, King would serve the fire-baptized church as a pastor until July 7, 1900, when he was elected as the new general overseer of the struggling Fire-Baptized Movement.[26]

With Irwin's defection sending shockwaves through the infant church, the Fire-Baptized Movement nearly went into extinction. Sensing that changes needed to be made, King's first action while in office was to diffuse the autocratic government that Irwin had established. By delegating the licensing and ordination responsibilities to local annual conventions, King attempted to slowly shift some of the church's tyrannical structure. He further established biennial meetings rather than allowing the general overseer to call meetings any time he pleased. At Lamont, Oklahoma, the association, under Kings' guidance, decided to change their name from the Fire-Baptized Holiness Association to the Fire-Baptized Holiness Church. Indeed, these were baby steps in the right direction; however, these steps were minimal at best. Dr. Synan notes that although the church did progress in becoming more democratic, the general overseer still retained office for life as well as the power to appoint and dismiss all ruling elders and pastors. Accordingly, these remaining facets of government, along with their rigid holiness views, still remained as a huge problems with A.B. Crumpler's Holiness Church.[27]

Evidently, the changing of the guard between Rev. B.H. Irwin and Rev. J.H. King meant very little to A.B. Crumpler. The war between both these holiness groups was still ripping through the state. As such, new tensions were now beginning to develop between J.H. King's leadership and A.B. Crumpler's. Although the newly elected King was more emotionally stable and grounded than Irwin, let's not forget that J.H. King was one of twenty men that participated in the public defiance of A.B. Crumpler and his preachers in the Dunn meeting led by Rev. Irwin. Evidence for this is shown in *The County Union,* which stated that Rev. B.H. Irwin and his gang were in both Dunn and Fayetteville holding annual conventions for the Fire-Baptized Holiness Association in April of 1899. In addition, J.H. King wrote in *Yet Speaketh* that he was present for these North Carolina convention meetings and even "preached a few times." Crumpler was very aware of this and most assuredly began to form his own opinion towards the new general overseer.[28]

Even though King's policies were less radical than Irwin's, Crumpler still remained strongly opposed towards J.H. King and the fire-movement. Perhaps it was because of meetings like the one in Sanford, North Carolina, where Fire-Baptized evangelist John Dull held a revival in which the "dynamite played quite an active part in unearthing the devil." The "devil," as Dull defines it, was none other than "The shallowness of the Holiness Movement in North Carolina." Such continued attacks on Crumpler's "shallowness" provoked him to print another intriguing response to the charges made by these fire-baptizers.[29]

Published on May 1, 1901, A.B. Crumpler responded with poetic power to J.H. King and the church being lead under his command. Crumpler writes:

> In some localities the holiness people feel called on to trim up one another. So they don't seem to be especially interested in the conversions of sinners and sanctification of believers; but their time is spent in discussing the swine, neck-tie, Sabbath-day and many other questions of equal size and consigning everybody to perdition who does not immediately kill all of his hogs, tear off his neck-tie, keep Saturday for Sunday, and pour his camphor out on the ground. "Who art thou that judgeth another man's (God's) servant? To his own master he standeth or falleth. Yea, he shall be holden up: for God is able to make him stand." Rom. 14:4. I invite the reader to examine the whole of the 14th chapter of Romans. There are some blessed good people who were once happy and free and whose lives were once full of tenderness, sweetness, and love, who have gotten in bondage to the old ceremonial law and to a morbid conscientiousness and into a spirit of judging and making their own consciences the standard for other people and lost their mellowness, sweetness, tenderness and unction out of their experience and life. (KJV)[30]

Knowing that good people everywhere in the South would read this article, Crumpler once again made a clear and distinctive statement revealing his position towards the Fire-Baptized Church. The Apostle of holiness realized that there were "some blessed good people" being misled by their teachings. In an effort to preach the truth, Crumpler hoped to reform some of their strenuous holiness views. His attempt however would be met with great opposition eventually leading to a "new regime" of holiness that was destined to emerge at Falcon, North Carolina, in 1911.

Amazingly, eight years before the alleged falling out between G.B. Cashwell and A.B. Crumpler was to occur, Rev. Crumpler was already at war with J.H. King, the Fire-Baptized Movement, and possibly J.A. Culbreth. Clearly, as the leader of the Holiness Church, A.B. Crumpler made it blatantly obvious that he wanted his converts not to be "yoked together" with these religious zealots. Yet, what we have to remember is that many of these North Carolina Fire-Baptized preachers were his friends at one time. For a season, Crumpler worked hand in hand with S.D. Page, W.W. Avant, Ed Kelly, S.M. Payne, and others. He knew that they generally loved the Lord and enjoyed winning souls to holiness, but he could not bring himself to agree with their new doctrines and strict holiness views. Thus, the internal war between Rev. Irwin, J.H. King, and A.B. Crumpler became a major point of division within the eastern North Carolina Holiness Movement between the years 1899 to 1906.[31]

So why has this issue remained silent? Why has this internal war remained hidden from the public? Furthermore, why has it taken one hundred and twelve years to grasp the truth of what really happened to the ministry of A.B. Crumpler? Perhaps there are those who wished never to disclose this information. Perhaps preachers inspired by Mr. Crumpler disliked the way the holiness church was heading. Maybe the good ole' boy spirit of church politics was beginning to manifest itself within the church. Given these new details, it seems only right that we raise such questions. Who knows, we just may find an answer.[32]

Chapter 11

THE AFTERMATH

As North Carolina progressed into the twentieth century, many things began to change for A.B. Crumpler, G.B. Cashwell, and the Tar Heel Holiness Movement. Both the wars of racism and religion had literally torn the movement in half. The South of old had been replaced with a new era of violence, hatred, and segregation. Born out of the White Supremacy Campaign of 1898, the Jim Crow era had officially started, and its effects were being felt in cities like Dunn, Greenville, Raleigh, Wilmington, Kinston, Clinton, and Goldsboro. Railcars, restaurants, restrooms, and many other public facilities were now separated and adorned signs that read "for whites only" or "no niggers allowed." A new level of racism was rising, one that would permeate through the minds of both races. The sociological impact this would have on both whites and people of color would be severely damaging for years to come.[1]

By being "put into their place," many of Carolina's African American and Native American populations struggled in finding their identity because of constant rejection, fear, and abuse. Playing upon these wounds were theatrical dramas like the *Clansman,* which, when released in 1903, became a major screen play. Canvassing many Carolina cities, this play portrayed people of color as barbarians who preyed on innocent white folks. Accordingly, author Newkirk wrote that after this play ran through Carolina theaters, mass lynchings, murder, and injustices soon followed. Black had never been blacker and white had never been whiter. Spreading like wildfire, this new southern mind-set invaded every aspect of life in North Carolina, especially A.B. Crumpler's Holiness Church of Goldsboro.[2]

A Great Falling-Away

Being situated in the middle of Goldsboro, the church suffered greatly. In rural areas, Jim Crowism was less prominent than it was in the town's limits. With no public restrooms, offices, or businesses to segregate in the country, the scope of these laws were generally limited. Although efforts were made to construct government legislation in favor of rural segregation, it failed to pass through North Carolina's legislature. However, in the city where segregation was everywhere, Crumpler's congregation of "poor folks and negroes" became a big target for segregation.[3]

The first Pentecostal Holiness Church, which had once thrived on its racial diversity, wealth, and creditability, was now becoming shunned and despised because of its members. Newspapers, which were known for carrying full front page articles about Rev. Crumpler's success, had all but disappeared. Being under Democratic rule, many Carolina news publications were in fear of having their offices burned by fire if they attempted to promote racial integration. This kind of media intimidation caused many editors to only allow Rev. Crumpler a brief mention on the third or fourth page. Perhaps this was another contributing factor that led Crumpler to publish his own paper, *The Holiness Advocate,* through a publishing company surrounded by Lumbee Indians in Lumberton, North Carolina.[4]

Naturally, the Masonic orders were also very upset with Crumpler, Lee, and other ministers. In relating some of these tensions between Masonry and the Holiness Church, Crumpler wrote, "Our Masonic friends are getting warm under the collar." By using brutal political tactics and wealthy influence over Carolina towns, these secret orders opposed A.B. Crumpler's Church. It seems that this response manifested itself through many different forms of pressures that eventually brought the church to its knees.[5]

Perhaps the greatest form of this pressure manifested when A.B. Crumpler's financial support was suddenly cut off. As early as 1903, articles began appearing in Crumpler's paper that revealed the Goldsboro tabernacle was drowning in debt. Owing two thousand dollars on the property and not the building, Crumpler appealed to readers to support the Goldsboro holiness center of eastern North Carolina. With a solid church membership at 125, some 300 to 400 congregants attending Sunday mornings, and 600 to 800 people attending the services at night, the Goldsboro church did not lack large crowds; however, what they did lack was money.[6]

Most members of the Goldsboro tabernacle were very poor and represented every racial class in the city. Occupationally, it seems many were tenet farmers who, according to Crumpler, did not even own a home. Thus, they were unable to supply the two thousand dollars that was needed to pay off the church's debt. This caused Crumpler to petition his followers all around the state to help in their cause. Sadly, his call for help fell upon deaf ears, and the movement would continue to struggle financially for the next few years.[7]

Crumpler's lack of financial support seems to always lead to the secret societies that the Holiness church was in contention with. Places like Goldsboro, Dunn, and Clinton all boasted of at least four different kinds of secret lodges within each of their towns. Generally speaking, lodge members were extremely wealthy during this time and did not wish to associate themselves with the rift-raft of Crumpler's church. By controlling a major portion of the town's revenue streams, it is very likely that these secret organizations possessed a lot of power. They could have easily discouraged other wealthy citizens, banks, or businesses from assisting the holiness cause. Most likely, this was the case for the Goldsboro church. Even though Crumpler had won several prominent and wealthy merchants to holiness in 1896, many of them seemed to disappear after rigid segregation laws kicked in during 1900. Outnumbered by Democratic secret orders such as the Freemasons, Odd Fellows, Knights of Pythias and Red Shirts, Eastern North Carolina's "best Negro Preacher," and his inter-racial church, stood very little chance in flourishing within any segregated city.[8]

Making matters worse, a wave of un-belief began to crash upon some of Crumpler's most loved and trusted preachers. Many of them, who had once professed their sanctification experiences, were abandoning the movement by 1903. Holiness pioneers such as D.H. Tuttle, J.T. Kendall, D.A. Futrell, W.A. Jenkins, W.F. Galloway, J.G. Johnson, D.C. Geddie, V.A. Royall, and T.J. Browning all soon returned to the comfort of prior careers. Arrayed like David's mighty men, these revivalists had conducted meetings all over the state. They introduced thousands to the fires of holiness. Under their preaching, the canopies of heaven invaded earth leaving countless of seekers on the ground like dead men. There is no telling how many souls were saved, sanctified, and healed through their efforts. Yet, as powerful as their ministries were, they stood no chance to the mounting waves of persecution that were beginning to collide upon the foundations of the movement. Reasons given for their dismissal always centered upon financial perplexity or zero support for their evangelistic zeal.[9]

Recalling how these "mighty have fallen" A.B. Crumpler writes, "They (above ministers) are as silent as the monuments are dead! The pressure, brought upon them in the matter of appointments, has silenced their guns." Being severely hurt by their choice to leave, a frustrated Crumpler goes on to pour out his heavy heart upon the pages of the *Advocate*. Many of these ministers had initially launched out into the evangelistic field with great fervor and revival power, but when they began to encounter persecution and opposition, they retreated. Unfortunately, as with every revival movement in church history, the sifting process had begun. Those not strong enough to endure were "burned like the chaff." Such was the case with some of these first holiness leaders in the state. Some returned back to their churches, some dropped out of ministry, and others even began to denounce the movement they once carried as a hoax or sham.[10]

In light of all these hardships, Crumpler's headquarters was torn apart. By May of 1906, the Goldsboro tabernacle had been lost and sold to a group of Quakers. Ironically, the flaming center of holiness for the Tar Heel state was dismantled on the same location where it was birthed, the Goldsboro Courthouse square. The fall of the Goldsboro Tabernacle marked the beginning of the end for A.B. Crumpler's rein in North Carolina. Soon, another thundering voice would arise from Sampson County, and take what Crumpler started beyond anything he could have ever imagined.[11]

In retrospect, the failure of Crumpler's church in Goldsboro has always been attributed to tobacco and divorce issues that were raised within the church. Though these issues did weigh heavily on the young church, it does not seem to fully explain the sudden collapse of the centralized hub of holiness for the state; however, racial segregation does. By 1905 the segregation law was clear. Town officials, law enforcement, and secret societies did not want black, white, or Indians meeting together in the same establishments. To do so could be punishable by beatings, floggings, imprisonment, or even lynching. Evidently, this is why Crumpler's other thirty plus churches thrived and the Goldsboro tabernacle went "down, down, down."[12]

Unlike the Goldsboro location, Crumpler's other churches were situated deep within the country where Jim Crowism was less enforced. This seems to also explain why Crumpler could not receive the financial support he needed to expand the church. During this time, people of wealth were generally members of a secret order or somehow affiliated with it. Whether through business partnerships, politics, or family ties, most in southeastern North Carolina were connected to the lodge. Cleary, Rev. Crumpler and the Holiness Church had fallen into the unpopular and minority category.

Before things got better, however, they got worse. J.A. Culbreth, one of Crumpler's wealthiest converts, decided to create another holiness center upon his own lands. Sensing the time was ripe, Culbreth initiated the Falcon Holiness Camp Meeting at the turn of the century. Unfortunately, Culbreth's actions also led to the decapitation of Crumpler's struggling ministry in Goldsboro. The Falcon encampment, therefore, quickly rose as the new "Mecca" of holiness for North Carolina.

The Shift: From Goldsboro to Falcon

Falcon's early success is traced back to A.B. Crumpler's historic revival that was held in Dunn, North Carolina, in May 1896. Having been converted through these meetings, J.A. Culbreth and several of Dunn's leading religious families joined themselves together in prayer. Among them were most likely the Goff's and the Lee's. It seems that they organized holiness prayer meetings in the town to keep the revival fire burning. Impacted by these sanctified meetings, several women from these families felt the need to establish a "Women's Christian Temperance Union." Both the Erasmus Lee and J.A. Culbreth families were providential in heading up this organization.[13]

Having grown up practically as neighbors, both the Erasmus Lee and J.A. Culbreth families seemed to have been very close. However, it soon became obvious that the Culbreths had to abandon the Dunn prayer meetings and forsake the sweet fellowship they shared with these saints. Culbreth writes:

> About four years ago it became evident that we must leave our home in Dunn, and move out here in this country place, our hearts would almost faint when we would think of leaving the "Holiness Prayer meetings," and breaking away from the sweet fellowship of the saints in Dunn, to come here where holiness has never been preached, and not a soul even understood what the profession of sanctification meant.[14]

Although reasons why they had to flee were never given, Mr. Culbreth decided to move back to his Falcon estate sometime in 1897. Mr. Culbreth, who had owned several stores and had inherited a fortune after his parents passing, sought to build a small tabernacle in the small village of Falcon, where holiness could be taught and practiced. In 1898, after a tornado had blown down some trees, Mr. Culbreth used the lumber to erect a small tabernacle building reminiscent to A.B. Crumpler's gospel tent.[15]

One year later (1899), after Mrs. Culbreth received her healing from the infamous B.H. Irwin, J.A. Culbreth felt prompted to initiate an interdenominational holiness camp meeting in his own backyard, Falcon. Coming off the heels of Rev. S.C. Todd's sermon on missions in the Falcon tabernacle, the Culbreth's gave two hundred and fifty dollars to his cause in return for the use of Todd's large gospel tent and fifty smaller tents. Todd, who had been looking for a place to hold a large camp meeting, found it through this meeting with J.A. Culbreth. Thus, on the last week of July in 1900, the first Falcon Camp Meeting was established.[16]

Assembling the campgrounds after the Vineland, New Jersey, model, the meeting was an immediate success which attracted thousands from around the surrounding areas. Mr. Morris records that under the encampment "Men fell under the power of God! God's presence was so real that both men and women lay in what were called trances." Having been established as an interdenominational camp meeting, Falcon attracted members of the fire-baptized, Free-will Baptist, and holiness churches within the area.[17]

Mr. Morris also notes that through the establishment of this meeting, "three faces merged in the forefront: Rev. S.C. Todd, Rev. G.D. Watson, and J.A. Culbreth." It is interesting to note that Rev. A.B. Crumpler, the "father of holiness" in eastern North Carolina, was not one of these emerging faces. Although Rev. Crumpler preached towards the end, his role in this camp meeting as well as future ones would be very limited. Nonetheless, with or without A.B. Crumpler, the Falcon Camp meeting era had officially begun in the summer of 1900. Soon, many of Crumpler's early converts would make their way to the annual Falcon Camp Meeting.[18]

For many years the general public has always associated the early Falcon ministries as being under A.B. Crumpler's reigns. However, this is not the case. Dr. York writes, "The first scheduled camp meeting at Falcon took place from July 19 to 29, 1900. It was held under the auspices of the Christian Missionary Alliance Church." Thus, Culbreth through another means other Crumpler's Holiness Church, conceived the "Falcon Camp Meeting Association." Though Crumpler and Culbreth would be connected, their ministries remained separate and independent of each other.[19]

While the Falcon Camp Meeting was beginning to experience tremendous growth between 1900 and 1904, A.B. Crumpler's holiness headquarters was experiencing bankruptcy. Despite his popularity, many of Crumpler's followers refrained from rescuing the debt of the Goldsboro church. One of the most notable laymen fully capable of assisting Crumpler was J. A. Culbreth. Mr. Culbreth, however, did not offer to help "the father of holiness" and the struggling Goldsboro Church. Why was this? Perhaps he no longer agreed with Crumpler's views and the direction he was taking the Holiness church. Certainly, befriending the fire-baptizers against Crumpler's better judgment suggested possibilities of this disagreement, but maybe there was more to it than that.

It is very possible that Culbreth could have disagreed with A.B. Crumpler over the racial issue. New facts are beginning to surface that show J.A. Culbreth opposed racial integration within every sphere of society, including the Holiness Church. Furthermore, Culbreth was a strong supporter of white supremacy and the Democratic campaign that stripped away rights from African Americans. Evidence for this is seen through a diary written by William Davis Jones III, a grandson of the late J.A. Culbreth. In reflecting upon the political life of Mr. Culbreth, Jones writes:

> Grandpa (J.A. Culbreth) was still one of the best known and most influential men in Cumberland County. He was a Democrat and an admirer of the Raleigh editor, Josephus Daniels. Though not a preacher he frequently spoke at church meetings, Cousin Mayo Bundy

> jokingly said that holding the Bible in one hand and The News and Observer in the other, Grandpa converted many Republican church-goers to the Democratic Party.[20]

Noted previously, Josephus Daniels was a key figure in the white supremacy Democratic campaign that strongly desired to choke the Cape Fear with the carcasses of African Americans. He, along with North Carolina Governor C.B. Aycock and Senator Furifold Simmons, used the *News and Observer* to kindle a movement of white anger during the 1898 Democratic campaign. There vial message was what induced the Jim Crow era in the Old North state as well as the entire South. Accordingly, one of the Democrats' favorite tactic was to visit local churches and persuade Republicans and Populists to join their bloody cause. Interestingly, J.A. Culbreth exemplified this same behavior according to his grandson's diary.

Undoubtedly, this would have been a point of difference given the fact that Crumpler was building his holiness organization on racial diversity. Authors have always recorded the willingness of Mr. Culbreth to entertain the idea of inter-denominationalism through his Falcon Camp meetings, but what about inter-racialism? The only indication that African Americans were allowed to attend the Falcon camp meetings does not occur until the 1920s and 1930s. Even then, Eddie Morris notes that they were only allowed to sit as spectators in reserved sections. Unlike the Falcon Camp Meetings, A.B. Crumpler's Holiness Church welcomed the idea of co-working with African Americans even after 1900. In many instances, there are records revealing that A.B. Crumpler, T.M. Lee, and G.B. Cashwell participated with "colored" preachers. However, there does not seem to be this same kind of partnership within the early history of the Falcon Camp Meeting, Holiness School, or the orphanage.[21]

Although Crumpler most likely disagreed with Mr. Culbreth's politics and attitude towards the race issue, he did not allow that to stop him from encouraging his holiness readers to attend. Advertisements would often appear in the *Advocate* to inform readers of the next camp meeting at Falcon. In addition, A.B. Crumpler was elected by the people to serve on the board of directors for the Falcon Camp Meeting Association that was organized following the second annual meeting in 1901. However, Crumpler's position on the board never materialized. Most likely, he was asked to serve out of respect, but for whatever reason he declined. By 1909, all ties between A.B. Crumpler and J.A. Culbreth would be totally served

PART IV

THE PENTECOSTAL EXPLOSION AND THE RISE OF G.B. CASHWELL

THE PRELUDE: A CONNECTION TO THE PAST

During January 2012, I had an incredible dream about the Azusa Street Revival and this generation's connection to it. In the dream, I was riding in a car that had departed from the east coast and was trekking west across the country. The car was being driven by an unidentified driver. My destination, however, was Los Angeles, California. When the car entered the city limits, I realized that I was no longer in the year 2012 but had been transported back to the year 1906. The driver pulled the car into the driveway of an old house. The address read: 214 North Bonnie Brae Street. Suddenly, I was aware that this was the house where the Azusa Street Revival began in 1906. After pulling into the driveway, I noticed on my right side stood a small cemetery which was adorned with small grave markers. Upon observing this site, I heard a voice speak, "Can these bones live again?" I was then awakened with an urgency to study just exactly what occurred at 214 North Bonnie Brae Street. What has been uncovered through this dream will provide additional insights into the miracle of Azusa Street, and how it claimed one of Pentecost's most influential leaders, Rev. Gaston B. Cashwell. Therefore, if we wish to grasp the fullness of Cashwell's legacy and our current connection to it, we must revisit 214 North Bonnie Brae Street and the leaders chosen to ignite the famed Pentecostal Revival.

Chapter 12

THE REAL MIRACLE OF AZUSA STREET

According to Christianity *Today*, the nations of the earth contain over 600 million Pentecostal believing Christians. With the exception of the Roman Catholic Church, global Pentecostalism has exploded to become the largest Christian church in the world. It is a world-wide movement that is still evolving and impacting every race, nation, and culture. Who would ever have thought that this "third force in Christendom" would have emerged to such heights given its unlikely founders and humble origins?[1]

Beginning with black washwomen, the famed Azusa Street Revival was first poured out upon the African-American community within the ghettos of Los Angeles, California, in April of 1906. Incredibly, at the height of an era of racial injustice, God chose a poor one-eyed black man, William J. Seymour, to spearhead this global revival that was destined to shake continents. The repercussions of this spiritual renewal being led by a black man would prove to be both transformational and deadly. Nevertheless, William Seymour, G.B. Cashwell, and others would go on to lead the nation and eventually the world in a movement that would seek to restore the apostolic ministry, and destroy one of the greatest evils of mankind, racism.[2]

Besides the tongues phenomenon, harmony between the races at Azusa became the major staple of the movement. This seems to be the real miracle of Azusa that is often overlooked by skeptics, Christian or not. For generations, scholars, historians, and researchers have expounded on the theological position of the Apostolic Faith Movement that began at 312 Azusa Street. Unfortunately, this emphasis has often placed the spotlight on "speaking in tongues" and not the Holy Spirit baptism itself. In fact, many charismatic believers today equate tongues as being the actual Pentecostal experience. This was not the case for the early founders of Azusa, however. Both their definition and experience of Pentecost would always center around one thing: love.[3]

To them, the Pentecostal encounter was an extraordinary endowment of Christ's own love manifesting through human actions. Confirming this romantic love-affair between God and man was the mysterious speaking of unknown tongues. However, Seymour and Cashwell never forced this experience on anyone as Pentecostals would do in later years. They simply set the stage for the Holy Spirit to move upon a broken and sanctified heart. Always urging their followers to seek the "Holy Ghost" Himself and not the manifestation of tongues, they worked tirelessly in trying to distinguish tongues from the actual baptism with the Holy Spirit.[4]

In articulating this point, G.B. Cashwell wrote, "When you receive your Pentecost, you will see that it is the Lover you receive-not only love, but the Lover." A Nazarene preacher who visited the Azusa Mission described his Pentecostal experience by declaring, "It was a baptism of love. Such abounding love! Such compassion seemed to almost kill me with sweetness!" William J. Seymour, leader of the Azusa Mission, defined the Pentecostal baptism as if Christ Himself came and enthroned His own love upon the "cleansed heart" of a believer. It would also be this transformational love between the heart of God and the seeker that would, in Frank Bartleman's words, "wash away the color line" in America.[5]

Seymour's Assignment

Everyone remembers their high school days when the annual year book furnished the picture of those most likely to succeed. Everyone also remembers, when gazing upon that picture, the face of who was least likely to succeed became evident as well. Prior to the heavenly visitation at 312 Azusa Street, this would have probably been the prevailing thought of William Joseph Seymour. Given his background, Seymour was no doubt the least likely to succeed at anything in life, much less in ushering a global movement that would reshape the face of Christianity. It seems however, that God wanted to make a point when He chose Seymour to take charge of the flock. Historically, the church often forgets that the Lord chooses the foolish things of the world to confound the wise. Certainly, Seymour's life and ministry reminded the body of Christ that the Father pleasures in choosing those least likely to succeed. Therefore, Rev. Seymour's story and how it intertwines with the "Apostle of Pentecost to the South" will add historical value in understanding why God chose the Azusa Street Mission to set forth a new pattern of ministry that would change the world.

William J. Seymour was born on May 2, 1870, and died on September

28, 1922. Being the son of former slaves, life was extremely difficult for Seymour during his youth. Having grown up in Centerville, Louisiana, following reconstruction, Seymour was no stranger to racial hatred. Like G.B. Cashwell, Rev. Seymour was born into a race war between white empowered secret societies and the colored population of Louisiana. One of Seymour's biographers, Graig Borlase, notes that these secret organizations terrorized the black community through the propagation lynchings and murder. Perhaps it was this racial climate that drove William Seymour's parents, Simon and Phillis Seymour, to find refuge in the local Catholic Church. Besides attending Baptist churches, the parents of Rev. Seymour were known to have been a part of the Catholic Church of the Assumption and possibly the Church of the Immaculate Conception just outside of Centerville. This, however, was not uncommon in the South during the years of reconstruction.[6]

At the same time, just several miles from the G.B. Cashwell farm in Sampson County, North Carolina, lived a prominent physician known as Dr. John Carr Monk. Dr. Monk, who was a member of the Goshen United Methodist Church, left the Methodist congregation over racial issues and converted to Catholicism during the 1860s. Reasons for his departure centered upon the church's action to dispel blacks from their church once they had been freed under the emancipation of 1863. Dr. Monk, being highly upset with the decision, also abandoned the church of his youth and sought a Christian faith that would treat "all men equal." He found it in the Catholic Church where he and his family were converted in 1873. Soon after their conversion, Dr. Monk moved his family a few miles north to Newton Grove, North Carolina, and organized St. Mark's Catholic Church in 1874. Teaching the Apostolic Faith, Monk encouraged all the African-Americans that had been rejected from Goshen Methodist and other congregations to attend his parish. Within a few short years, Dr. Monk built a school for African-Americans and established the largest inter-racial congregation in Sampson County. Today, St. Marks is known as Our Lady of Guadalupe and consists of over six hundred Spanish families, still making it one of the largest inter-racial congregations in the region.[7]

Unlike the Baptist, Methodist, and Presbyterian denominations following the Civil War, many of the South's Catholic churches welcomed all races. Most likely, this is what drew William J. Seymour's parents into attending Catholic services. Despite this early religious upbringing, Rev. Seymour in later years made a profession of faith in the African American Methodist Church. Subsequently, Seymour's journey led him to a Holiness

Church known as the Evening Light Saints. Here, Seymour came into contact with the National Holiness Movement that had swept the country.[8]

By 1905, Seymour found himself in Houston, Texas, as a student of the Charles Fox Parham's Apostolic Faith Bible School. Rev. Parham, whose Bible school had experienced the first rain drops of Pentecost in 1901, is credited with constructing the Pentecostal doctrine that Seymour carried with him to Los Angeles. This message included five steps:

1. Justification by Faith
2. Sanctification: Second work of grace subsequent to salvation.
3. The baptism with the Holy Spirit: With the "Bible Evidence" of speaking in tongues
4. Divine Healing: Applied through the atonement of Jesus Christ
5. The Second Coming of Jesus[9]

After accepting this teaching, Seymour received a request to preach in Los Angeles, California. Sister Hutchins, who contacted Seymour, asked if he could come and take charge of services at the Santa Fe Holiness Mission. Little did Rev. Seymour know that this invitation would change his life.

According to Dr. Sanders, William Seymour arrived in Los Angeles in February of 1906. Two months later, Dr. Sanders reveals that Seymour preached his first sermon at the Santa Fe Mission. Though he had not received the Baptism of the Holy Spirit nor spoke in tongues, Seymour fearlessly delivered a message from Acts 2:4 and proclaimed with power the message of Pentecost. The following week when Seymour returned, he found the doors of the mission padlocked. Unhappy with the newly constructed Pentecostal theology, Sister Hutchins and some of the members of the church barred Seymour from their congregation. Like many holiness advocates, Sister Hutchins and those in charge of the holiness work in Los Angeles believed that the Baptism of the Holy Spirit occurred in the sanctification process.[10]

In later months, Seymour would comment about this experience in his paper, *The Apostolic Faith*. He states:

> The Lord sent me the means, and I came to take charge of a mission on Santa Fe Street, and one night they locked the door against me, and afterwards got Bro. Roberts, the president of the Holiness Association, to come down and settle the doctrine of the Baptism with the Holy Ghost, that is simply sanctification. He came down and a good many holiness preachers with him, and they stated that sanctification was the Baptism with the Holy Ghost. But yet they did not

> have the evidence of the second chapter of Acts, for when the disciples were all filled with the Holy Ghost, they spoke in tongues as the Spirit gave utterance. After the president heard me speak of what the true Baptism of the Holy Ghost was, he said he wanted it too, and told me when I had received it to let him know.[11]

Often times God will chose the path of pain to bring about the beauty of His plan. Such was the case for William Seymour, who had been rejected, misunderstood, and homeless before stumbling right into his destiny.

Having heard of Seymour's misfortune, Mr. and Mrs. Richard Asbury invited the one-eyed preacher to stay in their home located at 214 N. Bonnie Brae Street. The Asburys, who were Baptists, initially did not agree with Seymour's view on Pentecost. Recognizing his relentless passion to preach this message, however, the Asburys allowed Seymour to hold underground prayer meetings in their home. Little did the Asburys know that these cottage prayer house meetings would set a major precedent for spreading the Pentecostal revival in the days to follow.[12]

Traditionally, these house meetings were known as tarrying services. Tarrying services were very organic in nature and spontaneous. In them, small groups of believers would wait for the Lord to move. Sometimes these meetings could last hours and even days. With no program, no worship band, and no sermon in the traditional sense, tarrying services created an atmosphere of freedom for the Holy Spirit to manifest. These services became the primary vehicle that expanded the Azusa Street Revival into the four corners of the earth. Just as John Inskip, William McDonald, and Phoebe Palmer utilized the camp meeting to establish the National Holiness Movement of the nineteenth century, so it was that Seymour, Cashwell, and other Pentecostal pioneers utilized tarrying services (cottage prayer meetings) to ignite the power of Pentecost. Given Seymour's transdenominational upbringing, he seemed to be the right man to facilitate these types of services. Among the first to attend were humble black washerwomen and their spouses.[13]

As soon as word spread of the prayer meetings, a small following of white believers began to show up at the Asburys' home. They included the McGowans; Arthur G. Osterberg, pastor of an independent Full Gospel Church; and Frank Bartleman, the prophetic voice of California. Incredibly, on April 9, 1906, in the midst of a racially segregated country, God and His mighty presence showed up at 214 N. Bonnie Brae Street among the interracial gathering. Apparently, the Holy Spirit had no regard for the Jim Crow laws that divided his children, and neither did the saints of the Bonnie Brae house. Frank Bartleman, who had been absent that day, recorded that the

"Spirit had fallen a few nights before, April 9, at the little cottage on Bonnie Brae Street. They had been tarrying very earnestly for some time for an outpouring. A handful of colored and white saints had been waiting there daily."[14]

In addition to the racial unity breaking forth, Dr. Synan notes that everyone present fell to the floor in religious ecstasy and began to speak in other tongues. Immediately, crowds from the surrounding areas began to show up in curiosity. Three days later, on April 12, 1906, Seymour himself received the Baptism with the Holy Spirit and spoke in unknown tongues. Running morning, noon, and night, the Bonnie Brae house meetings became a magnet for all people in the community.[15]

Seizing the moment, Seymour, like the Apostle Peter in Acts chapter two, rushed to the crowds and began to preach the message of Pentecost with supernatural signs following. Under this heavenly atmosphere, the inhabitants of the Bonnie Brae house and surrounding neighborhoods were baptized in the Holy Spirit. An eyewitness remembers, "It (Bonnie Brae house meetings) now flowed out to the front yard, the neighbors' yards, and onto the street as Brother Seymour preached from the porch." Author Roberts Liardon stated in his book, *God's Generals,* that the porch of the Bonnie Brae house became the stage and the streets the pews in which hundreds would congregate.[16]

The significance of what occurred at the Bonnie Brae home is important to note. Prior to Seymour's arrival in Los Angeles, southern California had been aching for a move of God. The forerunner spirit had been unleashed through ministers like Frank Bartleman, Joseph Smale, and others who began to prepare the way for Seymour's appearance. Biblically, the forerunner's job was to turn the hearts of a divided people for the purpose of unity. In the same way, the forerunner anointing running through California in 1906 was working to turn the hearts of two divided races towards each other. Bartleman and other key leaders seemed to recognize this supernatural manifestation of divine love.[17]

Surprisingly, the cries of their intercession were answered when a poor black preacher, blind in one eye, arrived at their door step. Although white and black holiness organizations had been working independent of each other, it was William J. Seymour, the message burning in his bones, and the Bonnie Brae meetings that brought both races together. Interestingly, once these pre-Azusa saints were in one accord the Baptism of the Holy Spirit with the evidence of speaking in tongues exploded. The result of this baptism triggered a world-wide movement of brotherly love that would challenge the body of Christ to tear down the newly formulized view of "separate but equal" that was sweeping the country.

Within a few days, Seymour and other leaders sought to secure a larger venue to hold the meetings. Their search ended when they found an old run down warehouse located at 312 Azusa Street. Located in the heart of a black neighborhood, this site would be forever immortalized as the place where God came and dwelt among men. At the time Seymour purchased the building, it was being used as a stable. With dirt floors and un-plastered walls, the future Azusa Mission was in terrible condition. Before Seymour purchased the two-story building, however, it was used as a house of worship for the First African-Methodist Church. Amazingly, in this barn of a building and under the leadership of a black minister, the glory of heaven invaded earth.[18]

The realities of the Azusa Mission are seen best through the eyes of those who were there. Rev. Bartleman, one of Seymour's converts, left behind a detailed account of how the Azusa Street meetings flowed. He writes:

> The meetings started themselves, spontaneously, in testimony, praise and worship. The testimonies were never hurried by a call for 'popcorn.' We had no prearranged programme (*sic*) to be jammed through on time. Our time was the Lord's. We had real testimonies, fresh heart experience. Brother Seymour generally sat behind two empty shoe boxes, one on top of the other. He usually kept his head inside the top one during the meeting, in prayer. There was no pride there. The services ran almost continuously. Seeking souls could be found under the power almost any hour, night and day. The place was never closed nor empty. The people came to meet God. He was always there. Hence a continuous meeting. The meeting did not depend on a human leader. God's presence became more and more wonderful. In that old building, with its low rafters and bare floors, God took strong men and women to pieces, and put them together again, for His glory. It was a tremendous overhauling process. Pride and self-assertion, self-importance and self-esteem, could not survive there. The religious ego preached its own funeral sermon quickly. No subjects or sermons were announced ahead of time, and no special speakers for such an hour. No one knew what might be coming, what God would do. All was spontaneous, ordered of the Spirit. We wanted to hear from God, through whoever he might speak. We had no 'respect of persons.' The rich and the educated were the same as the poor and ignorant, and found a much harder death to die. We only recognized God. All were equal.[19]

Under this atmosphere, the presence of God triumphed and freedom of the Spirit moved strongly. It was here in the "colored church" of Azusa that Mexicans could lay their hands upon whites, and black men could weep and pray over white women. Outside of the mission this behavior would constitute lynching; however, inside the mission it released an incredible surge of healing power between the races. Thus, the Azusa meetings quickly become a different type of revival than the Holiness Movement.

When the National Holiness Movement exploded following the Civil War, a great conviction seized the nation. Having seen slavery dismantled and battlefields overflowing with blood over racial indifferences, holiness prophets began the work of breaking down walls ridden with prejudice. Through their efforts, black churches and white churches began to work together. The message of sanctification became a rallying point in which divided races could agree on. Noted previously, this also became the identifying mark of A.B. Crumpler's Holiness Church in eastern North Carolina from 1896–1906.[20]

There are countless reports of Rev. Crumpler and others working closely with African-Americans. However, due to the increasing pressures of Jim Crowism after 1900, even the Holiness Church of North Carolina had its limits. Although A.B. Crumpler and T.M. Lee had worked closely with "colored congregations," there still remained zero black ministers within Crumpler's church. This brings up a point that needs to be addressed: It was one thing for a white preacher to shepherd over people of color, but it was an entirely different matter for a white preacher to submit under black leadership. The Azusa Street Mission, however, destroyed this mentality.[21]

At 312 Azusa Street, the ideology of Jim Crowism was beheaded. Under its rafters people of all color were equal. There was no black churches nor white churches; no teachers or students, but all were one body baptized into perfect unity. Although the tongues phenomenon was attracting the crowds, it was the baptism encounter of divine love that was quickly becoming the real miracle of Azusa. To substantiate this, one has to look no further then Seymour's paper, *The Apostolic Faith*.

In the November 1906, issue, a front page article appeared describing why the little "colored church" on 312 Azusa Street was advancing the Kingdom of God so powerfully. It reads:

> It is noticeable how free all nationalities feel. If a Mexican or German cannot speak English, he gets up and speaks in his own tongue and feels quite at home for the Spirit interprets through the face, and people say amen. No instrument that God can use is rejected on account of color or dress or lack of education. This is why God has so built up the work.[22]

The same article goes on to include miraculous healings, testimonies of speaking in tongues as well as other languages, and the restoration of all the spiritual gifts listed in the Bible. Toward the end of the article, the author sites what he believes is the most supernatural manifestation occurring at

312 Azusa Street: "The Sweetest thing of all is the loving harmony." In his eyes, racial harmony trumped the healings, tongues, and even restoration of spiritual gifts. Other articles agreed by saying, "God makes no difference in nationality. Ethiopians, Chinese, Indians, Mexicans, and other nationalities worship together."[23]

In addition, write-ups would often appear encouraging the believers not to seek for the manifestation of tongues, but the Lord Himself. One author wrote:

> In seeking the baptism with the Holy Spirit do not ask the Lord for tongues. Just pray the Lord to give you the baptism with the Holy Ghost as He gave his disciples, according to the second chapter of Acts, and wait before Him till the Lord verifies His promise in your precious souls.[24]

Rather than forcing or manipulating the people into speaking in tongues, these Azusa leaders seemed to understand that the real miracle of Azusa was not in the tongues phenomenon. According to them, the real miracle of Azusa was in the jaw-dropping experience of a white man laying down his life before a black man and vice-versa. In the midst of a black and white nation, the Pentecost they experienced was rooted in integration, not segregation.

In retrospect, it would be the integration of the races through the heavenly Holy Spirit baptism that cultivated an atmosphere for miracles, signs, and wonders. Furthermore, Seymour's extraordinary ability to facilitate the services is what sustained this supernatural environment. Perhaps it was this new heavenly experience that began to beckon the attention of a North Carolina Holiness preacher some three thousand miles away.

CASHWELL FLEES TO AZUSA STREET

It's hard to believe that Los Angeles, California, at one time, was under Carolina jurisdiction according to the Carolina Charter of 1663. Running directly west on the 35 degree latitude line, Los Angeles was nearly a three thousand mile straight shot to Dunn, North Carolina, where the Cashwell home stood. Historically, the story behind G.B. Cashwell's venture to Azusa Street has only been told through the IPHC lens. For decades, G.F. Taylor's accounts have shaped the public's understanding of G.B. Cashwell and the events that led him to seek his Pentecost. However, in light of new findings, it is appropriate to question the motives of G.F. Taylor, A.H. Butler, J.A. Culbreth, and the one-sided history that they left behind.[25]

In 1906 the North Carolina Holiness Movement was in disarray. With three different sects of holiness groups competing in the same area, the news of a fresh revival could not have come sooner for the Tar Heel revivalists. G.F.

Taylor remembered how North Carolina holiness ministers were longing for another powerful revival. After hearing of the Azusa Street meetings, Taylor noted that many of his peers were "deeply interested in it" but only a "few of us thought of going there after it." One of the reasons that most likely prevented these Southern holiness ministers in traveling to California was the fact that it was being conducted in a "colored church," and was being led by a son of ex-slaves. Being a few thousand miles away, Los Angeles would have certainly been a long trip in 1906; however, could it be possible that news of this inter-racial movement was too much to bear for Rev. G.F. Taylor and others within the North Carolina Holiness Church?[26]

Accordingly, Taylor admits that some in the Church had been following the Azusa meetings in detail for several months. Given the news accounts from the *Los Angeles Times*, and religious periodicals like the *Way of Faith* and *The Apostolic Faith*, it is highly likely that Rev. Taylor and others were well aware that Azusa was being spearheaded by a black man. This was a provoking thought that seemed to bother most Southern white preachers, even within the Holiness Movement. Perhaps this is why G.B. Cashwell was the only North Carolina preacher bold enough to venture out of the holiness boat and tread upon the waters of uncertainty to Los Angeles. His pilgrimage to Azusa has always been viewed in light of his spiritual hunger for more of God. Yet, it seems that other circumstances were pushing and even threatening Cashwell to leave for California.[27]

For unidentified reasons, tensions within the North Carolina Holiness Movement had been mounting against G.B. Cashwell just prior to his California departure. Intriguingly, these tensions always seem to center around Cashwell's good friend, A.B. Crumpler. Traditionally, Pentecostal historians have always pegged this belief upon two sources: G.F. Taylor's *Our Church History,* and J.E. Campbell's *History of the Pentecostal Holiness Church.* Campbell's account accuses G.B. Cashwell of being the preacher who was "least admired" by A.B. Crumpler. Mr. Campbell also referenced that "Mr. Crumpler did not have any confidence in Mr. Cashwell." Rev. G.F. Taylor also noted that there were a number of ministers "who had grievances against Bro. Cashwell" within the Holiness Church. What could these complaints against Cashwell be?[28]

Although no record has emerged to clarify G.F. Taylor's remarks, deeper observations reveal that all negative comments concerning G.B. Cashwell are based on opinion and speculations. Campbell's account gives no evidence whatsoever why A.B. Crumpler "least admired" Cashwell. It remains only as his personal opinion. Even though G.F. Taylor knew Cashwell and Crumpler firsthand, his testimony about them does not seem to fit new documents, photographs, and histories that are surfacing. Perhaps, when he wrote the history from his memory twenty years later, he may have left out a few other details about A.B. Crumpler and G.B. Cashwell. Currently, no documented accounts have surfaced written by either Crumpler or Cashwell that affirms these accusations between each other. In fact, the opposite exists. Just a few months before G.B. Cashwell ventured to Azusa Street, A.B. Crumpler mentions his co-founder. He writes:

> Bro. G.B. Cashwell and his good wife (Lovie Lee Cashwell) have been spending a few days recently among the good people at Goshen, and preaching at night. We were glad to have Bro. and Sister Cashwell with us at our last regular appointment at that place.[29]

According to Crumpler's own pen, there is no detection of any animosity between Crumpler and Cashwell. Instead, his letter reflects a personal and deep respect for the Cashwells. Crumpler also mentions that he was "glad to have Bro. and Sister Cashwell with us" indicating that he and the Cashwells had been recently ministering together.[30]

By 1906, A.B. Crumpler and G.B. Cashwell had a friendship of at least twenty-one years. In addition, Lee family history remembers that the Crumplers and Cashwells were very good friends. Photographs of both A.B. Crumpler and G.B. Cashwell have also been found hidden in each other's family albums. It is new discoveries like these that are beginning to cast doubt upon the traditional view of the Cashwell-Crumpler relationship as told by the founding fathers of the IPHC.[31]

Besides the negative opinions of Campbell, the most popular source of the Crumpler-Cashwell conflict derives from a mysterious letter that G.B. Cashwell allegedly wrote. According to G.F. Taylor, Cashwell authored and turned in a letter during his absence at the 1906 Lumberton Convention explaining why he went to California. It reads:

> Dear Brethren: If I have offended anyone of you, forgive me. I realize that my life has fallen short of the standard of holiness we preach; but I have repented in my home in Dunn, N.C., and I have been restored. I am unable to be with you this time, for I am now leaving for Los Angeles, Calif., where I shall seek for the Baptism of the Holy Ghost.[32]

Since 1930, this letter has gone unchallenged. It has also been framed to pinpoint the initial division between G.B. Cashwell and A.B. Crumpler. Interestingly, there is no trace that this letter ever actually existed. Moreover, Cashwell in all his writings, never mentions it or provides reference suggesting that he had "fallen short" of anything before traveling to Los Angeles; neither does A.B. Crumpler. Bizarrely, G.F. Taylor took it upon himself to create this letter from his own memory nearly thirty years after Cashwell boarded the train to California! Whether or not this letter ever existed is highly questionable.[33]

Why have G.F. Taylor, A.H. Butler, J.E. Campbell, and others framed Crumpler and Cashwell to appear as enemies? This is a question that has gone unexplored since Cashwell ignited the Pentecostal Movement in Dunn, North Carolina, on December 31, 1906. For years, there has never been any reason to question the relationship between Cashwell and Crumpler. However, for years, it has never been known that Crumpler and Cashwell were saved together under the same minister (J.T. Kendall), founded the Pentecostal Holiness Church together, and enjoyed a close friendship. Perhaps the IPHC founders were trying to hide something when they wrote their history. Maybe, they were ashamed in disclosing some of the details centered around Crumpler and Cashwell. Nonetheless, indicators are now pointing to a possible cover-up between A.B. Crumpler and G.B. Cashwell's estranged relationship as well as the strange events leading up to Cashwell's departure to Los Angeles in 1906. Sometimes, things are not as they appear.

This does not mean, however, that G.B. Cashwell was without enemies prior to leaving for California. Cashwell's own letter to *The Apostolic Faith* reveals that he and Lovie were deeply distressed over his decision to visit the Azusa Mission. Additionally, Cashwell wrote that after he received confirmation from the Lord to go to California, both he and his wife came under severe testing. He writes:

> After praying and weeping before God for many days, He put it into my heart to go to Los Angeles to seek the baptism with the Holy Ghost. My wife prayed and wept with me till we both got the witness that it was the will of God for me to go. The Devil fought me and laid the hand of affliction on my wife, and I felt it almost impossible to for me to come.[34]

Cashwell's biographer alludes that the affliction which came upon Lovie Cashwell was due to complications during her pregnancy. This certainly is a possibility. Unfortunately, there is no way to prove it.[35]

It's also important to remember that G.B. Cashwell grew up with a questionable past. Solid documents revealing his personal life are extremely rare. Could there have been something hiding in Cashwell's background that may have made its way into the public? The same letter by Cashwell goes on to add:

> The night I left home, wife and I prayed and wept before the Lord and God gave the victory, and we both consented on our knees that

> if we died we would be in the order of the Lord and that God would take us home.[36]

Cashwell's choice of words reveals that both he and Lovie were in danger of dying. Why would both of the Cashwells be in danger of death? Mr. G.B. Cashwell was the only one who boarded the train that evening. Were the Cashwell's being threatened by outside influences? Cashwell family history recounts that Gaston Cashwell left for California not only because he hungered for the fullness of God, but also because "he was very unhappy with the way things were going."[37] Although this reason has never been clarified, it does leave room to speculate that Cashwell's trip to Azusa may have been out of a life-saving necessity rather than just spiritual curiosity.

Even some of his fellow holiness ministers suggested this possibility. Many of them believed that G.B. Cashwell had permanently relocated to California when he left in November 1906. Taylor notes:

> When we (Holiness Ministers) learned that one had gone from Dunn, N.C., to Los Angeles, some of us thought he had moved out there, or at least he would be gone a year or more. Imagine our surprise when we learned about six weeks later that he was back in Dunn holding a meeting.[38]

Why would G.B. Cashwell need to relocate permanently in California? The only possible answer to this question seems to point back to G.B. Cashwell's obscure background. To complicate matters, church historians have suggested that a family member of G.B. Cashwell sold a piece of land to fund Gaston's west coast trip. Over the years, this theory has been interpreted to imply that the Cashwells were financially broke. This is not true. There has never been a land deed or any hard proof that supports this story.[39]

On the other hand, a search through the Harnett County, Sampson County, and Cumberland County registry of deeds will show that the Cashwells were wealthy. Both Lovie and Gaston had received handsome investments from their families and had attained a considerable amount of wealth. By 1906, Gaston and Lovie Cashwell had three small children, lived in a large house in Dunn, owned a second home in Ayden, and were extensive land owners. If one thing is clear, it is that Gaston certainly had the ability to purchase his own ticket to California. Thus, it stands to reason that G.B. Cashwell may have left for the Azusa Mission not only in fear of God, but possibly in fear of his life.[40]

Cashwell's Struggles

After boarding the train at Dunn, G.B. Cashwell set out for the Azusa Mission. He arrived at Los Angeles in November of 1906. During the six-day train ride, Cashwell had been spiritually preparing himself to encounter the presence of God. He wrote, "I was six days on the road, was fasting and praying to the Lord continually."[41] The incredible baptism of love with the Holy Spirit was not going to come easy, however. Frank Bartleman observed that "preachers usually died the hardest" at the Azusa Mission. The same would be true of Cashwell's experience. He states:

> As soon as I reached Azusa Mission, a new crucifixion began in my life and I had to die to many things, but God gave me the victory. The first alter call I went forward in earnest for my Pentecost. I struggled from Sunday till Thursday.[42]

Once Cashwell darkened the door of the old Azusa building, he realized something was terribly wrong within his own heart. Hidden from plain sight, this sin(s) manifested itself under the open heaven atmosphere at Azusa.

For decades scholars, historians, and church history buffs have always interpreted Cashwell's crucifixion as a personal death to his own racist views. Cashwell's only biography points this out by saying that "he had to die to two things: African Americans in leadership, and the intense worship between the different ethnic races."[43] Dr. Synan similarly noted, "At first, deeply prejudice against 'Negros,' he (G.B. Cashwell) saw his prejudice fading as interest in speaking with tongues began to overwhelm him." Since Cashwell's experience has first been recorded, this has been the defining moment in Rev. G.B. Cashwell's short but powerful Pentecostal career. It makes for an incredible story; however, in light of a Cashwell's interesting background, it seems to be no more than just that, a story.[44]

As stated above, G.B. Cashwell himself never wrote anything pertaining to such a "crucifixion." There is not even a brief reference that he ever struggled with racism, before or after his pilgrimage to Azusa. Interestingly, the only known letter written by Cashwell prior to his California trip shows the entire Cashwell family ministering with the "colored saints" near Goldsboro, North Carolina in 1903.

In view of this, it's very hard to believe that Gaston Cashwell was racist, struggled with racism, or had a problem with William J. Seymour's leadership prior to his Los Angeles conversion. Cashwell, like his fellow North Carolina holiness ministers, had been following the Azusa Revival closely. It is almost certain that Cashwell knew William J. Seymour was a black man leading the charge. Perhaps this is the real reason he boarded that train. Nonetheless, it seems that Cashwell sealed his fate in riding the rail to Los Angeles in 1906. So, if racism was not his personal crucifixion, then what was it? Due to a lack of Cashwell's writings, we just don't know.

Regardless of what his struggles were, the Spirit of God collided with the hungry heart of G.B. Cashwell after a few days in the Mission. His testimony in *The Apostolic Faith* goes to say:

> While seeking in an upstairs room in the Mission, the Lord opened up the windows of heaven and the light of God began to flow over me in such power as never before. I then went into the room where the service was held, and while Sister Lum was reading of how the Holy Ghost was falling in other places, before I knew it, I began to speak in tongues and praise God. A brother interpreted some of the words to be, "I love God with all my soul." He filled me with His Spirit and love, and I am now feasting and drinking at the fountain continually and speak as the Spirit gives utterance, both in my own language and in the unknown language. I find that all has to be surrendered to God, our own language and all, and He speaks through us English, German, Greek or any other tonge (*sic*) in His own will and way.[45]

Despite his troubles, Cashwell encountered the deep well of God's love through his Pentecostal experience. Like Seymour, Bartleman, and others, Rev. Cashwell defined the Baptism with the Holy Ghost as the Spirit's own love running through his veins. The aftermath of this bubbly encounter resulted in Cashwell speaking in an unknown language. This fresh touch from the Lord would become the basis of his new assignment as an Apostolic Faith representative.

At some point during his stay in the Mission, Cashwell received a word of knowledge to carry the presence of Pentecost back to North Carolina. Whether or not this was his primary intensions is not known. What is known, however, is that Cashwell returned to the Old North State rejoicing. Believing for someone to provide his "fare" home and a "new suite of clothes," Cashwell received these gifts most likely as a confirmation towards his new apostolic ministry. Surprisingly, these acts of faith point to the belief that Cashwell informally joined Seymour's "Apostolic Faith Movement." Being a member of A.B. Crumpler's inter-denominational Holiness Convention, it is possible that Cashwell could have united with the Azusa Street Church while still holding membership in Crumpler's Holiness Conventional body. Evidence for this is seen through several sources.[46]

First, according to *The Apostolic Faith* newspaper, William J. Seymour and a small Azusa committee were licensing preachers as Pentecostal missionaries and evangelists. Ministers like Frank Bartleman, A.G. Garr, Rachel Sizelove, and Lucy F. Farrow were all being sent out as Azusa representatives. Seymour, who headed up the committee, approved candidates after laying hands upon them. According to Dr. Synan, Cashwell went through an identical process in which black Azusa leaders laid hands upon the North Carolina heart preacher. Doug Beacham, Cashwell's biographer, even recognized this when he stated, "In one sense, Cashwell returned to North Carolina as an Azusa Street Mission 'missionary,' sent with a financial blessing that validated his faith and the work of the Spirit in his life."[47]

Second, after his Azusa Street trip, Cashwell's ministry was always detached and separate from A.B. Crumpler's Holiness Church. Although he worked closely with many of them, he was more of a lone wolf when it came to church politics. Rev. G.F. Taylor confirms this by saying, "In 1908 Rev. G.B. Cashwell established in Atlanta Ga., a paper known as the *Bridegrooms Messenger*. He was its editor, and there were several of our people on the editorial staff, but this paper was never under the auspices of this church."[48]

Third, Cashwell's newspaper, along with Pentecostal Missions he would help organize, were found listed under *The Apostolic Faith* newspaper as being a member of that movement and not the North Carolina Holiness Church. Nevertheless, with the fire of God's love burning through his bones, G.B. Cashwell now set his sights on eastern North Carolina. Since the North Carolina Holiness Movement had become sharply divided, it seems that Gaston longed to share his California experiences with his fellow ministers. Whether they would accept or reject his testimony really didn't seem to bother him. Love had transformed him from the inside out. Even Cashwell's enemies could not stop or hinder what was about to break out in the nation under his ministry. Having the powerful Azusa anointing flowing out of him, Rev. G.B. Cashwell quickly began planning to facilitate another Azusa Street Mission. Only this time, it would be in the racially heated atmosphere of the South.[49]

Chapter 13

FROM AZUSA TO DUNN, NORTH CAROLINA

By 1907, Eastern North Carolina had become one of the deepest wells of revival in the southern United States. It had witnessed wave after wave of heavenly glory under the preaching of Bishop Francis Asbury, A.B. Crumpler, Sam Jones, B.H. Irwin, J.H. King, L.L. Pickett, G.D. Watson, Seth Reese and many others. Interestingly, the small town of Dunn, North Carolina, became somewhat of a favorite location, where many of these burning revivalists ignited their powerful ministries. Although the newly established city had gained a reputation for being exceptionally violent, it was now turning into a habitation for God's holy presence. Perhaps this is why Rev. G.B. Cashwell selected the town of Dunn in hosting one the most significant meetings ever recorded within the annals of church history, the "Azusa East" revival! Before examining the Carolina interracial movement that would shake the Jim Crow South, it is necessary to record the first official site where G.B. Cashwell launched his North Carolina Pentecostal career, Sharecake.[1]

Share-The-Cake: G.B. Cashwell's First Pentecostal Meeting

Despite popular belief, the famous three-story tobacco warehouse revival in Dunn was not the first place where G.B. Cashwell ignited the flames of Pentecost in the South. Having arrived back in eastern North Carolina during the first week of December 1906, Cashwell first chose to share his Pentecostal experience somewhere deep in the country. An exuberant Cashwell briefly wrote about this initial meeting in *The Apostolic Faith*. He states:

> To the Saints in Azusa Mission, and through all California, greetings in Jesus Name! O praise Him! It is wonderful. Last week I held a few services in the country in one of the Holiness churches, and two

> received their Pentecost and spoke in tongues. The languages were as perfect as I ever heard. One was a Sunday school superintendent and the other an elder of the church.[2]

For years, no one has ever discovered where this first meeting was held. Fortunately, the Cashwell family history provides a solid answer. According to several direct descends of Cashwell, this initial meeting began under the auspices of St. Matthews Holiness Church.[3]

Located in the Sharecake area of Sampson County, St. Matthews was a family-friendly choice for Cashwell to hold his first Pentecostal meeting. Demographically, it is situated less than two miles from the Cashwell farm that he grew up on. Most likely, these first services centered around Cashwell's family and friends. Many of Cashwell's siblings had never traveled outside of southeastern North Carolina, much less across the country. Surely, their ears waited in expectation to hear firsthand accounts of the Azusa Street Mission and the one-eyed minister who "converted" their beloved preacher.[4]

Dr. McCullen also mentions the small farming community in an article he wrote entitled, "Sharecake, 1878." Here, he records an odd story about the small community, and their rejection of a young Gaston B. Cashwell. Accordingly, during his youthful years, Cashwell was not invited to an upscale wedding hosted by a prominent Sharecake family. In retaliation, Cashwell and some friends crashed the party and created quite the scene. The essence of the story explains how a certain class of people refused to share a joyous celebration with G.B. Cashwell because they were ashamed or embarrassed of who he was. Family members have speculated that Dr. McCullen purposely tailored this story to hold a symbolic meaning. Sharecake, or "Share-The-Cake" in Mr. McCullen's mind, was not only a geographical location, but also a type of mentality. According to McCullen, this mentality, developed by locals, seemed to exclude any credit due to G.B. Cashwell's colorful ministry.[5]

Another connection between G.B. Cashwell and Sharecake centers on his early holiness years. During the 1890s, after G.B. Cashwell embraced the holiness message, he was remembered for holding services around Sharecake in the "old Cindy House." The Cindy House group was eventually organized into St. Matthews Holiness Church shortly after the turn of the century. By December 1906, the humble congregation of St. Matthews became the first people in the entire South to experience the Baptism of the Holy Spirit under the powerful ministry of their very own G.B. Cashwell.[6]

Cashwell also had family ties at St. Matthews. According to Dr. McCullen, one of the charter members of St. Matthews was his father, Joseph T. McCullen Sr. A nephew of G.B. Cashwell, both he and his wife, Myrtie Gore McCullen, were among the first to be impacted by his California experiences. Being absorbed with the Pentecostal Movement until his death, J.T. McCullen Sr. helped build St. Matthews, donated land for the parsonage, and remained a faithful member until his death. Besides serving the church, Mr. McCullen Sr. also demonstrated his Pentecostal love by aiding African Americans in need. Amazingly, one of his greatest contributions to the local black community most likely came through the nudging of Uncle Gaston Cashwell.[7]

According to a land deed, dated August 1, 1908, J.T. McCullen Sr. gave one acre of his land to the Lee's Chapel Holiness Church Colored. The Church, which still functions today under the name St. Peters Holy Church, was given land to build a house of worship for Pentecostal-Holiness believing "colored saints." Interestingly, it butted up next to the old Cashwell farm. Being that Goshen Holiness church (five miles away) was possibly, at one time, racially mixed and was organized by Cashwell and Crumpler, it is very likely that St. Matthews was also initially mixed as well. With the unfortunate advent of white supremacy following 1900, many of these inter-racial congregations would be forced to segregate. Therefore, Lee's Chapel Holiness Church Colored was very possibly the black remnant of St. Matthews Holiness Church.[8]

Having nowhere to go, it seems G.B. Cashwell and J.T. McCullen Sr. aided their fellow African American brethren by giving them a place to worship. Certainly, this was also a pattern of love that Granny Susan Cashwell started fifty years prior. Although it is not known if Gaston pastored the congregation, it is believed by locals that he helped organize it. This would certainly add to the growing list of churches that G.B. Cashwell helped start during his ministry. Sadly, most of the information regarding Cashwell's amazing church planting abilities seems to have been intentionally forgotten. Most likely, this has occurred due to his passionate love and unyielding determination to serve "poor folks and Negros," despite the looming threat of white supremacy. Maybe one day we will discover just how many churches Cashwell really started. Perhaps then, we will finally be able to "share-the-cake" with him, and celebrate in all of the wonderful accomplishments he has made to Christianity.[9]

Background of the Dunn Revival

After seeing success among white and black folks out in the country, Cashwell quickly began to organize a meeting in the middle of Dunn's city limits. This proved to be a strategic choice. Nestled in the heart of North Carolina, Dunn was still a newly established city during Cashwell's day. Being charted in 1887, it was first ruled by thieves, drunks, and shifty loggers. Some historians even dubbed it, "hells half acre" during its infancy years. Despite these treacherous beginnings, Dunn began to grow rapidly with the arrival of the railroad during the early 1890s. Farmers, entrepreneurs, and businesses soon began to capitalize on this growth. By the turn of the century, Dunn had secured the best tobacco and cotton markets in the state. Such an achievement would beckon the attention of farmers from all over the country side.[10]

According to an article published in the local paper, thousands of people from the surrounding counties would flock to Dunn every day for a one month period. Most of them were farmers who came to the city looking to purchase farming supplies for the upcoming season. Having already a population of over two thousand people by 1902, these massive crowds caused Dunn to burst at the seam with seas of people. Incredibly, this designated month that swept in thousands occurred during January. This, of course, would be the same month that G.B. Cashwell chose to host his most famous Pentecostal meeting.[11]

Recognizing Dunn's strategic location, Cashwell sought a neutralized site where ministers and people of all backgrounds could gather as one. With the imprint of the Azusa Mission burning in his heart, Rev. G.B. Cashwell secured a three-story tobacco prize house on South Wilson Ave. The large prize house was first organized in August of 1899 and built sometime in 1900. On August 23, 1899, the County Union published an article announcing Dunn's newest building along with its dimensions. It states.

> A stock company composed of our businessmen has been organized and the bill has placed with the mill men for lumber to build a prize house. The house will be 40x80, three stories.[12]

Like the old abandoned Azusa Street Mission, this three-story tobacco prize house was an excellent choice. Being backed by no church, no denomination, or any other organization, it was perfect in creating an Azusa type atmosphere.

Burning with expectation, Gaston scheduled the first meeting to begin there on December 31, 1906. Rev. H.H. Goff's wife, Florence Goff, noted that Cashwell invited "every holiness preacher in the convention" to attend as well as any other person desiring to experience the baptism of love with the Holy Ghost. Soon, advertisements for the Pentecostal meeting were listed in A.B. Crumpler's Holiness Advocate and J.M. Pikes, Way of Faith holiness papers. Although the revival would be welcomed by some, for many of Dunn's residents and leading officials, Cashwell's meeting would serve as the ultimate rock of offense. Reasons for this date back to A.B. Crumpler's first holiness meeting and the white supremacy movement that put it down.[13]

When A.B. Crumpler pitched his 2,500 men tent in Dunn, during May of 1896, major breakthroughs were made. Under his leading, blacks and whites found sweet fellowship together. Denominational walls were beginning to break, and unity seemed to triumph within the pulpits of Dunn's leading churches. After 1900, however, everything changed. Being a heavenly recruited city for the white supremacy movement, the newly developed town soon became a hotbed for secrets societies and racial segregation. As noted previously, the North Carolina Democratic Party largely advanced white supremacy through the meeting of Masonic orders. The city of Dunn would be no exception.[14]

According to Herman Green, a Dunn historian and high-ranking Freemason, "Masonry continued to burn in the hearts" of Dunn's leading citizens between the years 1888–1915. Experiencing a boom in membership during this time, Dunn Freemasons began to secure a sweeping majority of Dunn's government offices. In fact, by the time G.B. Cashwell sparked the Dunn revival in January of 1907, four out of the last five Mayors of Dunn had been baptized into Masonry. Most city and county commissioners were also known to be members of the lodge. Most likely, the same results followed within the halls of city council, law enforcement, and Dunn's wealthy class. Besides the Masonic rooster, lodgers also had an option to join the Knights of Pythias or the Odd Fellows. Many of their records have yet to be explored. Given the strength of these secret orders, it is quite possible that nearly 50 percent of the towns 2,500 population in 1907 were joined to these pro-democratic secret societies.[15]

Dunn's newspaper also became a target for Democratic control. In 1902, the city's long standing paper The County Union was replaced by The Democratic Banner. Its new editor, W.A. Stewart, was another leading Mason. Through his efforts, The Banner quickly became the voice of white supremacist ideals for Dunn and the surrounding areas. In affirming their handle on Dunn's citizens, the paper published a candid article stating, "The policy of the paper will be strictly Democratic in politics, aligning itself earnestly and enthusiastically for the party's nominees, and using its strongest endeavor to put before the people the truth about political matters in general."[16]

In light of these factors, A.B. Crumpler's Holiness Church had no chance of surviving within the city limits of Dunn. Waves of political persecution and racial segregation were beginning to take their toll. The Dunn of 1907 was completely different from the Dunn of 1896. Thus, G.B. Cashwell would certainly have his work cut out for him in organizing an open-door meeting that would welcome Caucasians, African Americans, Native Americans, and the mixed multitudes.

Azusa Street, North Carolina!

When New Year's Eve struck the clock in 1906, a seismic shift took place in the little town of Dunn, North Carolina. The results forever changed the fate of several denominations and ultimately reshaped Christianity. Under the marvelous leading of G.B. Cashwell, the three-story prize house revival and the thousands who attended it shook and trembled. Through the Holy Spirit's presence, many succumbed to the new baptism of love and the wonderful experience of speaking in unknown languages.[17]

Unlike A.B. Crumpler's 1896 holiness revival that also took place in Dunn, the tobacco house meeting depended on no sermon or human effort. It was a personal appointment between the bride and bridegroom. Cashwell, like William J. Seymour, recognized this and seized the moment by surrendering all his rights to control the services. Operating under the colorblind anointing of Azusa Street, Cashwell reeked with a love so powerful, that all races were supernaturally drawn through the door. Even prideful preachers became gripped with the powerful, yet sweet conviction of the Holy Spirit. Unfortunately, Dunn's 1907 newspapers have been lost, and sources revealing what transpired inside the prize house are extremely rare. Thankfully, there are a few direct references that can lead us back into the revival that touched so many.[18]

The first comes from G.B. Cashwell's own pen. After witnessing the initial signs of a Pentecostal explosion, G.B. Cashwell wrote back to Los Angeles to share Dunn's results with the rest of the world. An excited Cashwell writes:

> This is only the third day here, and already about ten have received their Pentecost. Five preachers received the baptism and some of them have two or three languages already and can preach sermons and pray in tongues. The church is filled to overflow and people come from all over the country. Sinners are being converted and others repenting. This town of about 2,500 has never seen Pentecost before, but praise God, it has come and the town and is stirred from center to circumference. People have laid aside eating and business to a great extent and are going down before God in earnest. How I praise God for this wonderful salvation. All the signs follow me since I received the Pentecost. O let us trust only to the still, sweet voice of Jesus. He does it all. O how I praise God for sending me to Los Angeles, and for you all.[19]

Despite the backlash of town officials that would quickly rise, Cashwell observed a tremendous impact on numerous preachers in this meeting. Many of these holiness leaders had been sharply divided over internal conflicts and controversial issues. Under the Azusa type atmosphere, however, Fire-baptizers, Free Will-Baptist, and Crumpler's Holiness Church ministers became one. Preachers such as H.H. Goff, M.D. Sellars, J.A. Blaylock, A.H. Butler, G.F. Taylor, E.H. Blake, Pinkie Blake, and many others went down to Dunn and embraced the message of Pentecost. Their conversions would be paramount in spreading the fire all over the Carolinas. Imagine their surprise when they began to hear strange languages being uttered from the barn-like building and stumbled right into their new God-given destiny.[20]

Florence Goff, wife of Rev. H.H. Goff who married the Cashwell's, wrote about some of their struggles with the Dunn revival. Believing they had "all the Pentecost Brother Cashwell had after going to Los Angeles," the Goffs, along with many preachers in the convention, were very apprehensive about G.B. Cashwell's meeting. After scoping out one of the meetings, H.H. Goff confessed "something has surely struck Brother Cashwell; he spoke a few words in tongues." Within a few days, many of their Holiness Free Will-Baptist friends such as R.B. Jackson, Willie Strickland, J. A. Blaylock, and M.D. Sellars had all been swept into the new Pentecostal Movement. Stirred about this news, the Goffs wasted no time in going to Dunn to get their Pentecost. Mrs. Goff writes:

> When we reached the place, I heard sister McLaughlin (now in heaven) praying, "O God, do give Bro. Goff the Holy Ghost." As I went down the aisle they arose from prayer. She threw her arms around me and cried, "Sister Goff, the blessed Holy Ghost has come. He's come! Sit down!" Then she began to sing a heavenly song in other tongues, a new sound to me. About that time Bro. McIntosh arose and began talking in tongues. O! how I cried! I felt like God was speaking. I was as one standing before God, it seemed to me. I fell on my face at the altar by my husband and began to beg God to heal and baptize me with the Spirit.[21]

Mrs. Goff goes on to add:

> Brother Cashwell said, "Come to the altar." I went. Four or five saints came, laid hands on me, the Holy Ghost struck me; my hands began to draw; my jaws became stiff; the power went all over me. The saliva flew four feet from me; my tongue became first stiff; they said, "Praise God." I tried to; my tongue just flew. I arose knowing I was healed and baptized with the Holy Ghost. I had not been a day without a body supporter, and had not slept on my left side in months without terrible pain.[22]

After surrendering all to the Lord, Florence Goff encountered the experience of being baptized into the richness of Christ's love. Her husband, H.H. Goff, would have a bit more of a struggle before receiving his Pentecost.

Accordingly, on January 17, he really received the Holy Ghost through an experience that shook the entire tobacco three-story prize house.[23]

With meetings running nearly all day in the Dunn prize house, another location was needed to sustain the revival during the night. In Los Angeles, the Azusa Street Mission ran from about 10:00 a.m. until midnight. To keep the fire burning, night services were held back at the Bonnie Brae Home. These cottage house prayer meetings also became the same pattern G.B. Cashwell used in sustaining Pentecostal services in Dunn. According to Florence Goff, these meetings were held in the Cashwell home on Layton Ave. On the same day following her Pentecostal experience, Mrs. Goff stated, "That evening we went to Brother Cashwell's to a prayer meeting. Sister Cashwell received her Pentecost that evening." Mrs. Goff goes on to testify that the power of God became so strong in that meeting that she sung worship in over a dozen different languages.[24]

Another account that reveals the Cashwell home being used to facilitate Pentecostal services comes from the testimony of Frank Bartleman. In September of 1907, Rev. Frank Bartleman, one of the original pioneers of Azusa Street, went on a national rampage spreading the Pentecostal Movement. As an Apostolic Faith representative, he made a pit stop in Dunn, North Carolina, and preached there to the Pentecostal saints. Although Cashwell was far away "spreading the fire," Rev. Bartleman still ministered in Dunn. He wrote, "I dropped off at Dunn, North Carolina, where Brother Cashwell's family lived, and preached five times in the little Pentecostal Church there." [25] At this time, there was no Pentecostal church or gathering in Dunn, except for those that were meeting in Cashwell's home.

Contrary to some beliefs, the Cashwell's home was a very nice and large home. It had been the home of Lovie Cashwell's parents, Mr. and Mrs. Erasmus Lee. Owning entire city blocks of Dunn, as well as hundreds of acres of land throughout eastern North Carolina, the Erasmus Lee home was a home of nobility that sheltered the large Lee family. With their passing, it fell into the hands of the Cashwells, who by 1907, had five small children. Amazingly, the Cashwell home stood only several blocks away from the prize house. This made its location and size ideal for holding together a small congregation of Pentecostal believers. These underground meetings in the Cashwell home eventually gave birth to a large church body. This will be discussed in chapter sixteen.[26]

Keeping in step with the Azusa Street Mission, Cashwell welcomed all the races. In recounting the "colored people" who crowded into the Dunn meeting with their white brethren, Cashwell notes:

> Several colored people have received their Pentecost and speak in tongues God has wonderfully blessed some of the people with the gift of song. One colored sister, a school teacher, received the Pentecost the other night and spoke in tongues for some time. She has manifested a call to foreign fields. All the people of God are one here.[27]

Even in the midst of a town that legally prevented blacks from assembling with whites, Rev. G.B. Cashwell refused to bow his knee to segregation. He only believed in preaching an integrated Pentecost, not a segregated Pentecost. For him, it was non-negotiable. Cashwell, unlike some of his peers, understood that it was an impossibility to separate the baptism of love between blacks and whites. In his eyes, all people deserved a chance to experience this new and wonderful gift that was beginning to unite races around the country. Incredibly, using the Pentecostal baptism as his weapon, Cashwell spearheaded the Jim Crow ideology of the South. Certainly, this became his most undisclosed crowning achievement. Perhaps this is why he was chosen to hold the keys for the entire South.[28]

Besides Cashwell's pen, there is another eye-witness account of the Dunn Pentecostal revival. Rev. Sam Frann, who became a Pentecostal minister in later years, remembered Cashwell's Dunn meeting. When he was eighteen, Frann stumbled into the prize house to investigate the strange noises he was hearing. His experience, which was recorded in an unpublished paper by Dr. James Goff, sheds light on how Cashwell conducted the services that were so powerful. Frann's testimony, as told through Goff, states:

> The warehouse was overcrowded with people filling both the seating area and the rostrum. Cashwell sat in a chair in the middle of the rostrum facing the congregation. Fann remembers that the service was rather characteristically begun with singing and prayer. Rather than a single dominant sermon by Cashwell, the service consisted "short speeches" made by different ones. Cashwell, however, remained the center of attention as "whatever he said, they observed those things." The congregation sat quietly listening obviously waiting to see some demonstration by the Holy Spirit.[29]

According to this account, there are several comparisons between Rev. Seymour's Azusa Mission, and G.B. Cashwell's tobacco house revival.

First, Cashwell laid out the floor plan almost identical to how Seymour arranged the Azusa Mission. At Azusa Street, Rev. Seymour organized the first floor (40x60) with seating all around the two shoe boxes he used as a pulpit. With people all around him, Seymour remained the center of attention. Cashwell, in like manner, organized the prize house with this same layout and took up his seat in the "middle of the rostrum."

Second, shifting from preacher to facilitator, both Seymour and Cashwell understood how to give up their right to control the meetings. Through their ability to facilitate, the powerful and tangible presence of the Holy Spirit was maintained in great fashion.

Third, like Azusa Street, sermons, programs, schedules, or big name speakers found no place in Cashwell's meetings. Only Spirit led testimonies given by ordinary people who had encountered the Holy Spirit baptism.

Fourth, Cashwell's meetings were designed as "tarrying services." With the congregation sitting quietly and waiting, the Dunn meeting was unlike anything any Carolinian had seen up to this point. Under A.B. Crumpler and the Fire-baptized Holiness revivals, shouting, clapping, and loud singing were the trademarks of a good meeting; but not so with G.B. Cashwell's Dunn revival. Under his leadership, the people waited in desperate expectation until the Holy Spirit Himself showed up.

Certainly, the Dunn revival was identical to Azusa Street in many ways: in structure, leadership, style, and power. Perhaps this is why Pentecostal historian Dan Woods, has dubbed Cashwell's tobacco house meeting as the "Azusa East" of the east coast. However, there is one similarity between the Azusa Street Mission and Cashwell's meeting in Dunn that has never been explored, opposition.[30]

According to articles in The Apostolic Faith, opposition against the Azusa Street revival was fierce. Such an account is found on the front page of the November, 1906 issue. The report tells of an incident where a band of Azusa workers were arrested for speaking in tongues. In writing to Seymour, the four defendants wrote, "We are charged with using boisterous language, unusual noise, or in other words speaking in tongues." This was a tactic that local officials were using to break up Pentecostal inter-racial gatherings. For years no one has ever known of such political criticism breaking out against Cashwell's Dunn meeting until recently.[31]

On August 27, 2010, the city of Dunn, North Carolina, finally honored the achievements of G.B. Cashwell. Fueled by the findings of Mrs. Elisabeth Crudrup and Mr. Thomas Ellis of the Harnett County Historical Association, the state of North Carolina was prompted to erect a historical road marker in Rev. Cashwell's honor. Their diligent research, however, exposed a dark side of the Dunn revival that most are unfamiliar with. According to an interview with the Harnett County Historical Association about these new discoveries, The Daily Record recorded:

> Like the California revival. Mr. Cashwell welcomed all denominations and races, whites, blacks, Lumbee Indians, anyone interested in a deeper relationship with God. During their research, Mrs. Crudrup and Mr. Ellis found some interesting historical accounts. "During our

> research, we found that the newspapers of the day complained about the filth 'those people' left behind when they came to Dunn," Mrs. Crudrup said. "And at that time, if you worshiped with blacks and Indians, your church could get burned down. G.B. Cashwell refused to segregate, it was unheard of at the time," she said. "Dunn even imposed a $64 dollar fine on anyone caught speaking in tongues inside the city limits." "You have to remember, this was only eight years after the Wilmington Riots," Mr. Ellis said, "so on top of the normal racial intolerance of the time, there was a lot of white anger. But Cashwell overcame the sin of racism and welcomed everyone," he said.[32]

Given the political and racial atmosphere over Dunn at the time, local resistance against this revival was imminent. Although this outpouring of God's love awakened some, it enraged others, especially the town's leading Democratic elite. By this time, Dunn had already gained a reputation for harboring Ku Klux Klan activity. Additionally, the agricultural town boasted a strong presence of numerous Masonic orders. Most likely, the thought of blacks laying their hands on whites, and vice-versa, was a sickening thought for many of Dunn's residents.[33]

In taking his stand not to segregate, it is almost certain that G.B. Cashwell and his family received death threats. It's important to remember that Los Angeles, California, was extremely different from Dunn, North Carolina, in the year 1907. However, like many other facts in the Crumpler-Cashwell story, the opposition against them and their ministry always seems to be covered up. Perhaps this is why the Dunn revival was so quick in duration. Unlike the Azusa Street meetings that lasted for three years, the Dunn prize house meeting only lasted for about twenty-one days. Interestingly, sometime following the close of Cashwell's Dunn meeting, the three-story prize house mysteriously burned to the ground. No records, indications, or evidence has ever emerged revealing how or why this happened.[34]

Just as quickly as the historic Dunn revival began, it ended. Cashwell remarked to The Apostolic Faith that fifty or more had received the Pentecostal experience in the Dunn meetings. Fifteen of them, however, were preachers from North Carolina, South Carolina, and Georgia. Like Gideon's army, these newly converted ministers would shake the southeastern States with revival power. Many would travel back to their respective states and invite Cashwell to hold Dunn type meetings within their regions. Soon, the entire South would be baptized in the Holy Spirit through G.B. Cashwell and the message burning in his heart.[35]

Chapter 14

CASHWELL TRANSFORMS THE SOUTH

DESPITE LOOMING THREATS, political coercion, and resistance from conservative church leaders over the belief of the baptism with the Holy Spirit, G. B Cashwell couldn't be stopped. With fire in his eyes, Cashwell was a man consumed with the Holy Spirit. Burning from the inside out, hell and all its forces seemed powerless in defeating him. He quickly outgrew the boundaries of North Carolina and began to spread his message to other states. Under his unique ministry, Georgia, South Carolina, Tennessee, Florida, Alabama, and many other states would be baptized with Pentecostal power. The wake of his rumblings spawned multiple denominations, hundreds of churches, and left millions of lives transformed by the Gospel he preached.

Besides fighting the Jim Crow South, converting national and international denominational leaders became the staple of G.B. Cashwell's ministry. He was, without a doubt, a leader of leaders. Due to the success of the Dunn revival, ministers from around the country began to invite Cashwell to share his Pentecostal beliefs with their organizations. Whether Gaston knew it or not, these heavenly inspired meetings resulted in a cataclysmic shift in Christianity as we know it today. Like the Apostle Paul, Cashwell was handed spiritual keys over entire regions. His work in the South brought unity to many denominations still struggling to find their place within the broken Holiness Movement.

CASHWELL AND FIRE-BAPTIZED CHURCH

After stepping into the light of Pentecost, Cashwell immediately received all of the supernatural gifts of the Holy Spirit. According to him, one of these gifts was the discerning of spirits. Such a gift was needed when he began to expand the Pentecostal Movement from North Carolina to Toccoa, Georgia.

Toccoa became one of Cashwell's first major Pentecostal victories. It was here that J.H. King, general overseer of the Fire-Baptized Holiness Church, surrendered his intellectual struggle under Cashwell's meetings. Subsequently, the entire F.B.H.C. followed King's leading and were all swept into the new movement; however, it would not come without a struggle.[1]

With the moral failure of their founder, Rev. B.H. Irwin, the F.B.H.C. struggled to survive between the years 1900–1911. Even under the new leadership of J.H. King, the Fire-baptizers still suffered from the consequences of their rigid holiness views. Besides holding to the strict Old Testament dietary laws and having a zero tolerance policy for those who wore facial hair, Fire-baptizers also did not believe in the taking of medicine.[2]

Mattie Perry, who was a Fire-baptized advocate, operated a faith healing school in Marion, North Carolina, during the 1900s. Refusing to offer any medicine to her patients, Miss Perry made headline news in The Duplin Journal when two of her followers died of fevers. Rev. R.B. Hayes, a ruling elder for the F.B.H.C., also came under harsh scrutiny when he refused to give medicine to his dying son. After the boy's death, Rev. R.B. Hayes was apprehended by authorities and placed under their custody. Fortunately, he admitted his failure and was restored back to ministry after experiencing the baptism of love under the leading of G.B. Cashwell. Misguided though it was, the faith of these believers was never lacking. Nonetheless, such an extremist approach to ministry is what continued to provoke holiness wars between Fire-baptizers and the Holiness Church of North Carolina.[3]

Although many of their congregations in the Midwest had disappeared by 1907, the F.B.H.C. still had a strong presence in the Southern regions of the United States. For many of them, news of Cashwell's Dunn revival could not have come sooner. Though King was not present at the Dunn revival, many members of his church were. Among them were Rev. E.H. Blake and his sister, Pinkie Blake. After having received the Pentecostal Baptism in the prize house, the Blakes and others returned to Fire-baptized headquarters in Georgia. Fueled by the flames of love and the bewilderment of speaking in unknown languages, these Fire-baptizers requested Cashwell's services in Toccoa, Georgia. Little did Gaston know that this appointment would change a leader and produce a large Christian denomination that still thrives today, the International Pentecostal Holiness Church (IPHC).[4]

In early February of 1907, G.B. Cashwell arrived in Toccoa, Georgia, and held a series of revival meetings at the local Fire-baptized church. At the time, J.H. King was living in the small Georgia town and was serving as pastor of the church. Unlike many of his followers, King struggled with the idea of Pentecost. The thought of the Pentecostal baptism following the sanctified experience "pained" him. In his view, the Pentecostal Movement seemed to be "a denial of the work of God." In hearing about Cashwell's meetings in Dunn, King wrote, "The more I heard of the meeting in Dunn, the less I desired to go there."[5] He also felt that it was unscriptural, as well as dangerous. Moreover, the young Overseer publicly declared that he would "oppose Cashwell if he should teach the Pentecostal baptism with speaking in tongues." With many members of his own flock bursting with Pentecostal hunger, King had no choice but to host G.B. Cashwell and investigate the supernatural anointing surrounding his ministry.[6]

In the interim period prior to Cashwell's arrival, several meetings were held by those who had experienced Pentecost back in Dunn. King, being highly skeptical of his congregation's testimony, attended the meetings and quickly refuted their experiences. Scorning them for being disobedient, King exercised his church authority over them by controlling the services with an iron fist. By the time Gaston arrived, tensions were already riding high. Accordingly, King stated that the meeting "conducted by Rev. Cashwell started with little show of success."[7]

Why was J.H. King so apprehensive? What prevented him from believing in this wonderful gift? Certainly, being under the influence of needing several degrees of baptisms as taught by his mentor, B.H. Irwin, had something to do with it. However, like many other intellectuals, King's greatest battle would be fought within his own mind. Frank Bartleman said it best, when he declared, "At Azusa, preachers die the hardest." J.H. King would be no different. Desperate for the truth, King sought for answers in Dean Alford's Critical Notes on the New Testament in Greek. His searching came to an end on February 15, 1907.[8]

After having read multiple passages in the Bible about the Pentecostal experience and speaking in tongues, King realized that he was in error. Immediately, he began to seek the Pentecostal baptism as taught by Cashwell. Writing about his encounter, King testified:

There came into my heart something new, though the manifestation was not great. There was a moving of my tongue, though I cannot say that I was speaking a definite language. I only know that there was some moving of my tongue as I had never experienced before. I had some assurance that the Comforter had come into my heart.[9]

After his Pentecostal experience, J.H. King's heart began to soften and he embraced the meetings being led by G.B. Cashwell. He later wrote, "The meeting at Toccoa proved to be a very successful revival. Many sought and obtained the baptism of the Holy Spirit, and the power of God was present to heal in a marvelous manner."[10] As word spread, people from all over the state, and even South Carolina, began to flock towards Cashwell's services. Capitalizing on this curiosity, King and others quickly organized another meeting to take place about thirty miles away in Royston, Georgia.

Royston had become headquarters for the F.B.H.C. and is where the printing office for Live Coals had been established. This paper was a revised rendition of Irwin's Live Coals of Fire and was being edited by J.H. King and A.E. Robinson. Once Cashwell arrived, both he and King headed up the meeting. Although it started slowly, the Royston meetings also became a huge success for Cashwell and the Pentecostal Movement. As a result, all of the ministers and members associated with the Fire-Baptized Holiness Church embraced the Pentecostal revival and accepted its teachings. Soon, a church convention was held at Anderson, South Carolina, and the doctrines of the F.B.H.C. were revised "in harmony with the new revelation of the truth."[11]

Cashwell also recorded the success of his Georgia campaigns within the pages of The Apostolic Faith. From Royston, Cashwell wrote:

> Hundreds of souls in the South have received the baptism with the Holy Ghost and speak in other tongues. Closed a series of meetings at Toccoa, Georgia, Sunday night. God was with us in great power from start to finish. I did not keep an account of how many received their Pentecost, but they all spoke in tongues, and all that receive the baptism with the Holy Ghost will speak in tongues.[12]

Despite J.H. King's skeptical view of Gaston's ministry, the Pentecostal power flowing from Cashwell's presence proved to be too much for King. Like A.B. Crumpler, G.B. Cashwell discerned that many people in Toccoa had been, "gulled by take-it-by-faith, re-consecrate, baptism of fire, 'dynamite,' and 'lydite' beliefs" until the faith of the people was almost gone. Incredibly, through Cashwell's efforts, the Fire-Baptized Movement was literally transformed overnight.[13]

Indeed, the coming of Rev. Cashwell to Georgia would be transformational on many levels. The aftermath of these services resulted with the conversion of a major church leader and entire denomination. Georgia, however, was only to be the first of many stops that Cashwell would make during his Pentecostal missionary journeys.

Cashwell, Crumpler, and Pentecost

Historically, scholars have always attributed A.B. Crumpler as being G.B. Cashwell's biggest opponent concerning Pentecost. This belief has been firmly rooted in the IPHC history which was composed from the memory of G.F. Taylor, A.H. Butler, and J.H. King. It has been their own opinions and prejudices that have shaped the public's understanding of G.B. Cashwell and A.B. Crumpler's relationship.

According to their interpretation of the story, A.B. Crumpler was upset with Cashwell over the new Azusa Street theology and promised Taylor that he would oppose Cashwell should he teach that speaking in tongues was the evidence of the baptism of the Spirit. Additionally, Taylor wrote, "Our president and editor (A.B. Crumpler) was at first silent on the subject in the Advocate. Later he began to write against it, and soon grew very bitter in his attacks." Yet, no such comments have ever been found. As far as we know, there is not one documented account written by A.B. Crumpler that belittles, opposes, or refutes neither G.B. Cashwell nor the Pentecostal Movement in general. Instead, a deeper investigation into A.B. Crumpler's profile reveals that he embraced the baptism of the Holy Spirit with speaking in tongues and supported both the Pentecostal Movement and his old friend G.B. Cashwell.[14]

This is first evident in A.B. Crumpler's own Pentecostal encounter. About the same time J.H. King and the Fire-baptizers were experiencing the power of Pentecost, Cashwell's longtime friend, A.B. Crumpler, was also being filled with the Holy Ghost. Although Crumpler was absent for Cashwell's Dunn revival, its influence did captivate the "Father of Holiness." He published his Pentecostal experience in the Holiness Advocate on June 1, 1907. Entitled "He Satisfies: He Abides," Crumpler shares an interesting journey he had with the Holy Spirit. "On March 15, at 3 o'clock in the afternoon," the burning revivalist wrote that he had been filled with the "blessed Holy Ghost" resulting in him "begging forgiveness" from people he had offended. Gripped by the soul searching baptism of love, the Holy Spirit even revealed to Crumpler a twenty year old matter that he needed to repent of. Eager to answer the Holy Spirit's charge, Rev. Crumpler joyfully confessed, "But it is all over now! Praise our God. It was all accomplished through Him the blessed Comforter."[15]

Following this divine encounter, on April 23, 1907, while ministering at Walnut Creek Free Will Baptist Church, Crumpler wrote:

> I took off my hat and knelt down on the oak leaves, and began to pray in a low whisper. I soon began to weep; and in a few moments I had such a revelation of the awful doom of a soul lost in hell as I had never seen before. I began to groan and weep and pray aloud. Oh what an agony for lost souls! For quite a half an hour this awful burden rested upon me. I felt that my heart would break. Suddenly, the burden rolled away and I ceased to pray. Then in the next moment I began to pray in A Language such I had never heard; therefore unknown to me. It seemed that someone else was doing the praying, and yet I knew

> the sounds I heard were coming from my own lips. But not a word could I comprehend with my mental understanding (Bold print is on the original text).[16]

From this testimony, it is obvious that Rev. Crumpler received the Pentecostal experience as defined by the early Azusa Street founders. Even so, A.B. Crumpler's Pentecostal encounter was more convincing than that of J.H. King's and other ministers who would go on to form the IPHC. It is also important to remember that during the first few months in 1907, the Pentecostal spirit was loosed in the atmosphere. Revival was exploding all over eastern North Carolina and the nation. Nearly every one of Crumpler's co-ministers had accepted the Holy Spirit baptism by this point. Whether attending a prayer meeting, going to church, praying at home, or "kneeling down on the oak leaves," people everywhere were stepping into the fires of Pentecost.[17]

Over the next eight days at the Walnut Creek revival, A.B. Crumpler began to preach his recent and fresh encounter with the Holy Spirit. This resulted in many conversions and several country folks receiving the Pentecostal baptism. Crumpler writes:

> We had three services on the last day. The house was filled at the morning and afternoon hours, and at night the house was packed to overflowing, and people stood on the outside at the windows and doors to hear the Word. There were about 15 conversions; 5 or 6 sanctified, and 4 received the Holy Ghost in His abiding fullness.[18]

This testimony is significant. By distinguishing between those who were sanctified and those who were filled with the Holy Ghost, A.B. Crumpler's theological position on sanctification had shifted. Like many holiness proponents, Crumpler believed that the Pentecostal baptism occurred during the sanctified experience. He did not believe that the Baptism of the Holy Spirit was a third step transpiring after sanctification. Yet, after his own encounter with the Holy Spirit, A.B. Crumpler realized that the Pentecost G.B. Cashwell was preaching was the real thing, and that there was another step in "receiving the fullness of the Holy Ghost." Moreover, under A.B. Crumpler's new and Pentecostal inspired preaching, people were coming under the mantle of Pentecost.

Exciting as this sounds, the buck does not stop here. Also during April 1907, A.B. Crumpler joined the Pentecostal fraction of Free Will Baptists and formed a committee to help rescue the "fallen women" of Wilmington, North Carolina. Meeting at Lebanon F.W.B. Church outside Clinton, the Pentecostal believing Baptist chose a group of ministers that would oversee the Seaside Rescue Home which stood at 516 Church Street in Wilmington,

North Carolina. Among those serving on the committee were, W.W. Avant, O.B. Garris, J.A. Blalock, C.J. Carr, S.N. Thrower, E.L. Parker, Edith Pope, Florence Goff, Lazzetta McLaughlin, Berta Maxwell, and A.B. Crumpler. Interestingly, nearly all of these ministers (except Crumpler) had been present in Cashwell's Dunn revival in January 1907 and had been baptized in the Holy Spirit. In addition, Edith Pope was G.B. Cashwell's sister-in-law and next door neighbor to the Cashwells. Besides sitting on this Pentecostal committee, Crumpler had the Holiness Church elect three trustees to oversee the home's financial establishment. They were A.H. Butler. G.F. Taylor, and C.B. Strickland. In agreement, the Pentecostal Free Will Baptists also elected three trustees of the Cape Fear conference to make the home both interdenominational and Pentecostal.[19]

In addition, the committee agreed that sister McLaughlin would reside as the recognized leader of the women's home. According to Florence Goff, Mrs. McLaughlin was the Pentecostal saint who had been crying out, "O God, do give brother Goff the Holy Ghost," in G.B. Cashwell's Dunn meeting. She is also the same women who attended the 1907 Falcon Camp Meeting along with G.B. Cashwell and A.B. Crumpler. Accordingly, Eddie Morris noted that while at the Falcon encampment, she was the one who "moved softly across the tabernacle floor" while speaking in tongues.[20]

> Impressed with her ability to preach the Word, A.B. Crumpler wrote an article about Mrs. McLaughlin's Pentecostal work in eastern North Carolina. Published on May 15, 1907, Crumpler states, "While down in the Burgaw section at Bro. R.B. Jackson's meeting it was our pleasure and privilege to meet sister McLaughlin of the Pentecostal Mission, of Nashville, Tenn., who was working in the meeting. She is a devout child of God and a splendid worker and a clear and forceful preacher of the Word."

Although there is no information regarding the results of the Burgaw services, it's important to recognize that this meeting was a Pentecostal meeting, With R.B. Jackson and Mrs. McLaughlin leading the charge, A.B. Crumpler seemed to really have enjoyed himself and these two Pentecostal firebrands.[21]

In spite of A.B. Crumpler's renewed spiritual encounter, he began to sense that he was not fit to lead this new charge. Physically, his body was beginning to take a beating after spearheading the eastern North Carolina Holiness Movement for eleven years. After the Walnut Creek meeting closed on April 29, 1907, Crumpler wrote that he returned home "with a weak and broken down body." Though he had been spiritually refreshed, Crumpler retreated home and rested for about a week. Feeling better, Crumpler next traveled to La Grange,

North Carolina, and held a Pentecostal meeting during mid-May 1907. Here, two dear sisters had been baptized with the Holy Spirit under his preaching. Yet, because of physical conditions Crumpler had to bring the meeting to an early close. He wrote, "On account of my physical weakness which makes it necessary for me to rest a few days before our next meeting, we shall be forced to close here tomorrow night."[22] During this point, A.B. Crumpler began to slowly withdraw from the spotlight, while G.B. Cashwell began to advance the movement in great power.

In retrospect, it appears the A.B. Crumpler knew that his time as founder and church leader in the Holiness Movement was coming to a close. This, no doubt, was God's divine plan. Like John the Baptist prepared an entire nation to receive the new ministry of Jesus, so it seems that A.B. Crumpler prepared North Carolina and the South, to receive the ministry of Gaston Barnabas Cashwell. Perhaps this is who Crumpler had in mind when he confessed, "I am completely divested of all earthly plans. I have no engagements but what seems to me could be filled better by someone else..."[23] In that same last issue of A.B. Crumpler's paper (June 1, 1907), Crumpler listed Rev. G.B. Cashwell as one of "Our Evangelists" revealing his full support of the Pentecostal catalyst. Maybe they were not enemies after all.[24]

Cashwell and N.J. Holmes

After leaving Royston, Georgia, Cashwell made another historic stop in West Union, South Carolina, around March 23, 1907. West Union resided in the backyard of a Holiness-Presbyterian minister named Nickels John Holmes (N.J. Holmes). Rev. N.J. Holmes, a native of Laurens, South Carolina, grew up in a strong Christian home during the 1850s. Although his father (Rev. Zelotes Lee Holmes) was an ordained Presbyterian minister, it appears that N.J. Holmes path to salvation was largely influenced by his mother, Catherine Nickels Holmes. Catherine Holmes came to know the Lord through one of her father's slaves. In writing of the "colored women's" Godly example, Mrs. Nickels wrote, "When I was about seven-years-old there lived in our family a colored women, a slave, who seemed to think that it was her duty to teach the children in the family, white and black, their religious duties..."[25] Subsequently, Catherine N. Holmes found herself in church and began to develop a mature relationship with the Savior. The wisdom of Mrs. C.N. Holmes was later exposed when her son, Rev. N.J. Holmes, wrote, "I surly rejoice and thank God that He has led me, and enabled me in a measure to carry out what was on my mother's heart..." Unbeknownst to the slave women, her godly impact on the N.J. Holmes family would be critical in spreading the Holiness- Pentecostal Movement around the globe.[26]

Following his father's footsteps, N.J. Holmes was ordained in the South Carolina Presbyterian Church in 1888. Seven years later, while searching for a deeper Christian experience, N.J. Holmes found himself in a holiness prayer meeting. Being led by a band of burning Methodists, Mr. Holmes became "sanctified" during this meeting in July 1895. Like many other denominational ministers, N.J. Holmes soon broke away from the Presbyterian Church for his acceptance of the holiness doctrine. Undeterred, Holmes quickly began to spread holiness among his Presbyterian brothers and sisters. Dr. Synan notes that the outcome of this furious work resulted in about a "dozen churches known as the Brewerton Presbyterian Church." After forming themselves into a small Holiness denomination, Rev. N.J. Holmes organized the Altamont Bible and Missionary Institute in November of 1898.[27]

Similar to J.H. King, Holmes was initially skeptical of the Pentecostal explosion that was breaking out under G.B. Cashwell's ministry in 1907. Struggling with the theological expression of tongues, Holmes did not believe that the Pentecostal experienced was confirmed through the speaking of unknown tongues. When meetings began by the end of March 1907, Holmes attended merely as a spectator. In this service, Cashwell allowed Pinkie Blake to have charge of the meeting while he (G.B.) calmly remained in the backdrop waiting for the right time to give an alter call. Though many went forward and received their Pentecost, N.J. Holmes did not. Admittedly, Holmes confessed that when he heard Pinkie Blake singing in tongues it was like "the sweetest and most heavenly music" he had ever heard. However, N.J. Holmes continually struggled with the theological position that G.B. Cashwell was presenting before him.[28]

After the West Union meetings closed and Cashwell left, Holmes continued to seek God about the Pentecostal baptism. Accordingly, on April 22, 1907, Holmes had an encounter with the Holy Spirit where he wrote that the Holy Ghost "gave me at that time only the very rudiments of language." However, not fully convinced that the speaking of tongues was the initial evidence of the baptism itself, Holmes began to once again backtrack in his views towards Pentecost. This uncertainty came to an end when G.F. Taylor arrived in June 1907.[29]

Taylor, who received his Pentecost under Cashwell, led a Pentecostal revival that rocked the foundations of the small Bible school. During this meeting, N.J. Holmes, and "quite a number of the students, received the baptism of the Spirit." This fresh encounter made the Altamont Bible and Missionary Institute the first Pentecostal Bible college in the nation. In 1915, N.J. Holmes's denomination joined the ranks of the Pentecostal Holiness Church. The Altamont Bible Institute also followed. Today the Altamont school is the oldest Pentecostal College in the country. It located in Greenville, South Carolina, and is known as Holmes Bible College.[30]

Although N.J. Holmes wasn't directly converted under Cashwell's meeting, it was Gaston's fiery ministry that indirectly broke Rev. Holmes's doubt and unbelief. J.E. Campbell later wrote that N.J. Holmes and G.B. Cashwell conducted a service together the following summer in Clinton. Although Campbell does not list the state, it is almost certain that this joint meeting took place in Clinton, South Carolina, during the summer months of 1908. Nonetheless, with the conversion of N.J. Holmes and the small denomination under his care, G.B. Cashwell's blazingly ministry was beginning to catch national significance.[31]

Cashwell and the Assemblies of God

With N.J. Holmes and J.H. King under the Pentecostal banner, Cashwell set his sights on Birmingham, Alabama. Arriving in Birmingham on April 17, 1907, Gaston conducted a meeting that would have historic significance. It was here that Mack M. Pinson attended and first heard of Cashwell's powerful ministry. Born in 1873, M.M. Pinson grew up on a cotton farm in rural Georgia. At the age of twenty he was saved in a Missionary Baptist Church Revival. Feeling a deeper hunger for more of God, Pinson embraced the Holiness Movement around the turn of century. His own journey on the "highway of holiness" led him to J.O. McClurkan of Nashville, Tennessee, in 1902. In Nashville, McClurkan operated a holiness school known as the Pentecostal Mission Bible and Literary Institute. After becoming a holiness student, Pinson was ordained through McClurkan's ministry in 1903.[32]

Following the Pentecostal Movement closely, Pinson heard of G.B. Cashwell's meeting being held in Birmingham, in April 1907. Stirred with curiosity, M.M. Pinson and H.G. Rodgers, a friend of Pinson's, quickly rushed to see the large framed man burning with Pentecostal fire. During the brief two day meeting, many people were supernaturally healed and delivered. Others, like Anna Dean Cole, were experiencing the wondrous baptism with the Holy Spirit. Ms. Cole, a young teenager, became the first person in the Birmingham revival to receive the Pentecostal baptism. Doug Beacham notes that through this amazing encounter, this young lady was given the gift of languages. By 1912, the young Anna arrived in Hong Kong as a missionary and assisted her aunt, Anna Dean, who had founded the Wing Kwong School in 1910.[33]

Despite the success of Birmingham, Pinson and Rodgers still remained unsure of the message that Cashwell was laying down before them. As soon as the Birmingham meeting came to a close, Cashwell received an invitation to Memphis, Tennessee. Although not yet converted, Pinson and Rodgers still had a growing appetite for the Pentecostal experience. They both followed Cashwell to Memphis, where Gaston had been invited to lead a revival in a small Independent Holiness Church. This small congregation had been following the great Welsh revival of 1904 under Evan Roberts as well as the 1906 Pentecostal outbreak in Los Angeles. Hearing of Cashwell's southern travels, they were eager to receive the Pentecostal message from someone who had been in the Azusa Mission.[34]

Lasting for about a month, the Memphis meetings were full of both revival and warfare. Cashwell wrote a letter to The Apostolic Faith reporting the conditions deep in the South. He writes:

> May 2– The Lord our God is with us at this place, and that saints are receiving their Pentecost. I have never met with such power of the Devil as here. One man came to the service and dragged his wife from the alter by force and threatened to kill me and others. But, glory to God, he was overpowered by our God. His wife got the baptism and spoke in tongues, and last night he was back to the service and says he must have his Pentecost. Praise God.[35]

Although Cashwell fails to mention other details about opposition he was facing, it is important to remember that Gaston was preaching an integrated message under an integrated anointing in the deep South. During his ministry, many would reject his efforts on the basis of two things: speaking in tongues and his close relationship with the black race.

Despite strong resistance, Cashwell did witness a major victory while in Memphis. Here, Pinson and Rodgers's quest for Pentecost was finally fulfilled. Preaching with incredible authority, Cashwell's messages destroyed all of Pinson and Rodger's theological reservations. On May 8, while praying in bed, Pinson received his Pentecost. Shortly after, Pinson and Rodgers organized the Pentecostal Association of the Mississippi Valley. Organic, and loosely affiliated, this association embodied the states of Alabama and Mississippi and continued to expand into the Southern regions of the country. In 1914, Pinson and Rodger's association joined with other independent Pentecostal groups and formed what is now known as the Assemblies of God. Pinson, along with seven other ministers, resided on the First General Council of the Assemblies of God. In later years, the AG denomination grew to become the largest white Pentecostal body in the world.[36]

G.B. Cashwell also had another divine appointment while he was in Tennessee. His Memphis letter reveals that he met with Pentecostal catalyst, Charles H. Mason. Being the head of a large black holiness denomination,

Mason was another significant force in spreading the flames of Pentecost. Mason, who was a black minister, is most famously recognized for helping organize the Church of God in Christ. Born to former slaves, Mason was reared outside Memphis on the Prior plantation. Like G.B. Cashwell, Mason emerged from a Colored Missionary Baptist Church. He was baptized in 1880 and by 1891, was ordained and licensed to preach the good news. A few years later, Mason came into contact with the Holiness Movement through the writings of Amanda Smith. After reading Smith's life story, Mason claimed the sanctified experience of a clean heart.[37]

In 1895 C.H. Mason met another black Baptist minister named C.P. Jones. Together, they shook the South's black population with sanctified messages and powerful worship. Through their trailblazing efforts, many black holiness congregations appeared throughout the South. According to Jones, most of these churches were interdenominational and interracial. After becoming increasingly dissatisfied with the Baptists, however, Mason and Jones broke away from the Baptist Church and founded the Church of God in Christ (COGIC). The COGIC quickly became the largest black holiness denomination in the nation. During this time, Mason and Jones were inseparable. With the advent of Azusa Street, however, their relationship would be torn asunder.[38]

Hearing of the marvelous reports bursting from 312 Azusa Street, C.H. Mason traveled from Tennessee to Los Angeles. Directly under William Seymour's leading, Mason received the Pentecostal experience he longed for on March 19, 1907. After staying with Seymour for five weeks, Mason returned to Tennessee burning with a new message. Unfortunately, it was not well received by his co-laborer, C.P. Jones. Divided over the Azusa Street beliefs, Mason and Jones parted company causing a church split. As a result, Mason become the recognized head of the interracial COGIC, and brought the young denomination under the Pentecostal banner. Immediately, the young Pentecostal church began to spread like wild fire.[39]

By the time G.B. Cashwell arrived in Memphis in April 1907, Mason had just returned from the Azusa Mission on fire with the Pentecostal message. Cashwell briefly wrote of his time spent with "Bro. Mason" while in Tennessee. Of their meeting, Cashwell writes, "I heard from Bro. Mason's church. The power is falling and many souls are being filled and speaking in tongues. I met Bro. Mason last week and found him filled with the blessed Holy Ghost. He is a precious brother."[40] Cashwell's remarks about Mason are revealing and intriguing.

They show that Cashwell continued to build interracial, Pentecostal relationships and possibly ministered within Mason's church. According to Dr. Synan, Mason's followers made up the largest black denomination in the world during this time. Certainly, a welcoming reception from Mason would have opened numerous doors into the Southern black community for Cashwell's ministry. Cashwell also defined Mason as a "precious brother" which bears sociological significance. In a day when blacks were shown no reverence and were often referred to by whites as "auntie," "uncle," "boy" and so forth, G.B. Cashwell addressed Mason with an affectionate greeting of brotherly love-the lasting evidence of the Pentecostal baptism. Unfortunately, there are no other known sources revealing the relationship between C.H. Mason and G.B. Cashwell.[41]

In later years, under C.H. Mason's exceptional leadership, many white Pentecostal ministers came to him for ordination between 1907 and 1914. Being the only Pentecostal incorporated denomination at that time, many whites flocked to Mason for their preaching credentials. However, in 1914 when the American Pentecostal Movement began to bow her knee to the spirit of segregation, most of these ministers broke away from C.H. Mason and the COGIC. Disenchanted with the idea of submitting under black leadership, they formed their own all white Pentecostal denomination: The Assemblies of God. Even so, the lasting impact of Cashwell's and Mason's ministry is undeniable. Today, nearly every Southern Pentecostal denomination in the United States, white or black, can trace their roots to either G.B. Cashwell or C.H. Mason

THE BRIDEGROOM'S MESSENGER: THE VOICE OF THE SOUTH

Following his time spent in Birmingham and Memphis, G.B. Cashwell traveled to Atlanta, Georgia, in June 1907, and led another historic revival. Unfortunately, details about the Atlanta meetings remain absent; however, we do know that through these powerful meetings, the Atlanta Mission was birthed. Situated on 53 1–2 Auburn Ave., the Pentecostal Atlanta Mission quickly became a stronghold for the Pentecostal Movement in the South. Even after six months of operation, the Atlanta mission ran services night and day in order to host the open heaven atmosphere invading the city.[42]

Mrs. Sexton, G.B. Cashwell's future co-editor, described the Atlanta Mission revivals by writing:

> Every afternoon and every night meetings are held in the Pentecostal Mission, 53 1–2 Auburn Avenue. More than six months the revival has continued, and still the interest is kept up and the tide runs high. Sometimes the weather being inclement, perhaps a pouring rain, you decide surly no one will be there such a night as this, but if you go you will find them praising God, singing and talking in new tongues,

> praying for the sick and rejoicing together in His loving service. Pastors and workers from different churches have visited the mission with an honest desire to investigate and they have wondered what it all meant. They could not explain away the wonderful manifestation of the power of God in our midst; they could not fight it lest they be found fighting against God…Many who received the Pentecostal baptism have gone out into service, holding meetings where hungry souls were waiting for God to send someone to tell them about Pentecost.[43]

Indeed, through G.B. Cashwell's influence, the city of Atlanta was being shaken under the power of God. Under this atmosphere, tumors and diseases were falling off the sick, teenagers were burning hot with the love of Jesus, and the elderly were being "transported and filled unutterably full of glory and of God." Mrs. Sexton also notes that Pentecostal messengers were leaving the mission and scattering coals of revival fire all over the city.[44]

Besides the supernatural phenomena breaking out on Atlanta's streets, the Atlanta Mission also became the birthplace of G.B. Cashwell's Bridegroom's Messenger. Recognizing the national impact that his ministry was having, G.B. Cashwell was prompted to start a newspaper that would carry the "Pentecostal Truth" to the South. Due to the success of the Atlanta meetings, Cashwell chose the mission on Auburn Avenue to begin publication. Cashwell published the first copy on October 1, 1907, in which he was listed as its first editor. Although southern holiness papers like J.M. Pikes Way of Faith, King's Apostolic Evangel, and Crumpler's Holiness Advocate, did carry some Pentecostal testimonies, letters, and teachings, it would be G.B. Cashwell's Bridegroom's Messenger, that became the authoritative voice in the South for the Pentecostal Movement. This paper, however, would always remain separate and detached from the North Carolina Holiness Church. Reasons for this will be discussed in the next chapter.[45]

In addition to establishing a Pentecostal paper for the South, Cashwell also used the Bridegroom's Messenger to explain his theological views, record testimonies, and give southerners a view of the movement that was sweeping the world. Like Seymour's Apostolic Faith, Cashwell's paper also had a global dynamic to it. Many of its columns are littered with testimonies from Pentecostal missionaries that were being sent to the nations of the earth. Incredible reports from India, China, Japan, Africa, Egypt, England, Sweden, and Jerusalem revealed that the Pentecostal Movement was not only ripping through the nation, but the entire world.

Under the Holy Spirit baptism, all the nations of the earth were becoming one. Even among non-believing Jews in Palestine, the power of Pentecost was exploding throughout the Jewish population. Missionary

Lucy Leatherman, who received her Pentecost at Azusa Street, was sent to Jerusalem to spread the revival. She writes:

> Perhaps not far from this very spot where the first Pentecostal baptism fell on the 120 souls in the upper room, the same power is felt again. Hallelujah! Praises burst forth as we see, with prophetic vision, the dear old city of Jerusalem being shaken again by the power of God as on the day of Pentecost. Five have had the baptism of the Holy Ghost and speak in tongues as the Spirit gives utterance.[46]

Leatherman goes on to reveal that she, along with others, was trying to organize a rescue mission and an office for a printing press in the Holy city. Seized with an incredible conviction to help God's chosen people, Sister Lucy and others stopped at nothing to bring revival back to Israel.[47]

T.J. McIntosh was also in Jerusalem assisting sister Leatherman. McIntosh, who joined A.B. Crumpler's Holiness Convention at Lumberton in 1906, became an Apostolic Faith missionary after receiving his Pentecost. Having a heart for the nations, McIntosh traveled the four corners of the earth spreading the flames of Pentecost everywhere he went. While in Jerusalem, he visited the Garden of Gethsemane and had an amazing experience. McIntosh writes, "The Holy Spirit spoke with my tongue to a priest, and threw his arms around me, laughed and patted me on the shoulder, and repeated the same words that the Spirit spoke with my tongue."[48] G.B. Cashwell faithfully recorded and listed articles like these all throughout his paper. In addition, Cashwell also kept accounts of Jews returning to Palestine. He, like these missionaries, loved the Jewish people and desired for them to regain control of their land. Forty years later, in 1948, Cashwell's hopes were fulfilled when Israel became nation.[49]

Cashwell and the Church of God

As the year 1907 came to a close, Cashwell's whirlwind of ministry in the South had ushered in several denominations, hundreds of churches, countless ministers, and a major newspaper into the Pentecostal Movement. Amazingly, 1908 for G.B. Cashwell would start off no differently. Hearing of Cashwell's effects in the South, Church of God founder, A.J. Tomlinson, sought to host the son of Pentecost in January 1908. Tomlinson, who is credited for being "one of the great organizing geniuses of modern American church history," has one of the best documented accounts of a Pentecostal encounter. His Spirit-led journey to January 12, 1908, and how it intertwines with Cashwell as well as the Tar Heel state, is exciting.[50]

Ambrose Jessup Tomlinson (1865–1943) was born into an Indiana Quaker family in a small town known as Westfield. He was saved in the year 1889, and soon after embraced the holiness message. Gripped with a missionary calling for the South's rural populations, A.J. Tomlinson was divinely directed to the mountaineers of western North Carolina, eastern Tennessee, and northern Georgia. By 1899, Tomlinson and his family relocated to Culberson, North Carolina. Here, Tomlinson began the work that had been blazing within his heart. Dr. Roebuck notes that while in Culbertson, Tomlinson "founded a school for children, a Sunday school, a clothing distribution center, and an orphanage." In 1903, after several years of incredible ministry, Tomlinson found a home amidst a small Holiness Church in a neighboring community known as Camp Creek.[51]

The Holiness Church of Camp Creek had sprung to life through an extraordinary Holiness-Pentecostal revival that ripped through the area in 1896. Incredibly, ten years prior to Azusa Street, the mountains of North Carolina were rocked with the manifestations of speaking in tongues. More commonly known as the "Revival at Camp Creek," this heavenly outbreak started among North Carolina's Cherokee Indians and spread into parts of Tennessee and Georgia. Under this atmosphere, people in this remote community were falling into trances, shaking, jerking, and "speaking in other tongues as the Spirit gave utterance." It is the earliest account in American history where the baptism of the Holy Spirit with speaking in tongues was poured out. Incredibly, this initial outpouring of the Holy Spirit took place in North Carolina, adding to the rich spiritual legacy of the Old North State.[52]

The birth of this revival seems to have begun with the growing intercession of Richard Spurling and his son, R.G. Spurling Jr., in neighboring Tennessee. Ten years earlier, the father and son team organized the Christian Union, which was an independent body that sought to bring unity to all of the denominations. While R.G. Spurling Jr. was still ministering near the Tennessee-North Carolina boarder, the revival at Camp Creek erupted. Soon, word spread across the mountains and people from all over the region were flocking to the Camp Creek community. Meeting in the Shearer Schoolhouse, a one-room impoverished mountain school, the revival was unlike anything anyone had seen before.[53]

By 1903, the Holiness Church at Camp Creek was looking for someone to lead them into the future. They found it in the Indiana preacher, A.J. Tomlinson. Tomlinson's vision for the newly established congregation took the church far beyond the borders of Camp Creek. In December 1904, Tomlinson moved from Culbertson, North Carolina, to Cleveland, Tennessee. Located in Bradley County, Cleveland became Tomlinson's centralized hub of holiness activity, and in later years, a stronghold for

The Church of God (Cleveland, Tennessee). Still overseeing the Holiness Church at Camp Creek, Tomlinson and others impacted the surrounding region by establishing multiple churches. Sensing the need to unify all of their churches, the young holiness denomination called for their first general assembly in 1906. One year later, during their second general assembly, these holiness pioneers identified themselves as the Church of God. Under the outstanding leadership of A.J. Tomlinson, the Church of God planted churches throughout Tennessee, Georgia, Kentucky, West Virginia, and North Carolina.[54]

Having followed G.B. Cashwell's Pentecostal campaigns, A.J. Tomlinson was impressed to invite Cashwell to the Church of God's third general assembly in January 1908. Prior to Cashwell's arrival, Tomlinson had been holding tarrying meetings for several weeks in anticipation of the outpouring of the Holy Spirit. G.B. Cashwell arrived in Cleveland, Tennessee, on the evening of January 10, and began preaching the next night.[55]

Thankfully, Tomlinson recorded Cashwell's spectacular meeting in his diary. An exuberant Tomlinson writes:

> Our Assembly consumed the last three days of last week. Sat. night Bro. Cashwell preached and on Sunday, yesterday, at nearly the close of his discourse, the Spirit so affected me that I slid down off my chair onto the floor, on the rostrum, and as I went down I yielded myself up to God; and after a considerable agony and groans my jaws seemed to be set, my lips were moved and twisted about as if an examination of them were being made. After that my tongue was operated on in like manner, also my eyes. Several examinations seemed to be taken, and every limb of my body was operated on in like manner, and finally, while laying on my bath (sic) both of my feet were raised right up in the air several times. Then I felt myself lifted as in a great sheet of power of some kind, and moved in the air in the direction my feet pointed.

Tomlinson's remarkable testimony goes on explain that while on the floor, he was taken in the Spirit to ten different countries. With each country, he was given the tongue of that particular nation. From South America to Europe; from the Middle East to Africa; and from Russia back to Cleveland, Tomlinson visited the continents of the earth. His experience became a defining moment in his personal life and the denomination he helped build.[56]

As the Cleveland meeting progressed with great success, Cashwell reported to the Bridegroom's Messenger some of the results. Cashwell notes:

> I am, at this writing, in Cleveland, Tenn., with brother Tomlinson. Services have been held here for several days, the church at large being

> assembled in convention. Several of the preachers from different places came here after their regular services last night. I was asked to speak as the Lord might direct. I gave only few minutes' talk and asked the Holy Ghost to come to the altar. The altar was full in a minute and many knelt in the aisle. We are expecting great things here if everybody will stay out of the way of the Holy Ghost.[57] Continuing to operate as a spiritual facilitator rather than preacher, Cashwell allowed the Holy Spirit to have full control of the meetings. Even so, Cashwell ends the letter by revealing a certain degree of opposition while he was holding the Cleveland revival.

Tomlinson seems to identify Cashwell's struggle in his diary. Dated January 20, 1908, Tomlinson wrote:

> We have been continuing the meetings ever since I last wrote. Sat. night the house was full. Last night it was packed and many had to leave because they could not get in. Yesterday afternoon in the service an M.E. preacher withstood Bro. Cashwell to the face about tongues, but it all worked out for good. He made a fool of himself and showed it to the entire audience, and the affair won hearts to the truth. We raised $37.04 for Bro. Cashwell. I preached at night.[58]

Despite this personal attack, G.B. Cashwell was not moved. Handled by the Spirit of God, Gaston showed no signs of retaliation against the disgruntled preacher. Rather, he allowed God to fight his battle. This, as we shall later see, was a reoccurring theme within Cashwell's ministry. Impressed with Gaston's ability to handle conflict, Tomlinson and the Church of God raised "$37.04" for Cashwell's ministry during the Cleveland revival.

G.B. Cashwell Takes the Fire North

Although Cashwell is widely recognized for his southern influence, Gaston did fan the flames of Pentecost into northern states as well. According to a letter he wrote in the Bridegroom's Messenger, Cashwell made his northern journey sometime in May 1908. Cashwell states:

> My visit to the different missions in the northern states and Canada has given us great encouragement. I have found in many places increased power among the workers, in the healing of the sick, and casting out devils, and doing of the work of the ministry in general. My fist stop after I left home in Dunn, N.C., was at Dartmouth, V.A. There I met some as earnest souls as I ever met. The saints at Dartmouth have their regular meetings at private homes, and then hold street meetings in the city on Sunday. I had the blessed privilege of being with them in one of these meetings. There are several hungry saints seeking the baptism at Portsmouth. From Portsmouth we went

> to Washington D.C., and found many earnests and honest workers in the Pentecostal Movement.[59]

While in Washington D.C., Cashwell goes on to add:

> We had blessed fellowship with the saints in Washington, and some glorious services in Sister Perry's home. The regular meetings are held in Sister Perry's double parlors. One dear sister from Mississippi received while we were there. She had been seeking her baptism for several months. Praise God, the Comforter has come! We all went on Sunday to the colored Mission and held two of the most glorious services with Brother and Sister Thomas. The power of God is mightily moving on this mission. About $150 was raised on Sunday to get a larger hall for their services. Praise God take courage and move on.[60]

Although every stop Cashwell made was significant, his arrival in Portsmouth, Virginia and Washington D.C. seems to have been racially motivated. Evidence for this is seen through Lucy Farrow and C.H. Mason's early work in the Hampton Roads community.

In the fall of 1906 Portsmouth, Virginia, had been the site of a powerful Pentecostal revival under the preaching of Lucy Farrow. Sold into slavery as young girl in Norfolk, Virginia, Farrow, in later years, became a free women and a soldier for the gospel. She, along with William J. Seymour and J.A. Warren, were the original three that God used to spark the Azusa Street revival. Three months before G.B. Cashwell ignited the Pentecostal fire in Dunn, North Carolina, Sister Lucy was holding glorious meetings in Portsmouth, Virginia. Writing form 907 Glasken Street, Farrow reported that many had been baptized with the Holy Spirit in the October 1906 issue of Seymour's Apostolic Faith.[61]

C.H Mason, the African-American preacher from Memphis, also visited the city of Portsmouth, Virginia, in April 1907. Fueled by his Pentecostal baptism experience, Mason held a powerful revival that rocked the old waterside city. By its close, 6,000 people had received the Holy Spirit, and the Hampton roads area was set ablaze with revival fire. Unfortunately, there are no records revealing where Cashwell preached in Portsmouth. Being acquainted with both Mason and Farrow, G.B. Cashwell most likely followed the path of Sister Lucy and C.H. Mason when he arrived there in the spring of 1908.[62]

Cashwell's next stop after Portsmouth was in Washington D.C. Here, he ministered in the "colored mission" with Bro. and Sister Thomas. Though details remain absent, Cashwell's visit to the "colored mission" in the nation's capital reveals his lasting compassion towards the black community. Besides ministering there, Cashwell and others also aided the mission by raising money to support their vision. Interestingly enough, while he was with Bro. and Sister Thomas, Cashwell's own rescue mission was opening upon the streets of Wilmington, North Carolina. This will be discussed in the next chapter.[63]

Having boarded the train in Washington, Cashwell rode to Potter Brook, Pennsylvania. At Potter Brook, Cashwell reported a "blessed ingathering" of saints that came as far as New York to hear the burning revivalist. Described by Cashwell as the "Jerusalem" of that region, the Potter Brook meetings became a "feast of spiritual things" for hungry seekers. Leaving Pennsylvania, G.B. Cashwell went to Toronto, Canada, where he and others were in the "heat of battle at Brother Sawder's mission." Accordingly, Cashwell noted that some of Toronto's most prominent people were on their faces seeking God for the baptism of the Spirit at the mission. Cashwell left Toronto and traveled to Bristol, Florida, where he held special services at Florida's annual Camp Meeting.[64]

Amazingly, in less than two years, G.B. Cashwell's apostolic ministry shifted the entire atmosphere of the South. Compelled by passion and gripped with spiritual power, Cashwell empowered whole movements to love their brother regardless of color or doctrinal beliefs. Whether flowing as an apostle, prophet, evangelist, pastor, teacher, revivalist, writer, intercessor, or father of the movement, Cashwell moved an entire generation to seek the fullness of the Holy Ghost.

Through his leading, A.B. Crumpler, J.H. King, A.H. Butler, G.F. Taylor, N.J. Holmes, A.J. Tomlinson, M.M. Pinson, and other national church leaders were swept into his blazing message of love. The aftermath of this resulted in the conversions of the: Fire-Baptized Holiness Church, the Brewerton Presbyterian Church, the Church of God, Assemblies of God, the North Carolina Holiness Church, the Pentecostal Free Will-Baptist Church, and many others. Unfortunately, not everyone would rejoice in his accomplishments. Little did Gaston know that while spreading the Pentecostal fire around the nation, conditions in his own backyard would begin to deteriorate. Soon, his dynamic ministry would come to a mysterious and abrupt end.[65]

Chapter 15

G.B. CASHWELL'S APOSTOLIC VISION FOR NORTH CAROLINA

BY THE SPRING of 1908, G.B. Cashwell's ministry was exploding all around the world. Growing up in Sampson County, the humble tobacco farmer turned preacher probably never dreamed of becoming one of the most significant figures in American Church History. Yet, in less than two years, Gaston Cashwell had managed to spark massive revivals in North Carolina, South Carolina, Georgia, Florida, Alabama, Mississippi, Tennessee, Oklahoma, Virginia, Washington D.C., Pennsylvania, and Canada. He had crossed over segregated lines and brought spiritual unity among divided races and divided denominations. Even some of Cashwell's converts, like T.J. McIntosh, were flooding the globe and spreading the movement into parts of China, Jerusalem, and India. Having organized the South's leading Pentecostal paper (Bridegroom's Messenger), dozens of missions, and countless churches, G.B. Cashwell now began to set his sights on unfolding his apostolic vision for eastern North Carolina. However, many of his peers whom he had inspired would not be so receptive of Cashwell's ministry in North Carolina.

Internally, another spiritual war for control was about to erupt through the North Carolina Holiness-Pentecostal Movement. This time, the battle would center on G.B. Cashwell and his Pentecostal ministry. As stated in the last chapter, the traditional view advocates the main opponent against Cashwell's efforts was Holiness Church leader, A.B. Crumpler. This, however, may not have been the case. It seems Cashwell may have had other enemies within the North Carolina Holiness Church. Thus, the following chapter will unpack Cashwell's vision for the Old North State, and the events leading up to both his and A.B. Crumpler's mysterious withdrawal from the entire movement.

The Apostolic Mantle

When the Azusa Street Revival first exploded, William J. Seymour did not define the revival or movement as being Pentecostal, but rather Apostolic. In Seymour's view, the Pentecostal baptism experience was only an extension of the movement as a whole. Accordingly, Seymour gave identity to Holy Spirit baptism and the Azusa Street revival by labeling it as the Apostolic Faith Movement. In this first issue of his paper, Seymour published the beliefs of the movement (Azusa Mission). They included: Justification by faith, Sanctification, Baptism with the Holy Ghost as a "gift of power" evidenced by speaking in tongues, supernatural healing, and restoration of all the spiritual gifts.[1]

He also wrote that The Apostolic Faith Movement "stands for the restoration of the faith once delivered unto the saints—the old time religion, camp meetings, revivals, missions, street and prison work and Christian Unity everywhere."[2] Witnessing the sick miraculously healed, devils being cast out, speaking in tongues, prophetic declarations, words of knowledge, and unity between blacks and whites, Seymour and Azusa leaders strongly believed they were an apostolic generation. By identifying themselves as a movement, they also recognized that their apostolic authority was meant to be given away; not segregated nor organized into a denomination. Therefore, ministry to the poor, broken, and distressed became an outlet to manifest their apostolic mantle of ministry.

Having been converted by the "one-eyed black man" under this banner, G.B. Cashwell naturally picked up his apostolic mantle from William J. Seymour. Similar to Seymour, Cashwell manifested his apostolic calling through his dynamic ministry. Like Moses, David, Peter, or Paul of the Bible, Cashwell operated in all five offices of ministry. As an apostle, G.B. Cashwell empowered major church leaders to transform their denominations. As a prophet, he prophetically warned his followers of the dangers to come. As an evangelist, Gaston spread the flames of Pentecost throughout the country. As a pastor, Cashwell shepherded churches and mission halls. As a teacher, G.B. Cashwell theologically expounded upon the Pentecostal baptism as well as the restoration of spiritual gifts. Rather than taking an opportunity to proudly wear any of these titles, however, the rural Carolina preacher continued to humbly walk out his high calling.

By embracing the apostolic mantle of Azusa Street, Cashwell's ministry quickly became a breeding ground for miracles, signs, and wonders. After a very successful year in 1907, G.B. Cashwell began to reveal his apostolic vision for North Carolina in 1908. Like his predecessors at Azusa, Cashwell's vision for the Old North State was manifested through social reform. He began to establish "rescue missions" all around the state. Moving in true apostolic power, Cashwell humbled himself to reach out to those in whom much of the church had discarded—prostitutes.[3]

The Mission

Hearing the voice of his heavenly father, Cashwell's heart began to ache for the city of Wilmington, North Carolina. Ten years prior, in 1898, Wilmington's streets had been filled with bloodshed and violence through the racial massacre that left many homeless. It was also ground zero for the Jim Crow laws that were beginning to shape America's view of "separate but equal." Being sharply divided, Wilmington, in 1908, was quite possibly the most wicked city in North Carolina at this time.[4]

The Evening Dispatch, one of Wilmington's leading newspapers in 1908, confirmed Wilmington's troubles by publishing articles depicting a city on the verge of another wave of racial violence. In an article entitled "Warns Preachers," judges were warning ministers not to discuss the infamous "night riders," nor their activities. Another account reveals Joshua Holland, an African American citizen, being carried to jail for handing a small note to a white women. Convicted in the Mayor's court, Holland was charged with assault and sentenced to thirty days of hard labor. In addition to the usual white anger in Wilmington, 1908 also marked the ten year anniversary of the city's bloody political victory in the revolution of 1898. Meeting at Wilmington's Masonic Temple, many of North Carolina's politicians associated with organizing the race riots hosted a large banquet dinner. The evening was most likely filled with old stories which recounted various brutish tactics that turned a city inside-out, and a nation upside-down. This atmosphere is what most likely drew Cashwell to exhibit the profound love that had overtaken his life and ministry.[5]

Burning with compassion for Wilmington's "fallen women," G.B. Cashwell opened up a rescue home for prostitutes in response to the twenty or so brothels that decorated the city's downtown section. Located on No. 814 South Ninth Street, the home was strategically situated in one of the poorest districts of Wilmington. On April 1, 1908, Cashwell published an article in the Bridegroom's Messenger announcing his plans to dismantle Wilmington's stronghold for the sexually abused. He writes:

> I thank God for putting the rescue work on my heart. I am sure He will tell you how much to give for this cause. I am already receiving letters from some who love this blessed work, saying that they are praying with me for the Home in Wilmington, N.C., to open. One dear sister, a child of God, sent $5 to start with, another says she will

> help as the Lord may lead. Now, brothers, you are acquainted with the Lord and His Spirit, do just what He says in the matter. "Quench not the Spirit." We need one thousand dollars to start with.[6]

Despite his extensive travels, the Wilmington mission became a major point of emphasis for G.B. Cashwell's Tar Heel ministry. Working in full partnership with his wife, Lovie Cashwell, the Cashwell's organized the Wilmington rescue mission as an independent work. Together, along with some friends, the Cashwells sought to rescue homeless girls who were selling themselves into sexual bondage. Running with this vision, Lovie Cashwell served the mission by residing as both secretary and treasurer.[7]

Opening up on May 1, 1908, with Pinkie Blake of Georgia leading the charge, the Wilmington home became an instant success. A grateful Cashwell writes:

> Our hearts feel glad for what God is doing for the rescue work in Wilmington. Sister Pinkie Blake has gone to that place to take charge with those in the city who will assist, and until Sister Bowen or someone comes to help in that much needed work…Let us know of any rescued at other places, and we will do all in our power to find a place of rest and comfort for them in the home at Wilmington until we can open up others. This home is not for the fallen women in Wilmington, N.C., alone, but for any poor fallen girl who wants to reform and seek God and a better life. May God lay this work heavy upon your heart and may you know just what He would have you to do for Him. Send all contributions to Mrs. G.B. Cashwell, Dunn, N.C. If your child is lost in sin and gone from home and you do not know where she is, give us all the information you have and we will do all in our power to find and rescue her.[8]

Compassionately moved for even the "least of these," Cashwell's vision to rescue these girls began to stir the entire city of Wilmington. Unsatisfied with waiting for victims to flood the rescue home, Cashwell empowered Pinkie Blake and other leaders of the home to go on the offense and track down women in need of healing.

By the end of July 1908, the home had flourished to such an extent, a larger building was needed in order to house all of the women and children that were flooding its doors. In the Bridegroom's Messenger, Cashwell reported, "The rescue work in Wilmington, N.C., has increased to such an extent we feel that a larger house must be secured for those who are coming in for help and to God."[9] His request was quickly answered and the home was moved to No. 310 North Ninth Street, making it closer to downtown. Continuing to grow, the rescue home finally caught the attention of Wilmington's newspapers. On December 7, 1908, a beautiful article was published in The Evening Dispatch revealing the home's magnificent work among the downtrodden of Wilmington. It reads:

> The home was opened on the first day of May and eighteen girls and children have been rescued since that time, of which five have been restored to their families. One of the girls was given nice clothes and sent to an industrial school in Georgia. Two of the girls have homes here in Christian families, while three had to be sent from the Home for refusing to abide by the rules and regulations. The rest are all here in the Home at present and we have on record new applications for five others. We hope the time is near at hand when some good person of Wilmington who has several nice lots will feel interested enough in the work to give us a lot. One lumber mill man has given his name for $100 worth of lumber to build the house when we get the lot. We are going to call on the rest of them and sincerely trust that they will give us enough to finish with. We want a two story, twenty-room building in a desirable place and near the street car line. Now anyone wishing to aid us in this undertaking will do us a kind favor by communicating with us at your earliest convenience. Some of the kind ladies have asked in what way they could assist us as winter in now here. Clothing for the inmates and beds will be thankfully received, and we will not object to any thing for the pantry.[10]

Incredibly, the rescue home was impacting the entire city. Through Cashwell's Georgia connections, it seems both he and Pinkie Blake were sending girls to the peach state for further care. Also aiding in the success of the home was Bro. W.D. Beckam.

Beckam, a Free Will-Baptist minister converted under Cashwell's influence, became the mission's loudest voice. Holding massive tent revivals all around Wilmington, Beckam's meetings were filled with supernatural sings and wonders. From mass healings, demonic deliverance, angelic visitations, and an account that testified "Jesus Himself" even appeared in the tent service, Beckam's meetings were no less then jaw-dropping. When he wasn't taking the tent around Wilmington, brother Beckam was holding day and night tarrying services on Fourth and Dawson Street. By securing a meeting hall in the middle of the city, Beckam reported to the Bridegroom's Messenger that a small army of Pentecostal warriors had been assembled in the old historic city. Cashwell was known to have made several trips to the hall and most likely encouraged his ground troops to keep pressing on. In one accord with Cashwell's vision, Beckam frequently visited the rescue home and most likely raised funds, brought in girls, and prayerfully strengthened the home's purpose in the city.[11]

Despite the rescue home's expediential growth, opposition was mounting against the work that was beginning to transform lives. Unfortunately, the resistance to Cashwell's vision for redeemed prostitutes was through the "Pastors Association" of Wilmington. Strongly dissatisfied with the rescue home's efforts, several of the city's leading pastors met with the Mayor and Chief of Police and requested a legal investigation. Their rigid report made front page news and was published on December 15, 1908. Entitled "The Rescue Home," the article belittled the rescue home's staff and residents. It reads:

> The committee was convinced that the work was not wisely managed, however, honest the intention. In addition to the inmates, some of whom were very evidently using the Home as a temporary convenience, we found that children were being placed in the same Home, surrounded by what could be considered most unwholesome environment, that must prove hurtful to young minds. We have learned more recently, on efficient authority, that an agent of the Home is making a canvass of the state for the purpose of inducing persons to come to the Home—many of whom are manifestly making of it a convenience... We are unable to discover that any reputable or responsible organization is behind the work; and the official heads of the institutions are affiliated with the leaders of a seemingly fanatical set. In the judgment of the committee which has the endorsement of the Pastors Association, the work as at present conducted is not only unwise but dangerous; and until properly organized and administered in responsible manner, does not merit the support of the people here. And we further suggest that the mayor take the matter under consideration, as being a possible menace to our community by the introduction of an undescribable class of women into our community, together with their sinful offspring. Committee of Ministers.[12]

Being independent, unauthorized, and belonging to no church nor organization, G.B. Cashwell's rescue home really struck a nerve with Wilmington's officials. Judging by the tone in their report, the association strongly condemned the home and felt it necessary for it to close its doors in Wilmington. Disgusted with the "indescribable class of women" and their "sinful offspring," the Pastors Association may have found Cashwell's rescue home to have been a haven for sexually abused "colored" women. This best explains why the association wanted to include the Mayor and Chief of Police. With their approval, under the Jim Crow law, a racially mixed home for women would certainly be a legal reason to permanently remove the rescue home. Mysteriously, the Cashwell rescue home was shut down just a few months later. It only remained open for one year.

In retrospect, the fierce opposition against the Wilmington work served as an unexpected death blow towards Cashwell's vision. The home had been a ministry that Gaston and Lovie founded together. Serving as both secretary and treasurer, Lovie shared in her husband's passion to see these sexually abused women redeemed. When it shut down, the Cashwells quickly began to realize that they were gaining more enemies then supporters. Besides the critical response from the Wilmington Pastors Association, the Cashwells were most likely disappointed with the lack of support from their fellow North Carolina ministers. During the rescue home's one year of existence, Lovie faithfully posted the financial contributions that were made in the Bridegroom's Messenger. Interestingly, nearly all of their support came from individuals in other states around the country. Hardly anything was ever collected from any of their friends in North Carolina.[13]

The Mandate

Besides establishing multiple rescue homes for the sexually abused, G.B. Cashwell also envisioned a unified interracial apostolic church, both globally and locally. Like Seymour, Cashwell firmly believed that he had born into an apostolic generation after encountering the Holy Spirit at the Azusa Mission. Preaching that all the spiritual gifts had been restored to the church, Cashwell encouraged believers everywhere to flow in all of the supernatural giftings of the Holy Spirit. Unlike some of his Southern converts, Cashwell sensed that this restoration of gifts was for the purpose of bringing the body of Christ into perfect unity; not to organize another denomination or wear a title. In his view, "The Holy Ghost is the only One that can keep the church or the body of Christ in perfect unity, for He is the Overseer of the Church."[14]

As seen through the fruit of his ministry, unity, in Cashwell's perspective, was not limited to one race or denomination. Like William J. Seymour, Cashwell strongly desired for unity among all races as well as the global church. Amazingly, Cashwell's secret weapon in bringing this to pass was rooted in his humility. He firmly believed that a true apostolic church was only as powerful as it was humble. Confirming this claim, Cashwell wrote a front page editorial in the Bridegroom's Messenger on April 1, 1908. He states:

> Brethren, you will find the secret of this mighty work in the humblest attitude you can get in before Him, not in trying to show off or exhibit what He has done for us; but down, down let us go before Him in earnest prayer, believing that He will restore the gifts to the church of God, and that the work He said would be done if He went to His father may be done in us.[15]

Contrary to popular belief, G.B. Cashwell's vision extended beyond people receiving their personal Pentecost. Cashwell longed to see every tribe, tongue, and nation come into perfect unity through the power of the Holy

Spirit. Towards this end, G.B. Cashwell fought vigorously. He understood that the Pentecostal baptism experience was the key in breaking down the walls of racism, sexual perversion, denominationalism, and cold dead religion. Through the divine encounter of Pentecost, Cashwell stressed to his followers that "oneness" and spiritual unity could be achieved.[16]

Regrettably, not everyone was buying into Cashwell's vision. Between 1907 and 1908, G.B. Cashwell quickly became one of Pentecost's most thunderous voices. By 1909, however, his ministry began to rapidly decline. Perhaps one of the reasons for this was the growing temptation for church leaders to organize the Pentecostal Movement. B.S. O'Neal, the pastor of the Atlanta Mission that Cashwell frequently visited, wrote:

> There seems to be a cry on the part of some dear Pentecostal people for organization. To my mind this would be a backward step and a great mistake, and perhaps a fatal one. Organization means a return to the old way. It means multiplied reports and statistics of which we have neither time to listen or read. Organization will tend toward division rather than bringing about more unity. The Holy Ghost is leading this movement and will continue to do so as long as He has His way.[17]

Affirming O'Neal's convictions, Cashwell responded to his followers with an article rebuking the need for Pentecostal denominationalism. After a disappointed meeting in Slocomb, Alabama, Cashwell sounded the alarm against organization by crying out:

> To the servants of the Most High God: You, who are watchman over the flock cry out, the wolves are coming, and you, who are looking after the lost sheep, hurry, or they will not get in! There is no time to lose. Don't grieve over results and decide that it is all a failure, because we are defeated in accomplishing what we hoped to. This is the last call, and we will never pass this way again…There has never been such a drove of hungry wolves after the flock of God. All hell has been turned loose on this work of the preparation of the coming of Jesus, and many of God's sheep are being devoured by the wolves of the Devil, and many watchmen are failing to give the alarm, but are shearing the sheep and then throwing them to the wolves. There is awful desolation and destruction among the people of God…The gospel, as has been, and is now being preached, condemns, everything of the Devil from the least to the greatest, and it stands for the whole truth of God according to His word, and it shuts every mouth that opens against it. It condemns and seals the destiny of those who fight it. It is like a cyclone where it goes. It is not trying to build up any church or society to remain in the world. It is not God's intention to do this, but to make the world for the judgment, and the true church for the coming of Christ. No one trying to organize this work

> will prosper in their souls. You may be saved, but it will be only by fire...Brethren, tell the people to make ready for the coming of the Lord, and waste no time. We have all the churches and "isms and schisms" the world needs, and to organize anything in this movement will gender [sic] more strife and division. Let us know nothing but to love each other. It is wonderful.[18]

It is obvious from his passionate cry not to organize the movement that Cashwell's future hopes for a unified apostolic church were beginning to fade. He also signals to his audience that many "wolves" were now running after the flock of God. Just who were these wolves? Bishops, overseers, pastors, evangelists, teachers? Who else would seek to organize a church movement? If so, then who and where? Of course, we may not know exactly who Cashwell was referring to; however, it does seem highly likely that Gaston had certain church leaders in mind. Is it possible that even some of these wolves were beginning to rove across the Carolina countryside right into Cashwell's own backyard?

The Mystery

From 1906–1908 Cashwell's powerful ministry was well received and documented. In 1909 it begins to quickly fade away from the national spotlight. During this time, his speaking engagements tapered off dramatically. His appearance within the columns of the Bridegroom's Messenger started to cease. His Wilmington rescue home was dismantled by city authorities, and the explosive interracial revival held in Dunn's three-story prize biulding had been shut down by government officials. From this perspective, 1909 became a year of disappointment and discouragement for Gaston and Lovie Cashwell. Surprisingly, no one has ever discovered why Cashwell's Pentecostal ministry began to take a sudden nose dive just two years after it began. It has always remained a mystery.

Adding to G.B. Cashwell's problems in 1909 was the growing coldness towards his ministry from his friends in Falcon, North Carolina. Although many of them, including J.H. King, A.H. Butler, G.F. Taylor, J.A. Culbreth, C.B. Strickland, and H.H. Goff, had been converted under Cashwell's ministry, it seems that they did not share in his excitement for an integrated apostolic church. Reasons for this have never been explored. There simply has never been enough evidence to give an explanation, until now.[19]

Coming from an unlikely source, a letter written by A.B. Crumpler may reveal why some of Cashwell's converts in Falcon gave him the cold shoulder. Dated June 2, 1909, A.B. Crumpler wrote a personal letter disassociating himself from J.A. Culbreth and the Falcon ministry. It reads:

> My Dear Bro. Your very kind letter to hand and noted. I know that I did once hold an official relation to the Falcon School and Camp-meeting work as trustee of the property. But since there has come to the throne another "Pharaoh that knows not Joseph" I did not know but that I had been succeeded as trustee by some good brother having the qualifications required by the new regime at Falcon. It will be perfectly satisfactory to me for you to put someone else in my place as trustee; and I will appreciate your doing so. While I feel no interest in the work at Falcon whatever and have no sympathy for the errors and delusions into which it has fallen, you may regard me still your personal friend and brother in the Lord. With very best wishes for you and yours, I beg to remain your brother. In The Fullness of His Love, A.B. Crumpler.[20]

At first glance, it's easy to assume that Crumpler is referring to G.B. Cashwell and Falcon's acceptance of the new Azusa Street theology. However, given new insights, this does not appear to be the case.

Crumpler first reveals that a new "Pharaoh that knows not Joseph" had risen to power at Falcon. He also adds that because of this changing of the guard, he had been "succeeded as trustee" of the Falcon School and Camp meeting by "some good brother." G.B. Cashwell was never a trustee at Falcon, nor did he ever come close to holding any type of leadership position there. Besides being a guest speaker once in 1907, Cashwell never played a significant role at Falcon during his thirty plus years of his ministry. If A.B. Crumpler is not referring to Cashwell, then who is this new "Pharaoh" over Falcon? The likely answer points towards J.H. King of the F.B.H.C.[21]

Just a few months before Crumpler wrote this letter, J.A. Culbreth had quietly anointed J.H. King over the Falcon School, Camp-Meeting Association, and orphanage. Moreover, King and other FBHC members had already been installed as trustees over Falcon's ministries as early as 1904. In addition, Cumberland County deed records show that J.H. King, M.D. Sellars, and S.D. Page all relocated to Falcon around the same time. Interestingly, these land transactions occurred right before A.B. Crumpler wrote his letter to J.A. Culbreth on June 2, 1909. This political maneuver also sheds light on Crumpler's use of the word "regime," in his letter. Regime is a government term referring to an "administration" or a type of "government." Could it be that this new administration Crumpler was referring to was the strict and rigid order of the F.B.H.C? It appears so. One thing is for certain, this partnership did not begin overnight.[22]

Sometime before A.B. Crumpler withdrew from the Holiness Church of North Carolina (November 1908), J.A Culbreth began to build his new regime at Falcon. Having launched the Falcon Camp Meeting Association, tabernacle, and a holiness school, Culbreth was in need of some able leaders.

Topping the list was not Crumpler or Cashwell, but J.H. King, general overseer of the Fire-Baptized Holiness Church. Having approached King at the 1907 Falcon Camp meeting, Culbreth solicited for J.H. King to take charge of the Falcon encampment. Agreeing to his request, King embraced his new position at Falcon and moved there just one month after A.B. Crumpler resigned as president of the Holiness Church. He brought with him S.D. Page, M.D. Sellars, and several other key leaders of the F.B.H.C.[23]

Being independent and "undenominational," the Falcon ministry had always served as a rallying point for A.B. Crumpler's Holiness Church and other holiness believing Christians. With J.H. King at the helm, however, Falcon began to grow closer and closer to the F.B.H.C. Keep in mind, A.B. Crumpler was still head of the Holiness Church in 1907 and strongly discouraged a relationship with King and the F.B.H.C. Although King and the Fire-baptizers had been swept into Pentecost by 1908, they still held onto their legalistic views of holiness. Noted previously, these views forbid the wearing of mustaches, neckties, and the eating of pork products. It seems that this is something that both A.B. Crumpler and G.B. Cashwell strongly disagreed with. Nevertheless, the new administration at Falcon marched forward without Crumpler or Cashwell (the movement's two founders), and began to organize the Holiness- Pentecostal Movement into a denomination, the Pentecostal Holiness Church. Stated earlier, the organization of Pentecost into a denomination was something that Cashwell strongly opposed.[24]

Seeing the hand writing on the wall, A.B. Crumpler quietly withdrew from the Holiness Church at the annual convention held in Dunn, during November 1908. His removal caused a shift of leadership within the church. A.H. Butler became the new president, G.F. Taylor the vice-president, and C.B. Strickland became secretary. G.B. Cashwell was listed as being present, and helped the church formulate the Azusa Street theology. However, as soon as Crumpler left, Cashwell also disassociated himself with the new administration in 1908. Immediately following the 1908 convention, talks to organize a new Pentecostal denomination between the F.B.H.C. and the Holiness Church of North Carolina began without the presence of A.B. Crumpler or G.B. Cashwell. Excited about this possibility, J.H. King cancelled all his ministry appointments in 1909, and "returned to Falcon the last day of December to take up the work that should come to me there."[25]

Cashwell historians have always speculated that G.B. Cashwell did encourage the merger between the F.B.H.C and the Holiness Church of North Carolina. This belief has been asserted based upon Cashwell's presence at the Convention of the Holiness Church that met the following year at Falcon in November 1909. The problem with this view, however, is that

Cashwell was never there. Although the minutes record him as being present during the roll call of preachers and playing a small role in business matters, Gaston Cashwell never showed up in Falcon that day. Renowned Pentecostal scholar and historian, Dr. Vinson Synan, explains what happened:

> Other less happy possibilities were indicated by the unexplained absence of Cashwell from the 1909 Convention. For some reason he failed to appear, although he easily was the most important single individual in the previous convention...Despite his absence, his name was carried on the roll of the 1909 Convention, although he was not assigned a church.[26]

Strangely, the minutes counted Cashwell as being present, although he was absent. Cashwell's "unexplainable absence" at this meeting puts things in a different perspective.

First, it reveals that G.B. Cashwell was not in attendance for the 1906, 1907, 1909, or 1910 Conventions. Second, it shows that A.B. Crumpler and G.B. Cashwell left the North Carolina Holiness Church together at the same Convention in 1908. Third, with Crumpler and Cashwell gone, new president A.H. Butler, vice-president G.F. Taylor, and J.A. Culbreth quickly organized a committee to "confer with a like Committee from the Fire Baptized Holiness Church and a like Committee of the Pentecostal Conference of the Free Will Baptist Church." By the time Butler, Taylor, and Culbreth publically announced this union in 1909, J.H. King, S.D. page, and M.D. Sellars had been living in Falcon for nearly a year. Moreover, the Free Will Baptist never accepted the Culbreth, Butler, Taylor invitation and remained detached from the Falcon regime until they formed the Pentecostal Free Will Baptist Church in 1955.[27]

After the strange 1909 Convention that called for a new regime in Falcon, G.B. Cashwell disappeared from the movement. Surprisingly, the man responsible for bringing Pentecost to both organizations was never a part of the equation. Doug Beacham notes that Gaston preached once more in Atlanta and Palmetto, Georgia, in the early part of 1910, but completely vanished soon after. By the next Convention that met in La Grange, North Carolina in November 1910, G.B. Cashwell's name was dropped from the list of membership of the North Carolina Holiness Church. Two months later, on January 31, 1911, the F.B.H.C. and the Holiness Church of North Carolina merged together, and formed the Pentecostal Holiness Church. Dr. Synan writes that "no reason was given" for G.B. Cashwell's unexplained removal.[28]

What happened? Did Cashwell prophesy his own demise in Alabama when he cried "The wolves are coming?" Did he really disagree with the merger being presented at Falcon? Did other ministers disapprove of his vision not to organize and extend the Pentecostal Movement to include people of color? The most famous question that has been asked concerning the G.B. Cashwell mystery is why did he abandon the Pentecostal Movement? This question has gone unanswered since his name was removed in 1910. No one has ever come forward with a solid answer. Perhaps it is because people are asking the wrong question. Maybe a better question to ask is: who forced G.B. Cashwell out of the movement he helped start?

Chapter 16

CASHWELL AND CRUMPLER: THE MYSTERY REVEALED?

SINCE G.B. CASHWELL suddenly disappeared from the movement he was leading in 1910, not one piece of documentation has emerged explaining why he left. As a result, numerous theories have surfaced over the years. Most of them are harsh in nature and have led some to believe that he totally renounced Pentecost and even possibly had an affair. Author J.E. Campbell, of the Pentecostal Holiness Church, wrote that Cashwell did "grievously fail God and brought reproach on the cause of the full gospel of Pentecostal Holiness." Cashwell's biographer notes that M.M. Pinson, who received Pentecost under Cashwell's ministry in 1907, also suggested that Cashwell made a "shipwreck of his faith" when he left the movement. However, both Campbell and Pinson's account fail to offer any proof supporting their negative comments towards Cashwell. More recent authors, such as Dr. Synan and Dr. Beacham, suggest Cashwell left because he was never offered a position in the newly organized Pentecostal Holiness Church. Yet, this also appears to be given without any substantial evidence.[1]

Bizarrely, all of Cashwell's North Carolina converts in Falcon remained dead silent over the issue. Even after Cashwell's death when they began to publish their history in the 1920s and 1930s, church leaders such as J.H. King, G.F. Taylor, A.H. Butler, J.A. Culbreth, and H.H. Goff never mentioned a word explaining why Cashwell left. It should be noted that these men were his personal friends. H.H. Goff had married him and Lovie Cashwell in 1899. Taylor, Butler, and Culbreth had been impacted through the historic Dunn revival. King had ministered with Cashwell in several different states during 1907–1908. Why the silent treatment? What could G.B. Cashwell possibly have done to merit such a silent response from those who obviously knew him quite well?[2]

In years past, researchers have solely relied on IPHC founders and the Lee side of the family to draw conclusions about the Cashwell mystery. Rarely has anyone searched the Cashwell side of the family in Keener, North Carolina, for answers. Thankfully, a treasure chest of insight has been recently discovered that may lift the fog over both Crumpler and Cashwell's departure from the Holiness- Pentecostal Movement. It originates from Dr. J.T. McCullen's writings about his "Uncle Gaston Cashwell" and the Cashwell-McCullen family history.

Dr. McCullen was born on November 11, 1914, and was raised on the Cashwell farm. His parents, J.T. McCullen Sr. and Myrtie Gore McCullen, were among the very first to receive Pentecost under Cashwell's ministry when he returned to Sampson County from Los Angeles in 1906. "Daddy," as Dr. McCullen calls him, is also credited with helping build St. Matthews Pentecostal Holiness Church and was a faithful member there until his death in 1966. Dr. McCullen also grew up attending St. Matthews with the rest of his siblings. Having a unique thirst for knowledge, Dr. McCullen left the rural Keener farm and enrolled himself at the University of North Carolina. After graduating with his Doctorate in English, he furthered his education by attending Oxford College in England. Over time McCullen mastered English literature and became a recognized Shakespearian scholar.[3]

Besides becoming a prolific writer and professor of English, Dr. McCullen also served the U.S. Marines during World War II as an intelligence operative. When his duty was over, Dr. McCullen returned to the Cashwell farm and lived out the rest of his days writing. Among his greatest works is a series of unpublished books that he authored about the Cashwell family. In addition to studying history, genealogy, and literature, Dr. McCullen was extremely fascinated about his Cashwell family roots. He discovered many of the Cashwell family mysteries, and wrote about them in his books. Many of these secrets were made known to Dr. McCullen through personal interviews with Cashwell's siblings. Oddly, McCullen coded many of his answers from the naked eye using a Shakespearian form of code writing; however, he did decide to make some clear and plain to the average reader.[4]

Among them is included a brief article explaining what really happened to both A.B. Crumpler and G.B. Cashwell and the revival movement they founded. Entitled Antiquity Forgot, McCullen's book reveals several things about the Crumpler and Cashwell mystery:

> In 1901, a preacher (A.B. Crumpler) who grew up not far from our home established the first Pentecostal Holiness Church in North Carolina. In 1906, a great uncle of mine (G.B. Cashwell) returned from California speaking in unknown tongues, enthusiasm hailed

> as evidence that one has been baptized by the Holy Ghost. These two preachers of local origin roved throughout southeastern U.S.A. staging revivals characterized by emotional abandon that won multitudes of converts. Daddy (J.T. McCullen Sr.) affiliated with this movement and was absorbed in it until his death. Seldom—apparently—do enthusiasts caught up in any emotional fervor pause for analysis of handwriting on the wall. Quite rapidly, preachers inspired by these founders seized their mantle, as well as the limelight, and gained control of the movement. Be motivations whatever they may, the two founders of this movement soon abandoned it and returned to the more stable congregations in which they had been nurtured. Whether any, or how many, converts won by them paused to ask, "If this new religion is not good enough for its founders, is it good enough for me?" is an unanswered question.[5]

First, it is clear that A.B. Crumpler and G.B. Cashwell were never enemies as G.F. Taylor, A.H. Butler and others made them out to be. There is not even a hint of disagreement between the "two founders," but instead a partnership to spread the Holiness- Pentecostal Movement.

Second, A.B. Crumpler and G.B. Cashwell did have mutual enemies. Although McCullen fails to specifically identify who they are, it is obvious that he was referring to the new "regime" that was assembling at Falcon.

Third, it is apparent that there was an unknown explosive war for control between the two founders and their adversaries at Falcon. It also reveals that a strategy was devised to steal the movement away from Crumpler and Cashwell. By "seizing their mantle as well as the limelight," it seems that the preachers inspired by Crumpler and Cashwell conspired a way to remove both of them from the spotlight. Missing records, tainted church minutes, numerous historical discrepancies, and a failure to report the whole story all suggest possibilities of this.

Fourth, it is exceptionally clear that Crumpler and Cashwell did not abandon the movement, but that the movement abandoned them. Being forced out, it is important to note, that these two founders did not put up fight. They did not seek to justify their position. Instead, they maturely walked away from the powers that be, and returned to ministry apart and separate from the Pentecostal Holiness Church.

Crumpler and Cashwell: Life beyond the Holiness- Pentecostal Movement

After 1908, virtually nothing of A.B. Crumpler's life has ever been known. This is because most have been taught that he lived out the rest of his days as a bitter and cynical old man. Eddie Morris, a Pentecostal-Holiness historian, stated, "It is said that he (A.B. Crumpler) returned to his old church in Clinton and became a diminishing figure, declining in both health and intellect." However, nothing further from the truth has ever been written.[6]

When A.B. Crumpler was forced out of the church he helped found in 1908, serious repercussions followed for him. Noting his withdraw, A.H. Butler, G.F. Taylor, and the new leadership passed a law demanding his preaching credentials. It stated, "Resolved, That all ministers holding credentials from the North Carolina Holiness Convention, who have withdrawn themselves from said convention, be requested to surrender said credentials to said Convention."[7] Having left the Clinton Methodist Church in "good standing" during 1899, Crumpler placed his preaching credentials in the Holiness Convention in 1900. Now that he had left the church, Crumpler had no way to formally exercise his preaching gift. He had no choice but to return to the Methodist Church where he had first received his ordination.[8]

On December 9, 1913, the Charlotte Observer published a brief article revealing A.B. Crumpler's readmission back into the Methodist Church. It reads, "The question of restoring the credentials of A.B. Crumpler, of Clinton District, who left the Methodist Church and went to the Holiness Church, caused some debate. It was voted to restore the credentials." Soon, Rev. Crumpler returned to the place where it all started, Clinton Methodist Church. Here, he served the church as supply pastor, and most likely preached in local congregations. By 1916, however, Crumpler was again holding evangelistic campaigns all over eastern North Carolina. Clinton's newspaper The News Dispatch, lists Rev. Crumpler "conducting meetings" in Sampson, Johnston, and the surrounding counties during this time.[9]

Showing no signs of weakness, A.B. Crumpler continued to faithfully expand the gospel message over the next thirty years of his life. Although he was under the Methodist Church, Crumpler still ministered to all people and denominations. The Robesonian lists A.B. Crumpler's ministry as being exceptionally active and affective in Lumberton, North Carolina, throughout the 1920s and 1930s. Dated June 29, 1933, Lumberton's paper announces that "A.B. Crumpler, of Clinton, former pastor of the Gospel Tabernacle here, will fill the local pulpit Sunday at the 11:00 a.m. service and will preach in the court house at 3 and 8 p.m." Being a Gospel Tabernacle church in 1933, it is very likely that this congregation was a Lumbee Indian independent Pentecostal-Holiness church.[10]

Besides preaching the gospel, A.B. Crumpler also followed in his families legacy as being a very successful government official. Beginning in the spring of 1913, A.B. Crumpler began to announce his candidacy for mayor of Clinton. Entitled "A Preacher for Mayor," local newspapers ran brief ads of the former President of the Holiness Church running for office. Accordingly, A.B. Crumpler won the elections and served Clinton, North Carolina, as mayor from 1915–1916.[11]

While serving the town as mayor, Crumpler also decided to practice law again. On February 10, 1916, he passed the bar examination and reclaimed his license to practice law in North Carolina. After securing an office above Slossberg's Store in Clinton, the News Dispatch introduced A.B. Crumpler as an "Attorney-At-Law." Although there are no records indicating Rev. Crumpler's career as an attorney, his granddaughter, Mrs. Jane McGregor, remembers quite fondly some of Mr. Crumpler's cases. She notes that Mr. Crumpler was famous for defending clients who had no money. Graciously, he would take up their case free of charge and defend them as best as he could.[12]

One year later, on March 15, 1917, A.B. Crumpler decided to run again for mayor. Another announcement was also carried in the Dispatch. Written by Crumpler, it states, "At the earnest request of a number of friends I hereby announce myself a candidate for mayor subject to the will of the citizens of the town of Clinton in the coming municipal election."[13] Whether Crumpler won his second term is not known. Sometime after, Crumpler expanded his dynamic political career even further by running for another elected office, Clinton's justice of the peace. Having won, Crumpler served the town as a judge. Most likely, he presided over court cases and issues relating to legal matters during his tenure as justice of the peace. Amazingly, after leaving the Holiness- Pentecostal Movement in 1908, A.B. Crumpler ended up serving the community as a lawyer, mayor, justice of the peace, and most importantly, a powerful preacher.[14]

Rev. A.B. Crumpler lived to be eighty-nine-years-old and continued to serve God until his death. A family story that illustrates Crumpler's dedication to the Lord is offered by Mrs. McGregor, Crumpler's granddaughter. Having lived right next door to Mr. Crumpler, Mrs. McGregor remembers that her grandfather would turn up missing quite often during his later years. Although other family members would be worried, Mrs. McGregor always knew exactly where to find her aging grandfather, at the altar of the church praying to the Lord.[15]

The Apostle of Holiness for North Carolina passed away at his home in Clinton, on October 23, 1952. His death had a tremendous impact on people all over the state. Crumpler's obituary appeared in the Sampson Independent a week later on October 30, 1952. Entitled "Death Claims Aged Citizen," it reads:

> Rev. A.B. Crumpler 89, one of Clinton's oldest and best known citizens died at his home Thursday at 6:15 p.m. after extended illness. He was a native of Sampson County and spent most his life here. Mr. Crumpler was a licensed attorney and at one time practiced law in Clinton. Later he entered the ministry and at one time was a member of the Methodist Conference, having retired from the ministry several years ago. He also served as Justice of the Peace in Clinton and served the town as mayor in 1915–16. He numbered his friends by his acquaintances. Funeral services were conducted from the Crumpler-Honeycutt funeral parlor Friday afternoon at 4 o'clock by Pastor Rev. C. Freeman Heath. Interment was in the Clinton cemetery.[16]

The article follows with an impressive list of at least fifty notable ministers and government officials who took part in the services. Among them were former North Carolina senator Hennery Vann, and an unlikely close friend of A.B. Crumpler, Paul L. Cashwell.[17]

Surprisingly, both A.B. Crumpler's obituary and death certificate reveal that Paul L. Cashwell was one of Crumpler's six pallbearers. This is very revealing. Typically, the pallbearer position is regarded as "one of the highest honors that can be bestowed upon a family member or close friend." Surviving family members are primarily responsible for choosing pallbearers for the deceased. Although there is no documentation revealing dialogue between A.B. Crumpler and Paul Cashwell, it is certain that Paul and Rev. A.B. Crumpler shared a very close relationship and considered each other family. Moreover, it also shows that A.B. Crumpler did not hold G.B. Cashwell in contempt and adds creditability to Dr. McCullen's observations about the mutual friendship shared between the Crumpler and Cashwell families.[18]

No one from the Pentecostal-Holiness Church was listed as attending Crumpler's funeral. Sadly, there is no record of communication between A.B. Crumpler and his former friends in Falcon since he had disassociated himself from J.A. Culbreth forty-four years earlier. Rev. Crumpler was survived by one son, Dr. L.O. Crumpler of Danville, Virginia, and one daughter, Mrs. Grace Crumpler Vann of Clinton.[19]

G.B. Cashwell's Later Years

Unlike Rev. A.B. Crumpler, there is very little documentation revealing G.B. Cashwell's ministry after 1910. Fortunately, one letter, written by Cashwell, has surfaced since that time. It was published in September 1911 in the Word and Work, a northern Pentecostal paper. Surprisingly, it reveals a spiritually strong G.B. Cashwell returning to the place where his ministry had been informally excommunicated, Falcon, North Carolina.

Breaking his silence, Cashwell attended the annual Falcon Camp meeting during 1911. He attended to hear and observe the powerful ministry of Dr. F.E. Yoakum. Yoakum, a native of Los Angeles, had also been transformed at the Azusa Street Mission. Hearing of his visit to Falcon, Cashwell decided to go and meet the man who was "handled by the power of the Spirit of God." Motivations be whatever they may, Cashwell's presence at Falcon was quite revealing. He writes:

> The other day, wife read an account of Dr. Yoakum coming to Falcon Camp Meeting, and I told her if he went there and taught and practiced what he is teaching, and God recognizes it, she would see a stir, such as she had never seen before. I met him, and as soon as I did, I knew God was in the man and that he was handled by the power of the Spirit of God. I saw self was down and God had him under control. It brought conviction to my heart and I cried out, "Lord God, restore unto me the Joys of Thy salvation." Brother Yoakum laid his hands upon me and I was filled as never before by the Spirit of the Lord. He was so busy going and praying for the sick. The Lord was blessing, healing and saving people from the time that he got off the train. Then for the few days he was at Falcon, it was a real feast for the Lord's people. All dissension and strife seemed to disappear and people were baptized in the love of Jesus. I never saw anything like it. All the hatred, jealousy, and division among the people seemed to go as chaff before the wind. It was wonderful! Wonderful! Hundreds, yes, thousands of people embraced each other, who had been cold and dead while professing holiness. It was wonderful what a revival God sent to us through that man, and I am glad in my heart today. I praise God I ever met him. That the Lord sent him to us and that I am back here in the Spirit of the Lord among you people. Praise God. Glory be to God.[20]

In light of Dr. McCullen's insights, Dr. Yoakum's meeting in Falcon discloses two important details. First, it shows that Cashwell had a personal breakthrough. Given Cashwell's rejection from Falcon's leaders, he most likely struggled with forgiveness issues. Through God's presence in Yoakum, however, Cashwell was "filled as never before by the Spirit of the Lord." It seems that this was the breakthrough Cashwell needed in order to face his enemies.

Second, Cashwell reveals that "dissension, strife, hatred, jealously, and division" were all present at Falcon at the time of Dr. Yoakum's arrival. Certainly, these are essential ingredients needed to generate a spiritual war of control between "two founders" and the "preachers they inspired." Most importantly, Cashwell's last known letter exposes his greatest attribute, his humility.[21]

After G.B. Cashwell was forced out of the movement, Gaston's ministry returned to where it all began Keener, North Carolina. It seems between the years 1910 and 1915, Cashwell fed "more stable congregations" with the good news of the kingdom. Although he still resided in Dunn, family history remembers "Uncle Gaston" traveling back and forth to Keener, where he would preach to local churches. Many of the small congregations that Cashwell preached at during this time appear to have been racially mixed. One of them was Browns Missionary Baptist Church (African American).[22]

A current elder of Browns Church, whose grandfather was one of the original founding members in 1871, remembers that the "Cashwell man" use to come and teach African-Americans how to study and preach the Scriptures. When asked his first name, the elder responded "Gaston, Gaston Cashwell."[23]

More Secrets in the Graveyard: Cashwell's Mysterious Death

According to Doug Beacham, G.B. Cashwell's health started to decline by March 1914. Being fifty-two years of age and weighing in at over 250 pounds, doctors began to treat Cashwell for mitral valve problems. As his conditioned worsened, Gaston began to slip into congestive heart failure. On March 5, 1916, the "Son of Pentecost" passed away at fifty-four years of age. He was buried twenty-four hours later at Greenwood Cemetery in Dunn, on March 5, 1916. Beacham also noted that "there are no written records of an obituary or any type of funeral service, though probably a service was held on Sunday as part of the burial." Thankfully, a new record has emerged concerning the death of G.B. Cashwell.[24]

Besides his death certificate, there was another record kept by Cashwell's undertaker, Mr. Hatcher. Noted as "Gaston B. Cashwell's Record of Funeral," this report may answer some long asked questions about Cashwell, while digging up new ones. Filled out by Lovie, Gaston's funeral record discloses several important things about Cashwell at the time of his death.[25]

First, it shows that there was a small private funeral service held in the Cashwell home at three o'clock on March 5, 1916. Conducting the service was Rev. W.R. Cullom and Rev. H.A. Hockaday. Dr. Willis Richard Cullom was born on January 15, 1867 in Halifax County, North Carolina. Becoming a Southern Baptist minister, Cullom was widely known for his outstanding ability to teach the Bible to all people. Throughout his evangelistic career, Cullom preached to both black and white congregations all over the Tar Heel state. Cullom is most famously recognized for his leading role as professor at Wake Forrest University. There is not much known about Rev. Hockaday. Most likely he was a personal friend of Dr. Cullom, and accompanied him at G.B. Cashwell's funeral service.[26]

It appears that Dr. Cullom met G.B. Cashwell in his later years through

Dunn's First Baptist Church. Between 1905 and 1916, Dr. Cullom periodically served as a supply pastor for Dunn's First Baptist Church. According to Lovie Cashwell's obituary, G.B. Cashwell was a member of Dunn's First Baptist Church "at the time of his death."[27] Conveniently, the church was located right across the street from the Cashwell home. There are, however, no membership records of Cashwell listed. Most likely, when he wasn't preaching in Keener in his later years, Gaston attended First Baptist where he met Dr. Cullom and formed a close relationship with him.[28]

Second, Gaston's religion was recorded as being "M. Baptist" on the report. This seems to confirm Dr. J.T. McCullen's insights. Being ousted of the Pentecostal Movement, Cashwell returned to "more stable congregations in which he had nurtured." As noted previously, for many years Cashwell had nurtured the loosely affiliate Missionary Baptist Church, Persimmon College. This is also the same church body that Cashwell emerged from. After his removal in 1910, Cashwell, it appears, returned to his original church roots just as A.B. Crumpler returned to his.[29]

Third, Cashwell's funeral was mysteriously quite. There were no pallbearers, flowers, chairs, embalming services, last will and testament, city calls, death notices in newspapers, or any type of an obituary. Remember, his death was not sudden, but covered an extensive period of time. He was given a six foot-three inch state casket made of white pine wood and a black blood clothe to stretch over his body. His marker plainly read "Gaston B. Cashwell," with nothing to reference him being a minister. Besides the private service at his home for his wife and five children, no one else is recorded as attending. There was never a grave-side service. In addition, there is no record of anyone from the Pentecostal Holiness Church attending. Moreover, it seems that none of Cashwell's siblings or nieces and nephews came to Gaston's service either. Strangely, as soon as G.B. Cashwell was pronounced dead, he was buried, gone, and quickly forgotten by the local community. Having impacted Christianity in such a powerful way, could more have been done to honor the man who brought thousands into the Pentecostal Movement? Or was Cashwell's death and burial an actual relief to others?[30]

It wasn't long, however, before word spread across the nation of G.B. Cashwell's death. One report was given by A.J. Tomlinson of the Church of God. Published on March 18, 1916, within the columns of the Church of God Evangel, Tomlinson wrote:

> As we go to press we have just learned of the death of brother G.B. Cashwell, of Dunn, NC, having departed this life the 4th inst... Sister Cashwell has our heartfelt sympathy in this hour of bereavement. She has an interest in our prayers as she battles on in life to care for her

> children the fruit of their marriage since 1899. To brother Cashwell is due the honor of carrying the Pentecostal message first to many of us in the southeastern states eight years ago, having preached in his own North Carolina, Georgia, Florida, Alabama, and Tennessee, besides some of the western states. Though his career as a Pentecostal preacher was of short duration, he set the match to the prepared material and the fire he started is still blazing higher and still spreading.[31]

Besides Tomlinson's heartfelt response, Mrs. E.A. Sexton, editor of the Bridegroom's Messenger, also published a lengthy write up concerning G.B. Cashwell's death. Headlined "Brother G.B. Cashwell Dead," this article gave a similar outpouring of honor and love for the surviving Cashwell family members. Continuing in silence, no comments on Cashwell's death or his family has ever been found from the pen of any of Falcon's leaders.[32]

Lovie Cashwell: Dunn's Other Pentecostal Pioneer

After Gaston sparked the historic Dunn revival during January 1907, Pentecostal services were held nightly in the Cashwell home on Layton Ave. As noted previously, several people, including Lovie Cashwell, were baptized in the Holy Spirit during these meetings. The meetings were also largely attended by a Pentecostal fraction of the Free Will Baptist Church of Dunn. It seems that after Cashwell had been rejected from the movement, this group relocated their meetings to a small wood framed building up the street on N. Layton Ave. Detached and separate from the Pentecostal Holiness Church in Falcon, this congregation remained a Pentecostal Free Will Baptist Church for many years.[33]

In 1917, a year after G.B. Cashwell's death, the church secured Rev. J.L. Davis as its pastor. Rev. Davis first came to Dunn as a young man several years prior to 1917. During this time he began to date Ms. Emma Lee, sister of Lovie Cashwell. Having also been swept into the Pentecostal Movement, Davis left with Rev. J.H. King in 1910 on a Pentecostal missions trip around the world. Returning in 1912, he married Ms. Emma Lee and soon relocated to New York where attended Bible school. After leaving New York, the Davis family moved to Kentucky. While in Kentucky, Rev. Davis furthered his education by attending Asbury College. When he came back to Dunn, in 1917, he became pastor of the Pentecostal Free Will Baptist Church on N. Layton Ave. For unidentified reasons, the church during this time did not seek membership within the Pentecostal Holiness Church in Falcon.[34]

On April 19, 1919, Edith Pope, another sibling of Lovie Cashwell, donated land for the church. Interestingly, the lot was situated right next door to the Cashwell residence. With a growing congregation including

Lovie Cashwell, the Popes, the Davises, the Hoods, and several others, the church constructed a new building. This location made it very convenient for Lovie and the Cashwell children to attend. Three years later, on November 15, 1922, Rev. Davis had the congregation charted by the "State Corporation Commission as an independent church, subject to no association or conference." At this point, the independent church identified itself as Gospel Tabernacle. Over the next thirty years, Gospel Tabernacle remained an independent, thriving, and vibrant interdenominational and Pentecostal believing church. Rev. Davis's daughter, Mrs. Emma Lee Davis Laine, remembers that her father's vision was to keep the church open for all denominations. According to her, it wasn't unusual for "Methodists, Baptists, Presbyterian, or Pentecostal preachers" to visit and hold services at Gospel Tabernacle.[35]

The church suffered a death blow in October 1944, when one of its founding members, Lovie Cashwell, passed away. The Dunn Dispatch noted Mrs. Cashwell's passing and published an outstanding obituary on October 17, 1944. Headlined "PIONEER DUNN WOMEN PASSES," the article states:

> Mrs. Lovie H. Cashwell, 70, widow of the late Rev. G.B. Cashwell and one of Dunn's pioneer residents, died in the Harnett County Hospital here Monday night at 11:25. She had been in ill health for some time and her condition became worse about three weeks ago. Funeral services will be held Wednesday afternoon at 4 o'clock at the Gospel Tabernacle here. The Rev. J. Luther Davis, pastor, the Rev. Lewis Morgan, pastor of the First Baptist Church, and Dr. Angus R. McQueen of the Presbyterian Church will officiate. Burial will follow in Greenwood Cemetery. One of Dunn's best known and most beloved citizens, Mrs. Cashwell was a member of one of the town's leading families. She was born in the vicinity of Dunn and lived here all her life, with the exception of a few years when she left with her husband. Mrs. Cashwell was a charter member of the Gospel Tabernacle and has taken a leading part in the affairs of the church, and the civic and social activities of the town as well. As a young girl, she served as an organist for the Presbyterian Church. Her husband, a widely known minister and evangelists, died March 1916. At the time of his death, he was a member of the First Baptist Church here. She was the daughter of the late Erasmus and Lucinda Allen Lee. Surviving are three sons: Paul L. Cashwell of Clinton; G.B. Cashwell of Mount Airy and David H. Cashwell of Greensboro; two daughters, Mrs. J.H. Monds of Carolina Beach, and Mrs. Paul Darden of Siler City; three sisters, Mrs. Edith Lee Pope and Mrs. J. Luther Davis of Dunn, and Mrs. Kizzie Taylor of Greensboro; one brother, R.E. Lee of Toccoa, Ga.; also 17 grandchildren and one great grandchild.[36]

Lovie Cashwell was obviously a remarkable woman. From start to finish, her life was filled with amazing devotion to God, her husband, and the revival movement he led. Accordingly, this article reveals that Lovie, like her late husband, had a heart for all denominations. This is evidenced by the three different pastors that officiated her service. She was also credited as being a "charter member of Gospel Tabernacle" and taking up a leadership position within the church. Interestingly, Gospel Tabernacle's history also shows that Mr. G.B. Cashwell was a charter member of the church as well, although he had died just before Rev. Davis became its pastor. Given Gospel Tabernacle's beginning at the Cashwell's residence, it seems the church history wanted to count both Gaston and Lovie as charter members.[37]

The article also exposes G.B. Cashwell's church membership at the time of his death as, Dunn's First Baptist Church. Surprisingly, the Dunn First Baptist Church was first organized as a Missionary Baptist Church. Noted previously, however, there are no records revealing that Gaston was an official member of this church body. Most likely, he attended services there and with the Pentecostal fraction of Free Will Baptist over on N. Layton Ave until his death in 1916.

After Lovie Cashwell's death, many of Gospel Tabernacles original members also began to pass away. It was during this time that Rev. Luther Davis retired as the church's pastor due to health reasons. As a result, the church began a closer union with the Pentecostal Holiness Church. In 1950, Gospel Tabernacle joined the Pentecostal Holiness Church, and the Rev. Bane T. Underwood became the church's pastor in 1951. Yet, it only did so after Lovie and other original members had died. Mrs. Emma Lee Davis Lane noted that this was a trying time for the congregation. Accordingly, the church split over its decision to join the Pentecostal Holiness Church. Half of the congregation joined the Pentecostal Holiness Church while the other half joined the Assemblies of God and called themselves Glad Tidings. Nevertheless, these congregations can trace their Pentecostal heritage back to the Cashwell's home in 1907. Today, both churches are still active and are located in Dunn, North Carolina.[38]

The Authors Corner

The G.B. Cashwell mystery has been one the most intriguing mysteries ever recorded within the annals of church history. Up until this point, no one has come forward with any answers explaining his sudden disappearance from the Pentecostal Movement. However, like in every mystery, there is an answer, and it appears to be carried by one person: Granny Susan Cashwell, the mother of G.B. Cashwell. I believe her fascinating family heritage holds the key to all of the mysterious questions surrounding the life of Rev. G.B. Cashwell. Unfortunately, for now it must continue to remain a mystery. Thankfully, not all is lost.

Dr. McCullen's account is the first documented report to offer a valid explanation of what happed to the burning voice of Southern Pentecostalism. Based on McCullen's insights and other researched materials, it is very likely that G.B. Cashwell's passionate vision to keep the Pentecostal Movement racially integrated is what led to his demise within the Pentecostal Holiness Church at Falcon, North Carolina. When the American Pentecostal Movement began to organize themselves into denominations, Jim Crowism took front stage. As seen with Rev. C.H. Mason and the organizers of the Assemblies of God, Pentecostal congregations segregated all over the country. The Pentecostal Holiness Church in Falcon was no different.

After the F.B.H.C and the N.C.H.C merged in 1911, evidence of racism quickly sprang up. According to his grandson's diary, J.A. Culbreth was a staunch Democrat and supporter of the White Supremacy Movement. G.F. Taylor was known to "accept donations from whatsoever source they come" including the white knights of the Ku Klux Klan. Perhaps the most inexcusable account of racial discrimination within the church came from a statement given by the general board of the church in 1922. It revealed that no "colored people" were allowed membership in the church south of the Mason and Dixon. The board also barred "colored people" from any type of leadership role. Interestingly, all of these racial actions were made with J.H. King, G.F. Taylor, J.A. Culbreth, and A.H. Butler at the helm.[39]

This also leads me to question the sincerity of Kings, Taylors, Culbreths, and Butlers own Pentecostal experience. For William J. Seymour and G.B. Cashwell, the initial evidence that one had been baptized with the Holy Ghost was manifested through speaking of tongues. However, the lasting evidence of the baptism itself was unconditional love for your brother regardless of his or her skin color. This is what separated leaders like Cashwell from leaders like Culbreth, Butler, Taylor, and King. The latter preached the message of Pentecost, but the former was the message of Pentecost! The Pentecostal Holiness Church segregated the baptism of the Holy Spirit. G.B. Cashwell on the other hand, fought to integrate it. "How can one be Pentecostal but yet hate his brother," is a question that Cashwell no doubt asked himself many times. Is this so hard to believe? Even today, most churches in the South still remain racially segregated. This is the unhealed wound in America that no one wants to talk about.

To their credit, the International Pentecostal Holiness Church has since acknowledged racism within the church's history. On August 23, 1996, the church called for a solemn assembly and corporately confessed the sins of their fathers. Ranging from pride, male domination, and racism, the church openly confessed and repented for sins that "brought about division to the body of Christ." Today the IPHC is a thriving church body that consists of over two million members with affiliates in one hundred and three countries around the world.[40]

Incredibly, A.B. Crumpler and G.B. Cashwell's impact is still being felt today. With over 600 million Pentecostals currently in the world, their contributions towards furthering the kingdom of God have been indescribable. Clearly, these two spiritual giants were ahead of their time. We are just now beginning to comprehend the fullness of their ministry efforts in the southern portion of the United States. Nevertheless, one thing is for certain: G.B. Cashwell and A.B. Crumpler were extraordinary revivalists. They exhibited the highest forms of Christian love, especially in the midst of hostile situations.

In closing, this entire book has examined the lives of A.B. Crumpler, G.B. Cashwell, and the gripping inter-racial movement they lead. Together, these two country preachers from Sampson County, North Carolina, shifted Christianity on a global scale. Both started their ministries with incredible spiritual power and fierce determination. Both sought to destroy the segregated South through the message of sanctification and the Pentecostal baptism. Yet, I am firmly convinced that the fullness of their efforts was prematurely aborted. If we wish to really honor their legacy, than it is imperative that we pick up their mantles and finish what they started at the turn of the century: racial and denominational reconciliation within the family of God. At its very core, this is the spiritual inheritance that G.B. Cashwell and A.B. Crumpler left behind. This is Fire in the Carolinas!

The site of the Azusa Street Revival in Los Angeles, California

The site of Azusa East! This is the only known picture of where the Azusa Street of the east coast began. The small building located right below the arrow is where G.B. Cashwell held his historic meeting in Dunn, North Carolina on December 31, 1906. At this site, the Baptism with the Holy Spirit was restored in the South and 12 Pentecostal denominations were born. Courtesy of North Carolina State Archives.

This is another never before seen actual photgraph of G.B. Cashwell (holding Bible). The photo is belived to be taken in G.B. Cashwell's obsecure years sometime after 1910. It was taken at Docia "Cashwell" Gore's home (G.B. Cashwell's sister) in Keener. The man next to him remaines unidentifed. Interestingly, the only tw actual photographs that have surfaced in over 100 years, both reveal Cashwell holding a Bible. Courtesy of John Aman and Stanley Carr.

NOTES

Chapter 1

G.B. Cashwell and A.B. Crumpler: Family Origins

(Endnotes)

1. Record of Funeral for Gaston B. Cashwell, March 4, 1916, File No. 204. Skinner and Smith Funeral Home, Dunn, North Carolina. This report measures Cashwell's casket as being 6'3" in length. Given the possibility that human bodies shrink over the years, it is very likely that Cashwell could have been 6'4" or even 6'5" in his early years.

2. On March 5, 2011, I conducted a personal interview with Stanley Carr and learned just how powerful G.B. Cashwell's preaching ability was. Mr. Carr's mother, Lottie Bass Carr, was a niece of G.B. Cashwell and heard him speak personally on several different occasions. Accordingly, she and some of G.B. Cashwell's other siblings, loved to pass on vivid accounts of Gaston's preaching mannerisms to their children. Thankfully, these detailed accounts have been kept alive through Mr. Stanley Carr.

3. Vinson Synan, *The Old Time Power: A Centennial History of the International Holiness Church* (Franklin Springs, Georgia: LifeSprings Publishing, 1998), 101.

4. Vinson Synan, *The Century of the Holy Spirit: 100 Years of Pentecostal and Charismatic Renewal* (Nashville, Tennessee: Thomas Nelson, 2001), 109. See William J. Seymour's, *Apostolic Faith* January, 1907, p.1 for a descriptive account of G.B. Cashwell's interracial and interdenominational meeting held in Dunn, North Carolina, in January 1907. Also, during the height of A.B. Crumpler and G.B. Cashwell's ministry, the North Carolina White Supremacy Movement exploded in 1898 and progressed rapidly alongside the Holiness- Pentecostal Movement. For more information on the white supremacy campaign, see James L. Hunt's, *Marion Butler and American Populism* (Chapel Hill, North Carolina: The University of North Carolina Press, 2003) p. 140–155.

5. Joseph T. McCullen, Jr., *Descendants and Relatives of Joseph Thomas McCullen, Sr. And Myrtie Peal Gore McCullen* (No publisher: December 1981) n.p. This genealogical document of Dr. McCullen's family includes a brief biography on G.B. Cashwell's father, Herring Cashwell, and his "brothers." The 1850 Federal US Census of Bladen County, North Carolina, also reveals that Thomas Cashwell Sr. had two sets of families.

6. Betty Jean Chase, "Thornton Family History" (n. p., 1999). This family history gives Thomas Jr. Cashwell's birth and lists his family. Thomas Jr. Cashwell is also the author's great-great-great-great-grandfather. The 1860 Federal US Census also lists Catharine Cashwell as living with Thomas Jr. and Christian Cashwell.

7. Oscar M. Bizzell, "Confederate Soldiers From Sampson County," *Heritage of Sampson County, North Carolina*, 222.

8. The 1860 United States Census (Free Schedule), Halls Township, Sampson County, North Carolina; p. 504. This census record shows that William was married to Susan Bass Cashwell and

that the William Cashwell family lived on Abraham Brewers land. Two children were listed: John and Elizabeth Cashwell.

9. Deed of Sale from Herring Cashwell to William Cashwell, August 25, 1855 (filed 6 October 1855), Sampson County, North Carolina, Deed Book 0032, Page 0525. Sampson County Register of Deeds Office, Clinton, North Carolina.

10. Bizzell, "Confederate Soldiers From Sampson County," *Heritage of Sampson County, North Carolina*, p. 222.

11. Joseph T. McCullen, Jr., *Descendants and Relatives of Joseph Thomas McCullen, Sr. And Myrtie Peal Gore McCullen* (No publisher: December 1981) n.p. The 1850 US Federal Census of Bladen County, North Carolina, lists Herring Cashwell working as a "hired" farmer for Willie Hall of Bladen County, North Carolina.

12. Doug Beacham, Azusa *East: The Life and Times of G.B. Cashwell* (Franklin Springs, Georgia: LSR, 2006), 14. Beacham believed that Herring Cashwell served in the Civil War and his name was recorded as "William Cashwell" instead of Herring Cashwell. However, it was Herring's brother William Cashwell who served in the war, not Herring. Additionally, I searched L.H. Manarin, *North Carolina Troops 1861–1865, A Roster*, and did not find any reference of a Herring Cashwell serving in the Civil War. Oscar Bizzell's, The *Heritage of Sampson County, North Carolina*, also did not list Herring Cashwell under its Troop roster. The only Cashwells it listed were Thomas Jr. Cashwell and William Cashwell, Herring's two brothers, p.222. Moreover, I personally interviewed Mr. Stanly Carr on February 5, 2011, and learned that he had traveled to Appomattox, Virginia, and personally searched the Civil War records there. He informed me that he did not find any listing of Herring Cashwell either. He also told me that his grandmother "Pender Cashwell Bass," was born about the same time Lee surrendered at Appomattox, and that great-grandfather Herring Cashwell was home for her birth.

13. Stuart Berde and Oscar Bizzell, "Coharie Indian Churches," *Heritage of Sampson County, North Carolina*, p.83–84. This article reveals that Sampson County was and still is inhabited by a significant population of Coharie Indians. Before the Jim Crow era began, it was not uncommon to see white, black, Indian, and mixed people work together on farms in the Sampson and Harnett County areas of North Carolina.

14. 1850 United States Census (Free Schedule), Halls Township, Sampson County, North Carolina; dwelling 952, family 952. Susan Stanley is listed as being eighteen years of age. She resides under Stephan and Edney Stanley, along with her three sisters: Harriet, Rebecca, and Patience Stanley. In my personal interview with Mr. Stanley Carr on March 5, 2011, I learned where the Stanley Woods was located.

15. Articles written by J.T. McCullen Jr. and Mary McCullen Savage in *The Heritage of Sampson County, North Carolina* confirms Susan and Harriett Stanley's excellent reputation in the Keener community. They are: "Persimmon College an Early Name for Keener, p. 35." "The Medicine Women of Persimmon College, p. 196." and "A Country Midwife in Halls Township, p. 197."

16. J.T. McCullen Jr., "A Country Midwife in Halls Township," *The Heritage of Sampson County, North Carolina*, 197.

17. Ibid.

18. ibid, 197.

19. Ibid, 197.

20. Mother Teresa Quote. Available, at http://www.brainyquote.com/quotes/quotes/m/mothertere158109.html. Also see, Mary McCullen Savage, "The Medicine Women of Persimmon College," *The Heritage of Sampson County, North Carolina*, 196.

21. Savage, 196.

22. Ibid. On February 5, 2011, I also visited Herring and Susan Cashwell's grave site for an accurate record of their births and deaths.

23. J. T. McCullen, *Antiquity Forgot: Reminiscences* (n.p. 1989), p. 90. This is an unpublished book that follows many of the joys, hardships, and day-to-day simple farm living that many of the Cashwell descendants endured. It is filled with outstanding references and insights into Granny Susan's life as well as G.B. Cashwell's. More importantly, it gives creditability to the outstanding character of the entire Cashwell family.

24. Last Will and Testament of William Bass, January 1853, (recorded in will book in 1855), Sampson County, North Carolina. William Bass was wealthy famer and land owner that lived close to the Stanley Woods. Interestingly, William Bass addressed the young Susan Stanley as his "guardian" in the will.

25. Last Will and Testament of William Bass, January 1853, (recorded in will book in 1855), Sampson County, North Carolina. William Bass was wealthy famer and land owner that lived close to the Stanley Woods. Interestingly, William Bass addressed the young Susan Stanley as his "guardian" in the will.

26. Vinson Synan, Old Time Power (Georgia: Life Springs, 1998), 68. Also see, Eddie Morris, The *Vine and Branches John 15:5 Holiness and Pentecostal Movements*, 88. Very little has ever been known of A.B. Crumpler's origins until now. Historians of the Pentecostal Holiness Church have included him in their histories as it pertains to the beginning of their organization. However, very little research has been conducted on A.B. Crumpler's life before and after his brilliant career as a revivalist (1896–1908).

27. Ibid, 88.

28. Jeff Hubbard, "The John Crumpler Family Tree." Available at http://www.findagrave.com/cgi-bin. Mr. Hubbard is a local historian and outstanding genealogist in North Carolina. Through extensive research he has pieced together "The John Crumpler Family Tree" which includes A.B. Crumpler's genealogy. Thankfully, Mr. Hubbard has recently posted all of this information on the Find-a-Grave website and has made it available for the public. He also has included some rare photographs of A.B. Crumpler's family. Also see, "First Sampson County Tax List, September 1784," *Heritage of Sampson County North Carolina*, 14.

29. Mary Harper Crumpler, "Notes for John Crumpler." Available at http://familytreemaker.genealogy.com/users/h/a/r/Ron-A-Harvey/WEBSITE-0001/UHP-0152.html. Mrs. Crumpler transcribed several documents relating to John Crumpler Sr. Her notes reveal that John Crumpler was Sheriff of Duplin County, North Carolina, between 1765–1782. During this time, Sampson County had not yet been formed. In 1784, Sampson County was carved out of Duplin County, North Carolina.

30. Ibid.

31. Jeff Hubbard, "The John Crumpler Family Tree." http://www.findagrave.com/cgi-bin. Also see Bizzell, "Magistrates and Attorneys in Our Early Court," *Heritage of Sampson County, North Carolina*, 52.

32. Hubbard, "The John Crumpler Family Tree." Also see Bizzell, "Clinton Almost Had Another Name," *Heritage of Sampson County, North Carolina*, 28.

33. Deed of Sale from Thomas Sutton to Blackmon Crumpler, December 2, 1812 (filed 2 December 1813), Sampson County, North Carolina, Deed Book 16, Page 103. Register of Deeds Office, Clinton, North Carolina.

34. Deed of Sale from Blackmon Crumpler to Methodist Episcopal Church Trustees, February 10, 1842 (filed 18 April 1842), Sampson County, North Carolina, Deed Book 26, Page 421. Register of Deeds Office, Clinton, North Carolina.

35. Bizzell, "The Sheriff and other County Officials," *Heritage of Sampson County*, 53. Also see Jeff Hubbard, "The John Crumpler Family Tree." http://www.findagrave.com/cgi-bin.

36. Ibid. George W. Crumpler and Margret Crumpler were second cousins.

37. Ibid, 53. Also see, "Politics from Jeffersonian Democracy to Secession, 1800–1861," *Heritage of Sampson County, North Carolina*, 68.

Chapter 2
The Obscure Years

1. J.T. McCullen, "Siblings and their Children of Grandmother Lettie Docia Cashwell Gore," *Descendants and Relatives of Joseph Thomas McCullen, Sr. and Myrtie Peal Gore McCullen*, (n.p., 1981), n.p. This family history lists all of G. B. Cashwell's siblings as well as information regarding their families.

2. Ted Widmer, "Abraham Lincoln House Divided Speech," *American Speeches: Political Oratory from Patrick Henry to Barack Obama* (New York: Library of America Classics, 2011), 79. For the Civil Wars effect on churches see Richard Wentz, *American Religious Traditions: The Shaping of Religion in the United States* (Minneapolis: Fortress, 2003) 327.

3. Joe A. Mobley, *The Way We Lived in North Carolina* (Chapel Hill, North Carolina: University of North Carolina, 2003) 345, 348–349.

4. Life Application Study Bible (NIV): Lamentations 1:1–3.

5. Gerene L, Freeman "What About My 40 Acres and A Mule?" http://www.yale.edu/ynhti/curriculum/units/1994/4/94.04.01.x.html. 3–7. This article is based upon a Yale University

curriculum for High School Students. It defines the term "40 Acres and a Mule" and explores principles of reparations and retributions.

6. 1870 United States Census (Free Schedule), Halls Township, Sampson County, North Carolina; p. 24.

7. Death Certificate for Gaston B. Cashwell, March 4, 1916, certificate No. 10, North Carolina Board of Health.

G.B. Cashwell's death certificate lists that he had a "common school" education. His sister's death certificate, Docia Cashwell Gore, also reveals that she, too, had a "common school" education. During his ministry, G.B. Cashwell published and edited a national religious newspaper entitled, *The Bridegroom's Messenger.*

8. McCullen, *A Wild-Goose Miscellany* (n.p. 1988), 109–110. Also see McCullen, "The Country Store," *Antiquity Forgot: Reminiscences* (n.p. 1989), 45–46. Around 1871 Susan and Herring bought a piece of land joining their original farm and built another small house. The photograph of the old Cashwell home was taken sometime around the 1900s, when it was being used as the "old country store." Look carefully, and you can see the advertisements for coca-cola and tobacco hanging outside of the structure.

9. Ibid.

10. Mary McCullen Savage, the Medicine Women of Persimmon College," *Heritage of Sampson County, North Carolina*, 196. Dr. J.T. McCullen always referred to his grandparents, Docia and Jerry Gore, as "Ma and Pa Gore." On March 5, 2011, I personally interviewed G.B. Cashwell's great nephew Stanley Carr. I learned from that interview that "Ma" and "Pa Gore" ran the old country store after Gaston and his brother Billy Cashwell had left the area.

11. McCullen, "Gaston B. Cashwell Once A Prodigal Son," *Heritage of Sampson County, North Carolina*, 87–88.

12. McCullen, "A Country Midwife in Halls Township," *Heritage of Sampson County, North Carolina*, 196–197.

13. McCullen, "Gaston B. Cashwell Once a Prodigal Son," *Heritage of Sampson County, North Carolina*, 87.

14. Doug Beacham, *Azusa East: The Life and Times of G.B. Cashwell* (Franklin Springs, Georgia: LSR, 2006), 19.

15. Personal Study Bible of A.B. Crumpler. This is Rev. A.B. Crumpler's personal Bible that he used for Scripture study and preaching. In the "Family Record" section, A.B. Crumpler lists his birthday as June 9, 1864. The massive Bible was given to Rev. Crumpler as a college graduation present on March 30, 1888. It was personally given to him by B.N. Duke of Durham, North Carolina. Mr. Crumpler graduated from Duke University Law School in 1888. On May 28, 2011, I personally interviewed Jane McGregor, who is A.B. Crumpler's granddaughter. She knew him personally for many years before he passed away in 1952. Ms. McGregor has great insight into Rev. Crumpler's later years, and currently holds A.B. Crumpler's Bible. Jane is a member of Clinton's First Methodist Church, where her mother, Grace Crumpler Vann, and her grandfather, A.B. Crumpler, all were members.

16. The 1880 United Sates Census (Free Schedule), Honeycutt Township, Sampson County, North Carolina. Also, in the same interview with Ms. Jane McGregor, it was confirmed exactly where the A.B. Crumpler family farm was located. My father and I visited the location. We were quite surprised to learn that it was only seven miles from the G.B. Cashwell family farm.

17. Personal Study Bible of A.B. Crumpler.

18. Ibid.

Chapter 3
The Revival That Changed Everything

1. Quote is from Pastor Jim Wall of Community Church, Chesapeake, Virginia.

2. Ann Hobbs, "History of Keener United Methodist Church (1885–1997)," 1. This history lists G.B. Cashwell as playing an important role in the formation of the church through a powerful revival meeting conducted by Rev. James T. Kendall in August 1885. For A.B. Crumpler's salvation conversion under Rev. J.T. Kendall's ministry, see J.M. Pike, *Way of Faith*, December 23, 1896, 5.

3. The 1900 United States Census (Free Schedule), Goldsboro Township, Goldsboro City, Wayne County, North Carolina. For more information on Rev. Kendall, see Franklin Grill, *Methodism in the Upper Cape Fear Valley* (Nashville, Tennessee: Parthenon, 1966), 147.

4. Grill, 147–150.

5. Hobbs, "History of Keener United Methodist Church (1885–1997)," 1.

6. Joe Mobley, *The Way We Lived in North Carolina*, 325. This shows a North Carolina state map of railroads between 1850 and 1890. Keener is midway between Raleigh and Wilmington, North Carolina. Also see Bizzell, "From Reconstruction Through Populism," *Heritage of Sampson County, North Carolina*, 72.

7. Hobbs, "History of Keener United Methodist Church (1885–1997)," 1.

8. McCullen, *Antiquity Forgot: Reminiscences*, 52.

9. Hobbs, 1.

10. Ibid, 1.

11. Deed of Sale from B.C. Weeks and wife to Methodist Episcopal Church South, 18 January 1886, Sampson County, North Carolina, Deed Book 66, Page 266, Registrar of Deeds Office, Clinton, North Carolina. Keener Methodist Church History also reveals that Rev. J.T. Kendall pastored the church for one year. Also see Frank Sutton's, 1909 map of northern Sampson County for the church's location.

12. Hobbs, "History of Keener United Methodist Church (1885–1997)," 1. Also, in a personal interview with Stanley Carr on February 5, 2011, I learned that G.B. Cashwell was saved and greatly impacted by the 1885 Keener Revival held by Rev. J.T. Kendall in August 1885.

13. The 1881 North Carolina Methodist Handbook of Church Discipline.

14. Ibid, 1881 N.C. Methodist Handbook.

15. In testing the information provided by Ann Hobbs History of the Keener Methodist Church, Keener United Methodists original land deed, and the Cashwell families oral history about G.B. Cashwell's church membership, I personally researched numerous churches and denominations for G.B. Cashwell's name. They included: Southern Baptist, Free Will-Baptist, Methodist, Presbyterian, and Catholic. Rev. G.B. Cashwell's name is not found on any of these records. After endless phone calls and e-mails, I concluded that the histories provided here by Ann Hobbs and J.T. McCullen are completely accurate.

16. *The North Carolina Methodist Handbook of Discipline 1881*. Parts of this book were e-mailed to me by request from Laura Dallas of the N.C. United Methodist Church in Raleigh, North Carolina, on July 26, 2011. The provisions of trustees in the Methodist Church at this time are found under, "Section VVI Trustees."

17. J.T. McCullen, "Persimmon College an Early Name for Keener," *Heritage of Sampson County, North Carolina*, p. 35. Also see, McCullen, "Prayer Meeting At Persimmon College," *Not in Entire Forgetfulness* (n.p. 1990), 1–7.

18. Record of Funeral for Gaston B. Cashwell, March 4, 1916, File No. 204. Skinner and Smith Funeral Home, Dunn, North Carolina. After the initial year of the Keener Revival in 1885, G.B. Cashwell, A.H. Brewer, and J.F. Gore cease to be found on any more records of Keener United Methodist Church. There is no record that he preached there or was ever a member. For more information on the prayer services conducted in Persimmon College, see J.T. McCullen, "Prayer Meeting At Persimmon College," *Not in Entire Forgetfulness* (n.p. 1990), 1–7.

19. "Sparks Caught at the Tent Meeting: Crumpler's Hot Shots," *The County Union*. May 20, 1896, 3. For A.B. Crumpler's "sanctified" experience in 1890, see Vinson Synan, *Old Time Power*, 68.

20. Grace Crumpler Vann, "First United Methodist Church: 1854–1997," 19, 29. Grace Crumpler Vann is one of two children born to Abner Blackmon and Lilly Jane Crumpler. In 1954, Grace C. Vann compiled a significant amount research together and wrote this excellent history of Methodism in Clinton, North Carolina.

21. Personal Study Bible of A.B. Crumpler. In addition, A.B. Crumpler also wrote in the marriage date to his second wife, Pet Holland Crumpler. After the death of his first wife Lilly Jane Crumpler, on September 15, 1917, Rev. A.B. Crumpler remarried Pet Holland on November 15, 1921. Pet H. Crumpler passed away in 1950. Interestingly, Rev. A.B. Crumpler outlived both of his wives and didn't pass until 1952. He was eighty-nine-years-old.

22. J.M. Pike, *Way of Faith*, December 23, 1896, 5.

23. For early accounts of A.B. Crumpler and J.T. Kendall working together see, J.M. Pike, *Way of Faith*, December 4, 1895, 1. For an early account of A.B. Crumpler and G.B. Cashwell working together, see, "History of Goshen Pentecostal Holiness Church," 1. For a record of G.B. Cashwell and J.T. Kendall in 1886 see, Deed of Sale from B.C. Weeks and wife to Methodist Episcopal

Church South, January 18, 1886, Sampson County, North Carolina, Deed Book 66, Page 266, Registrar of Deeds Office, Clinton, North Carolina.

Chapter 4
Ancient Wells of Revival

1. In 1896 under the preaching of A.B. Crumpler, the Holiness Movement ripped through the coastal and piedmont regions of North Carolina. In the same year, the Cherokee Native Americans of Camp Creek, North Carolina, experienced the first outpouring of the Pentecostal baptism with the Holy Spirit. Known as the Shearer Schoolhouse Revival, this powerful outbreak occurred ten years before Azusa Street in 1906. For more on the North Carolina Shearer Schoolhouse revival in 1896 see Charles Conn, *Like a Mighty Army: A History of the Church of God 1886–1976* (Cleveland, Tennessee: Pathway, 1977), 13–21. According to an outstanding message preached by Perry Stone in 2011 entitled, "The Cherokee Link to the End Time Outpouring," the North Carolina Cherokee Native Americans were among the first to experience the baptism of the Holy Spirit and speaking in tongues. Interestingly, in eastern North Carolina, the Coharie and Lumbee Indian tribes, as well as African Americans, were among the first to experience fires of sanctification and love of Pentecost under the preaching of A.B. Crumpler and G.B. Cashwell.
2. Vinson Synan, *The Century of the Holy Spirit: 100 Years of Pentecostal and Charismatic Renewal*, 32.
3. Kenneth O. Brown, *Inskip, McDonald, Fowler: "Wholly and Forever Thine"* (Hazelton, Pennsylvania: Holiness Archives), 1999, 79, 81, 84. Very little information about the 1867 Vineland Holiness Camp Meeting has ever been published. Dr. Kenneth Brown has done an extraordinary job in researching and bringing to life just what occurred at Landis Park in July, 1867. *Inskip, McDonald, Fowler: Wholly and Forever Thine* is filled with rare photographs, vivid detail accounts, and excellent primary sources that gives readers a play-by-play of this powerful revival.
4. Ibid, 80.
5. Ibid, 80.
6. Ibid, 81.
7. Ibid, 81.
8. Ibid, 81. For more on the Moravian Love Feast see John R. Weinlick, *Count Zinzendorf* (New York: Abingdon, 1956), 85.
9. Eddie L. Hyatt, *2000 Years of Charismatic Christianity* (Lake Mary, Florida: Charisma House, 2002), 105. Also see Vinson Synan, *Old Time Power*, 70–71.
10. Kenneth Brown, 71–72, 78.
11. Ibid, 83.
12. Ibid, 84. On July 27, 2009, my family and I visited the Manheim, Pennsylvania site of the second annual Holiness Camp Meeting. Sitting on the property today is a private veterinarian business. There are no historic markers, landmarks, or signs stating what happed there in 1868. Using the old map in Dr. Brown's book, we were able to find the location. Interestingly, the land is still laid out in the Ezekiel wheel formation, and one of the old wells of water still survives. Stepping onto the property, I remember feeling something like lightening jolt through my body. It was and still is holy ground. We prayed and asked the Lord to stir up that ancient well again.
13. Barlow Gorham, *Camp Meeting Manual: A Practical Book for the Camp Ground in Two Parts* (Boston: H.V. Degen, 1854), 28–31.
14. Brown, 84–85.
15. Ibid, 85. With Bishop Alexander Wayman of African Methodist Church and Bishop Henry Boehm taking leading roles during the encampment, the Manheim Revival was a powerful spectacle of Christian unity.
16. William Kostlevy, "The Holiness Movement, the Manheim Camp Meeting and C. H. Balsbaugh: Christian Perfection in Pennsylvania Dutch Country." Brethren Life and Thought 48 (Winter and Spring 2003), 97.
17. Ibid, 97.
18. Ibid, 101–104.
19. Brown, 90.
20. Ibid, 91.
21. Ibid, 93.
22. Ibid, 93.

23. Ibid, 94.
24. Ibid, 95.
25. Ibid, 97.
26. W. McDonald and John E. Searles, *The Life of Rev. John S. Inskip* (New York: Garland, 1985), 263.
27. Ibid, 270–271.
28. Ibid, 271–272.
29. Grace Crumpler Vann, "First United Methodist Church 1854–1997," 19. I requested a copy of this history by contacting the First United Methodist Church in Clinton, North Carolina.
30. *The Discipline of the Holiness Church* (Goldsboro, NC: Nash Brothers, [c. 1902]) 3.
31. Ibid, 3.
32. *The Sampson Democrat,* November 15, 1894. I am indebted to John Aman for this information. While searching old newspapers, Mr. Aman found this reference to Rev. A.B. Crumpler. He transcribed the article on August 16, 2011, and mailed it to me.
33. J.M. Pike, *Way of Faith*, December 4, 1895, 1. Currently, this article is the earliest account written by Rev. A.B. Crumpler. It contains insightful information regarding Crumpler's early revivals in eastern North Carolina. Also see J.M. Pike, "Jesus Triumphs at Ingold, N.C." *Way of Faith*, January 15, 1896, 1.
34. J.M. Pike, *Way of Faith*, December 4, 1895, 1.
35. *The Apostolic Faith*, December 1906, 3. According to this article written by G.B. Cashwell to the Azusa Street Mission, Cashwell started preaching holiness around the year 1897. However, it does not reveal when he first encountered the Holiness Movement. For Cashwell's involvement with "colored saints" while preaching holiness, see *HA*, October 15, 1903, 8.
36. J.T. McCullen "Gaston B. Cashwell Once a Prodigal Son," *Heritage of Sampson County, North Carolina*, 87. Also see Kenneth O. Brown, *Inskip, McDonald, Fowler: Wholly and Forever Thine*, 268.
37. 1850 United States Census (Free Schedule), Dooly, Georgia. This census reveals that P.H. Crumpler's father was James H. Crumpler, who was born in Sampson County, North Carolina. Using www.ancestry.com, www.findagrave.com, and www.familysearch.org, I was able to confidently piece together P.H. Crumpler's family ties back to Rev. A.B. Crumpler.

P.H. Crumpler also descends from John Crumpler Sr., the Crumpler patriarch of Sampson County, North Carolina. This makes P.H. Crumpler and A.B. Crumpler second cousins. For unidentified reasons, P.H. Crumpler's grandfather, John B. Crumpler, uprooted his family from Sampson County and relocated to Dooly, Georgia, sometime during the 1830s.

38. *Minutes South Georgia [Methodist Episcopal Church South] Conference, 1920*, 86. On August 11, 2011, I received an exciting e-mail from Sandra Harris. Upon my request, she located these records of Rev. P.H. Crumpler as well as an old photo of the burning revivalist. She sent me this material from the Moore Methodist Museum. The museum is located in St. Simons Island, Georgia. The museum holds records for the South Georgia Conference of the United Methodist Church.
39. *The News and Observer*, December 17, 1897, 6. Also see *Fayetteville Observer*, March 4, 1897, n.p. A.B. Crumpler personally mentions P.H. Crumpler in a revival they both conducted in Clinton, North Carolina, on July 5, 1896. For this reference see J.M. Pike, *Way of Faith*, August 5, 1896, 5.
40. *Fayetteville Observer,* July 23, 1896, n.p.
41. This is quoted in Oscar Bizzell, "Abner B. Crumpler Was Clinton's Outstanding Evangelist," *Heritage of Sampson County*, 86.
42. *The News and Observer*, December 17, 1896, 6.
43. *Minutes South Georgia [Methodist Episcopal Church South] Conference, 1920*, 87.
44. Beacham, *Azusa East: The Life and Times of G.B. Cashwell*, 19–20.
45. At this time, there is no record to prove that P.H. Crumpler converted G.B. Cashwell to holiness. However, there is significance evidence that points to this possibility. Based on Dr. McCullen's account of G.B. Cashwell in "Gaston B. Cashwell Once a Prodigal Son," Cashwell indeed converted to the Holiness Movement while in Georgia in 1893. Rev. P.H. Crumpler seems to be the preacher responsible for bringing this about.
46. "Sparks Caught at the Tent Meeting," *The County Union*, May 27, 1896, 3.
47. J.M. Pike, "Warsaw, North Carolina." *Way of Faith*, September 2, 1896, 1.
48. Pike, "A New Evangelist on a New Line," *Way of Faith*, December 23, 1896, 5.
49. A.B. Crumpler moved from Clinton to Goldsboro, North Carolina, in January 1901. See, *The Goldsboro Weekly Argus*, January 24, 1901, 3. G.B. Cashwell moved to Ayden, North Carolina,

around the same time. See, *The Democratic Banner,* March 13, 1901, 3. Ayden is about twenty-five miles from Goldsboro. Riding the Atlantic Coastline railroad that ran through Ayden, G.B. Cashwell could have traveled to Goldsboro very quickly.

Chapter 5
Carolina Fire

1. William C. Turner, Jr. *The United Holy Church of America: A Study in Black Holiness-Pentecostalism* (Gorgias Press, 2006), 20.
2. Ibid., 21.
3. *HA*, September 16, 1901, 2.
4. Ibid. For more detailed information between A.B. Crumpler's Holiness Church and the United Holy Church working together see, *HA*, September 16, 1901, 2.
5. See J.M. Pike, *Way of Faith*, November 6, 1895, 5.
6. Pike, "God For Me: Man Against Me," *Way of Faith*, September, 23, 1896, 1. This article is W.W. Avant's personal testimony. It gives excellent insight into some of the rejection these ministers endured when they chose to embrace the holiness call.
7. Pike, *Way of Faith*, July 22, 1896, 5.
8. During 1896, Avant and Page cut their teeth in and around Roberson County, North Carolina. One of their greatest strongholds was in Lumberton, North Carolina. Lumberton is home to the Lumbee Indian Tribe. Today the N.C., Lumbee Tribe is the largest Indian tribe east of the Mississippi. For Avant and Pages work in Lumberton see Pike, *Way of Faith*, September 16, 1896, 4. For holiness partnerships between The United Holy Church of America and some of these independent white holiness ministers see Pike, "Holiness Among the Colored People in North Carolina," *Way of Faith*, March 14, 1900, 1.
9. Pike, "Vineland Tabernacle Meeting Near Whiteville, N.C.," *Way of Faith*, May 20, 1896, 1. Also see, www.vinelanddepot.com
10. *The News and Observer*, July 25, 1896, 5.
11. Ibid, 5. Trances were quite common for folks who attended A.B. Crumpler's meetings. This article highlights how country people in Wayne County, North Carolina, laid in trances under the power of God.
12. *Plessy v. Ferguson*, 163 U.S. 537, 16 S. Ct. 1138, 41 L. Ed. 256 (1896). Available at http://www.lawnix.com/cases/plessy-ferguson.htm. This was a landmark Supreme Court case that ruled in favor of "separate but equal" as a federal law.
13. J.M. Pike, *Way of Faith*, January 15, 1896, 1.
14. *The County Union*, April 1, 1896, 3.
15. *The County Union*, May 20, 1896, 3. Also see, *The County Union*, May 27, 1896, 3.
16. Ibid., 3. In light of national and state interests over *Plessy v. Ferguson*, there was a lot of political aggression towards the race issue during 1896. Additionally, North Carolina was becoming a hotbed for the KKK and Red Shirt activity. Thus, A.B. Crumpler was making a bold statement during his famous "Sermon to the Colored." Vigorously, Crumpler fought to bring the Holiness Movement to all people; especially poor Native-Americans, African Americans, and those who were mixed. Without these articles, this wonderful aspect of A.B. Crumpler's ministry would be lost.
17. For a glimpse into Sampson County, North Carolina's racial and political atmosphere during this time, see Vann R. Newkirk, *Lynching in North Carolina: A History, 1865–1941*, 3–6.
18. *The County Union*, June 17, 1896, 3. A week after Crumpler left Dunn for another meeting in Goldsboro, in June 1896, the paper was recoding the revival spirit amidst the African American and Native American portions of Dunn.
19. Ibid., 3
20. Ibid.
21. *The County Union*, May 27, 1896, 3. Also see, *The County Union*, June 17, 1896, 3.
22. See Vinson Synan, *Old Time Power*, 69, 87.
23. Florence Goff, *Fifty Years on the Battlefield for God* (Falcon, North Carolina: self-published, 1948), 20.
24. "History of the Pentecostal Free Will Baptist Church," by Preston Heath, Herbert F. Carter, Don Sauls, R.M. Brown. Available at, www.pfwb.org/history/htm. Also see, "A Summary of the Conference Minutes 1855–2010," by Alan K. Lamm, Gary Barefoot, Michael Pelt, and Ricky Warren. Both of these accounts are un-published histories about the early years of the North Carolina Cape

Fear Conference of the Free Will-Baptist Church. I received a copy of "A Summary of the Conference Minuets 1855–2010" through Gary Barefoot on March 1, 2012. Mr. Barefoot is the curator of Mt. Olive College in Mt. Olive, North Carolina. I am indebted to Mr. Barefoot's hard work and faithful correspondence that has helped me learn more about G.B. Cashwell and A.B. Crumpler.

25. Goff, *Fifty Years on the Battlefield for God*, 20. Florence Goff's account mentions all of these preachers names in connection with the sweeping Holiness Movement through the Cape Fear Conference of the North Carolina Free Will-Baptist Church.

Chapter 6
Merging Holiness Streams

1. Vinson Synan, *The Century of the Holy Spirit: 100 Years of Pentecostal and Charismatic Renewal*, 32.

2. For Jewish inspired methods for camp meeting holiness revivalism see Barlow Gorham, *Camp Meeting Manual: A Practical Book for the Camp Ground in Two Parts*, 28–31. For other holiness methods including: location, relationship building, love feasts and unity see Kenneth O. Brown, *Inskip, McDonald, Fowler: Wholly and Forever Thine*, 76–79. Dr. Brown's book covers all of the State Holiness Associations that were birthed through the historic Vineland, New Jersey Camp Meeting. He also lists the date and location for every annual National Holiness Camp Meeting.

3. *The Pentecostal Holiness Advocate*, January 27, 1921, 6.

4. J.M. Pike, "North Carolina Holiness Association," *Way of Faith,* May 20, 1896, 5. This very rare article shows that the North Carolina State Holiness Association was organized in Vineland, North Carolina, during April 19–May 3, 1896.

5. J.M. Pike, *Way of Faith*, November 17, 1895, 5.

6. See *Constitution and By-Laws, and Minutes of the First Session of the North Carolina Holiness Convention*, (Goldsboro, North Carolina: Nash Brothers, 1899), 7.

7. *Way of Faith*, November 17, 1895, 5.

8. J.M. Pike, "Vineland Tabernacle Meeting Near Whiteville, N.C.," *Way of Faith*, May 20, 1896, 1.

9. *Way of Faith*, May 20, 1896, 5.

10. *The Fayetteville Observer*, July 23, 1896, n.p.

11. J.M. Pike, *Way of Faith*, July 22, 1896, 5. Rev. Ed Kelly played an important role in the formation of the North Carolina Holiness Association in Vineland, North Carolina, during 1896. Rev. Kelly came out of the Methodist Church in Wilmington, N.C., See Pike, *Way of Faith*, November 6, 1895, 2.

12. J.M. Pike, *Way of Faith*, August 5, 1896, 5.

13. The belief that G.B. Cashwell was a part of this Clinton revival is based upon Dr. McCullen's, *Antiquity Forgot: Reminiscences*, 88–95. According to McCullen, G.B. Cashwell's immediate family members were known for helping inmates in the county jail. In addition, Cashwell descendants also visited and encouraged residents in Clinton's "poor house." G.B. Cashwell's nieces, Myrtie McCullen and Poca Gore baked teacakes, and the children would gather various fruits. As a family, they would take their offerings of love and kindness and share them with some of Sampson County's worst of criminals—white and black.

Further evidence is seen in A.B. Crumpler's, *Holiness Advocate*, October 15, 1903, 8. Here G.B. Cashwell preaches to the "colored saints" of Hood Swamp, located in Wayne County, North Carolina. This occurred three years before he traveled to the Azusa Street Mission in November 1906. Although these seem to be noble feats today, in Cashwell's time, this kind of ministry was very unpopular. Perhaps this is why G.B. Cashwell and his family always seemed to remain under the radar and out of the spotlight.

14. J.M. Pike, *Way of Faith*, September 16, 1896, 4.

15. Ibid., 4.

16. *PHA*, January 27, 1921, 6.

17. Harold Stan York, *George Floyd Taylor: The Life of an Early Southern Pentecostal Leader.* Unpublished dissertation, 5–6, 33. Dr. York submitted this very well researched dissertation to Regent University in March 2012.

18. J.M Pike, *Way of Faith*, March 14, 1900, 1. Also see, *Third Annual Session Holiness Convocation of North Carolina, September 1897.* These are the minutes for the third Holiness

Convocation for the United Holy Church of America. The meetings took place in Durham, North Carolina, during September 5–12, 1897. G.A. Mial is recorded as the church's secretary.

19. Pike, March 14, 1900, 1.

20. See Pike, *Way of Faith,* October 13, 1897, 5. This article reveals Rev. P.H. Crumpler working with "Bro. Williams" among the "colored people" of Robeson County, North Carolina. Following the victory, P.H. Crumpler and other burning revivalist met at Vineland, North Carolina. The "cyclone" refers to Rev. B.H. Irwin and the Fire-Baptized Movement.

21. *HA*, September 16, 1901, 2.

Chapter 7
Goldsboro: The Gateway City

1. *Goldsboro: The Gate City of Eastern North Carolina* (n.p., 1923), 1, 3. This was retrieved from the Digital Collections of East Carolina University. Available at, http://digital.lib.ecu.edu/16980.2

2. Ibid., 3.

3. Vinson Synan, *Old Time Power*, 82.

4. "The Crumpler Meetings at Goldsboro," *The County Union*, June 17, 1896, 3. Originally, this article was published first in the *Goldsboro Daily Argus*. Dunn's newspaper, *The County Union,* re-published the article for local residents to see.

5. J.M. Pike, *Way of Faith*, June 24, 1896, 5. Pike's paper also re-published articles of Crumpler's historic meeting in Goldsboro during June 1896. Also see, *Way of Faith*, August 12, 1896, 5.

6. *Way of Faith*, June 24, 1896, 5.

7. Ibid. The article reveals that Crumpler's later work in Goldsboro was first built upon inter-denominational and inter-racial gatherings. Most of these converts would become the first members of the Pentecostal Holiness Church in Goldsboro.

8. Proof of this early association is found in Pike's, *Way of Faith*, October 20, 1897, 5. This reference reveals that Rev. Edward Kelly was scheduled to attend the "Goldsboro, North Carolina Holiness Association" on November 10, 1897. This can potentially open a new argument of when exactly the first Goldsboro Pentecostal Holiness Church was organized. The earliest account comes from Rev. A.H. Butler in 1898; however, this Goldsboro association could prove that there was a holiness church in Goldsboro in 1897 and possibly in the fall of 1896 following A.B. Crumpler's historic revival. Rev. H.W. Jernigan's account is found in *The County Union*, April 7, 1897, 3. Rev. J.T. Kendall's account is found in *Way of Faith*, December 23, 1896. 5.

9. See Vinson Synan, *Old Time Power*, 73–74.

10. *PHA*, January 20, 1921, 9. Rev. G.F. Taylor's assertion, along with numerous reports in *The County Union*, *The Goldsboro Daily Argus*, and *The News and Observer* all reveal and confirm that Eastern North Carolina's Holiness Movement began among African Americans, Native Americans, and poor country folks.

11. A.B. Crumpler, *The Discipline of the Holiness Church* (Goldsboro, North Carolina: Nash Brothers, 1902), 4.

12. Vinson Synan, *Old Time Power*, 76.

13. *The Goldsboro Weekly Argus*, January 6, 1898, 3. Also see, *The Goldsboro Weekly Argus*, March 17, 1898, 3.

14. *The Goldsboro Weekly Argus*, March 24, 1898, 3.

15. Ibid.

16. *The Goldsboro Weekly Argus*, April 21, 1898, 3. See chapter nine for more details about the Wilmington's Race Riots of 1898.

17. See Catherine W. Bishir, "Landmarks of Power: Building a Southern Past, 1885-–1915," *Where These Memories Grow: History and Southern Identity*, 15.

18. Synan, Old Time Power, 81.

19. Eddie Morris, *The Vine and Branches John15:5*, 28–29. See Synan, *Old Time Power*, 75-76.

20. I searched *The Goldsboro Weekly Argus* from years 1897–1908. After the April 21, 1898, reference of Crumpler folding up his tent, the *Argus* did not mention A.B. Crumpler until he returned to Goldsboro and attended the Holiness Convention on February 15, 1900.

21. Morris, *The Vine and Branches John15: 5*, 29.

22. Synan, *Old Time Power*, 80.

23. *Fayetteville Observer*, December 31, 1896, n.p. Crumpler was undeterred by this display of vandalism. The article goes on to say that "the next night the meeting was held in the open air, and a collection amounting to nearly one hundred dollars was taken up to replace it."

24. Synan, *Old Time Power*, 74.

25. J.M. Pike, *Way of Faith*, July 5, 1898, 2. On September 7, 2011, I received an outstanding e-mail from Mr. Gary Barefoot of Mt. Olive College about the missing issue of Pike's *Way of Faith*. Mr. Barefoot writes, "Here is an article I found in a copy of The Way of Faith (Pike newspaper) by A.B. Crumpler. This was done about the time he was preaching at the FWB church, St. Paul that I sent you yesterday. It says much about his relationship with the Methodist church and gives some time frame of his membership with them. Incidentally, this copy of the paper was a personal copy of T. F. Harrison, the first husband of Lovie Lee. He was co-author of History of North Carolina Free Will Baptists, done in 1897 with J. M Barfield. Both were of course, FWB preachers. It also says that Harrison was subscribing to the paper himself." Amazingly, this lost issue was found with Lovie Lee Cashwell's first husband, T.F. Harrison.

26. Ibid. It is interesting to note that A.B. Crumpler left the Methodist Church in very good standing. Although he was firm and aggressive in his preaching, Rev. Crumpler still demonstrated spiritual maturity by submitting to church authorities.

27. Ibid., 2.

28. *HA*, June 1, 1904, 4.

29. Ibid., 4, 5.

30. A.B. Crumpler, *The Disciple of The Holiness Church*, 3.

31. *HA*, August 1, 1901, 2. In A.B. Crumpler's "Articles of Faith" for the Holiness Church, Crumpler states that his congregations would be set like the Missionary Baptist Church. This is found in section XXI: The Ministry. Even after Crumpler wrote a more formal church *Discipline* in 1902, he still made it clear that the Holiness Church congregations would be independent, congregational, and inter-denominational. Furthermore, under Section 2, Article 2, of the 1902 *Discipline*, A.B. Crumpler encouraged holiness people to be joined with other denominations. In essence, these early holiness churches were no more than meetinghouses for sanctified Christians, where both white and black followers of holiness could come and worship together while retaining their original church membership.

32. *H.A.* July 15, 1904, 4.

33. Vinson Synan, *Old Time Power*, 80–81.

34. Although the exact date of A.B. Crumpler's pastoral position is not known, the Goldsboro newspaper lists A.B. Crumpler as the "pastor of the Pentecostal Holiness Church in this city." See, *Goldsboro Weekly Argus*, August 9, 1900, 3. For more on the Goldsboro Tabernacle see *PHA*, March 3, 10, 1921, 8.

35. *HA*, May 1, 1903, 4. For A.B. Crumpler's work among Goldsboro's African Americans see Pike's *Way of Faith*, June 24, 1896, 5.

36. "Our Local Optic," *Goldsboro Weekly Argus*, August 9, 1900, 3.

37. *Goldsboro Weekly Argus*, August 16, 1900, 3.

38. *Goldsboro Weekly Argus*, September 6, 1900, 3.

39. *Goldsboro Weekly Argus*, August 9, 1900, 3.

40. *HA*, April 15, 1901, 2.

Chapter 8
G.B. Cashwells Missing Holiness Years

1. *HA*, September 2, 1901, 2. This article reveals that Crumpler did not allow "preachers" within the Holiness Church to use tobacco. However, Crumpler never puts this same stipulation upon local farmers and sharecroppers most of which were members of the Holiness Church. According to G.F. Taylor, it was J.A. Culbreth in 1903 who forced a rule into the Holiness Church that forbade laymen to use, cultivate, and manufacture tobacco, not A.B. Crumpler. See *PHA*, March 3, 10, 1921. 9.

2. J.T. McCullen, *A Wild-Goose Miscellany* (n.p. 1988)25. Also see Mary McCullen Savage, "The Medicine Women of Persimmon College," *Heritage of Sampson County, North Carolina*, 196. Looking at tobacco from this perspective, it is easy to understand how this issue ripped congregations apart during the turn of the century in rural in North Carolina.

3. Margret Bass Gore, "John R. and Ann Pender Bass Family," *Heritage of Sampson County, North Carolina*, 297–298. In my interview with Stanley Carr on March 5, 2011, I learned that G.B. Cashwell and his brother-in-law, John R. Bass, made good money growing and selling tobacco.

4. Doug Beacham, *Azusa East: The Life and Times of G.B. Cashwell*, 20.

5. Ibid., 20, 21.

6. J.T. McCullen, "Prayer Meeting at Persimmon College," *Not In Entire Forgetfulness* (n.p. 1990) 1–2.

7. See notes in chapter 4, "G.B. Cashwell's Holiness Conversion."

8. McCullen, *Antiquity Forgot: Reminiscences*, 6.

9. Elizabeth Ross, *Sampson County Will Abstracts 1784–1900*, 22. This is the Last Will and Testament of Herring Cashwell, dated October 12, 1878, probated November 2, 1878. According to this will, Herring Cashwell left his son, G.B. Cashwell fifty acres of land. This land is currently situated where Halls Fire Department stands today. Somewhere in this vicinity was where G.B. Cashwell's tobacco barn once stood.

10. At the present time, no existence of G.B. Cashwell's ordination papers or license to preach has ever been found.

11. *The Apostolic Faith*, December 1906, 3.

12. HA, October 15, 1903, 8. Also see, HA, July 15, 1904, 8 for G.B. Cashwell holding meetings in "Keeners School House."

13. In my personal interview with Stanley Carr on March 5, 2011, I realized that G.B. Cashwell's early ministry most likely evolved around Sampson County's minority population. For an excellent source showing A.B. Crumpler and G.B. Cashwell working together prior to 1903, see "History of Goshen Pentecostal Holiness Church," 1.

14. *PHA*, February 24, 1921, 8. Rev. G.F. Taylor notes that Cashwell joined the Holiness Church at Dunn in 1903. However, the Goshen P.H. Church history reveals that Crumpler and Cashwell were organizing holiness churches during March of 1900, and possibly earlier.

15. Record of Funeral for Gaston B. Cashwell, March 4, 1916, Harnett County, North Carolina. The original record is located at Skinner and Smith Funeral Home, Dunn, North Carolina. Lovie Cashwell, Gaston's wife, filled out this record as soon as G.B. Cashwell passed away. She listed his religious affiliation as being "M. Baptist."

16. For Cashwell's admittance in the Goldsboro Holiness Convention see, *Proceedings of the Eighth Annual Convention of the Holiness Church of North Carolina*, November 20, 1907, 15. The minutes list G.B. Cashwell as having joined the Holiness Convention at Goldsboro in 1903. This must have been a typo. The Holiness Convention did not meet in Goldsboro in 1903. The Goldsboro Convention met in February 1900. By 1903, G.B. Cashwell and A.B. Crumpler had already established numerous Holiness Congregations in southeastern North Carolina. See, "History of Goshen Pentecostal Holiness Church," 1. For the early structure of these holiness churches see A.B. Crumpler, *The Discipline of the Holiness Church* (Goldsboro, North Carolina: Nash Brothers, 1902), 14

17. A.B. Crumpler, *The Discipline of the Holiness Church* (Goldsboro, North Carolina: Nash Brothers, 1902), 14. Also see Florence Goff, *Fifty Years on the Battlefield for God*, 40–41. This book reveals Rev. H.H. Goff's involvement with A.B. Crumpler while a member of the Free Will Baptist Church.

18. *Proceedings of the Eighth Annual Convention of the Holiness Church of North Carolina*, November 20, 1907, 15. Also see, *Goldsboro Weekly Argus*, February 15, 1900, 3.

19. J.M. Pike, *Way of Faith*, January 8, 1896, 1. Also see, *Way of Faith*, January 15, 1896, 1. Both issues reveal that A.B. Crumpler's early revivals started in Bladen and Sampson Counties. Most of them occurred within several miles of the G.B. Cashwell farm.

20. Pike, "The Victory at Goshen," *Way of Faith*, March 25, 1896, 2. This is the only vivid account of the powerful revival that A.B. Crumpler conducted at Goshen. This revival spawned Goshen Holiness Church four years later in March 1900. Interestingly, G.B. Cashwell organized the church along with A.B. Crumpler. Cashwell also became the churches first pastor in 1900. See, "Goshen P.H. Church History," 1. There is also a photograph of the old Goshen Holiness Church circulating. It was taken in the early 1900s when G.B. Cashwell was ministering there. The photograph appeared in a Newton Grove newspaper sometime during the year 2000.

21. *The Fayetteville Observer*, July 23, 1896, n.p.

22. In a phone interview with Stanley Carr on September 24, 2011, I was informed that G.B. Cashwell helped A.B. Crumpler start the First Pentecostal Holiness Church around 1900. Mr. Carr was told this by his mother, Lottie Carr, who knew Rev. G.B. Cashwell personally.

23. *HA*, August 1, 1901, 2

24. Ibid.

25. *The County Union*, March 22, 1899, 3. Never seen before, this is the belated wedding announcement of Lovie and the "Rev. G.B. Cashwell."

26. See Chapter three's footnotes concerning the connections between J.T. Kendall, A.B. Crumpler, and G.B. Cashwell.

27. For the Holiness Convention's early protocol for issuing preaching credentials within Holiness Churches see, *Constitution and By-Laws, and Minuets of the First Session of the North Carolina Holiness Convention*, October 26–28, 1899 (Goldsboro, North Carolina: Nash Brothers, 1899), 7.

28. Record of Funeral for Lovie H. Cashwell, October 16, 1944, Harnett County, North Carolina. The original record is located at Cromartie-Miller and Lee Funeral Home, Dunn, North Carolina. For Mrs. G.B. Cashwell's obituary see, *The Dunn Dispatch*, October 17, 1944, n.p. Lovie's father's side of the family, the Lees, were a deeply rooted Masonic family. For Erasmus Lee's Masonic afflation in the Mingo Masonic Lodge, see, *The County Union,* February 9, 1898, 3.

29. In a personal interview with Emma Lee Laine on March 1, 2012, I learned that Erasmus Lee and his family settled in the Black River Township. Emma Lee Laine is Erasmus Lee's granddaughter and Lovie Cashwell's niece. For the Culbreth's move to the same area see V. Mayo Bundy, *A History of Falcon, North Carolina* (Charlotte, North Carolina: Herb Eaton, 1980), 14.

30. *The Dunn Dispatch*, October 17, 1944, n.p.

31. In a personal interview with Gary Barefoot on April 5, 2011, I learned of Rev. T. F. Harrison's impact within the Free Will Baptist Church. Mr. Barefoot is the curator for Mt. Olive College in Mt. Olive, North Carolina. The archives of this college hold excellent historical documents and rare photographs of T.F. Harrison and his contributions to Christianity.

32. *The County Union*, April 24, 1895, 3.

33. "Marriage Just Over the County Line in Cumberland," *The Central Times*, May 15, 1895, 3.

34. Beacham, *Azusa East: The Life and Times of G.B. Cashwell*, 21–22. In my interview with Mr. Barefoot, he informed me that Rev. T.F. Harrison passed away due to a severe case of typhoid fever.

35. J.M. Pike, *Way of Faith*, April 7, 1897, n.p. I am indebted to Mr. Barefoot and the Free Will Baptist Church for saving this rare and missing issue of Pikes' *Way of Faith.*

36. Alan K. Lamm, Gary Barefoot, Michael Pelt, and Ricky Warren, "A Summary of the Conference Minutes 1855-2010," (n.p., 2010), 12–13. Unpublished manuscript.

37. *The County Union*, April 29, 1896, 3. In our interview, Mr. Barefoot also revealed that Emma Lee, Lovie Cashwell's sister, became a teacher at the Free Will Baptist Seminary in Ayden. The archives of Mt. Olive College holds a photograph of the old FWB seminary while it was in Ayden, North Carolina. Taken in May 1902, the picture shows Emma Lee, and Paul L. Cashwell. Paul was the Cashwell's first son and he was born in Ayden in 1902. Lovie and G.B. Cashwell are not in the picture, but were most likely preaching in the area.

38. Personal Interview with Emma Lee Laine on March 1, 2012.

39. Certificate of Marriage, Gaston B. Cashwell to Lovie L. Harrison, March 7, 1899, Harnett County, North Carolina. Harnett County Register of Deeds Office, Lillington, North Carolina.

40. For the Goff's interaction with Cashwells, see Florence Goff, *Fifty Years on the Battlefield for God*, 52.

41. *The County Union*, March 22, 1899, 3.

42. Ibid.

43. Doug Beacham, *Azusa East: The Life and Times of G.B. Cashwell*, 22.

44. "Pleasant H. Crumpler," *Minuets South Georgia Conference, 1920* (n.p.), 87.

45. *The Democratic Banner*, March 13, 1901, 3.

46. "The History of Goshen Pentecostal Holiness Church," 1.

47. For G.B. Cashwell's early holiness ministry in this section of North Carolina see *HA*, August 1, 1902, 8. *HA*, September 15, 1902, 4. *HA*, October 15, 1903, 8.

48. Ibid.

49. *HA,* August 1, 1902, 8.

50. *HA*, September 15, 1902, 4.

51. *HA*, October 15, 1903, 8.

52. "From the Field: Goshen, N.C.," *HA*, April 1, 1904, 8.

53. Personal Interview with Stanley Carr on March 5, 2011.

54. Jimmy Swinson, "St. Matthews Pentecostal Holiness Church History," 1. This history was compiled in later years by Jimmy Swinson, who is a pastor with the Pentecostal Holiness Church. Unfortunately, this history leaves out G.B. Cashwell's involvement with the church. According to Stanley Carr,

G.B. Cashwell played a huge role in founding the church and later brought it to the Pentecostal Movement. It seems that when Mr. Swinson wrote the history, he never had a chance to explore in depth the origins of the church that stood no less than two miles from the old Cashwell farm.

55. *HA*, May 15, 1904, 2. This article, written by Rev. A.H. Butler, reveals that the origins of St. Matthew's Pentecostal Holiness Church were rooted in the "old Cindy House." The Cindy House was an old ran down tenet house, where people went for sanctified meetings. In my interview with Stanley Carr, he revealed to me that Gaston aided in the Cindy House Prayer Meetings in the 1800s by holding brush arbor revivals.

56. Ibid.

57. Demographically, I used a 1909 map of Sampson County to estimate the distances of these churches. The map was constructed by Frank Sutton, Sampson Counties Geographer at the time.

Chapter 9
The External War:
White Supremacy vs. Holiness Church

1. Timothy B. Tyson, "The Ghosts of 1898: Wilmington's Race Riot and the Rise of White Supremacy," *The News and Observer*, November 17, 2006, 3.

2. Ibid., 3.

3. James L. Hunt, *Marion Butler and American Populism* (Chapel Hill, North Carolina: The University of North Carolina Press, 2003), 56.

4. Ibid., 10. For information on Senator Vance's Masonic Political career see Walter J. Klein, *He ain't heavy he's my BROTHER ZEB* (Raleigh, North Carolina: The Grand Lodge of A.F. and A.M. of North Carolina, 2005). For more information regarding Wilmington's African American population during this time, see, Timothy B. Tyson, 4.

5. Jerry B. Gershenhorn, *The Rise and Fall of Fusion Politics in North Carolina, 1880–1900*. Unpublished paper, 3. Dr. Gershenhorn is a distinguished author and professor at North Carolina Central University. This paper is an outstanding source for understanding the Fusion Political Movement in North Carolina during the late 1800s.

6. Ibid., 4.

7. Timothy B. Tyson, 6. For more information regarding white supremacy organization rallies see, *The County Union*, July 27, 1898, 3.

8. Timothy B. Tyson, 9. On March 24, 2011, my father and I spent several hours at the Grand Masonic Lodge in Raleigh, North Carolina. They permitted us to search through their membership records. Incredibly, they have a record of nearly every member of North Carolina Masonic Lodges dating back to the 1700s. Their records indicated that James Sprunt, C.B. Aycock, Robert Glenn, and Furifold Simmons were all members of the Masonic Lodges in North Carolina. Also see William R. Denslow, *10,000 Famous Freemasons vol. 1–4* (Richmond, Virginia: Macoy, 1957) for additional conformation concerning these North Carolina leaders and their Masonic membership.

9. Ibid. For A.M. Waddell's favorable disposition towards the KKK, see A.M. Waddell, *Some Memories of My Life* (Raleigh, North Carolina: Raleigh: Edwards and Broughton, 1908) 109–112.

10. "Ku Klux Klan," *Encyclopedia of Oklahoma History and Culture*. Available at http://digital.library.okstate.edu/encyclopedia/entires/k/ku001.html. For Nathaniel B. Forrest Masonic membership see William Denslow, *10, 000 Famous Freemasons vol. 2, n.p.* For a statement of the KKK's government structure see, *Klansman's Manual (1925),* Article II section IV, 2. Available online at http://history.hanover.edu/courses/excerpts/227kkkmanual.html.

11. Herman Green, *A History of Palmyra Lodge No. 147, A.F. and A.M. Dunn, North Carolina* (Dunn, North Carolina: n.p., 1963) 17-18. For news articles revealing these tactics of recruitment see *The County Union*, August 17, 1898, 3.

12. Timothy B. Tyson, 6. This outstanding article reveals powerful pictures of the infamous Carolina Red Shirts of 1898.

13. *The County Union*, November 9, 1898, 1.

14. Timothy B. Tyson, 9.

15. Ibid.

16. Ibid. Also see, Catherine W. Bishir, "Landmarks of Power: Building a Southern Past, 1885–1915," *Where the Memories Grow: History Memory and Southern Identity* (Chapel Hill, North Carolina: University of North Carolina Press, 2000) 15–18.

17. Timothy B. Tyson, 10.

18. Ibid., 11.
19. Ibid., 11.
20. Ibid., 3,8.
21. *Jim Crow Laws: North Carolina*. Available at http://www.findingsources.com/sitebuildercontent/sitebuilderfiles/jimcrowlawsnorthcarolina.pdf.

Also see, *Equal Protection of the Laws in North Carolina: A Report of the North Carolina Advisory Committee to the United States Commission on Civil Rights 1959–62* (n.p. 1962) 206.

22. Catherine W. Bishir, "Landmarks of Power: Building a Southern Past, 1885–1915," *Where the Memories Grow: History Memory and Southern Identity*, 21–25.
23. For some of A.B. Crumpler's articles against Freemasonry see:

Holiness Advocate, April 15, 1902, 1, 5; August 15, 1902, 5; June 1, 1903, 7; October 1, 1903, 3; October 15, 1903, 6; May 15, 1904, 4-5; June 1, 1904, 5; June 15, 1904, 4-5; July 15, 1904, 6.

24. Tobias Churton, *The Magus of Freemasonry: The Mysterious Life of Elias Ashmole-Scientists, Alchemist, and founder of the Royal Society* (Rochester, Vermont: Inner Traditions, 2006) 120–121. Interestingly, the Carolina Charter of 1663 covered every southern state in America. For its original boundaries see, *Original Boundaries of Carolina (1663/1665)*. Available at http://www.learnnc.org/lp/multimedia/6182. Also see, *Carolina Charter 1663*. Available at http://www.carolana.com/Carolina/Documents/charter1663.html.
25. Joe A. Mobley, *The Way We Lived in North Carolina* (Chapel Hill, North Carolina: The University of North Carolina Press, 2003), 30, 50–60. Also see Arwin D. Smallwood, *Bertie County: An Eastern Carolina History* (Charleston, South Carolina: Arcadia, 2002), 12–17, 100–102.
26. *Historical Table of Lodges Which Founded The Grand Lodge of North Carolina, Extinct Lodges, and Lodges Created By The Grand Lodge of North Carolina Since Its Organization in 1787.* (n.p.), 1. This is an extensive chart which reveals the location, year charted, and disposition of every Masonic Lodge in North Carolina since 1735. On March 24, 2011, I personally visited the Grand Masonic Lodge in Raleigh, North Carolina and received a copy of the chart. An excellent localized example of this is seen through the history of St. John's Lodge No. 13, A.F. and A.M. of Duplin County, North Carolina. For this history see Faison and Peal McGowen, *Flashes of Duplin's History and Government* (Raleigh, North Carolina: Edwards and Broughton, 1971), 169.
27. "The Origins of the Scottish Rite," *History of the Rite*. T*his material is taken from S. Brent Morris, The Complete Idiot's Guide to Freemasonry, Chapter 9: The Scottish Rite (New York: Alpha Books/Penguin, 2006). It is also available at http://scottishrite.org/about/history/*
28. *HA*, April 15, 1902, 1. See, William F. Whalen, *Christianity and American Freemasonry* (San Francisco, California: Ignatius, 1958), 16-18. Also see Timothy B. Tyson, 6, 8. Tyson charges Wilmington's "Secret Nine" along with N.C. Governor C.B. Aycock, N.C. Senator Furnifold Simmons, and N.C. Congressman Alfred M. Waddell as being the force behind the Democratic White Supremacy Campaign of 1898. All were active N.C. Freemasons during this time and promoted their agendas through lodge meetings.
29. Vann R. Newkirk, *Lynching in North Carolina: A History, 1865–1941* (Jefferson: McFarland, 2009), 9.
30. *The Democratic Banner*, April 3, 1901, n.p. Also see, *The County Union*, March 30, 1898, 2. Rev. J.A. Campbell was very well known Baptist minister who founded Campbell University in Busies Creek, North Carolina. Many are unaware of his involvement with Freemasonry, however. According to the Grand Masonic Lodge of North Carolina Records, Rev. J.A. Campbell was a charter member of the Busies Creek Masonic Lodge in June 1900. A brief bibliography of his achievements can be found on Campbell Universities website at http://www.campbell.edu/about/history-quick-facts.
31. *The Democratic Banner*, January 16, 1901, 3.
32. *HA*, June 1, 1904, 5. A.B. Crumpler despised the teachings of Freemasonry. As evident in this article, Crumpler took a strong stand against secret societies. Although it may not mean much today, in A.B. Crumpler's time, to come against the lodge was dangerous. Coming from a prestigious family that was rooted in local politics, A.B. Crumpler set himself apart as a man of holy fire. If you collectively observe all of the remaining issues of Crumpler's *Holiness Advocate*, you will find that articles against freemasonry take up more column space than tobacco and divorce.
33. Ibid., 5.
34. Ibid., 5.
35. *HA*, October 15, 1903, 6; October 1, 1903, 3.

36. *HA*, April 15, 1901, 2.

37. "Past Masters," *History of Hiram Lodge No. 98 AF and AM*. Available at http://www.hiramlodge98.com/pdf/Past-Masters.pdf.

38. *HA*, April 15, 1902, 5. This extensive article against Masonic Orders begins on page one and continues on page five. Rev. T.M. Lee's brother, R.E. Lee was also a member of the same Clinton lodge during this time. His membership record is also found at "Past Masters," *History of Hiram Lodge No. 98 AF and AM*. http://www.hiramlodge98.com/pdf/Past-Masters.pdf.

39. *Membership Records The Grand Lodge of North Carolina*. There office is located in Raleigh, North Carolina. They allow the public to access past membership records. According to these records John R. Bass, G.B. Cashwell's brother-in-law, was "initiated and raised" in 1888. He was a member of Hiram Lodge No. 98 AF and AM in Clinton, North Carolina. This was the same lodge Rev. T.M. Lee was once a member of. For Erasmus Lee's Masonic membership see Herman Green, *A History of Palmyra Lodge No. 147, A.F. and A.M. Dunn, North Carolina*, 46. This book reveals that many of the Lovie Lee family members were active in Freemasonry in Dunn. Given the fact that G.B. Cashwell was surrounded by so many in secret societies is interesting.

Chapter 10
The Internal War:
The Fire-Baptized Way vs. The Holiness Church

1. Kenneth O. Brown, *Inskip, McDonald, Fowler: Wholly and Forever Thine*, 114.

2. Vinson Synan, *Old Time Power*, 45.

3. J.M. Pike, *Way of Faith*, November 13, 1895.

4. Ibid., 2.

5. Harold D. Hunter, "Fire-Baptized Holiness Church," *International Pentecostal Holiness Church* (n.p., 2011), 1. This is a well-researched and written online history of the International Pentecostal Holiness Church (IPHC). It is available at http://www.pctii.org/iphc.html.

6. Ibid., 2.

7. Ibid., 2. Also see Synan, *Old Time Power*, 47.

8. Synan, *Old Time Power*, 48.

9. Ibid., 49. Also see, *Way of Faith*, February 12, 1896, 5.

10. Synan, *Old Time Power*, 52. For the *Holiness Advocates* position against the Fire-Baptizers see *HA*, April 1, 1903, 5.

11. *The County Union*, May 3, 1899, 2.

12. Ibid.

13. B.H. Irwin, *Live Coals of Fire*, October 6, 1899, 8. This was the official voice for the Fire-Baptized Movement that was sweeping the nation. Edited by Rev. B.H. Irwin, it reveals the official members list. This list shows that by 1899, nearly every holiness minister that was once with A.B. Crumpler during 1896 was now joined to B.H. Irwin's Fire-Baptized Association. Also see Vinson Synan, *Old Time Power*, 52–53.

14. "Letter From A.B. Crumpler," *The County Union*, May 10, 1899, 1.

15. *The County Union*, May 10, 1899, 3.

16. Ibid., 3. Also see, Bertha Westbrook and F.W. Wiegmann, *History of Hood Memorial Christian Church Dunn, North Carolina* (n.p., 1939), 4. This brief history reveals strong disapproval of the Fire-baptized ministers that swept through Dunn, N.C,, in 1899. There is, however, no mention or negative comments towards A.B. Crumpler and his following.

17. *Constitution and By-Laws, and Minutes of the First Session of the North Carolina Holiness Convention*, October 26-28, in Goldsboro, 1899, 1.

18. Mayo Bundy, *A History of Falcon*, North Carolina, 14, 20.

19. *The Democratic Banner*, January 9, 1901, 2. This publication of debt, which was owed to the Culbreth's, reveals the scope of wealth and influence that J.A. Culbreth had received through his father's estate. For additional land that J.A. Culbreth owned in downtown Dunn, see *The County Union*, November 18, 1896, 2. Also see Mayo Bundy, *A History of Falcon, North Carolina*, 21–22.

20. Bundy, 25.

21. Deed of Sale from J.A. Culbreth Commissioner, to H.L. Godwin, February 7, 1902 (Filed September 10, 1903), Harnett County, North Carolina. Register of Deed's Office, Lillington, North Carolina. According to the old index books at this office, J.A. Culbreth served as Commissioner of the Superior Court in Harnett County between 1896 and 1905. For J.A. Culbreth's support of

White Supremacy for the Democrats of 1898, see William Davis Jones III, *Recollections 1926–1953*, 23.

22. Joseph E. Campbell, *The Pentecostal Holiness Church 1898–1948: Its Background and History* (Franklin Springs, Georgia: Life Springs, 1951), 361.

23. Ibid., 361–362.

24. Synan, *Old Time Power*, 56.

25. Ibid., 56. Later, Rev. B.H. Irwin would be restored and is noted for playing a small role in Pentecostal Movement that broke out in Azusa Street during 1906.

26. Joseph H. King, *Yet Speaketh* (Franklin Springs, Georgia: The Publishing House of the Pentecostal Holiness Church, 1949), 11, 86.

27. Vinson Synan, *Old Time Power*, 59–60.

28. *The County Union*, May 10, 1899, 1. For J.H. King's participation in the Dunn meetings see J.H. King, *Yet Speaketh*, 98. Nothing has ever been written concerning J.H. King's relationship with A.B. Crumpler. Unfortunately, there is no record of dialogue between these two revival leaders. However, it seems quite clear that King and Crumpler strongly opposed each other. For the most part, their two organizations sharply disagreed during this time.

29. *Live Coals of Fire*, October 13, 1899, 3.

30. *HA*, May 1, 1901, 2.

31. For articles revealing a partnership between A.B. Crumpler and these ministers prior to the arrival of the Fire-Baptized Holiness Church see J.M. Pike, *Way of Faith*, September 16, 1896, 4. By 1899 there is no fellowship between these two organizations. They remain divided until 1906, when Gaston B. Cashwell returned with the burning message of Pentecostal love and unity.

32. See *PHA*, March 24, 1921, 8. In recounting the history of the Pentecostal Holiness Church, Rev. G.F. Taylor hinted to the disturbance between the Fire-Baptized Church and A.B. Crumpler's Holiness Church before the Pentecostal revival in 1907. However, details surrounding this conflict have always been left out. Based on these new articles between A.B. Crumpler and the Fire-Baptized Church, it seems the internal holiness war ran a lot deeper than what most have thought.

Chapter 11
The Aftermath

1. See Timothy B. Tyson, "The Ghosts of 1898: Wilmington's Race Riot and the Rise of White Supremacy," *The News and Observer*, November 17, 2006, 13. This section, which is entitled, "The Impact of 1898," reveals how Wilmington's massacre affected the entire South through the new Jim Crow Laws of segregation.

2. Vann R. Newkirk, *Lynching in North Carolina: A History, 1865–1941*, 29.

3. Ibid., 28. For Crumpler's work among African Americans in Goldsboro see Pike, *Way of Faith*, June 24, 1896, 5. For Goldsboro "sharecropper" membership of Crumpler's Church see *HA*, May 1, 1903, 4.

4. Timothy B. Tyson, 8. After researching volumes of eastern North Carolina newspapers on microfilm, I have arrived at this conclusion: Between 1896 and 1899, the papers I researched including the *Dunn County Union*, *Goldsboro Weekly Argus*, *Clinton Dispatch*, *Robesonian*, and the *Fayetteville Observer*, all recorded favorable stories about A.B. Crumpler and the Holiness Church. Between 1900 and 1906, however, these same papers became silent of A.B. Crumpler and the Holiness Church. I contribute this silence towards the pressing racial hatred that was overflowing from North Carolina's political system during this time. How could pro-white supremacy papers endorse or support a white preacher who ministers to the "colored" population of eastern North Carolina? (I have kept a large file of all these papers and dates pertaining to this conclusion.) For more on Crumpler's publication in Lumberton, North Carolina, see Vinson Synan, *Old Time Power*, 82.

5. *HA*, June 14, 1904, 4.

6. *HA*, May 1, 1903, 4.

7. Ibid.

8. For a list of Goldsboro's secret societies at this time see *Goldsboro Weekly Argus*, March 14, 1901, 3. This reference lists four lodges: Neuse Lodge, No. 6, I.O.O.F., Wayne Lodge No. 112, A.F. and A.M., Ruffin Lodge, No. 6, K. of P., and the Goldsboro Council No. 39, Jr. O. U. A. M. C.B. Aycock, the North Carolina Governor that championed the white supremacy campaign of 1898, was a member of the Masonic Wayne Lodge. A native of Goldsboro, Aycock was known to have

stirred his fellow Masons with passionate declarations of white supremacy. For a social description of Freemasons in contention with A.B. Crumpler's Holiness Church, see *HA*, April 15, 1902, 1.

9. *HA*, April 1, 1904, 5.

10. Ibid.

11. *PHA*, March 3, 10, 1921, 8.

12. Ibid., 9. According to Rev. G.F. Taylor, two major issues ripped the Goldsboro Church in half: tobacco and divorce. For years, many scholars have placed a great emphasis upon Taylor's account. However, in addition to tobacco and divorce, it seems that the integration of the races may have also lead to the demise of Crumpler's Holiness Church in Goldsboro, North Carolina. Taylor, in this history, admits that Crumpler's following was made up "poor folks and Negros," but he never expounds beyond this remark.

13. "W. C. T. U. Organized," *The County Union*, August 19, 1896, n.p.

14. *HA*, August 15, 1901, 3.

15. Eddie Morris, *The Vine and Braches John 15: 5: Holiness and Pentecostal Movements*, 86.

16. Ibid., 87.

17. Ibid., 88.

18. Ibid., 87.

19. Harold S. York, *George Floyd Taylor: The Life of an Early Southern Pentecostal Leader*, 28.

20. William Davis, *Recollections: 1926–1953*, 23. Written by William Davis III, grandson of J.A. Culbreth, this diary recounts William's personal relationship with his grandfather. According to this record, there is a different side of Mr. Culbreth that has not been explored. Being a strong advocate for white supremacy, it seems Mr. Culbreth had zero tolerance for interracial meetings at his beloved Falcon Camp Meeting Association. A.B. Crumpler, on the other hand, encouraged it. This racial disagreement would also become another point of division between G.B. Cashwell and the early Falcon leaders.

21. For Falcon's mission as being an inter-denominational organization see *HA,* August 15, 1901, 3. For a segregated appearance of African Americans at Falcon Camp Meeting's during the 1920s and 1930s, see Eddie Morris, *The Vine and Braches John 15:5: Holiness and Pentecostal Movements,* 84. To date, there is no record of any African Americans involved in any extension of Falcon's early ministries.

Chapter 12
The Real Miracle of Azusa Street

1. Robert C. Crosby, "A New Kind of Pentecostal," *Christianity Today*, 1. Published on August 3, 2011, this article is an excellent source which reveals the global impact of Pentecostalism in today's world. Also, see Vinson Synan, *The Century of the Holy Spirit: 100 Years of Pentecostal and Charismatic Renewal* (Nashville, Tennessee: Thomas Nelson, 2001).

2. *AF*, September 1906, 3. *The Apostolic Faith* was the original news publication that was being published from the Azusa Street Mission during the height of the Pentecostal revival. Edited by William J. Seymour, it is a wonderful primary source that enriches our understanding of what really transpired at 312 Azusa Street. It is filled with gripping testimonies, brief histories, and un-ending columns of the supernatural. Many books have been written explaining the theological foundations of the Pentecostal Baptism. Very little attention however, has been given to the integration of races at Azusa Street. Yet it would be the mixing of races, under the banner of love that would spark national and international interest amidst a segregated nation. Tongues, therefore, became the battering ram that broke down walls of racism, division, and religious complicacy while catapulting an entire generation into apostolic power.

3. *AF*, November 1906, 1. Also see Ithiel C. Clemons, *Bishop C.H. Mason and the Roots of the Church of God in Christ* (Bakersfield, California: Pneuma Life, 1996), 45.

4. *AF*, "The Baptism of the Holy Ghost," February–March 1907, 7. This article was written by William J. Seymour, and explains his personal definition of the Holy Spirit baptism.

5. For G.B. Cashwell's perspective on the Pentecostal experience as a love encounter, see *HA*, June 1, 1907, 5. For the Nazarene brother's testimony see *AF*, September 1906, 1. William Seymour's account is also found in *AF*, September 1906, 2. Also see Frank Bartleman, *Another Wave Rolls In!: What Really Happened at Azusa Street* (Monroeville, Pa: Whitaker Books, 1970), 55.

6. Rufus G.W. Sanders, *William Joseph Seymour Black Father of the Twentieth Century Pentecostal/Charismatic Movement* (Sandusky, OH: Xulon Press, 2003), 24. For William Seymour's social

conditions while growing up see Craig Borlase, *William Seymour: A Biography* (Lake Mary, Florida: Charisma House, 2006), 18–21.

7. *A Short Story of Our Past*. This brief history is taken from the website of "Our Lady of Guadalupe Catholic Church" in Newton Grove, North Carolina. Today Our Lady of Guadalupe Church holds 600 hundred Spanish families. It still remains one of the largest inter-racial congregations in the region. Available online at http://www.ourladyofguadalupe.catholicweb.com.

8. Vinson Synan, *The Century of the Holy Spirit: 100 Years of Pentecostal and Charismatic Renewal*, 46.

9. Doug Beacham, *Azusa East: The Life and Times of G.B. Cashwell*, 43.

10. Rufus Sanders, *William Joseph Seymour Black Father of the Twentieth Century Pentecostal/Charismatic Movement,* 84.

11. *AF*, September 1906, 1.

12. Vinson Synan, *The Century of the Holy Spirit: 100 Years of Pentecostal and Charismatic Renewal*, 47.

13. Frank Bartleman, *Azusa Street,* foreword by Dr. Vinson Synan (Plainfield, New Jersey: Bridge Publishing, 1980), 58–60. Also see Synan, 47.

14. Synan, 48. Also see Frank Bartleman, *Azusa Street*, 43.

15. Synan, 49.

16. Roberts Liardon, *God's Generals: Why They Succeeded and Why Some Failed* (Tulsa, Oklahoma: Albury, 1996), 146–147.

17. Ibid., 144.

18. *AF*, "Bible Pentecost," November 1906, 1. This article reveals that locals referred to the Azusa Mission as the "colored church." Also see Rufus Sanders, *William Joseph Seymour Black Father of the Twentieth Century Pentecostal/Charismatic Movement*, 93, 95.

19. Frank Bartleman, *Azusa Street*, 58–59.

20. See chapter six. Though there are articles revealing A.B. Crumpler's work among African Americans, there is currently no membership record of any black minister during his reign as president of the Holiness Church (1898–1908).

21. Such was the case for Charles F. Parham. Parham, who is also credited as a "Father of Pentecost," went to the Azusa Mission upon William J. Seymour's request. When he arrived, he was "sick to his stomach" at the scene of white women and black men praying and weeping over each other. Filled with bitterness over this racial harmony, Parham traveled north and began to hold meetings opposing Seymour and the Azusa Street Mission. For more on Parham's disgust of Azusa, see, Ithiel C. Clemmons, *Bishop C.H. Mason and the Roots of the Church of God in Christ*, 46–48.

22. *AF*, "Bible Pentecost," November 1906, 1.

23. Ibid., 1. Also see *AF*, "The Same Old-Way," September 1906, 3.

24. *AF*, "Pentecost With Signs Following," December 1906, 1.

25. For a map of the original Carolina Charter boundaries, see *Original Boundaries of Carolina (1663/1665)*. Available at http://www.learnnc.org/lp/multimedia/6182. G.B. Cashwell's home was located near the corner Layton Avenue and West Cumberland Street in Dunn, North Carolina. The railroad depot was only a few blocks away. For years, there has never been any solid reason to question the early Pentecostal Holiness Church history, as told by G.F. Taylor, A.H. Butler, J.H. King, and J.A. Culbreth. In light of new findings, however, it is becoming increasingly clear that their interpretation history is not exactly accurate. Many important details have been left out. Especially, details concerning the firebrand who helped bring them into existence, Rev. G.B. Cashwell.

26. *PHA*, May 29, 1930, 1. By the time G.B. Cashwell boarded the train to Los Angeles in November 1906, the Azusa Street revival had been going on for nearly a year. Both secular newspapers as well as Christian publications were carrying the news of the explosive interracial gatherings occurring at 312 Azusa Street. Taylor and the rest of North Carolina's holiness leaders were well aware of this.

27. For early accounts of Azusa Street in the Los Angeles newspapers, see Ithiel C. Clemmons, *Bishop C.H. Mason and the Roots of the Church of God in Christ*, 45. As well as Vinson Synan, *The Century of the Holy Spirit*, 39.

28. For Campbell's account of Cashwell, see J.E. Campbell, *The Pentecostal Holiness Church: 1898–1948*, 241. For Taylor's account of Cashwell's turbulent relationship with Holiness Church see *PHA*, March 17, 1921, 8. By these remarks, it is clear that Cashwell did have some enemies within the Holiness Church prior to his California trip in 1906.

29. *HA*, June 15, 1906, 4.
30. Ibid.
31. In my personal interview with Emma Lee Laine on March 1, 2012, I was informed that the A.B. Crumpler and G.B. Cashwell families were "very good friends." Emma also informed us that Lovie Cashwell, her aunt, had left some belongings to Emma after she died. Among them, was an original issue of J.M. Pike's *Way of Faith* noting Lovie and Rev. T.F. Harrison's holiness conversions, and an old photograph of Rev. A.B. Crumpler. No photo of Cashwell or the Cashwell children were left, only a picture of Mr. A.B. Crumpler.
32. *PHA*, May 29, 1930, 1.
33. See Doug Beacham, *Azusa East: The Life and Times of G.B. Cashwell*, chapter two, footnote 10, 56. After searching through several different avenues, I have never found any trace of this letter. Cashwell family members also have no recollection of hearing anything about this alleged confessional from Gaston Cashwell.
34. *AF*, "Came 3,000 Miles for His Pentecost," December 1906, 3.
35. Doug Beacham, *Azusa East: The Life and Times of G.B. Cashwell*, 46–47.
36. *AF*, December 1906, 3 (Emphasis is mine).
37. Personal interview with Stanley Carr on March 5, 2011. After leaving this interview, I realized for the first time that G.B. Cashwell may have been forced to leave Dunn, North Carolina, in 1906.
38. *PHA*, May 29, 1930, 1. This question of Cashwell moving permanently to California has never been explored. Understandably so, no evidence has ever surfaced to offer such an explanation. Perhaps Cashwell's obscure background is a good starting point to launch such an investigation.
39. The assumption of Cashwell's family member selling property to fund Gaston's trip to Los Angeles was told by Rev. J. Doner Lee, a distant Lee family member. More details are found in Doug Beacham, *Azusa East: The Life and Times of G.B. Cashwell*, 57, chapter two, footnote, 29. According to Rev. Lee, Lovie Cashwell sold a piece of her land and gave the money to G.B. Cashwell to purchase a train ticket. For several months I searched through Harnett, Sampson, and Cumberland counties' land deed records, but found no record of any such transaction. Furthermore, in a personal interview with Stanley Carr on March 5, 2011, I was told that Gaston Cashwell bought his own ticket to California. This stands to reason, given Cashwell's success as a tobacco farmer. Lovie Cashwell also received a handsome inheritance when her father, Erasmus Lee, passed away in 1898. This reveals that the Cashwells were not as poor as some have suggested.
40. For Lovie H. Cashwell's inheritance from her father, see Division of Estate of E. Lee to Edith Pope and J.H. Pope, W.B. Warren and wife Katurah E. Warren, J.W. Taylor and wife Kesiah A. Taylor, L.H. Lee, G.B. Cashwell and wife Lovie H. Cashwell, Robert E. Lee, Emma Lee, Henry Lee, May 1, 1900, Harnett County, North Carolina, Harnett County Register of Deeds Office, Lillington, North Carolina.

Interestingly, the Cashwells were not poor. They owned hundreds of acres of land in several North Carolina counties including Harnett, Sampson, Ayden, and possibly Cumberland. They also owned a second home in Ayden, North Carolina, from Lovie's first marriage to Rev. T.F. Harrison.
41. *AF*, December 1906, 3.
42. Ibid.
43. Doug Beacham, *Azusa East: The Life and Times of G.B. Cashwell*, 50.
44. Vinson Synan, *The Holiness-Pentecostal Tradition*, 114.
45. *AF*, December 1906, 3.
46. *AF*, December, 1906, 3. Proving that Cashwell was not broke opens up new suggestions for this reference. Its seems, that Cashwell's request for a train ticket home, and a new suite of clothes was his "fleece" or sign of approval from God to travel back to North Carolina. The possibility of Cashwell informally joining the Apostolic Faith Movement is very likely.
47. See Fred T. Corum, *Like As of Fire: Reprint of the Old Azusa Street Papers* (Wilmington, Mass: n.p., 1981), n.p. This is a reprint of the old Azusa Street Papers, which were collected by Mr. Corum. In the introduction section, Mr. Corum reveals that William Seymour and the other Azusa leaders were "examining candidates for licenses" as Apostolic Faith missionaries and evangelist. In commissioning those who were called, the Azusa leadership team "laid hands and prayed" for potential candidates to be released in apostolic power. Recognizing his unique call, Seymour and the leadership team laid hands upon G.B. Cashwell and apostolically sent him back to North

Carolina as an Apostolic Faith messenger. See, Vinson Synan, *The Holiness-Pentecostal Tradition*, 114. Also see, Doug Beacham, *Azusa East: The Life and Times of G.B. Cashwell*, 54, 55.

48. *PHA*, April 14, 21, 1921, 9. Adding to this belief is the fact that G.B. Cashwell is only listed as attending only one Convention of the Holiness Church. Since 1899, the Holiness Convention had met in various eastern North Carolina towns. However, G.B. Cashwell's only confirmed attendance came in the 1908 convention in Dunn, North Carolina, where the Holiness Church adopted the new Azusa Street theology he was preaching. Although his name was recorded at the 1909 convention in Falcon, North Carolina, he never showed up. By the 1910 convention, G.B. Cashwell had mysteriously disappeared from the ministry. Thus, out of eleven Holiness Convention meetings between 1899 and 1910, G.B. Cashwell is only known to have attended one—the one held in1908.

Another point of discussion centers around the fact that during the height of his Pentecostal reign, G.B. Cashwell made Atlanta, Georgia, his headquarters and not Falcon nor Goldsboro, North Carolina. This is where he organized a mission, published his paper the *Bridegroom's Messenger*, and established himself as national voice for the Pentecostal Movement. For more details about Cashwell's connections with Atlanta see, *BGM*, October 1, 1907, 3. Also see *BGM*, November 1, 1907, 3.

49. See, *AF*, October 1908, 5. This shows that G.B. Cashwell's newspaper as well as the mission he helped start in Atlanta, Georgia, in 1907, are listed as belonging to the "Apostolic Faith Movement." Additionally, it reveals that T.J. McIntosh, an A.B. Crumpler Holiness Church member and Cashwell Pentecostal convert, is listed as an "Apostolic Faith Missionary."

Chapter 13
From Azusa to Dunn, North Carolina

1. For Francis Asbury's remarkable tour through eastern North Carolina, see"How the Gospel got to Goshen," *The News and Observer*, July 3, 1955, 3. For details on A.B. Crumpler's famed Dunn revival in May 1896, see *The County Union*, May 27, 1896, 3. Also see *The County Union*, May 1, 1895, 3.

2. *AF*, "Pentecost in North Carolina," January 1907, 1.

3. On March 5, 2011, I personally interviewed Stanley Carr. In this meeting, Mr. Carr informed me that the very first place G.B. Cashwell preached the Pentecostal message was at St. Matthews Holiness Church.

4. *HA*, July 15, 1904, 8.

5. J.T McCullen, "Sharecake, 1878," *The Heritage of Sampson County, North Carolina*, 34.

6. See chapter 8, footnote 278.

7. J.T. McCullen, *Antiquity Forgot: Reminiscence*, 68.

8. Deed of Sale from J.T. McCullen and wife to Lee's Chapel Church (Col.), August 31, 1908, Sampson County, North Carolina, Deed Book 212, Page 466. Register of Deeds Office Clinton, North Carolina. Having been involved in numerous church plants for bi-racial churches, there is no question that G.B. Cashwell helped organize this church. If not directly, then indirectly through the Pentecostal conversion of J.T. McCullen Sr.

9. McCullen, 68.

10. Herman Green, *A History of Dunn, N.C.*, (Dunn, North Carolina: Twyford, 1985), 8–14. Also see, "The Town of Dunn," *The Democratic Banner*, June 19, 1901, 2.

11. "People Wanted," *The Democratic Banner*, January 16, 1901, n.p. Also see, *The Democratic Banner*, June 19, 1901, 2. G.B. Cashwell opened the Dunn revival on December 31, 1906.

12. *The County Union*, August 23, 1899, 3. The exact location of the tobacco prize house that Cashwell used is on South Wilson Avenue, Dunn, North Carolina. Today, a small black Pentecostal Holiness Church occupies where the prize house once stood.

13. Florence Goff, *Fifty Years on the Battlefield for God*, 49.

14. See chapter nine, footnote 308.

15. Herman Green, *A History of Palmyra Lodge No. 147, A.F. and A.M. Dunn, North Carolina*, 11. This book records every member that joined the Masonic Lodge in Dunn, North Carolina, between the years 1852-1963. Also see Herman Green, *A History of Dunn, N.C.*, 24–29. This history of Dunn records every town mayor between the years 1887–1983. In piecing both books together, I was able to identify how many of Dunn's mayors and leading officials were Freemasons. Surprisingly, nearly the entire town's leading officials were members of secret lodges. Also see, "City Minutes of Dunn, North Carolina, 1907–1920." On April 11, 2011, I received a microfilm copy of

these minuets from Dunn's Fire Chief, Mr. Tew. The minutes list all of Dunn's government officials between the years 1907–1920.

16. *The Democratic Banner*, May 28, 1902, 2. For Stewarts Masonic membership record see Herman Green, *A History of Palmyra Lodge No. 147, A.F. and A.M. Dunn, North Carolina*, 52.

17. Doug Beacham, *Azusa East: The Life and Times of G.B. Cashwell*, 62.

18. "Highway Marker to Honor Dunn's Pentecostal Son," *The Daily Record*, August 3, 2010, 3. This excellent article celebrates Cashwell's achievements by erecting a North Carolina state marker at the original site of the Dunn revival. Lead by Elizabeth Crudup and Thomas Ellis II of the Harnett Historical Association, the news piece uncovers remarkable new insights into Cashwell's Dunn meeting. Accordingly, it shows that the meeting was attended by "whites, blacks, Lumbee Indians" and anyone else who was interested in the meeting.

19. "Pentecost in North Carolina," *AF*, January 1907, 1.

20. Doug Beacham, *Azusa East: The Life and Times of G.B. Cashwell*, 63.

21. Florence Goff, *Fifty Years on the Battlefield for God*, 51.

22. Ibid., 52.

23. Ibid., 52.

24. For references on Azusa Street's night meetings at the Bonnie Brae Home see *AF*, September 1906, 1. For night meetings at the G.B. Cashwell residence see Florence Goff, *Fifty Years on the Battlefield for God*, 52.

25. Frank Bartleman, *Azusa Street*, 110. The first documented account of a Pentecostal believing congregation did not emerge in Dunn until 1917, when Pastor Luter Davis organized "Gospel Tabernacle." Being the old Lee homestead, the Cashwell home was certainly large enough to entertain a small gathering of Pentecostals.

26. Division of Estate of E. Lee to Edith Pope and J.H. Pope, W.B. Warren and wife Katurah E. Warren, J.W. Taylor and wife Kesiah A. Taylor, L.H. Lee, G.B. Cashwell and wife Lovie H. Cashwell, Robert E. Lee, Emma Lee, Henry Lee, May 1, 1900, 501. Harnett County, North Carolina. Register of Deeds Office, Lillington, North Carolina.

This document reveals that all of the Lee children including, Lovie and Gaston Cashwell, inherited several city blocks in Dunn. Shortly after, Lovie and her sister Edith Lee Pope made arraignments to swap properties. The lot originally portioned to Edith Pope located near "the Presbyterian Church" on the corner of Cumberland and Layton Street soon became the Cashwell home. The Cashwell's house location was also confirmed to me through my personal interview with Emma Lee Laine on March 1, 2012. Emma, Lovie and Gaston Cashwell's niece, was born and raised in the house right next door to the Cashwell's. Thus, she and her Aunt Lovie Cashwell were neighbors, until Lovie passed way in 1944.

27. *AF*, January 1907, 1.

28. Ibid., 52.

29. James R. Goff, Jr., "The Pentecostal Catalyst to the South: G.B. Cashwell (1906–1909)." Unpublished manuscript, April 2, 1980, 4, 5. Dr. Goff interviewed Rev. Frann on March 11, 1980.

30. Ibid., 52.

31. Ibid., 52.

32. Ibid., 52.

33. See Malcolm Fowler, *They Passed This Way: A Personal Narrative of Harnett County History* (North Carolina: Harnett County Centennial, 1955), 122–123. Also see, Lloyd Johnson, "Averasboro (Town of)," *North Carolina History Project*. Available at http://www.northcarolinahistory.org/commentary/102/entry.

34. Charles H. Cookman, Fenton L. Jones, David B. Crabtree, Mark A. Muirhead, *Never Let Go: The Dramatic Story of the North Carolina District of the Assemblies of God* (Dunn, North Carolina: North Carolina Assemblies of God, 1994), 11. This is the only account in existence that reveals the fate of the historic prize house in Dunn. No information has ever surfaced to shed any more light on this topic.

35. *AF*, February-March 1907, 3.

Chapter 14
Cashwell Transforms the South

1. *AF*, February-March 1907, 3. Cashwell flowed powerfully in all the spiritual gifts. Among the ones he frequently used for spreading Pentecost was, "casting out devils, healing the sick, and

discerning of spirits." For J.H. King's personal account of Pentecost, see J.H. King, *Yet Speaketh*, 113–121.

2. For Cashwell's disapproval of the practices of the Fire-Baptized Church see *AF*, February–March 1907, 3.

3. "Faith Cure Believers Die of Fever," *The Duplin Journal*, November 20, 1902, 3. Also see W.M. Hayes, *Memoirs of Richard Baxter Hayes* (Greer, South Carolina: n.p., 1945), 61–67.

4. J.H. King, *Yet Speaketh*, 115. The IPHC currently has around two million members worldwide. For more information about the church see, http://www.iphc.org/.

5. King, 114.

6. Ibid., 115.

7. Ibid., 115–116.

8. Ibid., 116. Also see Frank Bartleman, *Azusa Street*, 60.

9. Ibid., 120.

10. Ibid., 121.

11. King, Yet Speaketh, 122, 124.

12. *AF*, February-March 1907, 3.

13. Ibid., 3.

14. *PHA*, March 17, 1921, 8–9. This personal account, written by G.F. Taylor, is the root of the alleged Cashwell-Crumpler conflict. Since 1921 it has shaped everything we have come to believe about G.B. Cashwell and A.B. Crumpler. Given Taylor's esteemed position within the Pentecostal Holiness Church, his writings have gone unchallenged. However, new findings are beginning to cast a cloud of doubt over Taylor's original account of the church's early history.

15. *HA*, June 1, 1907, 1.

16. Ibid.

17. Interestingly, A.B. Crumpler's Pentecostal experience is more vivid, accurate, and spirit-filled then J.H. King's, A.H. Butler's, G.F. Taylor's, and J.A. Culbreth's. In *Yet Speaketh*, an indecisive J.H. King is not sure if he received the Pentecostal baptism or not. G.F. Taylor, in the *PHA*, confesses that he was forcing people to speak in tongues, but remains silent about his own experience. In addition, A.H. Butler admitted that he received the Holy Spirit baptism while alone in his house, but does not give any details. Mayo Bundy, author of Falcon's history, writes that J.A. Culbreth never even spoke in tongues at all, but claimed the Pentecostal experience. A.B. Crumpler's testimony, however, reflects deep conviction over hidden sins, a genuine repentance, and an infilling of the Holy Spirit evidenced by speaking in "A language."

18. *HA*, May 15, 19007, 1.

19. *HA*, June 1, 1906, 8. The IPHC archives department listed this issue under June of 1906. However, the paper is actually from the spring 1907, after the Pentecostal revival in Dunn. Knowing this adds more understanding as to what was happening among Crumpler's Holiness Church during the Pentecostal outpouring in eastern North Carolina. Incredibly, this misplaced article reveals A.B. Crumpler was working hand in hand with all those who experienced the Pentecostal baptism under G.B. Cashwell's ministry. For more on this Pentecostal partnership with the Sea-Side Rescue Home see, *1907 Minutes of the Cape Fear Conference of the Free Will-Baptist Church*, November 1907, 7, 8. These minutes are located in archives section of the Mt. Olive College Library in Mt. Olive, North Carolina. For the mentioning of Butler and Taylor's name as trustees, see *1908 Minutes of the Cape Fear Conference of the Free Will-Baptist Church*, November 1908, 11. Also, see *Proceedings of the Eighth Annual Convention of the Holiness Church of North Carolina*, November 1907, 5–6.

20. *HA*, June 1, 1906, 8. Florence Goff, *Fifty Years on the Battlefield for God*, 51. Also see Eddie Morris, *The Vine and the Braches John 15:5*, 90–91. Mr. Morris seems to have misspelled her name "McGlothem." However, Sister McLaughlin was no doubt, an instrumental advocate for spreading the Pentecostal message around eastern North Carolina in 1907.

21. *HA*, May 15, 1907, 4.

22. Ibid., 1.

23. *HA*, June 1, 1907, 1.

24. *HA*, June 1, 1906, 7. This is the misplaced issue. The actual date is June 1907. Interestingly, this listing reveals that G.B. Cashwell was a supported evangelist of A.B. Crumpler. This is the only listing of G.B. Cashwell as an endorsed "evangelists" within Crumpler's paper between the years 1901 and 1907.

25. J.E. Campbell, *The Pentecostal Holiness Church 1898–1948*, 425.

26. Ibid., 424–425.

27. Ibid., 426, 430. Also see, Vinson Synan, *Old Time Power*, 103; *The Altamont Witness*, October 23, 1911, 1.

28. Doug Beacham, *Azusa East: The Life and Times of G.B. Cashwell*, 102, 104.

29. Ibid., 105.

30. Ibid., 105. Also see, "Holmes, Nickels John," *The New International Dictionary of Pentecostal and Charismatic Movements* (Grand Rapids, Michigan, Zondervan, 2002), 730.

31. Campbell, 264.

32. "Pinson, Mack M," *New International Dictionary of Pentecostal and Charismatic Movements*, 989.

33. Doug Beacham, *Azusa East: The Life and Times of G.B. Cashwell*, 107.

34. J. Samuel Rasnake, *Stones by the River: A History of the Tennessee District of the Assemblies of God* (Bristol, Tennessee: Westhighlands Church, 1975), 38.

35. *AF*, May 1907, 1.

36. Rasnake, 46. Also see, *New International Dictionary of Pentecostal and Charismatic Movements*, 989.

37. Ithiel C. Clemmons, *Bishop C.H. Mason and the Roots of the Church of God in Christ*, 4-5. C.H. Mason was heavily influenced through Amanda Smith. Smith, the dynamic "Coloured Evangelists," ministered alongside with John Inskip, on the fathers of the National Holiness Movement.

38. Clemmons, 6, 14–16.

39. Ibid., 26. Also see Vinson Synan, *The Century of the Holy Spirit*, 102.

40. *AF*, May 1907, 1.

41. Vinson Synan, *The Holiness-Pentecostal Tradition: Charismatic Movements in the Twentieth Century* (Grand Rapids, Michigan: Eerdmans, 1997), 126.

42. *BGM*, October 1, 1907, 3.

43. *BGM*, January 1, 1908, 1.

44. Ibid.

45. *BGM*, October 1, 1907, 1, 3.

46. *BGM*, "Pentecost in Jerusalem, Palestine," June 15, 1908, 1.

47. Ibid.

48. *BGM*, July 1, 1908, 1. For McIntosh's membership in the Holiness Convention see *Proceedings of the Eighth Annual Convention of the Holiness Church of North Carolina*, November 20, 1907, 15.

49. See *BGM*, May 1, 1908, 1.

50. See Vinson Synan, *The Century of the Holy Spirit*, 116.

51. Harold D. Hunter, Cecil M. Robeck, Jr., *The Azusa Street Revival and its Legacy* (Cleveland, Tennessee: Pathway Press, 2006), 112.

52. See Charles Conn, *Like A Mighty Army: A History of the Church of God 1886–1976* (Cleveland, Tennessee: Pathway, 1977), 18, 24. In 1896, under the preaching of A.B. Crumpler, the Holiness Movement ripped through coastal and piedmont regions of North Carolina. In the same year, the Cherokee Native Americans of Camp Creek, North Carolina, experienced the first outpouring of the Pentecostal baptism with the Holy Spirit. According to an outstanding message preached by Perry Stone in 2011, entitled "The Cherokee Link to the End Time Outpouring," the North Carolina Cherokee Native Americans were among the first to experience the baptism of the Holy Spirit and speaking in tongues in America. Rev. Stone reveals that the North Carolina Cherokee tribe was who many of the people present when the revival broke out in the Shearer Schoolhouse. Rev. Perry Stone's message is available online at, http://www.voe.org/store/11hx-d07-the-cherokee-link-to-the-end-time-outpouring-dvd.

53. Conn, *Like A Mighty Army: A History of the Church of God 1886–1976*, 13–15. In addition, Rev. Perry Stone's message unveils the true identity of R. G. Spurling's wife. According to Stone, she was a full blooded Cherokee Indian, and her father was the chief of the Carolina Cherokee's. For a copy of this outstanding sermon see, http://www.voe.org/store/11hx-d07-the-cherokee-link-to-the-end-time-outpouring-dvd.

54. Harold D. Hunter, Cecil M. Robeck, Jr., *The Azusa Street Revival and its Legacy*, 113, 115. Also see Synan, *The Century of the Holy Spirit*, 116–117.

55. A.J. Tomlinson, "The Work at Cleveland, Tenn.," *BGM*, February 1, 1908, 4.

56. A.J. Tomlinson, *Diary of Happenings*, January 13, 1908.
57. *BGM*, January 15, 1908, 2.
58. A.J. Tomlinson, *Diary of Happenings*, January 20, 1908.
59. *BGM*, June 15, 1908, 2.
60. Ibid.
61. *AF*, September 1906, 1, 3.
62. For Mason's massive Pentecostal Revival in Norfolk, Virginia, see "History of the Church of God in Christ," available online at http://www.detourstodestiny.net/cooper/id14.html.
63. *BGM*, June 15, 1908, 2.
64. Ibid.
65. For Cashwell's impact in the South see Doug Beacham, *Azusa East: The Life and Times of G.B. Cashwell*, 175.

Chapter 15
G.B. Cashwell's Apostolic Vision for North Carolina

1. *AF*, September 1906, 2.
2. Ibid.
3. *BGM*, April 15, 1908, 2. Also see *BGM*, May 1, 1908, 1. After organizing a women's rescue home in Winston-Salem, North Carolina, G.B. Cashwell aimed to open these homes everywhere he went. Cashwell also set his sights on Wilmington, North Carolina, where "250 or 300 fallen women" were crying out for help. According to Cashwell, these women dwelled in various "public houses of illfame." Houses of illfame was a term used to described brothels or whorehouses. See, *Merriam-Webster Dictionary Online*. Available at http://www.merriam-webster.com/dictionary/house of ill fame.
4. *BGM*, April 1, 1908, 1.
5. *The Evening Dispatch*, December 19, 1908, 1; November 24, 1908, 6; November 11, 1908, 6.
6. *BGM*, April 1, 1908, 1. For the Wilmington, N.C., rescue homes location see *BGM*, August 1, 1908, 4.
7. See, *BGM*, September 15, 1908, 2.
8. *BGM*, May 1, 1908, 1.
9. Ibid, August 1, 1908, 1.
10. "The Rescue Home," *The Evening Dispatch*, December 7, 1908, 5. For notification of the rescue home's address change see "Location of the Home Changed," *The Evening Dispatch*, August 24, 1908, 6.
11. *BGM*, February 15, 1909, 3. For additional articles about Beckam's meetings in Wilmington see, *BGM*, February 1, 1908, 3; May 1, 1909, 3; May 15, 1909, 2; July 1, 1909, 1; August 1, 1909 3.
12. *The Evening Dispatch*, December 15, 1908, 1.
13. See Doug Beacham, *Azusa East: The Life and Times of G.B. Cashwell*, 185.
14. *BGM*, August 15, 1909, 4.
15. *BGM*, April 1, 1908, 1.
16. *BGM*, August 15, 1909, 4.
17. *BGM*, January 1, 1909, 4.
18. *BGM*, March 1, 1909, 2.
19. Unfortunately, neither G.B. Cashwell or any of his acquaintances associated with Falcon commented on their relationship. Even so, Florence Goff, G.F. Taylor, J.H. King and others, went on to write and publish histories concerning their early Pentecostal conversions under G.B. Cashwell's ministry. Beyond their initial experiences, these authors remained dead silent when it came to the fate of G.B. Cashwell.
20. A.B. Crumpler, Letter to J.A. Culbreth, June 2, 1909. The original letter is located at the IPHC Archives and Research Center in Oklahoma City, Oklahoma. On March 18, 2011, I received a copy of this letter via e-mail from Erica Rutland, who works at the IPHC Archives and Research Center. I am very grateful for her assistance and the diligence of the IPHC Archives department to assist me in the endeavour.
21. Eddie Morris, *The Vine and Braches: John 15:5*, 90. Morris records that Cashwell spoke at the 1907 Falcon Camp Meeting. There is however, no other documented account of Cashwell preaching in Falcon, N.C., before or after this date. Moreover, there is no record or recollection of G.B. Cashwell holding an official position at Falcon.

22. J.H. King, *Yet Speaketh*, 133. For a list of Falcon's trustees in 1904, see Deed of Sale from J.A. Culbreth and wife to Trustees Falcon Holiness School and Camp Meeting Association, May 4, 1904, Cumberland County, North Carolina, Deed Book 174, Page 165, Cumberland County, North Carolina, Register of Deeds Office, Fayetteville, North Carolina.

23. For land transactions between J. A. Culbreth and J.H. King, M.D. Sellars, and S.D. Page see, Deed of Sale from J.A. Culbreth and wife to J.H. King, December 26, 1908, Cumberland County, North Carolina, Deed Book 153, Page 47. Register of Deeds Office, Fayetteville, North Carolina; Deed of Sale from J.A. Culbreth and wife to M.D. Sellars, April 23, 1909, Cumberland County, North Carolina, Deed Book 153, Page 61; Deed of Sale from G.F. Taylor and wife to S.D. Page, February 14, 1908, Cumberland County, North Carolina, Deed Book 146, Page 324.

24. For a legal definition of regime see, *The Free Dictionary*. It is available online at http://www.legal-dictionary.thefreedictionary.com/regime. It is noteworthy to observe that a strong percentage of leadership in the F.B.H.C. all moved to Falcon, North Carolina, between 1908 and 1909. This was still several years before the historic merger between the FBHC and Crumpler's Holiness Church took place in 1911.

25. Ibid. King, 133, 138.

26. See *PHA*, March 24, 1921, 8. For Cashwell's cry against organizing Pentecost into a denomination see *BGM*, March 1, 1909, 2.

27. *Proceedings of the Ninth Annual Convention of the Holiness Church of North Carolina*, November 26, 1908, 2–3. Also see, King, 139.

28. Vinson Synan, *Old Time Power*, 110. Also see, *Proceeding of the Tenth Annual Convention of the Pentecostal Holiness Church of North Carolina,* November 23, 1909, 4. The minuets also recorded that "G.B. Cashwell gave a good talk concerning supplying the churches with pastors," but it seems that this too, was carried over from the previous convention in 1908, where Cashwell was present. Why did the church count Cashwell present at the 1909 Convention although he never showed? This is another question that still remains unanswered.

29. *Proceeding of the Tenth Annual Convention of the Pentecostal Holiness Church of North Carolina,* November 23, 1909, 7. The failure of the Holiness-Pentecostal Free Will-Baptists to join the merger is another point of debate. Currently, there is no record revealing why they choose not to accept the invention. For their history, see "History of the Pentecostal Free Will Baptist Church." It is available online at httpp://www.pfwb.org/history/htm.

30. Doug Beacham, *Azusa East: The Life and Times of G.B. Cashwell*, 196. See, *Proceedings of the Eleventh Annual Convention of the Pentecostal Holiness Church of North Carolina*, November 1910, 4. For Dr. Synan's remarks see Vinson Synan, *Old Time Power*, 110.

Chapter 16
Cashwell and Crumpler: The Mystery Revealed?

1. J.E. Campbell, *The Pentecostal Holiness Church 1898–1948*, 241. Doug Beacham, *Azusa East: The Life and Times of G.B. Cashwell,* 213. Vinson Synan, *Old Time Power*, 110.

2. There has never been one published account explaining what really happened to G.B. Cashwell. Even from these ministers who personally knew him. It seems that they wanted him to be forgotten.

3. *Descendants and Relatives of Joseph Thomas McCullen Sr. and Myrtie Peal Gore McCullen*, n.p. This brief McCullen family history records geological information about Dr. McCullen, the Cashwells, and several other joining families in the Sampson County area. Also see J.T. McCullen, *Antiquity Forgot: Reminiscences*, 68. For Dr. McCullen's achievements, see Doug Beacham, *Azusa East: The Life and Times of G.B. Cashwell*, chapter one, endnote six, 31. Beacham interviewed McCullen right before he passed away on November 21, 2005.

4. Dr. McCullen's books include: *Antiquity Forgot: Reminiscence*; *Wild-Goose Miscellany*; *By the Soul Only*; *Not in Entire Forgetfulness*. These books cover a wide variety of topics that occupied Dr. McCullen's attention. Ranging from his time in war to growing up near the old Cashwell farm, McCullen's writings leave behind a rich heritage of the Cashwell family and their descendants. However, in writing about some of his ancestors such as Granny Susan Cashwell or G.B. Cashwell, Dr. McCullen always manages to code certain details. Namely, details pointing to the genealogical makeup of Cashwell family members. Thus, the only way to decode his writings is to understand the rural South during the post-civil war era.

5. J.T. McCullen, *Antiquity Forgot: Reminiscences*, 68.

6. Eddie Morris, *The Vine and Braches: John 15:5*, 14.

7. *Proceedings of the Ninth Annual Convention of the Holiness Church of North Carolina*, November 26, 1908, 5.

8. J.M. Pike, *Way of Faith*, July 5, 1898, 2. A.B. Crumpler withdrew from the Methodist Church at Clinton United Methodist Church in Clinton, North Carolina. This was the very same church that A.B. Crumpler emerged from in 1886. After leaving 1899, Crumpler transferred his preaching credentials to the Holiness Convention in Goldsboro, North Carolina, in 1900. G.B. Cashwell also joined the Convention at Goldsboro in the same year.

9. "Alternate Clerical Delegates to Conference," *Charlotte Daily Observer*, December 9, 1913, 9. For A.B. Crumpler's revival meetings in 1916, see *The News Dispatch*, January 6, 1916, 3; March 2, 1916, 3.

10. *The Robesonian*, June 29, 1933, 1; "Musicians, Singers Invited to Join in Evangelic Services," *The Robesonian*, June 29, 1933, 6. For information regarding Pentecostal "Gospel Tabernacles," see Stanley Burgess, *Dictionary of Pentecostal and Charismatic Movements* (Grand Rapids MI: Zondervan, 1993), 166. This source reveals that after the Christian Missionary Alliance Church began to accept the Pentecostal Movement, it labeled many of its churches as "Gospel Tabernacles." Thus, churches with these names were generally Holiness-Pentecostal believing churches.

11. "A Preacher for Mayor," *Charlotte Daily Observer*, March 30, 1913, 4. This article was originally published in *The Clinton Democrat*, and then republished in the Charlotte Observer. For a listing of A.B. Crumpler's tenure as the Mayor of Clinton and Justice of the Peace, see *Heritage of Sampson County, North Carolina*, 56.

12. "Fifty-Five Receive License to Practice Law in State," *Charlotte Daily Observer*, February 11, 1916, 1. Also see, *The News Dispatch*, March 22, 1917, n.p. On May 28, 2011, I personally interviewed Jane McGregor, who is A.B. Crumpler's granddaughter. She knew him personally for many years before he passed away in 1952. Ms. McGregor informed of these wonderful stories about her amazing grandfather, A.B. Crumpler.

13. *The News Dispatch*, March 15, 1917, n.p.

14. See, *Heritage of Sampson County, North Carolina*, 56

15. Personal Interview with Jane McGregor, A.B. Crumpler's granddaughter, on May 28, 2011.

16. "Death Claims Aged Citizen," *The Sampson Independent*, October 30, 1952, n.p. I am extremely grateful for Candace Atwood, librarian of the J.C. Holiday Library in Clinton, North Carolina. On March 1, 2011, Mrs. Atwood found and emailed me a copy of A.B. Crumpler's lengthy obituary.

17. Ibid.

18. "Choosing the Pallbearers for a Funeral," *Funeral Guide*. This article is available online at: http://www.funeralhomesguide.com/pallbearer/html.

19. See A.B. Crumpler's obituary, "Death Claims Aged Citizen," *The Sampson Independent*, October 30, 1952, n.p.

20. Doug Beacham, *Azusa East: The Life and Times of G.B. Cashwell*, 203–206. Beacham records the full length of Cashwell's letter from *Word and Work* publication in his book. See, *Word and Work*, September 1911, 278, 279.

21. After nearly two years of silence, G.B. Cashwell revisits the Pentecostal world and pours his heart in the letter. Looking through Dr. McCullen's lens, it seems Cashwell went back to Falcon and attempted to reconcile himself back to those who "stole the lime light and gained control of the movement." Judging by the tone in his letter, Cashwell continued to firmly believe in the power of Pentecost as well as divine healing. However, it takes two to reconcile. Unfortunately, no one at Falcon has ever commented on G.B. Cashwell's appearance at the 1911 Falcon Camp Meeting. For some reason, it appears they still wanted no part of the preacher who helped formed their denomination in 1900, and brought it into the Pentecostal Movement in 1908.

22. J.T. McCullen, *Antiquity Forgot: Reminiscence*, 68. In a personal interview with Stanley Carr on March 5, 2011, I learned that G.B. Cashwell returned to Kenner after 1910 and preached in various churches in the local area. He continued to minister until his health began to fail in 1915. Interestingly, it seems that Cashwell spent most of his time preaching in small black churches in rural Sampson County. This also explains why he may have remained hidden from the spotlight. Some of these congregations may have included Lee's Holiness Chapel (now St. Peters Untied Holy Church), and Brown's Missionary Baptist (African American).

23. On August 1, 2011, I conducted a phone interview with Pastor Jeffery White of Browns Missionary Baptist Church (African American). I learned that over the years, the G.B. Cashwell family had strong ties to this local African American Baptist church. Browns broke off of the white

Browns Missionary Baptist Church following the Emancipation Proclamation (1860s), in which President Lincoln freed the slaves. After being forced out of the original Browns Baptist Church, the newly freed slaves organized their own church around 1871. Some believe that Granny Susan Cashwell, G.B. Cashwell's mother, helped organized Browns in the 1870s. Nonetheless, current members of Browns M. Baptist Church remember hearing that Gaston Cashwell used to come and assist the local black congregation by teaching them how to preach the Scriptures.

24. Doug Beacham, *Azusa East: The Life and Times of G.B. Cashwell*, 208–209.

25. Funeral Record for Gaston B. Cashwell, March 4, 1916, Harnett County, North Carolina, Page 204. Skinner and Smith Funeral Home, Dunn, North Carolina. On February 5, 2011, I personally visited Skinner and Smith Funeral Home and found the original funeral record for G.B. Cashwell. Being a distant family member, they gave me a copy of this insightful document.

26. Ibid. James H. Blackmore, *The Cullom Lantern: A Biography of W.R. Cullom of Wake Forrest* (Raleigh, North Carolina: Edwards and Broughton, 1963), 2, 131–132, 154. Dr. Cullom was an outstanding minister. He was noted for being more a father type figure to younger ministers. More of a teacher rather than a preacher, Dr. Cullom had a great ability to encourage and empower younger ministers.

27. *The Dunn Dispatch*, October 17, 1944, n.p.

28. For Dr. Cullom's relation to Dunn's First Baptist Church see, Herman P. Green, *A History of First Baptist Church Dunn, North Carolina, 1885–1981* (Dunn, North Carolina: Twyford Printing, 1981), 36. It seems, during his obscure later years, G.B. Cashwell confided in the comfort and wisdom of Dr. Cullom

29. See, Funeral Record for Gaston B. Cashwell, March 4, 1916, Harnett County, North Carolina, Page 204.

30. Ibid. G.B. Cashwell's death has been a complete mystery. A deeper investigation of his burial stone also reveals another question. Being flat and level with the ground, G.B. Cashwell's grave marker is conducive for modern day lawnmowers. However, in 1916 these stones were non-existent. In addition, Lovie Cashwell's grave stone is identical with G.B. Cashwell's. Lovie didn't pass away until 1944, nearly thirty years later. It seems when Lovie died, the flat stone for both Gaston and Lovie Cashwell were laid at the same time. From this, we can conclude that G.B. Cashwell may have not even had a grave marker when he was originally buried on March 5, 1916.

31. A. J. Tomlinson, "G.B. Cashwell Passes Over," *Church of God Evangel*, March 18, 1916, 2. This was quoted in David G. Roebuck, *Azusa Street Revival and Its Legacy*, 111.

32. For Mrs. Sexton's full length comments on G.B. Cashwell's death see Doug Beacham, *Azusa East*, 212. It very important to remember that the only references of Cashwell's death in the Pentecostal world were from people outside the state of North Carolina. There has never been one recorded comment on G.B. Cashwell's death by J.H. King, A.H. Butler, G.F. Taylor, J.A. Culbreth, S.D. Page, F.M. Britton, H.H. and Florence Goff, A.E. Robinson, or any other member of the Pentecostal Holiness Church.

33. Florence Goff, *Fifty Years on the Battlefield*, 52. Also see, Faye Miller Stancil, "Rev. J. Luther Davis," *The Heritage of Harnett County, North Carolina*, 479.

34. Personal Interview with Emma Lee Laine on March 1, 2012. Emma is the daughter of Rev. Luther Davis and Emma Lee. She is also the niece of Gaston and Lovie Cashwell.

35. Deed of Sale from J.H. Pope and wife Edith Pope to J.A. Blaylock, J.L. Davis, J.H. Pope: Trustees of the Free Will-Baptist Church, April 10, 1919, Harnett County, North Carolina. Register of Deeds Office, Lillington, North Carolina. Personal Interview with Emma Lee Laine on March 1, 2012. For more on this congregation see, Faye M. Stancil, "Rev. J.L. Davis," *The Heritage of Harnett County, North Carolina*, 479.

36. *The Dunn Dispatch*, October 17, 1944, n.p.

37. *Fortieth Anniversary Gospel Tabernacle.* This brief history of Gospel Tabernacle lists G.B. Cashwell and Lovie Cashwell as charter members.

38. Ibid. Personal Interview with Emma Lee Laine on March 1, 2012.

39. For G.F. Taylor's support of the Ku Klux Klan, see *Minutes of the Fifth General Conference*... 1925, 5. For the Pentecostal Holiness Church's banishment of "colored people" see Vinson Synan, *Old Time Power*, 329.

40. Synan, *Old Time Power*, 329. For the success of the IPHC see, http://www.iphc.org/

BIBLIOGRAPHY

ARCHIVES AND COLLECTIONS

Archives of the International Pentecostal Holiness Church. Bethany, Oklahoma Housed in the Archives and Research Center.

Archives of the North Carolina Conference of the Pentecostal Holiness Church. Falcon, North Carolina. Located in archives department. Memorial Library.

Archives of the Church of God. Cleveland, Tennessee. Found in the Dixon Pentecostal Research Center.

Archives of Regent University. Virginia Beach, Virginia. Housed in the Classical Pentecostal Sections.

Archives of Mt. Olive College. Mt. Olive, North Carolina. Located in the Free Will Baptist Historical Collection.

Archives of East Carolina University. Greenville, North Carolina. Situated in the Joyner Library Archives department.

Archives of Wake Forrest University. Winston-Salem, North Carolina. Found in Special Collections and Archives department.

Archives of the Grand Masonic Lodge of North Carolina. Raleigh, North Carolina. Membership records are stored in the grand lodge headquarters building.

North Carolina State Archives. Raleigh, North Carolina. Located in the Archives Information Circulars.

North Carolina State Library. Raleigh, North Carolina. Found in Government and Heritage Library Catalog.

North Carolina Room of the New Hanover County Public Library. Wilmington, North Carolina. Housed in the North Carolina Room.

MINUETS, DISCIPLINES AND GOVERNING DOCUMENTS

Charter of Carolina, 1663. Raleigh, North Carolina: North Carolina State Archives.

Constitution and By-Laws, and Minuets of the First Session of the North Carolina Holiness Convention. Goldsboro, North Carolina, 1899.

The Discipline of the Holiness Church. Goldsboro, North Carolina: Nash Brothers, Book and Job Printers, 1902

Discipline of the Methodist Episcopal Church, South. 1881.

Historical Table of Lodges, Extinct Lodges, and Lodges Created by the Grand Lodge of North Carolina. Raleigh, North Carolina, 1787.

Ku Klux Klan Manual. Hanover, Indiana: Hanover Historical Texts Collection, 1925.

Minutes of the Cape Fear Conference of the Free Will Baptist Church. The First, Mt. Olive, North Carolina, 1907; The Second, Mt. Olive, North Carolina, 1908.

Minuets of City Commissioners of Dunn, North Carolina. Dunn, North Carolina, 1907–1920.

Minutes of County Commissioners of Harnett County, North Carolina. Lillington, North Carolina, 1905–1931.

Minutes of the Sampson County Court. Sampson County, North Carolina: Sampson County Historical Society, 1784–1800; 1800-1810; 1810–1820.

Minutes of the South Georgia Conference of the Methodist Episcopal Church, South. 1920. Minuets of the Third Annual Session of the Holiness Convocation of North Carolina. Durham, North Carolina, 1897.

Proceedings of the Annual Conference of the Holiness Church of North Carolina. Goldsboro, North Carolina: Nash Brothers, Printers and Binders, 1907, 1908, 1909, 1910.

Report of the North Carolina Advisory Committee to the United States Commission on Civil Rights. Washington D.C: United States Government Printing Office, 1962.

Holiness-Pentecostal Periodicals

Altamont Witness. Greenville, South Carolina, 1914.

Apostolic Evangel. Falcon, North Carolina, 1907–1917.

Apostolic Faith. Houston, Texas, October 1908, 1–4.

Apostolic Faith. Los Angeles, California, 1905, 1906.

Bridegroom's Messenger. Atlanta, Georgia, 1907.

Confidence. Sunderland, England, 1908.

Holiness Advocate. Goldsboro, North Carolina, 1901.

Live Coals of Fire. Lincoln, Nebraska, 1899.

The Messenger. Dunn, North Carolina, 2007.

Pentecostal Holiness Advocate. Franklin Springs, Georgia, 1917–1996.

Way of Faith. Columbia, South Carolina, 1894–1925.

Newspapers

The Atlanta Constitution. Atlanta, Georgia, 1893.

The Caucasian. Clinton, North Carolina, 1892–1900.

The Central Times. Dunn, North Carolina, 1896.

Charlotte Daily Observer. Charlotte, North Carolina, 1896–1916.

The Daily Record. Dunn, North Carolina, 2011.

The Democratic Banner. Dunn, North Carolina, 1901–1902.

The Dunn County Union. Dunn, North Carolina, 1895–1899.

The Dunn Dispatch. Dunn, North Carolina, 1944.

The Duplin Journal. Kenansville, North Carolina, 1902.

Eastern Carolina News. Kenansville, North Carolina, 1908.

The Evening Dispatch. Wilmington, North Carolina, 1898–1908.

The Fayetteville Observer. Fayetteville, North Carolina, 1896–1897.

The Goldsboro Weekly Argus. Goldsboro, North Carolina, 1896–1908.

The News Dispatch. Clinton, North Carolina, 1909–1917.

The News and Observer. Raleigh, North Carolina, 1896–1897, 1955, 2006.

The Robesonian. Lumberton, North Carolina, 1897, 1900–1939.

The Sampson Independent. Clinton, North Carolina, 1952.

The Weekly Guide. Dunn, North Carolina, 1913.

Official Records:

Vital Records

Certificate of Marriage, T.F. Harrison to Lovie H. Lee, May 1895, Cumberland County, North Carolina. North Carolina State Archives, Raleigh, North Carolina.

Certificate of Marriage, Gaston B. Cashwell to Lovie Lee Harrison, March 7, 1899, Harnett County, North Carolina. Register of Deeds Office, Lillington, North Carolina.

Death Certificate for A. Blackmon Crumpler, October 23, 1952, File No. 25382, North Carolina State Board of Health.

Death Certificate for Gaston B. Cashwell, March 4, 1916, File No. 10, North Carolina State Board of Health.

Record of Funeral for A. Blackmon Crumpler, October 24, 1952. Crumpler-Honeycutt Funeral Home, Clinton, North Carolina.

Record of Funeral for Gaston B. Cashwell, March 4, 1916, File No. 204. Skinner and Smith Funeral Home, Dunn, North Carolina

Record of Funeral for Lovie H. Cashwell, October 16, 1944, File No. 226.Cromartie-Miller and Lee Funeral Home, Dunn, North Carolina.

Census Records

1850 United States Census (Free Schedule), Northeast Cape Fear Subdivision, Bladen County, North Carolina.

1850 United States Census (Free Schedule), Halls Township, Sampson County, North Carolina.

1850 United States Census (Slave Schedule), Halls Township, Sampson County, North Carolina.

1860 United States Census (Free Schedule), Halls Township, Sampson County, North Carolina.

1870 United States Census (Free Schedule), Halls Township, Sampson County, North Carolina.

1880 United States Census (Free Schedule), Honeycutt Township, Sampson County, North Carolina.

1900 United States Census (Free Schedule), Halls Township, Sampson County, North Carolina.

1900 United States Census (Free Schedule), Goldsboro Township, Goldsboro, North Carolina.

Legal Records

Deed of Sale from Thomas Sutton to Blackmon Crumpler, December 2, 1812, Sampson County, North Carolina, Deed Book 16, Page 103. Register of Deeds Office, Clinton, North Carolina.

Deed of Sale from Blackmon Crumpler to Methodist Episcopal Church Trustees, 10 February 1842, Sampson County, North Carolina, Deed Book 26, Page 421. Register of Deeds Office, Clinton, North Carolina.

Deed of Sale from Joshua Bass to Herring Cashwell, February 9, 1855, Sampson County, North Carolina, Deed Book 37, Page 254. Register of Deeds Office, Clinton, North Carolina.

Deed of Sale from Herring Cashwell to William Cashwell, August 25, 1855, Sampson County, North Carolina, Deed Book 32, Page 525. Register of Deeds Office, Clinton, North Carolina.

Deed of Sale from B. F. Hargrove to Herring Cashwell, April 15, 1871, Sampson County, North Carolina, Deed Book 38, Page 81. Register of Deeds Office, Clinton, North Carolina.

Deed of Sale from B.C. Weeks and wife to M.E. Church, South, January 18, 1886, Sampson County, North Carolina, Deed Book 66, Page 266. Register of Deeds Office, Clinton, North Carolina.

Deed of Sale from David R. Watson to G.B. Cashwell, December 17, 1890, Sampson County, North Carolina, Deed Book 76, Page 305. Register of Deeds Office, Clinton, North Carolina.

Deed of Sale from G.B. Cashwell to Docia Cashwell Gore, October 13, 1891, Sampson County, North Carolina, Deed Book 83, Page 111. Register of Deed Office, Clinton, North Carolina.

Deed of Sale from William Culbreth and wife Nancy J. Culbreth to J.A. Culbreth, May 11, 1894, Harnett County, North Carolina, Page 46. Register of Deeds Office Lillington, North Carolina.

Deed of Sale from G.B. Cashwell to James Stackhouse, May 4, 1892, Sampson County, North Carolina, Deed Book 81, Page 150. Register of Deeds Office, Clinton, North Carolina.

Deed of Sale from J.A. Culbreth Commissioner to H.L. Godwin, February 7, 1902, Harnett County, North Carolina, Page 92. Register of Deeds Office, Lillington, North Carolina.

Deed of Sale from J.A. Culbreth and wife to Trustees Falcon Holiness School and Campmeeting Association, May 4, 1904, Cumberland County, North Carolina, Deed Book 174, Page 165. Register of Deeds Office, Fayetteville, North Carolina.

Deed of Sale from G.F. Taylor and wife to S.D. Page, February 14, 1908, Cumberland County, North Carolina, Deed Book 146, Page 324. Register of Deeds Office, Fayetteville, North Carolina.

Deed of Sale from J.T. McCullen and wife to Lee's Chapel Church (Col.), August 31, 1908, Sampson County, North Carolina, Deed Book 212, Page 466. Register of Deeds Office, Clinton, North Carolina.

Deed of Sale from J.A. Culbreth and wife to J.H. King, December 26, 1908, Cumberland County, North Carolina, Deed Book 153, Page 47. Register of Deeds Office, Fayetteville, North Carolina.

Deed of Sale from J.A. Culbreth and wife to M.D. Sellars, April 23, 1909, Cumberland County, North Carolina, Deed Book 153, Page 61. Register of Deeds Office, Fayetteville, North Carolina.

Deed of Sale from J.H. Melvin to Lovie Cashwell, January 10, 1913, Sampson County, North Carolina, Deed Book 222, Page 221. Register of Deeds Office, Clinton, North Carolina.

Deed of Sale from G.B. Cashwell and wife to Alex Stewart and wife, May 25, 1915, Sampson County, North Carolina, Deed Book 265, Page 15. Register of Deeds Office, Clinton, North Carolina.

Deed of Sale from J.H. Pope and wife Edith Pope to J.A. Blalock, J.L. Davis, and J.H. Pope-Trustees of the Free Will Baptist Church of Dunn, N.C., April 10, 1919, Harnett County, North Carolina. Register of Deeds Office, Lillington, North Carolina.

Deed of Sale from D.H. Hood, J.L. Davis, Mrs. Edith Pope, and Mrs. Lizzie Monds to Lovie H. Cashwell, November 23, 1922, Harnett County, North Carolina. Register of Deeds Office, Lillington, North Carolina.

Last Will and Testaments

Division of the Negros of W. Everett Bass to William Bass, Joshua Bass, Richard Bass, John Bass, and Everett Bass, February 16, 1835, Sampson County, North Carolina.

Division Estate of E. Lee to Edith Pope and J.H. Pope, W.B. Warren and wife Katurah E. Warren, J.W. Taylor and wife Kesiah A. Taylor, L.H. Lee, G.B. Cashwell and wife Lovie H. Cashwell, Robert E. Lee, Emma Lee, and Henry Lee, April 15, 1901, Harnett County, North Carolina.

Last Will and Testament of John Bass to grandson John Bass, October 2, 1885, Sampson County, North Carolina.

Last Will and Testament of William Bass to Susan Stanley, January 24, 1853, Sampson County, North Carolina.

Last Will and Testament of Herring Cashwell to wife Susan Cashwell, William H. Cashwell, Gaston B. Cashwell, Ann Henderson Cashwell, Lettie Docia Cashwell, and oldest daughter Susan Cashwell, October 12, 1878, Sampson County, North Carolina. (Sampson County Will Abstracts 1784-1900.)

Unpublished Manuscripts

Beacham Doug. "Remembering the Outpouring: The Dunn Revival Past, Present, Future." Unpublished manuscript read at Gospel Tabernacle Pentecostal Holiness Church in Dunn, North Carolina, on January 13, 2004.

Gershenhorn, Jerry. "The Rise and Fall of Fusion Politics in North Carolina, 1880–1900." Unpublished essay.

Goff, James R., "The Pentecostal Catalyst to the South: G.B. Cashwell (1906–1908)." Unpublished manuscript, April 2, 1980.

Jones, William. "Recollections: 1926–1953." Diary at the Archives of the North Carolina Conference of the Pentecostal Holiness Church. Falcon, North Carolina.

Lamm, Alan K., Gary Barefoot, Michael Pelt, and Ricky Warren. "A History of the Cape Fear Conference." Unpublished History of the Cape Fear Conference of the Free Will Baptist Church. Located in the FWB Historical Collection and Archives department of Moye Library at Mt. Olive College. Mt Olive, North Carolina, 2011.

McCullen, J.T. "Antiquity Forgot: Reminiscences." Unpublished manuscript of the Cashwell, Gore, and McCullen families, written in 1989.

________. "By the Soul Only." Unpublished manuscript of Dr. J.T. McCullen's military experiences during World War II, written in 1989.

________. "Descendants and Relatives of Joseph Thomas McCullen, Sr. and Myrtie Peal Gore McCullen." Unpublished genealogical document, written December, 1981.

________. "Not in Entire Forgetfulness." Unpublished manuscript of Dr. McCullen's recollections, written in 1990.

________. "A Wild-Goose Miscellany." Unpublished book of Dr. McCullen's academic essays, written in 1988.

Smith, Maude P., "Magnolia United Methodist Church History: 1700–2011." Unpublished manuscript of the churches history. Written in 2011, and found at Magnolia United Methodist Church, Magnolia, North Carolina.

Tomlinson, A.J. "Journal of Happenings." Unpublished diary of A.J. Tomlinson. Diary at Church of God Headquarters in Cleveland, Tennessee. January 13, 1908, January 20, 1908.

York, Stanley. "George Floyd Taylor: The Life of an Early Southern Pentecostal Leader." P.H. Dissertation. Regent University, 2012.

Personal Interviews

Gary Barefoot. March 29, 2011.

Stanley Carr. March 5, September 24, 2011.

Dr. Herbert Carter. April, 2012.

Elizabeth Crudup. January 10, 2011.

Thomas Ellis II. January 10, 2011.

Dr. James Goff Jr. January 17, 2011.

Ann Hobbs. April 15, 2011.

Moses King. February 1, 2012.

Emma Lee Laine. March 1, 2012.

Robert Lindsay. January 26, 2011.

Allie Ray McCullen. February 23, 2011.

Jane McGregor. May 28, 2011.

Rev. Jeffery White. August 1, 2011.

Rev. John Wilkins. January 10, 2011.

Local Church Histories

The History of Brown's Baptist Church on the Occasion of the Bicentennial of the Founding of the Church. Author unknown. Organized 1778, Sampson County, North Carolina.

History of Brown Baptist Church Clinton, North Carolina (African American). Complied by Mr. Claude Moore. Organized 1871, Sampson County, North Carolina.

History of Clinton First United Methodist Church: 1854-1997. Compiled and written by Grace Crumpler Vann. Organized 1854, Sampson County, North Carolina.

History of Goshen Pentecostal Holiness Church. Author unknown. Organized March 1900, Sampson County, North Carolina.

Historyof Gospel Tabernacle Pentecostal Holiness Church. Author unknown. Organized 1917, Dunn, North Carolina.

History of Hood Memorial Christian Church Dunn, North Carolina. Compiled and written by Bertha Westbrook and F.W. Wiegmann. Organized 1889, Dunn, North Carolina

History of Keener United Methodist Church (1885–1997). Complied by Ann Hobbs. Organized 1885, Keener, North Carolina.

History of Magnolia United Methodist Church: 1700–2011. Complied by Maude P. Smith. Organized 1785, Magnolia, North Carolina.

History of the Pentecostal Free Will Baptist Church Inc. Written by Preston Heath, Herbert F. Carter, Don Sauls, and R.M. Brown. http://www.pfwb.org/history.html (Accessed September 13, 2012).

History of Thunder Swamp Pentecostal Holiness Church. Complied by Rev. Jimmy Whitfield. Organized August 1904, Wayne County, North Carolina.

History of St. Matthews Pentecostal Holiness Church. Written by Rev. Jimmy Swinson. Organized 1903, Sampson County, North Carolina.

Books and Articles

Bailey, Clyde S. *Pioneer Marvels of Faith*. Morristown, Tennessee, n.d.

Bartleman, Frank. *Azusa Street*. S. Plainfield, New Jersey: Bridge Publishing, 1980.

Beacham, Doug. *Azusa East: The Life and Times of G.B. Cashwell*. Franklin Springs, Georgia: LSR Publishing, 2006.

Bizzell, Oscar M. *The Heritage of Sampson County, North Carolina*. Sampson County, North Carolina: Sampson County Historical Society, 1983.

Blackmore, James H. *The Cullom Lantern*. Raleigh, North Carolina: Edwards and Broughton Company, 1963.

Blaisdell, Bob. *The Wit and Wisdom of Abraham Lincoln*. Mineola, New York: Dover Publishing, 2005.

Borlase, Craig. *William Seymour: A Biography.* Lake Mary, Florida: Charisma House, 2006.

Bradshaw, Charles E. *Profiles of Faith.* Franklin Springs, Georgia: Advocate Press, 1984.

Brown, Kenneth O. *Inskip, McDonald, Fowler: "Wholly And Forever Thine."* Hazelton, Pennsylvania: Holiness Archives Publishing, 1999.

Brundage, Fitzhugh W. *Where These Memories Grow: History, Memory, and Southern Identity.* Chapel Hill, North Carolina: University of North Carolina Press, 2000.

Bundy, Mayo V. *A History of Falcon, North Carolina.* Charlotte, North Carolina: Walsworth Publishing, 1980.

Burgess, Stanley M. *The New International Dictionary of Pentecostal and Charismatic Movements.* Grand Rapids, Michigan: Zondervan, 2002.

Butler, A.H. "His Dealings with Me." *The Holiness Advocate.* (May 15, 1904), 2.

Butler, George E. *The Croatan Indians of Sampson County, North Carolina: Their Origin and Racial Status. A Plea for Separate Schools.* Durham, North Carolina: Seeman Printing, 1916.

Cashwell, G.B. "Came 3,000 Miles for His Pentecost." *The Apostolic Faith.* (December, 1906), 3.

_______. "Pentecost in North Carolina." *The Apostolic Faith.* (January, 1907), 1.

_______. "G.B. Cashwell's Letter." *The Holiness Advocate.* (June 1, 1907), 5.

Campbell, Joseph E. *The Pentecostal Holiness Church: 1898–1948 Its Background and History.* Franklin Springs, Georgia: Publishing House of the Pentecostal Holiness Church, 1951.

Clemons, Ithiel C. *Bishop C.H. Mason and the Roots of the Church of God in Christ.* Bakersfield, California: Pneuma Life Publishing, 1996.

Conn, Charles W. *Like A Mighty Army: A History of the Church of God: 1886–1976.* Cleveland, Tennessee: Pathway Press, 1977.

Crumpler, A.B. "From North Carolina." *The Way of Faith.* (December 4, 1895), 1.

_______. "Clinton, N.C.," *The Way of Faith.* (January 8, 1896), 1.

_______. "Jesus Triumphs at Ingold, N.C.," *The Way of Faith.* (January 15, 1896), 1.

_______. "The Devil Kept Hustling." *The Way of Faith.* (February 12, 1896), 5.

_______. "The Victory at Goshen." *The Way of Faith.* (March 25, 1896), 2.

_______.**"Hard** at Work." *The Way of Faith.* (August 5, 1896), 5.

_______." Warsaw, North Carolina." *The Way of Faith.* (September 2, 1896), 1.

Fowler, Malcolm. *They Passed This Way: A Personal Narrative of Harnett County History.* Harnett County, North Carolina: Harnett County Centennial Inc., 1955.

Freeman, Gerene L. "What About My 40 Acres and A Mule?" *Racism and Nativism in American Political Culture.* vol. 4, 1994. Curriculum Unit 94.04.01. http://www.yale.edu/ynhti/curriculum/units/1994/4/94.04.01.x.html (Accessed September 4, 2012).

Frodsham, Stanley H. *With Signs Following: The Story of the Pentecostal Revival in the Twentieth Century*. Springfield, Missouri: Gospel Publishing, 1946.

Gerber, Scott D. "Carolina Charter of 1663," *North Carolina History.org: An Online Encyclopedia,* North Carolina History Project, http://www.northcarolinahistory.org/encyclopedia/154/entry (Accessed September 30, 2010).

Goff, Florence. *Fifty Years on the Battlefield For God*. Falcon, North Carolina: Self Published, 1948.

_______. *Tests and Triumphs*. Falcon, North Carolina. 1924.

Green, Herman P. *A History of Dunn,* N.C., *Dunn, North Carolina*: Twyford Printing Company, 1985.

_______. *A History of First Baptist Church: Dunn, North Carolina 1885–1981*. Dunn, North Carolina: Twyford Printing Company, 1981.

_______. *A History of Palmyra Lodge No. 147, A.F. and A.M. Dunn, North Carolina*. Dunn, North Carolina: Self-Published, 1963.

Grill, Franklin C. *Methodism in the Upper Cape Fear Valley*. Nashville, Tennessee: Parthenon Press, 1966.

Hasty, Mary A. *The Heritage of Harnett County, North Carolina, vol.* 1. Harnett County, North Carolina: Delmar Printing, 1993.

Hayes, W.M. *Memoirs of Richard Baxter Hayes*. Greer, South Carolina: Self Published, 1945.

Hubbard, Jeff. "The John Crumpler Family Tree." *Find A Grave*. December 21, 2010. http://www.findagrave.com (Accessed September 1, 2012).

Hunt, Jams L. *Marion Butler and American Populism*. Chapel Hill, North Carolina: University of North Carolina Press, 2003.

Hunter, Harold D. and Cecil M. Robeck. *The Azusa Street Revival and Its Legacy*. Cleveland, Tennessee: Pathway Press, 2006.

Hunter, Harold D. "International Pentecostal Holiness Church." Revised August 13, 2012. http://www.pctii.org/iphc.html (Accessed February 2, 2011).

Hyatt, Eddie L. *2000 Years of Charismatic Christianity*. Lake Mary, Florida: Charisma House, 2002.

Johnson, Lloyd. "Averasboro," *North Carolina History.org: An Online Encyclopedia,* North Carolina History Project, http://www.northcarolinahistory.org/commentary/102/entry (Accessed January 16, 2011).

Kendall, J.T. "A New Evangelists on a New Line." *The Way of Faith* (December 23, 1896), 5.

King, J.H., and King, Blanche L. *Yet Speaketh: Memoirs of the Late Bishop Joseph H. King*. Franklin Springs, Georgia: Publishing House of Pentecostal Holiness Church, 1949. King, J.H. "History of the Fire-Baptized Holiness Church." *The Pentecostal Holiness Advocate*. (March–April, 1921), a succession of four articles.

Klein, Walter J. *He ain't heavy he's my Brother Zeb*. Raleigh, North Carolina: Published by North Carolina Grand Lodge of A.F. and A.M., 2005.

Kostlevy, William. "The Holiness Movement, The Manheim Camp Meeting, and C.H. Balsbaugh: Christian Perfection in Pennsylvania Dutch Country," *Brethren Life and Thought 48* (Winter and Spring 2003): 91–109.

Liardon, Roberts. *God's Generals: Why They Succeeded and Why Some Failed.* Tulsa, Oklahoma: Albury Publishing, 1996.

McCullen, J.T. "Gaston B. Cashwell Once a Prodigal Son." *Heritage of Sampson County, North Carolina*, 87.

_______. "Sharecake, 1878." *Heritage of Sampson County, North Carolina,* 34–35.

_______. "Persimmon College an Early Name for Keener, 1880." *Heritage of Sampson County, North Carolina*, 35.

_______. "A Country Midwife in Halls Township." *Heritage of Sampson County, North Carolina*, 197.

McDonald, W. and John E. Searles. *Life of Rev. John S. Inskip*. New York: Garland Publishing, 1985.

Mobley, Joe A. *The Way We Lived in North Carolina*. Chapel Hill, North Carolina: University of North Carolina Press, 2003.

Morris, Eddie W. *The Vine and Braches John 15:5: Holiness and Pentecostal Movements*. Franklin Springs, Georgia: Advocate Press, 1981.

Newkirk, Vann R. *Lynching in North Carolina: A History, 1865–1941*. Jefferson, North Carolina: McFarland and Company Publishing, 2009.

Paris, Arthur E. *Black Pentecostalism: Southern Religion in an Urban World*. Amherst, Massachusetts: University of Massachusetts Press, 1982.

Rasnake, Samuel. *Stones By the River: A History of the Tennessee District of the Assemblies of God*. Bristol, Tennessee: Westhighlands Church, 1975.

Sanders, Rufus. *William Joseph Seymour Black Father of the Twentieth Century Pentecostal/Charismatic Movement*. Sandusky, Ohio: Xulon Press, 2003.

Synan, Vinson. *The Century of the Holy Spirit: 100 Years of Pentecostal and Charismatic Renewal*. Nashville, Tennessee: Thomas Nelson, 2001.

_______. *The Holiness-Pentecostal Tradition: Charismatic Movements in the Twentieth Century*. Grand Rapids: Michigan, William B. Eerdmans Publishing, 1997.

_______. *Old Time Power: A Centennial History of the International Pentecostal Holiness Church*. Franklin Springs, Georgia: LifeSprings, 1998.

Taylor, G.F. "Our Church History." *The Pentecostal Holiness Advocate*. (January 20–April 14, 1921), a series of twelve articles.

Turner, William C. *The United Holy Church of America: A Study in Black Holiness-Pentecostalism*. Durham, North Carolina: Gorgias Press, 2006.

Weinlick, John R. *Count Zinzendorf.* New York: Abingdon Press, 1956.

Welchel, Tom. *Azusa Street: They Told Me Their Stories*. Mustang, Oklahoma: Dare 2 Dream Printing, 2006

Wentz, Richard E. *American Religious Traditions: The Shaping of Religion in the United States*. Minneapolis, Minnesota: Fortress Press, 2003.

Widmer, Ted. *American Speeches: Political Oratory from Patrick Henry to Barack Obama*. New York: Penguin Group (USA) Inc., 2011.

Wood, Daniel L. and William H. Preskitt, Jr. *Baptized With Fire: A History of the Pentecostal Fire-Baptized Holiness Church*. Franklin Springs, Georgia: Advocate Press, 1982

ABOUT THE AUTHOR

BEFORE ANSWERING GOD'S call, Michael Thornton was hopelessly addicted to life destroying drugs for nearly a decade. After entering into a Christian Recovery Center, Michael encountered the powerful love of Jesus. All of his chains of addiction were finally broken. Following his completion of the program, God called Michael to school, where he met his wife Amber Thornton. In May of 2007, both Amber and Michael graduated from Heritage Bible College in Dunn, North Carolina, and continued to further their education at Regent University. In May 2012, Michael received a Master's degree in Public Administration/Non-profit Organizations from Regent University.

During this time, God began to stir in Michael's heart the flames of revival. God quickly opened some amazing doors, and Michael was able to share his story among different denominations and cultures. His testimony was featured on the 700 Club and was aired several times all over the world. Continuing to follow the call for a national and global spiritual awakening, the Lord led Michael to re-dig the ancient wells of revival in North Carolina. Fruit from this assignment led to this book—*Fire in the Carolinas*. This work has resulted in a great hunger and passion to see North Carolina lead the nation in another global healing revival between divided races and churches. Additionally, God has blessed the Thorntons with four beautiful daughters: Jordan, Abigail, Briella, and Bethany Thornton.

CONTACT THE AUTHOR

Email:
mthornton80@yahoo.com